TH
DIVINE
OF
CHURCH
GOVERNMENT:

BY SUNDRY MINISTERS
OF CHRIST WITHIN THE
CITY OF LONDON

THE EDITOR TO THE READER.

After what the authors of the following Treatise have said in their preface, the Editor judges it unnecessary for him to detain the reader long with any observations of his upon the subject. He, however, could sincerely wish that the friends of Christ would pay that attention to the government and discipline of his Church which it justly deserves. Although this subject should not be placed among the things essential to the being of a Christian; yet if it be found among the things that Christ has commanded, it is at our peril if we continue wilfully ignorant of, or despise it. He has expressly declared, that he who breaks one of the *least* of his commandments, and teacheth men to do so, shall be called least in the kingdom of heaven. It is an opinion too common, that if we believe the *essentials* of religion, there is no occasion for so much preciseness about the forms of church government, which are only *circumstantials*, as there will be no inquiry made about these at the tribunal of Christ. But whatever relative importance the things of religion may have, when compared with one another, we ought to reckon nothing which God hath appointed, nothing which Jesus hath ratified with his blood, nothing which the Holy Spirit hath indited, so *circumstantial*, as to be unworthy of our serious regard. It is at least very rash, if not presumptuous, to say, that nothing about the circumstantials of religion will be inquired into at the tribunal of Christ. God has expressly said, that every work, good or evil, every idle word, and every deed done in the body, shall be brought into judgment; and false worshippers will, perhaps, find that their form of worship consisted in something worse than idle words, or sinful words either, even in sinful deeds, for which they will be accountable at the judgment. As Christ laid down his life for his people, has instructed them, and has set a hedge about all that they have, it would be most ungrateful to requite him with pouring the highest contempt on his kingly honor and authority; and when his worship is polluted, his truth perverted, and the walls of his New Testament Zion broken down, to care for none of those things. Government and discipline are the hedge of his garden, the Church; and how will what men call the essentials of religion remain in their glory, when this is broken down, the present state of affairs can sufficiently attest, when the most damnable errors are propagated with impunity.

In our times the enemies of the scriptural order of the house of God are very numerous and very active, exerting all their power to break down the carved work of God's sanctuary. The present spirit for novelty and innovation, together with the rage for infidelity so prevalent, strongly favors the opposition made to every thing which has a tendency to bind men closely to God, to his truths, to the purity of his worship and ordinances, or to one another by a holy profession. The design, therefore, of republishing this Treatise is to assist Presbyterians of all denominations in the understanding of those passages of Scripture upon which their wall is built, that they be not led aside by the cunning speeches of false teachers, whereby they deceive and draw aside the hearts of the simple.

This work was first published at London, at the time when the controversy between the Presbyterians and ancient Independents ran very high, and every intelligent and unprejudiced reader will see, that the Holy Scriptures have been carefully perused, accurately compared, wisely collected, and judiciously explained, in order to evince that the Presbyterian government has the only lawful claim to a divine right, and is the only form appointed by Christ in his Church. It is, therefore, to be wished, that all his people would endeavor, in the strength of Divine grace, to observe the laws of his house, and to walk in all his ordinances and commandments blameless.

Considerable pains have been taken to make this edition more easily understood by common readers than the former, and yet several difficult and hard words have passed unnoticed. The Latin quotations from the Fathers have been omitted, because they contain nothing materially different from what is in the body of the work, and modern Independents pay little regard to any human authorities but their own. It was proposed to have added a few extracts from Messrs. Rutherford and Gillespie, but upon looking into their works nothing of consequence was observed, that tended to cast any new light upon the subject. It is hoped, however, that the Appendix is filled up with extracts from other authors upon subjects of considerable importance, and very necessary for these times, concerning the scriptural qualifications and duties of church members; the divine right of the gospel ministry; the people's divine right to choose their own pastors; with an abstract of Dr. Owen's arguments in favor of the divine right of the ruling elder: and as there are many serious Christians who have not a capacity to take up and retain a long chain of reasoning, a summary of the whole Treatise is given by way of question and answer as a conclusion.

The Editor is not to be understood as approving of, or vindicating every single sentiment, or mode of expression, used in this Treatise: at the same time, next to the Holy Scriptures, he recommends it as one of the best defences of presbytery which he has seen.

That it may be blessed of God for informing the ignorant, settling the wavering, and establishing the believers of *the present Truth*, is the earnest desire of,

Christian reader,

Your humble servant in the Gospel,

T.H.

Paisley, 28th February, 1799.

PREFACE
TO THE PIOUS AND JUDICIOUS READER.

CHRISTIAN READER:

Thou hast in the ensuing treatise, 1st, a brief delineation of the nature of a divine right, wherein it consists, and how many ways a thing may be accounted of divine right, according to the Scriptures; as also, 2d, a plain and familiar description of that church government which seems to have the clearest divine right for it, and (of all other contended for) to be the most consonant and agreeable to the word of Christ; which description (comprehending in itself the whole frame and system of the government) is in the several branches thereof explained and confirmed by testimonies or arguments from Scripture; more briefly, in particulars which are easily granted; more largely, in particulars which are commonly controverted; yet as perspicuously and concisely in both as the nature of this unusual and comprehensive subject insisted upon would permit. Things are handled rather by way of positive assertion, than of polemical dissertation, (which too commonly degenerates into verbal strifes, 1 Tim. vi. 3, 4; 2 Tim. ii. 23; and vain-jangling, 1 Tim. i. 6,) and where any dissenting opinions or objections are refuted, we hope it is with that sobriety, meekness, and moderation of spirit, that any unprejudiced judgment may perceive, that we had rather gain than grieve those who dissent from us; that we endeavor rather to heal up than to tear open the rent; and that we contend more for truth than for victory.

To the publication hereof we have been inclinable (after much importunity) principally upon deliberate and serious consideration of, 1st, the necessity of a treatise of this kind; 2d, the advantage likely to accrue thereupon; and, 3d, the seasonable opportunity of sending it abroad at such a time as this is.

I. The necessity of a treatise of this nature, is evident and urgent. For,

1. We hold ourselves obliged, not only by the common duty of our ministerial calling, but also by the special bond of our solemn covenant with God, especially in Art. 1, to bend all our best endeavors to help forward a reformation of religion according to the word of God, which can never be effected without a due establishment of the scripture-government and discipline in the Church of God. And to make known what this government is from the law and testimony, by preaching or writing, comes properly and peculiarly within the sphere of our place and vocation.

2. A cloud of darkness and prejudice, in reference to this matter of church government, too generally rests upon the judgments and apprehensions of men (yea of God's own people) among us, either, 1st, through the difficulty or uncommonness of this matter of church government, (though ancient and familiar in other reformed churches, yet new and strange to us;) or, 2d, through the strange misrepresentations that are made hereof, by those that are small friends to the true presbyterial government, or that are enemies to all church government whatsoever; or, 3d, through the different opinions about church government, which are to be found among pious people and ministers: by all which the weak

and unstable minds of many are cast into a maze of many confused thoughts and irresolutions.

3. Though many learned treatises have been published, some whereof have positively asserted, others have polemically vindicated divers parts of church government, and the divine right thereof, yet hitherto no treatise of this nature is extant, positively laying open the nature of a divine right, what it is, and a system of that government, which is so, and proving both by the Scriptures; without which, how shall the judgments and consciences of men be satisfied, that this is that church government, according to the word of God, which they have covenanted to endeavor to promote, and whereto they are obliged to submit? And since it is our lot to travel in an unbeaten path, we, therefore, promise to ourselves, from all sober and judicious readers, the greater candor and ingenuity in their measuring of our steps and progress herein.

II. The advantage which may probably accrue hereupon, we hope shall be manifold: For, 1. Who can tell but that some of them, that in some things are misled and contrary-minded, may be convinced and regained? and it will be no small reward of our labors if but one erring brother may be brought back. 2. Some satisfaction may redound to such as are of doubtful, unresolved minds, by removing of their doubts and scruples, and ripening of their resolutions, to settle more safely in point of church government. 3. Those that as yet are unseen in the matter of church government, or that want money to buy, or leisure to read many books upon this subject, may here have much in a little, and competently inform themselves of the whole body of the government. 4. Consequently upon the attaining of the former ends, the work of reformation will be much facilitated and smoothed, the hearts of the people being prepared for the Lord and his ordinances. 5. The present attempt (if it reach not to that completeness and satisfactoriness which is desired) may yet incite some of our brethren of more acute and polished judgments to embark themselves in some further discoveries for the public benefit of the Church. 6. But though it should fall out that in all the former we should be utterly disappointed, we shall have this peace and comfort upon our own spirits, that we have not hid our talent in the earth, nor neglected to bear witness to this part of Christ's truth, touching the government of his Church, by his kingly power, wherein Christ was opposed so much in all ages, Psalm ii. 1, 2, 3; Luke xix. 14, 27; Acts iv., and for which Christ did suffer so much in a special and immediate manner, as1 some have observed. For this end Christ came into the world, (and for this end we came into the ministerial calling,) to bear witness to the truth.

III. Finally, the present opportunity of publishing a treatise on this subject doth much incite and encourage us therein. For at this time we are beginning, in this province of London, (and we hope the whole kingdom will, with all convenient speed, and due caution, second us,) to put that covenanted church government into actual execution, which we have a long time intended in our deliberate resolutions. So that generally we shall be engaged in the government one way or other, either as acting in it as the church officers, or as submitting to it as church members: now, how shall any truly conscientious person, either act in it, or conform and submit unto it with faith, judgment, and alacrity, till he be in some competent measure satisfied of the divine right thereof?

Will mere prudence, without a divine right, be a sufficient basis to erect the whole frame of church government upon, as some conceive? Prudentials, according to general rules of Scripture, may be of use in circumstantials, but will bare prudentials in substantials also satisfy either our God, our covenant, our consciences, or our end in this great work of reformation? What conscientious person durst have a hand in acting as a ruling elder, did he not apprehend the word of God holds forth a divine right for the ruling elder? Who durst have a hand in the censures of admonishing the unruly, excommunicating the scandalous and obstinate, and of restoring the penitent, were there not a divine right hereof revealed in the Scripture, &c. Now, therefore, that ruling elders, and the rest of the people, may begin this happy work conscientiously, judiciously, cheerfully, in some measure perceiving the divine right of the whole government, wherein they engage themselves, cleared by Scripture, we hope, by God's blessing, that this small tract will afford some seasonable assistance, which will be unto us a very acceptable recompense.

Thus far of the nature of this treatise, and the grounds of our publishing thereof. In the next place, a few doubts or scruples touching church government here asserted, being succinctly resolved, we shall preface no further.

Doubt 1. Many scruple, and much question the divine right of the whole frame of church government; as, 1. Whether there be any particular church government of divine right? 2. What that government is? 3. What church officers or members of elderships are of divine right? 4. Whether parochial or congregational elderships be of divine right? 5. Whether classical presbyteries be of divine right? 6. Whether provincial, national, and ecumenical assemblies be of divine right? 7. Whether appeals from congregational to classical, provincial, national, and ecumenical assemblies, and their power to determine upon such appeals, be of divine right? 8. Whether the power of censures in the congregational eldership, or any other assembly, be of divine right? 9. Whether there be any particular rules in the Scripture directing persons or assemblies in the exercise of their power? 10. Whether the civil magistrates, or their committees' and commissioners' execution of church censures be contrary to that way of government which Christ hath appointed in his Church?

Resol. To all or most of these doubts some competent satisfaction may be had from this treatise ensuing, if seriously considered. For, 1. That there is a church government of divine right, now under the New Testament, declared in Scripture, is proved, Part I. 2. What that government is in particular, is evidenced both by the description of church government, and the confirmation of the parts thereof by Scripture, Part. II. chap. 1, and so to the end of the book: whereby it is cleared that the presbyterial government is that particular government which is of divine right, according to the word of God. 3. What ordinary church officers, (members of the several elderships,) are of divine right, is proved, Part II, chap. 11, sect. 1, viz. pastors and teachers, with ruling elders. 4. That parochial or congregational elderships, consisting of preaching and ruling elders, are of divine right, is manifested, Part II. chap. 12. 5. That classical presbyteries, or assemblies, and their power in church government, are of divine right, is demonstrated, Part II. chap. 13. 6. That synodical assemblies, or councils in general, (consequently provincial, national, or ecumenical councils in particular,) and their power in church government, are of divine right, is cleared, Part II. chap. 14. 7. That appeals from congregational elderships, to classical and synodical assemblies, from lesser to greater assemblies associated, and power in those assemblies to determine authoritatively in such, appeals, are of divine right, is proved, Part II. chap. 15. 8. That the power of church censures is in Christ's own church officers only as the first subject and proper receptacle there of divine right, is cleared, Part II. chap. 11, sect. 2, which officers of Christ have and execute the said power respectively, in all the ruling assemblies, congregational, classical, or synodical. See section 3, and chap. 12, 13, 14, 15. 9. That the Scriptures hold forth, touching church government, not only general, but also many particular rules, sufficiently directing both persons and assemblies how they should duly put in execution their power of church, government. This is made good, Part II. chap. 4; and those that desire to know which are these rules in particular, may consult those learned2 centuriators of Magdeburg, who have collected and methodically digested, in the very words of the Scripture, a system of canons or rules, touching church government, as in the preface to those rules they do profess, saying, touching things pertaining to the government of the Church, the apostles delivered certain canons, which we will add in order, &c., the very heads of which would be too prolix to recite. 10. Finally, that neither the supreme civil magistrate, as such, nor consequently any commissioner or committees whatsoever, devised and erected by his authority, are the proper subject of the formal power of church government, nor may lawfully, by any virtue of the magistratical office, dispense any ecclesiastical censures or ordinances: but that such undertakings are inconsistent with that way of government which Christ hath appointed in his Church, is evidenced, Part II. chap. 9, well compared with chap. 11.

Doubt 2. But this presbyterial government is likely to be an arbitrary and tyrannical government, forasmuch as the presbyters of the assembly of divines and others (who, Diotrephes-like, generally affect domineering) have desired an unlimited power, according to their own judgments and prudence, in excommunicating men from the ordinances in cases of scandal.

Resol. A heinous charge, could it be proved against the presbyterial government. Now for wiping off this black aspersion, consider two things, viz: I. The imputation itself, which is unjust and groundless; II. The pretended ground hereof, which is false or frivolous.

I. The imputation itself is, that the presbyterial government is likely to be an arbitrary and tyrannical government. *Ans.* How unjust this aspersion! I. What likelihood of arbitrary conduct in this government, that is, that it should be managed and carried on according to men's mere will and pleasure? For, 1. The presbyterial government (truly so called) is not in the nature of it any invention of man, but an ordinance of Christ; nor in the execution of it to be stated by the will of man, but only by the sure word of prophecy, the sacred Scriptures. This government allows not of one church officer at all; nor of one ruling assembly made up of those officers; nor of one censure or act of power to be done by any officer or assembly; nor of one ordinance to be managed in the Church of God, but what are grounded upon, and warranted by the word of God. This government allows no execution of any part thereof, neither in substantials, nor circumstantials, but according to the particular, or at least, the general rules of Scripture respectively. And can that be arbitrary, which is not at all according to man's will, but only according to Christ's rule, limiting and ordering man's will? Or is not the Scripture a better and safer provision against all arbitrary government in the Church, than all the ordinances, decrees, statutes, or whatsoever municipal laws in the world of man's devising, can be against all arbitrary government in the commonwealth? Let not men put out their own eyes, though others would cast a mist before them. 2. Who can justly challenge the reformed presbyterial churches for arbitrary proceedings in matters of church government, practised in some of them for above these fourscore years? Or where are their accusers? 3. Why should the presbyterial government, to be erected in England, be prejudged as arbitrary, before the government be put in execution? When arbitrary conduct appears, let the adversaries complain. 4. If any arbitrary conduct hath been discovered in any reformed church, or shall fall out in ours, it is or shall be more justly reputed the infirmity and fault of the governors, than of the government itself.

II. What probability or possibility of tyranny in the presbyterial government? For, 1. Who should tyrannize, what persons, what ruling assemblies? Not the ministers; for, hitherto they have given no just cause of any suspicion, since this government was in hand: and they are counterpoised in all assemblies with a plurality of ruling elders, it being already studiously provided that there be always two ruling elders to one minister: if there be still two to one, how should they tyrannize if they would? Neither ministers nor ruling elders are likely to tyrannize, if due care be taken by them, whom it doth concern, to elect, place, and appoint, conscientious, prudent, and gracious ministers and ruling elders over all congregations. Nor yet the ruling assemblies, lesser or greater; for in the presbyterial government all lesser ruling assemblies (though now at first, perhaps, some of them consisting of more weak and less experienced members) are subordinate to the greater authoritatively; and persons aggrieved by any mal-administrations have liberty to appeal from inferior to superior: and the very national assembly itself, though not properly subordinate, yet is it to be responsible to the supreme political magistracy in all their proceedings so far as subjects and members of the commonwealth.

III. How can they tyrannize over any? Or in what respects? Not over their estates: for they claim no secular power at all over men's estates, by fines, penalties, forfeitures, or confiscations. Not over their bodies, for they inflict no corporal punishment, by banishment, imprisonment, branding, slitting, cropping, striking, whipping, dismembering, or killing. Not over their souls; for, them they desire by this government to gain, Matth. xviii. 15; to edify, 2 Cor. x. 8, and xiii. 10; and to save, 1 Cor. v. 5. Only this government ought to be impartial and severe against sin, that the flesh may be destroyed, 1 Cor. v. 5. It is only destructive to corruption, which is deadly and destructive to the soul. Thus the imputation itself of arbitrary conduct and tyranny to the presbyterial government is unjust and groundless.

II. The pretended ground of this aspersion is false and frivolous. The presbyters of the Assembly of Divines, and others (*Diotrephes*-like, affecting pre-eminence) have desired an unlimited power, according to their own prudence and judgment, in keeping men from the ordinances in cases of scandal not enumerated. *Ans.* 1. The presbyters of the Assembly and others, are so far from the domineering humor of Diotrephes, that they could gladly and

5

heartily have quitted all intermeddling in church government, if Jesus Christ had not by office engaged them thereto, only to have dispensed the word and sacraments would have procured them less hatred, and more ease. 2. They desired liberty to keep from the ordinances, not only persons guilty of the scandals enumerated, but of all such like scandals, (and to judge which are those scandals, not according to their minds unlimitedly, but according to the mind of Christ in his word, more sure than all ordinances or acts of Parliament in the world.) And was this so hideous a desire? This liberty was desired, not for themselves, but for well-constituted elderships. As great power was granted by the very service-book to every single curate; (see the Rubric before the communion.) A perfect enumeration and description of scandals can be made in no book but in the Scriptures; and when all is done, must we not refer thither? All scandals are punishable, as well as any, and to inflict penalties on some, and not on others as bad or worse, is inexcusable partiality. Why should not presbyteries duly constituted, especially the greater, be accounted, at least, as faithful, intelligent, prudent, and every way as competent judges of what is scandal, and what not, according to the Scriptures, and that without arbitrary conduct and tyranny, as any civil court, committees, or commissioners whatsoever? Ruling church assemblies are intrusted with the whole government in the church, consequently with this, and every part. The best reformed churches allow to their presbyteries power to keep from the ordinances scandalous persons, not only for scandals enumerated, but for scandals of like nature not enumerated, with some general clause or other, as may appear in eight several churches, according to the allegations here in the foot-note;4 and, therefore, no new thing is desired, but what is commonly practised in the reformed churches, whom we should imitate so far as they lead us on towards purity and perfection.

Doubt 3. But the independent government seems to be a far more excellent way, and it is embraced by many godly and precious people and ministers.

Ans. 1. What true excellency is there at all in the whole independent government, save only in those particulars wherein it agrees with the presbyterial government; and only so far as it is presbyterial? Therefore, the presbyterial government is equally, yea, primarily and principally excellent. Wherein is the excellency of the independent way of government? 1st. Have they only those officers which Christ himself hath appointed, pastors and teachers, ruling elders and deacons? So the Presbyterians. 2d. Have they those spiritual censures, of admonishing, excommunicating, and receiving again into communion, which Christ ordained in his Church, for guarding his ordinances, and well guiding of the flock? So the Presbyterians. 3d. Have they congregational presbyteries duly elected, and constituted for the exercise of all acts of government, proper and necessary for their respective congregations? So the Presbyterians. 4th. Have they liberty of electing their own5 officers, pastors, elders, and deacons? So the Presbyterians. 5th. Have they power to keep the whole lump of the Church from being leavened, and purely to preserve the ordinances of Christ, from pollution and profanation, &c.? So the Presbyterians, &c. So that whereinsoever the independent government is truly excellent, the presbyterial government stands in a full equipage and equality of excellence.

II. What one true excellence is there in the whole independent government in any one point, wherein it really differs from the presbyterial government? Take for instance a few points of difference.

In the independent government.	*In the presbyterial government.*
No other visible Church of Christ is acknowledged, but only a single congregational meeting in one place to partake of all ordinances.	One general visible Church of Christ on earth is acknowledged, and all particular churches; and single congregations are but as similar parts of that whole.
The matter of their visible Church must be to their utmost judgment of discerning such as have true grace, real saints.	The matter of the Church invisible are only true believers, but of the Church visible persons professing true faith in Christ, and obedience to him according to the rules of the Gospel.

Their churches are gathered out of other true visible churches of Christ, without any leave or consent of pastor or flock; yea, against their wills, receiving such as tender themselves, yea, too often by themselves or others, directly or indirectly seducing disciples after them.	Parochial churches are received as true visible churches of Christ, and most convenient for mutual edification. Gathering churches out of churches, hath no footsteps in Scripture; is contrary to apostolical practice; is the scattering of churches, the daughter of schism, the mother of confusion, but the stepmother to edification.
Preaching elders are only elected, not ordained.	Preaching elders are both elected and ordained.
Ruling elders also preach.	Ruling elders only rule, preach not, 1 Tim. v. 17.
The subject of church government is the community of the faithful.	The subject of church government is only Christ's own church officers.
The church officers act immediately as the servants of the church, and deputed thereby.	The church governors act immediately as the servants of Christ, and as appointed by him.
All censures and acts of government are dispensed in single congregations ultimately, independently, without all liberty of appeal from them to any superior church assembly; so the parties grieved are left without remedy.	All censures and acts of government are dispensed in congregational presbyteries subordinately, dependently, with liberty of appeal in all cases to presbyterial or synodal assemblies; where parties grieved have sufficient remedy.
There are acknowledged no authoritative classes or synods, in common, great, difficult cases, and in matters of appeals, but only suasive and consultative; and in case advice be not followed, they proceed only to a non-communion.	There are acknowledged, and with happy success used, not only suasive and consultative; but also authoritative classes and synods, in cases of great importance, difficulty, common concernment, or appeals; which have power to dispense all church censures, as need shall require.

Let these and such like particulars in the independent way, differing from the presbyterial, be duly pondered, and then let the impartial and indifferent reader judge, whether they be not the deformities, at least the infirmities of that way.

III. How many true excellences are there in the way of the presbyterial government, wherein it utterly surpasses the independent government! Read but the particulars of the former parallel in the presbyterial government, and then consider how far this transcends, yea, how the independent government is indeed no government at all, to the presbyterial government; wherein is to be found such ample provision, and that according to the word of God, for comely order against confusion; for peace and unity of the Church against schism and division; for truth of the faith against all error and heresy; for piety and unblamableness against all impiety and scandal of conversation; for equity and right against all mal-administrations, whether ignorant, arbitrary, or tyrannical; for the honor and purity of all Christ's ordinances against all contempt, pollution, and profanation; for comfort, quickening, and encouragement of the saints in all the ways of Christ; and consequently for the honor of God and our Lord Jesus Christ in all the mysterious services of his spiritual sanctuary: all which rich advantages, how impossible is it they should ever be found in the independent government so long as it continues independent? And what though some pious minister and people embrace the independent way! This dazzles not the eyes of the intelligent, but of the infirm; we are to be regulated by Scripture warrant, not by human examples. The best of saints have failed in the ecclesiastical affairs; what a sharp contention was there between Paul and Barnabas, Acts xv. 39, &c.; what a dangerous dissimulation was there in Peter, the Jews, and Barnabas! Gal. ii. 11, 12, 13, &c.; and, therefore, it is not safe, prudent, or conscientious, to imitate all the examples of the best, and yet how few are those that have engaged themselves in the independent way, in comparison to the multitude of precious ministers and people, inferior to them neither in parts, learning, piety, nor any other spiritual gift, who are for the presbyterial way of church government! Notwithstanding, let all the true Israel of God constantly follow, not the doubtful practices of unglorified saints, but the written pleasure of the most glorious King of saints; and as many as walk according to this rule, peace shall be on them, and upon the Israel of God.

THE DIVINE RIGHT OF CHURCH GOVERNMENT.

PART I.
OF THE NATURE OF A DIVINE RIGHT: AND HOW MANY WAYS A THING MAY BE OF DIVINE RIGHT.

CHAPTER I.
That there is a Government in the Church of DIVINE RIGHT *now under the New Testament.*

Jesus Christ our Mediator hath *the government* (both of the Church, and of all things for the Church) laid *upon his shoulder*, Isa. ix. 6, and to that end hath *all power in heaven and earth given to him*, Matth. xxviii. 18, John v. 22, Ephes. i. 22. But lapsed man (being full of pride, Psal. x. 2, 4, and enmity against the law of God, Rom. viii. 7) is most impatient of all government of God and of Christ, Ps. ii. 1, 2, 3, with Luke xix. 14, 27; whence it comes to pass, that the *governing* and *kingly power* of Christ hath been opposed in all ages, and especially in this of ours, by quarrelsome queries, wrangling disputes, plausible pretences, subtle policies, strong self-interests, and mere violent wilfulness of many in England, even after they are brought under the *oath of God to reform church government according to the word of God.* Yet it will be easily granted *that there should be a government in the Church of God*, otherwise the Church would become a mere *Babel* and *chaos* of confusion, and be in a far worse condition than all human societies in the whole world: and *that some one church government is much to be preferred before another, yea, before all other*, as being most desirable in itself, and most suitable to this state; otherwise, why is the *Prelatical* government rejected, that another and a better may be erected instead thereof? But the pinch lies in this, *Whether there be any government in the Church visible of divine right?* And, if so, *which of those church governments* (which lay claim to a divine right for their foundation) *may be most clearly evinced by the Scriptures to be of* divine right *indeed?* If the former be convincingly affirmed, the fancy of the *Erastians* and *semi-Erastians* of these things will vanish, that deny all government to the Church distinct from that of the civil magistrate. If the latter be solidly proved by Scripture, it will appear, whether the *monarchical government* of the pope and prelates; or the *mere democratical government* of all the people in an equal level of authority, as among the Brownists; or the *mixed democratical government* of both elders and people within their own single congregation only, without all subordination of Assemblies, and benefit of appeals, as among the Independents; or rather the *pure representative government* of the presbytery or church rulers only, chosen by the people, in subordination to superior synodical assemblies, and with appeals thereto, as it is among the Presbyterians, be that peculiar government which Jesus Christ hath left unto his church, by divine right, and in comparison of which all others are to be rejected.

To draw things therefore to a clear and speedy issue about the divine right of church government, let this general proposition be laid down—

The Scriptures declare, That there is a government of DIVINE RIGHT *in the visible Church of Christ now under the New Testament.*

This is evident, 1 Cor. xii. 28, *God hath set some in the Church, first, Apostles, secondly, Prophets, thirdly, Teachers—Helps, Governments;* in which place these things are plain: 1. That here the Apostle speaks of the visible Church: for he had formerly spoken of visible gifts and *manifestations of the Spirit given to profit this* Church *withal*, ver. 7 to 12. He also compares this Church of God to a visible organical body, consisting of many visible members, ver. 12, 13, &c. And in this 28th verse he enumerates the visible officers of this Church. 2. That here the Apostle speaks of one general visible Church; for he saith not *churches*, but *church*, in the singular number, that is, of one; besides, he speaks here of the Church in such a latitude as to comprehend in itself all gifts of the Spirit, all members, and all officers, both extraordinary and ordinary, which cannot be meant of the church of Corinth, or any one particular church, but only of that one general Church on earth. 3. That this general visible Church here meant, is the Church of Christ now under the New Testament, and not under the Old Testament; for he mentions here the New Testament officers only, ver. 28. 4. That in the visible Church now under the New Testament, there is a government settled; for besides *Apostles, Prophets*, and *Teachers*, here is mention of another sort of officer distinct from them all, called, in the abstract, *Governments*, a metaphor from pilots, mariners, or shipmasters, who by their helm, card, or compass, cables, and other tacklings, guide, and order, turn and twine the ship as necessity shall require; so these officers called *Governments*, have a power of governing and steering the spiritual vessel of the Church; thus, Beza on this place, says he declares the order of Presbyters, *who are keepers of discipline and church polity*. For how improperly should these, or any officers be styled *Governments in the Church*, if they had not a power of government in the Church settled upon them? Nor can this be interpreted of the civil magistrate; for, when the Apostle wrote this, the Church had her government, when yet she had no civil magistrate to protect her; and when did God ever take this power from the Church and settle it upon the civil magistrate? Besides, all the other officers here enumerated are purely ecclesiastical officers; how groundless then and inconsistent is it under this name of *Governments* to introduce a foreign power, viz. the political magistrate, into the list and roll of mere church officers? Finally, the civil magistrate, as a magistrate, is not so much as a member of the visible Church, (for then all Pagan magistrates should be members of the Church,) much less a governor in the Church of Christ. 5. That this government settled in the Church is of divine right; for, of those *Governments*, as well as of *Apostles, Prophets*, and *Teachers*, it is said, *God hath set* them *in the Church. God hath set* them, *hath put, set*—Tremellius out of the Syriac. Hath *constituted, ordained*—Beza out of the Greek. Now, if they be set in the Church and God hath set them there, here is a plain divine right for government in the Church.

Add hereto, 2 Cor. x. 8, "Of our authority, which the Lord hath given to us for the edification, and not for the destruction of you." Here are mentioned—1. Church power or authority for government in the Church. 2. The end of this power—positively, for the edification; negatively, not for the destruction of the Church. 3. The Author or Fountain of this authority—the Lord Christ hath given it, dispensed it; there is the divine right. 4. The proper subjects intrusted with this authority, viz: the church guides, our authority, which he hath given to us. They are the receptacle of power for the Church, and the government thereof. Compare also 1 Thes. v. 12, Matth. xvi. 19, 20, with xviii. 11, and John xx. 21, 22, 23. In which and divers like places the divine right of church government is apparently vouched by the Scripture, as will hereafter more fully appear; but this may suffice in general for the confirmation of this general proposition.

CHAPTER II.
Of the Nature of a DIVINE RIGHT in general.

Now touching this divine right of church government, two things are yet more particularly to be opened and proved, for the more satisfactory clearing thereof unto sober minds, to unprejudiced and unpre-engaged judgments, viz:—1. What the nature of a divine right is, and how many ways a thing may be said to be of divine right, and that by warrant of Scripture. 2. What the nature of the government of the Church under the New Testament is, which is vouched by the Scripture to be of divine right.

For the first—viz. What the nature of a divine right is—consider both what a divine right is in general, and how many ways a thing may be said by Scripture warrant to be of divine right in particular.

Right is that which is most proper, just, or equal; or that which is prescribed or commanded by some statute law, and is just to be received in virtue of said law.

Divine sometimes points out a divine warrant or authority from God, engraven or enstamped upon any thing, whereby it is exalted above all human or created authority and power. And thus, all Scripture is styled divinely breathed or inspired of God. Hence is the divine authority of Scripture asserted, 2 Tim. iii. 16, 17; and in this sense divine right is here spoken of, in reference to church government, as it signifies a divine warrant and authority from God himself, engraven upon that church government and discipline, (hereafter to be handled,) and revealed to us in his holy Scriptures, the infallible and perfect oracles. So that divine right, according to this interpretation of the terms, is that which is either just, meet, and equal; or commanded and enjoined by any divine warrant or authority. And generally, a thing may be said to be of divine right, which is any way divinely just, equal, &c.; or divinely commanded by any law of God, or by that which is equivalent to a divine law. And whatsoever matters in church government can be proved by Scripture to have this stamp of divine warrant and authority set upon them, they may properly be said to be of divine right, and that by the will and appointment of Jesus Christ, to whom God hath delegated all power and authority for the government of his Church, Matth. xxviii. 18, 19, 20, Isa. ix. 6, John v. 22, Eph. i. 22. In this sense, if church government, or any part of it, be found to be of divine right, then consequently—1. It is above all mere human power and created authority in the world whatsoever, and that supereminently. A divine right is the highest and best tenure whereby the Church can hold of Christ any doctrine, worship, or government; only God can stamp such a divine right upon any of these things, whereby conscience shall be obliged. All human inventions herein, whether devised of our own hearts, or derived as traditions from others, are incompatible and inconsistent herewith; vain in themselves, and to all that use them, and condemned of God. See 1 Kings xii. 32, 33, Isa. xxix. 4, Matth. xv. 6, 7, 8, 9. 2. It is beyond all just, human, or created power, to abolish or oppose the same, or the due execution thereof in the Church of Christ; for what is of divine right, is held of God, and not of man; and to oppose that, were to fight against God. The supreme magistrates in such cases should be nurse-fathers, Isa. xlix. 23, not step-fathers to the Church; their power being cumulative and perfective, not privative and destructive unto her; for she both had and exercised a power in church government, long before there was any Christian magistrate in the world; and it cannot be proved that ever Christ took away that power from his Church, or translated it to the political magistrate, when he became Christian. 3. It is so obligatory upon all churches in the whole Christian world, that they ought uniformly to submit themselves unto it; for a divine right is equally obligatory on one church as well as on another. And it is so obligatory on all persons, states, and degrees, that none ought to be exempted from that church government which is of divine right, nor to be *tolerated* in another church government, which is but of human invention; nor ought any Christian to seek after, or content himself with any such exemption or *toleration*; for in so doing, the inventions of men should be preferred before the ordinances of God; our own wisdom, will, and authority, before the wisdom, will, and authority of Christ: and we should in effect say, *We will not have this man to reign over us*, Luke xix. 27. *Let us break their bands asunder, and cast their cords away from us*, Psalm ii. 3.

CHAPTER III.
Of the Nature of a DIVINE RIGHT *in particular. How many ways a thing may be of* DIVINE RIGHT. *And first, of a* DIVINE RIGHT *by the true light of nature.*

Thus we see in general what a divine right is: now in particular let us come to consider how many ways a thing may be said to be of divine right by scripture-warrant, keeping still our eye upon this subject of church government, at which all particulars are to be levelled for the clearing of it.

A thing may be said to be of divine right, or (which is the same for substance) of divine institution, divers ways. 1. *By the true light of nature.* 2. *By obligatory scripture examples.* 3. *By divine approbation*. 4. *By divine acts*. 5. *By divine precepts or mandates*. All may be reduced to these five heads, ascending by degrees from the lowest to the highest divine right.

I. *By light of nature*. That which is evident by, and consonant to the true light of nature, or natural reason, is to be accounted of divine right in matters of religion. Hence two things are to be made out by Scripture. 1. What is meant by the true light of nature. 2. How it may be proved, that what things in religion are evident by, or consonant to this true light of nature, are of divine right.

1. For the first, What is meant by the true light of nature, or natural reason? Thus conceive. The light of nature may be considered two ways. 1. As it was in man before the fall, and so it was that image and similitude of God, in which man was at first created, Gen. i. 26, 27, or at least part of that image; which image of God, and light of nature, was con-created with man, and was perfect: viz. so perfect as the sphere of humanity and state of innocency did require; there was no sinful darkness, crookedness, or imperfection in it; and whatsoever was evident by, or consonant to this pure and perfect light of nature, in respect either of theory or practice, was doubtless of divine right, because correspondent to that divine law of God's image naturally engraved in Adam's heart. But man being lapsed, this will not be now our question, as it is not our case. 2. As it is now in man after the fall. The light of nature and image of God in man is not totally abolished and utterly razed by the fall; there remain still some relics and fragments thereof, some glimmerings, dawnings, and common principles of light, both touching piety to God, equity to man, and sobriety to a man's self, &c., as is evident by comparing these places, Psal. xix. 1, 2, &c., Acts xiv. 17, and xvii. 27, 28; Rom. i. 18-21, and ii. 12, 14, 15; 2 Cor. v. 1: in which places it is plain, 1. That the book of the creature is able (without the scriptures, or divine revelations) to make known to man much of God, his invisible Godhead and attributes, Psalm xix. 1, 2, &c.; Acts xiv. 17, and xvii. 27, 28; yea, so far as to leave them without excuse, Rom. i. 18-21. 2. That there remained so much natural light in the minds even of the heathens, as to render them capable of instruction by the creature in the invisible things of God; yea, and that they actually in some measure did know God, and because they walked not up to this knowledge, were plagued, Rom. i. 18-21, 24, &c. 3. That the work of the law (though not the right ground, manner, and end of that work, which is the blessing of the new covenant, Jer. xxxi. 33; Heb. viii. 10) was materially written in some measure in their hearts. Partly because they did by nature without the law the things contained in the law, so being a law to themselves, Rom. ii. 14, 15; partly, because they by nature forbore some of those sins which were forbidden in the law, and were practised by some that had the law, as 2 Cor. v. 1; and partly, because according to the good and bad they did, &c., their conscience did accuse or excuse, Rom. ii. 15. Now conscience doth not accuse or excuse but according to some rule, principle, or law of God, (which is above the conscience,) or at least so supposed to be. And they had no law but the imperfect characters thereof in their own hearts, which were not quite obliterated by the fall. Now so far as this light of nature after the fall, is a true relic of the light of nature before the fall, that which is according to this light may be counted of divine right in matters of religion, which is the next thing to be proved.

For the second, how it may be proved that what things in religion are evident by, or consonant to this true light of nature, are of divine right. Thus briefly,

1. Because that knowledge which by the light of nature Gentiles have of the invisible things of God, is a beam of divine light, as the apostle, speaking of the Gentiles' light of nature, saith, That which may be known of God is manifest in them—for God hath showed it to them. For the invisible things, &c., Rom. i. 19, 20. God himself is the Fountain and Author of the true light of nature; hence some not unfitly call it the divine light of nature, not only because it hath God for its object, but also God for its principle; now that which is according to God's manifestation, must needs be of divine right.

2. Because the Spirit of God and of Christ in the New Testament is pleased often to argue from the light of nature in condemning of sin, in commending and urging of duty, as in the case of the incestuous Corinthian; "It is reported commonly, that there is fornication among you, and such fornication as is not so much as named among the Gentiles," (who had only the light of nature to guide them,) 1 Cor. v. 1. In case of the habits of men and women in their public church assemblies, that women's heads should be covered, men's uncovered

in praying or prophesying. "Judge in yourselves, is it comely that a woman pray unto God uncovered? Doth not even nature itself teach you, that if a man hath long hair, it is a shame to him? but if a woman have long hair it is a glory to her," &c., 1 Cor. xi. 13-15. Here the apostle appeals plainly to the very light of nature for the regulating and directing of their habits in church assemblies; and thus, in case of praying or prophesying in the congregation in an unknown tongue, (unless some do interpret,) he strongly argues against it from the light of nature, 1 Cor. xiv. 7-11, and afterwards urges that women be silent in their churches, from the natural uncomeliness of their speaking there, for it is a shame for women to speak in the church, 1 Cor. xiv. 34, 35.

Now, if the Spirit of God condemn things as vicious, and commend things as virtuous from the light of nature, is there not divine right in the light of nature? May we not say, that which is repugnant to the light of nature in matters of religion, is condemned by divine right; and what is correspondent to the light of nature, is prescribed by divine right? And if not, where is the strength or force of this kind of arguing from the light of nature?

Consequently, in the present case of church government, that which is agreeable to the true light of nature, must needs be confessed to be of divine right. Though the light of nature be but dim, yet it will lend some help in this particular: e.g. the light of nature teaches, 1. That as every society in the world hath a distinct government of its own within itself, without which it could not subsist, so must the Church, which is a society, have its own distinct government within itself, without which it cannot subsist more than any other society. 2. That in all matters of difference the lesser number in every society should give way to, and the matters controverted be determined and concluded by the major part; else there would never be an end: and why not so in the Church? 3. That in every ill administration in inferior societies the parties aggrieved should have liberty to appeal from them to superior societies, that equity may take place; and why not from inferior to superior church assemblies?

CHAPTER IV.
II. *Of a Divine Right by obligatory Scripture Examples.*

II. By obligatory scripture examples (which God's people are bound to follow and imitate) matters of religion become of divine right, and by the will and appointment of Jesus Christ, by whose Spirit those examples were recorded in Scripture, and propounded for imitation to the saints. The light of nature in this case helps something; but the light of obligatory scripture examples helps much more, as being more clear, distinct, and particular. We say scripture examples; for only these examples are held forth to us by an infallible, impartial, divine hand, and those scripture examples obligatory, or binding; for there are many sorts of scripture examples that oblige not us to imitation of them, being written for other uses and purposes.

Great use is to be made of such examples in matters of religion, and particularly in matters of church government, for the clearing of the divine right thereof; and great opposition is made by some against the binding force of examples, especially by men of perverse spirits, (as too many of the Erastian party are;) therefore it will be of great consequence to unfold and clear this matter of scripture examples, and the obliging power thereof, that we may see how far examples are to be a law and rule for us by divine right. In general, this proposition seems to be unquestionable, that whatsoever matter or act of religion Jesus Christ makes known to his Church and people, by or under any binding scripture example, that matter or act of religion so made known, is of divine right, and by the will and appointment of Jesus Christ: But to evince this more satisfactorily, these several particulars are to be distinctly made good and manifested: 1. That some scripture examples are obligatory and binding on Christians in matters of religion. 2. Which are those obligatory scripture examples? These things being made out, we shall see with what strength scripture examples hold forth a divine right to us in the mysteries of religion, and particularly in church government.

12

I. That some scripture examples in matters of religion are obligatory on Christians, as patterns and rules, which they are bound in conscience to follow and imitate, is evident,

1. By the divine intention of the Spirit of God, in recording and propounding of examples in Scripture: for he records and propounds them for this very end, that they may be imitated. Thus Christ's humility, in washing the feet of his disciples, was intentionally propounded as an obligatory example, binding both the disciples, and us after them, to perform the meanest offices of love in humility to one another. "If I then, your Lord and Master, have washed your feet, ye ought also to wash one another's feet. For I have given you an example, that ye should do as I have done to you," John xiii. 4, &c., 13-15. Thus Christ's suffering with innocence and unprovoked patience, not reviling again, &c., is purposely propounded for all Christians to imitate, and they are bound in conscience as well as they can to follow it—"Christ suffered for us, leaving us an example, that ye should follow his steps," &c., 1 Pet. ii. 21-23. Hence, the apostle so urges the example of Christ for the Corinthians to follow in their bounty to the poor saints, yea, though to their own impoverishing, "For you know the grace of our Lord Jesus Christ, that though he was rich, yet for your sakes he became poor, that ye through his poverty might be rich," 2 Cor. viii. 9. Nor was the example of Christ only written for our imitation; but the examples of the apostles also in the primitive churches were intentionally left upon record for this end, that they might be binding patterns for us to follow in like cases in after ages. And in particular, this seems to be one singular ground, scope, and intention of Christ's Spirit in writing the history of the Acts of the Apostles, that the apostles' acts in the primitive churches might be our rules in successive churches. For, 1. Though this book contain in it many things dogmatical, that is, divers doctrines of the apostles, yet it is not styled the book of the doctrine, but of the Acts of the Apostles, that we may learn to act as they acted. This being one main difference between profane and sacred histories; those are for speculation, these also for admonition and imitation, 1 Cor. x. 11. The history, therefore, of the Acts propounds examples admonitory and obligatory upon us, that we should express like acts in like cases. 2. Luke (the penman of the Acts) makes such a transition from his history of Christ, to this history of Christ's apostles, as to unite and knit them into one volume, Acts i. 1; whence we are given to understand, that if the Church wanted this history of the apostles, she should want that perfect direction which the Spirit intended for her: as also that this book is useful and needful to her as well as the other. 3. In the very front of the Acts it is said, that *Christ after his resurrection* (and before his ascension) *gave commandments to the apostles— and spake of the things pertaining to the kingdom of God*, Acts i. 2, 3; viz. of the polity of the Church, say some.6 Of the kingdom of grace, say others.7 Judicious Calvin8 interprets it partly of church government, saying, Luke admonisheth us, that Christ did not so depart out of the world, as to cast off all care of us: for by this doctrine he shows that he hath constituted a perpetual government in his Church. Therefore Luke signifies, that Christ departed not, before he had provided for his Church's government. Now those expressions are set in the frontispiece, to stamp the greater authority and obligatory power upon the acts after recorded, being done according to Christ's commandments; Christ intending their acts in the first founding of his kingdom and polity ecclesiastic to be the rule for after churches. For what Christ spoke of his kingdom to the apostles is like that, "What I say to you, I say to all," Matt. xiii. 37, as what was said to the apostles touching preaching and baptizing, remitting and retaining of sins, was said to all the apostles' successors, "to the end of the world," John xx. 21, 23, with Matt, xxviii. 18-20.

2. By God's approving and commending such as were followers not only of the doctrine, but also of the examples of the Lord, his apostles, and primitive churches; "And ye became followers" (or imitators) "of us and of the Lord," 1 Thess. i. 6, 7; and again, "Ye, brethren, became followers" (or imitators) "of the churches of God, which in Judea are in Christ Jesus: for ye also have suffered like things of your own countrymen, even as they have of the Jews," 1 Thess. ii. 14. In which places the Holy Ghost recites the Thessalonians imitating of the Lord, of the apostles, and of the churches, to the praise of the Thessalonians, by which they are given to understand that they did well, and discharged their duty in such imitations: for God's condemning or commending any thing, is virtually a prohibiting or prescribing thereof.

3. By the Lord's commanding some examples to be imitated. Commands of this nature are frequent. In general, "Beloved, imitate not that which is evil, but that which is good," 3 John 11. In particular, 1. Imitating of God and Christ; "Be ye, therefore, followers of God as dear children: and walk in love, as Christ also hath loved us," Eph. v. 1, 2, with Eph. iv. 32. "He that saith he abideth in him, ought himself also to walk, even as he walked," 1 John ii. 6. 2. Imitating the apostles and other saints of God. "I beseech you, be ye imitators of me: for this cause have I sent unto you Timothy—who shall bring you into remembrance of my ways which be in Christ," 1 Cor. iv. 16, 17. "Be ye imitators of me, even as I also am of Christ," 1 Cor. xi. 1.

"Those things which you have both learned, and received, and heard, and seen in me, do: and the God of peace shall be with you," Phil. iv. 9. "Be not slothful, but imitators of them who through faith and patience inherit the promises," Heb. vi. 12. "Whose faith imitate, considering the end of their conversation," Heb. xiii. 7. "Take, my brethren, the prophets, who have spoken in the name of the Lord, for an example" (or pattern) "of suffering affliction, and of patience," James v. 10. These and like divine commands infallibly evidence that many scripture examples are obligatory, and do bind our consciences to the imitation of them.

4. By consent of orthodox and learned writers, both ancient and modern, acknowledging an obligatory force in some scripture examples, as being left upon record for our imitation. As among others Chrysostom,9 and Greg. Nyssen10 well observe.

Among modern writers, Mr. Perkins excellently observes, This is a rule in divinity, that the ordinary examples of the godly approved in Scripture, being against no general precept, have the force of a general rule, and are to be followed. See also Pet. Martyr, Calvin, and others.11

II. Thus, it is clear that some scripture examples are obligatory. Now (to come closer to the matter) consider which scripture examples are obligatory. 1. How many sorts of binding examples are propounded to us in Scripture. 2. What rules we may walk by for finding out the obligatory force of such examples.

How many sorts of binding examples are propounded unto us in Scripture, and which are those examples? Ans. There are principally three sorts, viz: Examples of God, of Christ, of Christians.

I. Of God. The example of God is propounded in Scripture as obligatory on us in all moral excellencies and actions: e.g. Matt. v. 44, 45, 48; Eph. v. 1; 1 Pet. i. 14-16; 1 John iv. 10, 11.

II. Of Christ. That the example of Christ is obligatory, and a binding rule to us for imitation, is evident by these and like testimonies of Scripture, Matt. xi. 29; 1 Cor. xi. 11; Eph. v. 2, 3, 25, &c.; 1 John ii. 6; 1 Pet. ii. 21-23. "If I then, your Lord and Master, have washed your feet, ye ought also to wash one another's feet. For I have given you an example, that ye should do as I have done to you," John xiii. 14, 15. In this place we must follow the reason of the example, rather than the individual act, viz: after Christ's example, we must be ready to perform the lowest and meanest offices of love and service to one another.

But which of Christ's examples are obligatory on Christians, will better appear, by distinguishing the several sorts of Christ's actions. Christ's actions were of several kinds; and to imitate them all is neither needful, nor possible, nor warrantable. Orthodox writers thus rank Christ's actions:

1. Some of Christ's actions were of divine power and virtue; as his miracles, turning water into wine, John ii. 7, &c.; walking on the sea, Mark vi. 48, 49; dispossessing of devils by his word, Mark i. 27; Luke iv. 36; curing one born blind with clay and spittle, John ix.; healing the sick by his word or touch, John iv. 50; Mark vi. 56; raising the dead to life again, as John xii. 1; Matt. xi. 5; Luke vii. 22.

2. Some were acts of divine prerogative, as sending for the ass and colt, without first asking the owner's leave, Matt. xxi. 2, &c.

3. Some mediatory, done by him as Mediator, Prophet, Priest, and King of his Church: e.g. inditing the Scripture, called therefore the word of Christ, Col. iii. 16; laying down his life *for the sheep*, John x. 15, &c.; giving of the Spirit, John xx. 22; Acts ii.; appointing of his own officers, and giving them commissions, Eph. iv. 7, 10, 11; Matt. x. and xxviii. 18-

20; instituting of new, and thereby abrogating of old ordinances, Matt. xxviii. 18, 19; 1 Cor. xi. 23, &c.

4. Some accidental, occasional, incidental, or circumstantial, as in the case of his celebrating his supper, that it was at night, not in the morning; after supper, not before; with none but men, none but ministers; with unleavened, not with leavened bread, &c.; these circumstantials were accidentally occasioned by the passover, nature of his family, &c.

5. Some acts of Christ were moral, as Matt. xi. 29; Eph. v. 2, 3, 25, &c.; or at least founded upon a moral reason and foundation, as John xiii. 14,15.

To imitate Christ in his three first sort of acts, is utterly unlawful, and in part impossible. To imitate him in his circumstantial acts from necessity, were to make accidentals necessary, and happily to border upon superstition; for, to urge any thing above what is appointed, as absolutely necessary, is to urge superstition; and to yield to any thing above what is appointed, as simply necessary, were to yield to superstition. But to imitate Christ in his moral acts, or acts grounded upon a moral reason, is our duty: such acts of Christ ought to be the Christian's rules.

III. Of prophets, apostles, saints, or primitive churches. That their examples are obligatory, is evident by these places, 1 Cor. xi. 1; Phil. iv. 8, 9; 1 Pet. iii. 4, 5, 6; 1 Thess. i. 6, and ii. 14; Heb. xiii. 7; James v. 10, 11; 3 John 11.

Which of their examples are obligatory, may be thus resolved, by distinguishing of their actions.

1. Some were sinful; written for our caution and admonition, not for our imitation: as 1 Cor. x. 5, 6, 10, 12. That neither the just be lifted up into pride by security, nor the unjust be hardened against the medicine through despair. See the fourth rule following.

2. Some were heroical; done by singular instinct and instigation of the Spirit of God; as divers acts may be presumed to be, (though we read not the instinct clearly recorded:) as, Elias's calling for fire from heaven, 2 Kings i. 10; which the very apostles might not imitate, not having his spirit, Luke ix. 54, 55; Phinehas's killing the adulterer and adulteress, Numb. xxv. 7, 8; Samson's avenging himself upon his enemies by his own death, Judges xvi. 30, of which, saith Bernard, if it be defended not to have been his sin, it is undoubtedly to be believed he had private counsel, viz. from God, for his fact; David's fighting with Goliath of Gath the giant, hand to hand, 1 Sam. xvii. 32, &c., which is no warrant for private duels and quarrels. Such heroic acts are not imitable but by men furnished with like heroic spirit, and instinct divine.

3. Some were by special calling, and singular extraordinary dispensation: as Abraham's call to leave his own country for pilgrimage in Canaan, Gen. xii. 1, 4, which is no warrant for popish pilgrimages to the holy land, &c.; Abraham's attempts, upon God's special trying commands, to kill and sacrifice his son, Gen. xxii. 10, no warrant for parents to kill or sacrifice their children; the Israelites borrowing of, and robbing the Egyptians, Exod. xii. 35, no warrant for cozenage, stealing, or for borrowing with intent not to pay again: compare Rom. xiii. 8; 1 Thess. iv. 6; Psal. xxxvii. 21; the Israelites taking usury of the Canaanitish strangers, (who were destined to ruin both in their states and persons, Deut. xx. 15-17,) Deut. xxiii. 20, which justifies neither their nor our taking usury of our brethren, Lev. xxv. 36, 37; Deut. xxiii. 19, 20; Neh. v. 7, 10; Psal. xv. 5; Prov. xxviii. 8; Ezek. xviii. 8, 13, 17, and xxii. 12; John Baptist's living in the desert, Mat. iii., no protection for popish hermitage, or proof that it is a state of greater perfection, &c.

4. Some were only accidental or occasional, occasioned by special necessity of times and seasons, or some present appearance of scandal, or some such accidental emergency. Thus primitive Christians had all things common, Acts iv. 32, but that is no ground for anabaptistical community. Paul wrought at his trade of tent-making, made his hands *minister to his necessities*, Acts xx. 34; would not take wages for preaching to the church of Corinth, 2 Cor. xi. 7-9; but this lays no necessity on ministers to preach the gospel *gratis*, and maintain themselves by their own manual labors, except when cases and seasons are alike, Gal. vi. 6-8; 1 Cor. ix. 6-13; 1 Tim. v. 17, 18.

5. Some were of a moral nature, and upon moral grounds, wherein they followed Christ, and we are to follow them, 1 Cor. xi. 1; Phil. iv. 8, 9, and other places forementioned; for, whatsoever actions were done then, upon such grounds as are of a moral, perpetual, and

common concernment to one person as well as another, to one church as well as another, in one age as well as another, those actions are obligatory on all, and a rule to after generations. Thus the baptizing of women in the primitive churches, Acts viii. 12, and xvi. 15, though only the males were circumcised under the Old Testament, is a rule for our baptizing of women as well as men, they being *all one in Christ*, Gal. iii. 28. So the admitting of infants to the first initiating sacrament of the Old Testament, circumcision, because they with their parents' were accounted within the covenant of grace by God, Gen. xvii., is a rule for us now to admit infants to the first initiating sacrament of the New Testament, baptism, because infants are federally holy, and within the covenant with their believing parents now, as well as then, Rom. xi. 16; 1 Cor. vii. 14; Col. ii. 11, 12. Thus the baptizing of divers persons formerly, though into no particular congregation, nor as members of any particular congregation, as the eunuch, Acts viii.; Lydia, Acts xvi.; the jailer, Acts xvi.; because it was sufficient they were baptized into that one general visible body of Christ, 1 Cor. xii. 12, 13, is a rule for us what to do in like cases upon the same common ground. Thus the Church's practice of preaching the word, and breaking bread on the first day of the week, Acts xx. 7, &c., is our rule for sanctifying the Lord's day, by celebrating the word, sacraments, and other holy ordinances, at these times. And in like manner, the primitive practices of ordaining preaching presbyters, by laying on of hands, 1 Tim. iv. 14; 2 Tim. i. 6; Acts xiii. 3; of governing all the congregations of a city by one common presbytery, in which respect they are all called by the name of one church, as the church of Jerusalem, Acts viii. 1, and xv. 4; the church of Antioch, Acts xiii. 1, and xi. 25, 26; the church of Corinth, 1 Cor. i. 2, 2 Cor. i. 1; which had churches in it, 1 Cor. xiv. 34. Of healing common scandals and errors, troubling divers presbyterial churches by the authoritative decrees of a synod, made up of members from divers presbyterial churches, as Acts xv., and such like, are our rules in like particulars, which the Lord hath left for our direction, the same grounds of such actions reaching us as well as them.

Now this last kind of examples are those which we are, by divers divine commands, especially enjoined to follow; and therefore such examples amount to a divine right or institution; and what we ought to do by virtue of such binding examples is of divine right, and by the will and appointment of Jesus Christ.

What discriminatory notes or rules may we walk by, for finding out the obligatory force of scripture examples; and what manner of examples those be? For discovery hereof, take these ensuing general rules:

1. Those examples in Scripture, which the Spirit of Christ commands us to imitate, are undoubtedly obligatory. Such are the moral examples of God, Christ, apostles, prophets, saints, and churches, recorded in Scripture, with command to follow them, Eph. iv. 32, and v. 1, 2; 1 John ii. 6; 1 Cor. xi. 1; Phil. iv. 6; Heb. vi. 12, and xiii. 7; James v. 10; 3 John 11.

2. Those examples in Scripture, which the Spirit of Christ commends and praises, are obligatory; his commendings are virtual commandings; and we ought to follow whatsoever is praiseworthy, especially in God's account, Phil. iv. 8, 9; 2 Cor. x. 18. Now the Spirit of Christ commends many examples to us: as, *Enoch's walking with God*, Gen. v. 24; *Noah's uprightness*, Gen. vi.; *Abraham's faith*, Rom. iv., *and obedience*, Gen. xxii.; *Lot's zeal against Sodom's sins*, 2 Pet. ii. 9; *Job's patience*, James v. 10, 11. And in a word, all the examples of the saints, which the Lord approves and speaks well of; as Heb. xi.; 1 Pet. iii. 5, 6: together with all such examples, whose imitation by others is commended in Scripture; as, 1 Thess. i. 6, 7, and ii. 14.

3. Those examples in Scripture are obligatory, whose ground, reason, scope, or end, are obligatory, and of a moral nature, and as much concern one Christian as another, one church as another, one time as another, &c., whether they be the examples under the Old or New Testament. Thus the example of the church of Corinth, in excommunicating the incestuous person, because he was a wicked person—and lest he should *leaven the whole lump;* and that they might keep the evangelical passover sincerely, and for that they had power *to judge them within*; and that his "flesh might be destroyed, and his spirit saved in the day of the Lord Jesus," 1 Cor. v. 5-8, 11-13: which grounds and ends being moral, oblige us to use the like remedy against all wicked and scandalous persons.

16

4. Those acts which are propounded in Scripture as patterns or examples, that we should act the like good, or avoid the like ill, are an obligatory law to us. There is an example of caution, and an example of imitation.

Thus in reference to well-doing, or suffering for well-doing, the examples of Christ, his apostles, and other saints, are propounded as patterns to write after, as John xiii. 14, 15; Heb. xi. tot. with Heb. xii. 1, *with such a cloud of witnesses.* This verse is as the epilogue of the former chapter, (saith the learned Calvin,) showing to what end the catalogue of saints was reckoned up, who under the law excelled in faith, viz: that every one may fit himself to imitate them. Another adds,12 He calls them a cloud, whereby we may be directed; in allusion to that cloud that went before Israel in the wilderness, to conduct them to the land of Canaan. See also 1 Pet. ii. 21-23; James v. 10.

Thus also, in reference to ill-doing, that it may be avoided by us, the bad examples of saints and others are laid before us as warnings and cautions to us, binding us to eschew like evils, 1 Cor. x. 5, 6, 11. "Now these things were our examples, to the intent we should not lust after evil things, as they also lusted. Now all these things happened unto them for examples," &c., Jude 7.

5. Those acts of saints or Christians, which were done by them as saints and Christians, are obligatory upon, and to be followed by all Christians; but those acts which are done by magistrates, prophets, apostles, ministers, &c., only as such, are only obligatory on such as have like offices, not on all; according to the maxim, that which agrees to any thing as such, agrees to every thing that is such. Thus James urges the example of Elias in praying, James v. 17. Paul presses the example of Abraham in being justified by believing, Rom. iv. 23,24. Peter prescribes, as a pattern to wives, the example of Sarah, and other holy women of old, for "adorning themselves with a meek and quiet spirit,—being in subjection to their own husbands," 1 Pet. iii. 4-6.

6. Those acts that were commonly and ordinarily done, are ordinarily to be imitated; as, baptizing *in water only,* and not in any other element, was the ordinary practice of the New Testament, Matt. iii. 11, 16; Mark i. 6, 10; Luke iii. 16; John i. 26, 31, 33; Acts i. 5, and viii. 36, 38, and x. 47, and xi. 16; and by that practice we are obliged to baptize in water only. Joining of many Christians together in receiving the Lord's supper was an ordinary practice, Matt. xxvi. 20, 26, 27; Acts ii. 42, and xx. 7, &c.; 1 Cor. xi. 20, and by us ordinarily to be imitated, how else is it a communion? 1 Cor. x. 16, 17.

But such acts as were done only upon special causes or singular reasons, are only to be imitated in like cases. Thus Christ argues from a like special cause, that he was not to do miracles at Nazareth without a call, as he did in other places where he had a call of God; from the particular example of Elijah and Elisha, who only went to them to whom God called them, Luke ix. 25-27; so he proves that in like case of necessity it was lawful for his disciples on the sabbath-day to rub ears of corn and eat them, &c., from David's example of eating show-bread when he had need, Matt. xii. 1-5.

7. Those acts that were done from extraordinary calling and gifts, are to be imitated (in regard of their special way of acting) only by those that have such extraordinary calling and gifts. Christ therefore blames his apostles for desiring to imitate Elijah's extraordinary act in calling for fire from heaven, &c., when they had not his spirit, Luke ix. 54, 55. Papists are blameworthy for imitating the extraordinary forty days' and nights' fast of Moses, Elijah, and Christ, in their Lent fast. Prelates argue corruptly for bishops' prelacy over their brethren the ministers, from the superiority of the apostles over presbyters.

CHAPTER V.
Of a Divine Right by Divine Approbation.

III. By divine approbation of the Spirit of Jesus Christ in his word. Whatsoever in matters of religion hath the divine approbation of the Spirit of Christ in the Scriptures, that is of divine right, and by the will and appointment of Jesus Christ. God's approving or allowing of any thing, plainly implies that it is according to his will and pleasure, and so is equivalent to a divine institution or appointment; for what is a divine institution or law but the publishing of the divine will of the legislator, touching things to be acted or omitted? and God cannot approve any thing that is against his will. Contrariwise, God's disallowing of any thing, plainly implies that it is against his will, and so of divine right prohibited, and unlawful. God allows or disallows things not because they are good or evil; but things are, therefore, good or evil, because he approves or disallows them.

Now God approves or disallows things divers ways:

1. By commending or discommending. God commended king Josiah for his zeal and impartiality in completing of the reformation of religion, 1 Kings xiii. 25. This is a rule for all princes and magistrates how they should reform. The angel of the church of Ephesus is commended, for not bearing of those that were evil, for trying and detecting the false apostles, and for hating the works of the Nicolaitans, Rev. ii. 2, 3, 6. The angel of the church of Pergamus is praised, for holding fast Christ's name, and not denying his faith in places of danger, and days of deepest persecution, Rev. ii. 13: a rule for all pastors and churches, how in all such cases they should carry themselves. God's commendings are divine commandings. On the contrary, God dispraises Ephesus, for falling from her first love, Rev. ii. 4. Pergamus, for holding the doctrine of Balaam, and the doctrine of the Nicolaitans, Rev. ii. 14, 15. Thyatira, for tolerating the false prophetess Jezebel, to teach and seduce his servants, &c., Rev. ii. 20. Laodicea, because she was neither hot nor cold, but lukewarm, Rev. iii. 15. The church of Corinth, for coming together in public assemblies, not for better but for worse, by reason of schisms, scandals, and other disorders about the Lord's supper, 1 Cor. xi. 17, &c. In these and all such divine discommendings of the churches for their corruptions, all succeeding churches are strongly forbidden the like corruptions: God's dispraises are divine prohibitions. Thus good church elders are commended in this notion, that they are *elders ruling well*, 1 Tim. v. 17; therefore, that elders in the church should rule, and rule well, is by this commendation of divine right.

2. By promising and threatening. What promise did God ever make to any act or performance, which was not a duty? or what threatening against any act which was not a sin? He promises to them that forsake all for Christ, a "hundred-fold now in this time, and in the world to come eternal life," Mark x. 29, 30; therefore it is our duty to forsake all for Christ. He promised to ratify in heaven his disciples' sentences of *building or loosing on earth*, and to*be with them* whensoever *two or three of them were met together* for that end, Matt. xvi. 19, and xviii. 18-20, and John xx. 23. Therefore binding and loosing, remitting and retaining of sins, and meeting together for that end, belong to them by divine right. He promised to be with them that baptize, preach, remit, and retain sins in his name, &c., *always, to the end of the world*, John xx. 23; with Matt, xxviii. 18-20, which promise shows, that these works and employments belong to all succeeding ministers to the world's end, as well as to the apostles by divine right. On the contrary, the Lord threatens Ephesus for decay of first love, Rev. ii. 4, 5; Pergamus, for holding false doctrine, Rev. ii. 14, 15; Thyatira, for tolerating of Jezebel and her false teaching, &c., Rev. ii. 21, 21, 23; and Laodicea, for lukewarmness, Rev. iii. 15, 16. Therefore, all these were their sins, and we are bound, even by this divine threatening, to avoid the like by a divine warrant.

3. By remunerating or rewarding; whether he reward with blessings or with judgments. With blessings God rewarded the Hebrew midwives, because they preserved the male children of Israel, contrary to Pharaoh's bloody command; *God made them houses*, Exod. i. 17, 20, 21. He will have the elders that rule well *counted worthy of double honor*, &c.; i.e. rewarded with a bountiful, plentiful maintenance, 1 Tim. v. 17. Therefore, their ruling in the church is of divine right, for which God appoints such a good reward. Contrariwise, with judgments God rewarded king Saul, for offering a burnt-offering himself, 1 Sam. xiii. 12-14; Uzzah, for touching the ark, though it was ready to fall, 2 Sam. vi. 6, 7; and king Uzziah, for going into the temple to burn incense, 2 Chron. xxvi. 16. None of these being priests, yet presuming to meddle with the priest's office. A rule for all persons, being not church officers, yea, though they be princes or supreme magistrates, that they are hereby warned by the divine law, not to usurp church authority or offices to themselves. God rewarded the Corinthians with the judgments of weakness, sickness, and death, for unworthy receiving of the Lord's supper, 1 Cor. xi. 30. So that this is a divine warning for all after churches against unworthy communicating.

18

CHAPTER VI.
IV. *Of a Divine Right by Divine Acts.*

IV. By divine acts. Whatsoever matters of religion were erected in, or conferred upon the Church of God, by God, or any person of the blessed Trinity, and are left recorded in the Scripture, they are of divine right, by the will and appointment of Jesus Christ. Shall divine approbation, yea, shall the saints' binding example hold forth to us a divine right, and shall not the divine actions of God, Christ, and the Spirit, do it much more? Take some instances: the Lord's-day sabbath, under the New Testament, was it not instituted (the seventh day being changed to the first day of the week) by the acts of Christ, having now perfected the spiritual creation of the new world? viz: by his resurrection and apparitions to his disciples on that day, and miraculous blessing and sanctifying of that day, by pouring forth the gifts of the Holy Ghost, Acts ii., all which were seconded with the apostolical practice in the primitive churches, Acts xx. 7, &c.; 1 Cor. xvi. 1, 2. And do not the churches of Christ generally conclude upon these grounds, that the Lord's-day sabbath is of divine warrant? Thus circumcision is abrogated of divine right, by Christ's act, instituting baptism instead thereof, Col. ii. 11, 12. The passover is abolished of divine right, by Christ himself, our true passover,*being sacrificed for us*, 1 Cor. v. 7; and the Lord's supper being instituted a memorial of Christ's death instead of it, Matt, xxvi., Mark xiv., Luke xxii. And the whole ceremonial law is antiquated and made void by Christ's death, accomplishing all those dark types; therefore Christ, immediately before his yielding up the ghost, cried, *It is finished,* John xix. 30. See Col. ii. 14; Eph. ii. 14, 15; *abolishing the law of commandments in ordinances*, Heb. viii. 13, and x. 4, 5, &c. Thus by Christ's act of giving the keys of the kingdom of heaven to Peter and the apostles, Matt. xvi. 19, and xviii. 18, 19, the keys belong to the officers of the church by divine right. By God's act of *setting in the Church some, first apostles*, &c., 1 Cor. xii. 28, all those officers belong to the general visible Church by divine right. By Christ's act of bounty upon his triumphant ascension into heaven, *in giving gifts to men*, Eph. iv. 7, 11, 12; all those church officers being Christ's gifts, are of divine right. Finally, by the Holy Ghost's act, in setting elders, overseers over the flock, Acts xx. 28, elders are such overseers by divine right.

CHAPTER VII.
V. *Of a Divine Right by Divine Precepts.*

V. Finally, and primarily, by divine precepts, whatsoever in matters of religion is commanded or forbidden by God in his word, that is accordingly a duty or sin, by divine right: as, the duties of the whole moral law, the ten words, commanded of God, Exod. xx.; Deut. v. Believing in Christ, commanded of God, 1 John iii. 23. The plentiful and honorable maintenance of ministers, commanded of God, 1 Tim. v. 17, 18; 1 Cor. ix. 9-11, 13, 14; Gal. vi. 6. The people's esteeming, loving, and obeying their pastors and teachers, commanded of God, 1 Thess. v. 12; Heb. xiii. 7, 17. Ministers' diligence and faithfulness, in feeding and watching over their flocks, commanded of God, Acts xx. 28; 2 Tim. iv. 1-3; 1 Pet. iv. 1-3; with innumerable commands and precepts of all sorts: now all things so commanded are evidently of divine right, and without gainsaying, granted on all hands, even by Erastians themselves. But the question will be, how far we shall extend this head of *divine commands.* For clearness' sake, thus distinguish, thus resolve:

God's commands are either immediate or mediate.

1. Immediate divine commands: as those which God propounds and urges; as the ten commandments, Exod. xx., Deut. v., and all other injunctions of his in his word positively laid down. Of such commands, the apostle saith, "I command, yet not I, but the Lord," 1 Cor. vii. 10.

Now these immediate commands of God, in regard of their manner of publishing and propounding, are either explicit or implicit.

19

1. Explicit: which are expressly and in plain terms laid down, as the letter of the commandments of the decalogue, Exod. xx. The commands of Christ, "Feed my lambs, feed my sheep," John xxi.; "Go, disciple ye all nations," &c., Matt, xxviii. 19; "Do this in remembrance of me," Matt, xxvi; 1 Cor. xi. 23, 24, &c. Now whatsoever is expressly commanded of God in plain, evident terms, that is of divine right, without all color of controversy. Only take this caution, the divine right of things enjoined by God's express command, is to be interpreted according to the nature of the thing commanded, and the end or scope of the Lord in commanding: e.g. 1. Some things God commands morally, to be of perpetual use; as to honor father and mother, &c.; these are of divine right forever. 2. Some things he commands but positively, to be of use for a certain season; as the ceremonial administrations till Christ should come, for the Jewish church, and the judicial observances for their Jewish polity; and all these positive laws were of divine right till Christ abrogated them. 3. Some things he commands only by way of trial, not with intention that the things commanded should be done, but that his people's fear, love, and obedience may be proved, tried, &c. Thus God commanded Abraham to offer up his son Isaac for a burnt-offering, Gen. xxii.: such things are of divine right only in such cases of special infallible command. 4. Some things he commands extraordinarily in certain select and special cases: as, *Israel to borrow jewels of the Egyptians to rob them*, without intention ever to restore them, Exod. xi. 2, &c. The disciples to *go preach*—yet to *provide neither gold nor silver*, &c. Matt. x. 7-10. The elders of the church (while miracles were of use in the church) *to anoint the sick with oil in the name of the Lord*, for their recovery, James v. 14. These and like extraordinary commands were only of force by divine right, in these extraordinary select cases, when they were propounded.

1. Implicit, or implied: which are either comprehensively contained in or under the express terms and letter of the command; or, consequentially, are deducible from the express command.

Comprehensively, many things are contained in a command, that are not expressed in the very letter of the command. Thus sound interpreters of the decalogue generally confess, that all precepts thereof include the whole parts under the general term, and God wills many things by them more than the bare words signify: e.g. in negative commands, forbidding sin, we are to understand the positive precepts prescribing the contrary duties; and so, on the contrary, under affirmative commands, we are to understand the negative thereof: thus Christ expounds the sixth commandment, Matt. v. 21-27, and ver. 43, to the end of the chapter. So when any evil is forbidden, not only the outward gross acts, but all inward acts and degrees thereof, with all causes and occasions, all fruits and effects thereof, are forbidden likewise: as, under killing, provoking terms, rash anger, Matt. v. 21, 22; under adultery, wanton looks, lustful thoughts, &c., Matt. v. 27-30. Now all things comprehended in a command (though not expressed) are of divine right.

Consequentially, many things are clearly deducible from express commands in Scripture, by clear, unforced, infallible, and undeniable consequence. Now what things are commanded by necessary consequence, they are of divine right, as well as things in express terms prescribed: e.g. in the case of baptism, have the ordinary ministers of the New Testament any punctual express command to baptize? yet, by consequence, it is evident infallibly, the apostles are commanded to baptize, and the promise is made to them by Christ, that he *will be with them always to the end of the world*, Matt, xxviii. 18-20, which cannot be interpreted of the apostles' persons only; for they were not to live till the world's end, but are dead and gone long ago; but of the apostles and their successors, the ministers of the gospel to the world's end; now to whom the promise of Christ's presence is here to be applied, to them the precept of baptizing and teaching is intended by clear consequence and deduction. So, infants of Christian parents under the New Testament are commanded to be baptized by consequence; for that the infants of God's people under the Old Testament were commanded to be circumcised, Gen. xvii.; for, the privileges of believers under the New Testament are as large as the privileges of believers under the Old Testament: and the children of believers under the New Testament are federally holy, and within the covenant of God, as well as the children of believers under the Old Testament, Gen. xvii., compared with Rom. xi. 16; 1 Cor. vii. 14: and what objections can be made from infants' incapacity now, against their baptism, might as well then have been made against their being circumcised: and why children should once be admitted to the initiating sacrament, and not still be admitted to the like initiating sacrament, (the Lord of the covenant and sacrament nowhere forbidding them,) there can be no just ground. And baptism succeeds in the room of circumcision, Col. ii. 11, 12. *Thus in case of the Lord's supper*, apostles were commanded to dispense it, and men commanded to receive it. "Do ye this in remembrance of me," Matt. xxvi., 1 Cor. xi. 24, 25; yet by consequence, the ministers of the gospel succeeding the apostles, being stewards of the mysteries of God, have the same charge laid upon them; and women as well as men are enjoined to keep that sacrament, whole families communicating in the passover, the forerunner of the Lord's supper, Exod. xiv., and male and female being *all one in Christ*, Gal. iii. 28. *Thus in case of the maintenance of ministers under the New Testament*: the apostle proves it by consequence to be commanded, God hath ordained, &c., from God's command of not *muzzling the ox that treads out the corn*, and of maintaining the priests under the Old Testament, 1 Cor. ix. 14, &c.; 1 Tim. v. 17, 18. And thus, in case of church polity, the Hebrews are commanded to obey and be subordinate to their rulers in the Lord, Heb. xiii. 17; consequently, other churches are commanded not only to have rulers, but to obey and submit to their rule and government. Timothy is commanded to lay hands *suddenly on none*, &c., in ordaining of preaching elders, 1 Tim. v. 21, 22; consequently, such as succeed Timothy in ordaining of preaching elders are enjoined therein to do nothing suddenly, hastily, &c., but upon mature deliberation. The apostle commands, that men must *first be proved, and found blameless, before they execute the deacon's office*, 1 Tim. iii. 10; by consequence, it is much more necessarily commanded, that ruling elders should first be proved, and be found blameless, before they exercise rule; and that ministers be examined, and found blameless, before they be ordained to or execute the ministerial function, for these offices are of greater and higher concernment than the deacon's office.

2. Mediate divine commands, which are mediately from God, but immediately from men; and these come under a double consideration, being either,

1. Such commands whose general principles are immediately the Lord's, yet accommodations and determinations of particulars are from men, by apparent deductions from those grounds. Of such the apostle saith, "But to the rest speak I, not the Lord," 1 Cor. vii. 12; not that Paul delivered any commands merely of his own head, (for he had "obtained mercy of the Lord to be faithful," ver. 25, and did *think that he had the Spirit of the Lord*, ver. 40,) but grounded his commands upon the word of God, whereof the apostle was the interpreter. The case is concerning divorce when it fell out that believer and unbeliever were married together: the Lord had given general rules about divorce, but no particular rule about this case, (it being not incident to the Jews;) the apostle, therefore, accommodates the general rule to the particular case; he, not the Lord, determined the particular. This sound interpreters conceive to be the apostle's meaning: Thus the apostle, treating of order in public assemblies, saith, "The prophet and the spiritual man must acknowledge the things which I write, to be the commandments of the Lord," 1 Cor. xiv. 37. Understand it mediately, as being agreeable to the Lord's principles revealed: for otherwise how should the prophet know what the Lord immediately revealed to the apostle? or why should we think it probable that what Paul here speaks of order and decency in church assemblies, was immediately and expressly delivered him by speech or revelation from the Lord, seeing these particulars have such easy and apparent deduction from general principles, and revelations are not unnecessarily multiplied? Yet these particular deductions and determinations are here styled the commandments of the Lord.

2. Such commands, which are accidental and occasional, whose grounds and general principles are also the Lord's; yet determination or deduction of particulars can hardly be made, but in such emergent cases and occasions accidentally falling out, as necessitate thereunto. As in that case, Acts xv., when the synod commands abstinence *from blood, and things strangled*, and that necessarily, (though the Levitical law was now abrogated,) because the common use thereof by accident grew very scandalous: therefore, by the law of charity, the use of Christian liberty is to be suspended, when otherwise the scandal of my brother is endangered; yet from any ground of equity to have provided such a particular rule as this, without such a case occurring, would scarce have been possible. Now the synod saith of this determination, "It seemed good unto the Holy Ghost, and unto us," Acts xv. And another

synod, walking by the like light and rule of the Scripture as they did, may say of themselves as the apostles said.

PART II.
OF THE NATURE OF THAT CHURCH GOVERNMENT WHICH IS OF DIVINE RIGHT, ACCORDING TO SCRIPTURE.

CHAPTER I.
The Description of Church Government.

The nature of that church government which is of divine right according to Scripture, comes next to be considered; (having so fully seen what the nature of a divine right is, and how many several ways matters in religion may be said to be of divine right.) For the fuller and clearer unfolding whereof, let us first see how church government may be described; and then how that description may be explained and justified by the word of God, in the branches of it.

Church government may be thus described:

Church government is a power13 or authority spiritual,14 revealed in the holy Scriptures,15 derived from Jesus Christ16 our Mediator,17 only to his own officers, and by them exercised in dispensing of the word,18 seals,19 censures,20 and all other ordinances of Christ,21 for the edifying of the Church of Christ.22

This description of church government may be thus explained and proved. Three things are principally considerable herein, viz: 1. The thing defined, or described, viz. church government. 2. The general nature of this government which it hath in common with all other governments, viz. power or authority.

3. The special difference whereby it is distinguished from all other governments whatsoever. Herein six things are observable. 1. The special rule, wherein it is revealed, and whereby it is to be measured, viz. the holy Scriptures. 2. The proper author, or fountain, whence this power is derived, viz. from Jesus Christ our Mediator, peculiarly. 3. The special kind of this power or authority, viz. it is a spiritual power, it is a derived power. 4. The several parts or acts wherein this power sets forth itself, viz. in dispensing the word, seals, censures, and all other ordinances of Christ. 5. The special end or scope of this power, viz. the edifying of the Church of Christ. 6. The proper and distinct subject or receptacle wherein Christ hath placed and intrusted all this power, viz. only his own officers. All these things are comprehended in this description, and unto these several heads the whole nature of church government may be reduced. So that, these being explained and confirmed by the Scriptures, it will easily and fully be discovered, what that church government is which is of divine right, and by the will and appointment of Jesus Christ, our Mediator.

CHAPTER II.
Of the Subject Described, viz. Church Government, the terms being briefly opened.

Touching the thing defined or described, it is church government. Here two terms are to be a little explained: 1. What is meant by church? 2. What is meant by government?

1. Church is originally derived from a Greek word,23 which signifies to call forth. Hence church properly signifies a company or multitude, called forth; and so in this notation of the word, three things are implied: 1. The term from which they are called. 2. The term to which they are called. 3. The medium or mean by which they are brought from one term to another, viz. by calling. And these things thus generally laid down, do agree to every company that may properly be called a church. Now, this word translated church, never signifies one particular person, but many congregated, gathered, or called together; and it

hath several acceptations or uses in the New Testament: 1. It is used in a common and civil sense, for any civil meeting, or concourse of people together: thus that tumultuous and riotous assembly is called a church, Acts xix. 32, 39, 40. 2. It is used in a special religious sense, for a sacred meeting or assembly of God's people together: and thus it signifies the Church of God, either, 1. Invisible, comprehending only the elect of God, as Heb. xii. 23, "and Church of the first-born," Eph. v. 23, &c., "Even as Christ is the head of the Church." 2. Or, visible, comprehending the company of those that are called to the visible profession of the faith in Christ, and obedience unto Christ, according to the gospel, as Acts ii. 47, and v. 11, and viii. 3, and xii. 1, 5; 1 Cor. xii. 23, and often elsewhere. Now in this description, church is not understood of a civil assembly; for such assemblies are governed by civil power. Nor of the invisible Church of Christ; for, as the Church is invisible, (to speak properly,) it is invisibly governed by Christ and his Spirit, Rom. viii. 14; Gal. ii. 20. But of the visible Church of Christ, for which Christ hath provided a visible polity, a visible government, by visible officers and ordinances, for the good both of the visible and invisible members thereof, which is that church government here spoken of.

2. Government is the translation of a Greek word, which properly signifies the government of a ship with chart, &c., by the pilot or mariner, and thence metaphorically is used to signify any government, political or ecclesiastical. But the word is only once used in all the New Testament, viz. 1 Cor. xii. 28: *Governments*, h.e. ruling elders in the church; the abstract being put for the concrete, governments for governors. But whatever be the terms or names whereby government is expressed, government generally considered seems still to signify a superiority of office, power, and authority, which one hath and exerciseth over another. This is the notion of government in general. So that church government, in general, notes that pre-eminence or superiority of office, power, and authority, which some have and exercise over others in spiritual matters, in church affairs. And here we are further to consider, that church government is either, 1. Magisterial, lordly, and supreme; and so it is primitively and absolutely in God, Matt. xxviii. 18. Dispensatorily and mediatorily in Jesus Christ our Mediator only, whom God hath made both Lord and Christ, Acts ii. 36; Matt, xxiii. 8, 10; 1 Cor. viii. 6, and to whom God alone hath dispensed all authority and power, Matt, xxviii. 18, 19; John v. 22. Now church government, as settled on Christ only, is monarchical. 2. Ministerial, stewardly, and subordinate; and this power Jesus Christ our Mediator hath committed to his church guides and officers in his Church, 2 Cor. x. 8, and xiii. 10; and church government, as intrusted in the hands of church guides, is representative. This ministerial church government, committed by Christ to his officers, may be considered either, 1. As it was dispensed under the Old Testament, in a Mosaical, Levitical polity; in which sense we here speak not of church government; (that polity being dissolved and antiquated.) 2. Or, as it is to be dispensed now under the New Testament, in an evangelical Christian polity, by Christ's New Testament officers; and this is that church government which is here described, viz. not the supreme magisterial government of Christ, but the subordinate ministerial government of Christ's officers; and this not as it was under the Old Testament, but as it ought to be now under the New Testament.

CHAPTER III.
Of the general Nature of Church Government, viz. Power or Authority.

Touching the general nature of this government, which it participates in common with all other governments, it is power or authority. Here divers particulars are to be cleared and proved, viz:

1. What is meant by power or authority? The word chiefly used in the New Testament for power or authority is used not only to denote Christ's supreme power, as Luke iv. 36; Mark i. 17, with Luke vi. 19; but also his officers' derived power, as with 2 Cor. x. 8, and xiii. 10. It is used to signify divers things: as, 1. Dignity, privilege, prerogative. "To them he gave prerogative to be the sons of God," John i. 12. 2. Liberty, leave, license; as, 1 Cor. viii. 9, "But so that your liberty become not an offence to the weak;" and 1 Cor. ix. 4, 5, "Have not we liberty to eat and drink? Have not we liberty to lead about a sister, a wife?" 3.

But most usually right and authority; as, Matt. xxi. 23, 24, 27, and xxviii. 18; so 2 Cor. x. 8, and xiii. 10: in this last sense especially it is here to be taken in this description of church government.

Power or authority in general is by some24 thus described: that whereby one may claim or challenge any thing to one's self, without the injury of any other. Power is exercised either about things, or actions, or persons. 1. About things, as when a man disposes of his own goods, which he may do without wrong to any. 2. About actions, as when a man acts that which offends no law. 3. About persons, as when a man commands his children or servants that are under his own power.—Proportionably, the power of the Church in government is exercised, 1. About things, as when it is to be determined by the word, what the Church may call her own of right; as, that all the officers are hers, Eph; iv. 7, 8, 10, 11; 1 Cor. xii. 28: that all the promises are hers, 2 Pet. i. 4; 1 Tim. iv. 8: that Jesus Christ, and with Christ all things, are hers, 1 Cor. iii. 21, 22. The keys of the kingdom of heaven are hers, Matt. xvi. 19, and xviii. 18, &c.; John xx. 21, 23, &c.: these things the Church may challenge without wrong to any. 2. About actions. As when it is to be determined by the word, what the Church of divine right may do, or not do: as, the Church may not *bear with them that are evil*, Rev. ii. 2; *nor tolerate women to teach*, or false doctrine to be broached, Rev. ii. 20, &c. The Church may*warn the unruly*, 1 Thess. v. 14: excommunicate the obstinate and incorrigible, Matt. xviii. 17, 18; 1 Cor. v. 4, 5, 13: receive again penitent persons to the communion of the faithful, 2 Cor. ii. 7, 8: make binding decrees in synods, even to the restraining of the outward exercise of due Christian liberty for a time, for prevention of scandal, Acts xv. 3. About persons. The Church also hath a power to be exercised, for calling them to their duty, and keeping them in their duty according to the word of God: as, to *rebuke them before all*, that sin before all, 1 Tim. v. 20: to prove deacons, Acts vi. 2, 3, &c.; 1 Tim. iii. 10: *to ordain elders*, Tit. i. 5; Acts xiv. 23: to use the *keys of the kingdom of heaven*, in the dispensing of all ordinances, Matt, xviii. 18-20, and John xx. 21, 23, with Matt, xxviii. 18-20: and, in a word, (as the cause shall require,) to judge of all them that are within the Church, 1 Cor. v. 12.

This is the power and authority wherein the nature of church government generally doth consist.

2. That all governments in Scripture are styled by the common names of power or authority: e.g. the absolute government of God over all things, is power, Acts i. 7: the supreme government of Jesus Christ, is power, Matt, xxviii. 18; Rev. xii. 10: the political government of the magistrate in commonwealths, is power, as John xix. 10; Rom. xiii. 1-3; Luke xxiii. 7: the military government of soldiers under superior commanders, is power, &c., Matt. viii. 9: the family government that the master of a family hath over his household, is power, 1 Tim. iii. 5, "If any man know not how to rule his own house." Yea, the very tyrannical rule that sin and Satan exercise over carnal men, is styled power, Acts xxvi. 18; Col. i. 13. Thus, generally, all sorts of government are commonly called power or authority.

3. That thus the Scripture also styles church government, viz. power or authority, as 2 Cor. x. 8, "Of our authority" (or power) "which the Lord hath given us for your edification." Paul speaks it of this power of church government. And again, speaking of the same subject, he saith, "Lest being present, I should use sharpness, according to the power which the Lord hath given me to edification, and not to destruction." 2 Cor. xiii. 10.

For further clearing hereof, consider the several sorts or kinds of ecclesiastical power, according to this type or scheme of ecclesiastical power and authority here subjoined.

Ecclesiastical power is either supreme and magisterial; or subordinate and ministerial.

I. Supreme magisterial power, consisting in a lordly dominion and sovereignty over the Church; and may come under a double consideration, viz:

1. As it is justly attributed to God alone. Thus the absolute sovereignty and supreme power (to speak properly) is only his over the Church, and all creatures in the whole universe: now this supreme divine power is either essential or mediatorial.

1. Essential, viz. that power which belongs to the essence of God, and to every person of the Trinity in common, as God. "His kingdom ruleth over all," Psal. ciii. 19. "God ruleth in Jacob to the ends of the earth," Psal. lix. 13. "The kingdom is the Lord's, and he is the Governor among the nations," Psal. xxii. 28.

2. Mediatorial, viz. that magisterial, lordly, and sovereign power or dominion, which God hath dispensed, delegated, or committed to Christ as Mediator, being both head of the Church, and over all things to the Church. This power is peculiar only to Jesus Christ our Mediator. "All power is given to me both in heaven and in earth," Matt. xxviii. 18. "The Father loveth the Son, and hath given all things into his hand," John iii. 35. "The Father judgeth no man, but hath committed all judgment to the Son," John v. 22. "One is your Master, even Christ," Matt. xxiii. 8, 10. "God hath put all things under his feet, and gave him to be head over all things to the Church," Eph. i. 20-23.—This power of Christ is the only proper fountain whence all ecclesiastical power flows to the Church.

II. As it is unjustly arrogated and usurped by man; whether, 1. By the pope to himself; who arrogates to himself to be Christ's vicar, the supreme visible head on earth of the visible catholic Church of Christ; who exalts himself above all that is called God on earth, over magistrates, princes, kings, yea, over the souls and consciences of men, and the holy Scriptures of God themselves, &c., 2 Thess. ii. 4; Rev. xviii. 10-13.

2. By earthly princes to themselves: as, King Henry VIII., who, casting off the papal power and primacy, was vested with it himself within his own dominions, over the Church, accounting himself the fountain of all ecclesiastical power, (it being by statute law annexed to the crown,) and assuming to himself that papal title of supreme head of the Church, &c., which is sharply taxed by orthodox divines of foreign churches. Thus, that most learned Rivet, taxing Bishop Gardiner for extolling the king's primacy, saith, "For, he that did as yet nourish the doctrine of the papacy, as after it appeared, did erect a new papacy in the person of the king."—Andrew Rivet, *Expli. Decalog. Edit.* ii. page 203. Judicious Calvin saith thus: "And to this day how many are there in the papacy that heap upon kings whatsoever right and power they can possibly, so that there may not be any dispute of religion; but should this power be in one king, to decree according to his own pleasure whatsoever he pleaseth, and that should remain fixed without controversy? They that at first so much extolled Henry, king of England, (certainly they were inconsiderate men,) gave unto him supreme power of all things, and this grievously wounded me always; for they were blasphemers, when they called him the supreme head of the Church under Christ: certainly this was too much. But let this remain buried, because they sinned by an inconsiderate zeal. But when that impostor, (he means Bishop Gardiner, as Rivet notes,) which after was chancellor of this Proserpina, which there at this day overcometh all the devils, he when he was at Ratisbon did not contend with reasons, (I speak of this last chancellor, who was Bishop of Winchester,) but as I now began to say, he much regarded not scripture testimonies; but said, it was at the pleasure of the king to abrogate the statutes, and institute new rites. Touching fasting, there the king can enjoin and command the people, that this or that day the people may eat flesh: yea, that it is lawful for the king to forbid priests to marry; yea, that it is lawful for the king to forbid to the people the use of the cup in the Lord's supper; that it is lawful for the king to decree this or that in his kingdom. Why? Because the king hath the supreme power. It is certain, if kings do their duty, they are both patrons of religion, and nurse-fathers of the Church, as Isaiah calls them, Isa. xlix. 23. This, therefore, is principally required of kings, that they use the sword wherewith they are furnished, for the maintaining of God's worship. But in the mean time there are inconsiderate men, that make them too spiritual; and this fault reigns up and down Germany; yea, spreads too much in these countries. And now we perceive what fruits spring from this root, viz: that princes, and all that are in place of government, think themselves to be so spiritual, that there is no other ecclesiastical government. And this sacrilege creeps among us, because they cannot measure their office with certain and lawful bounds, but are of opinion they cannot reign, unless they abolish all the authority of the Church, and become the chief judges both in doctrine, and in the whole spiritual government. At the beginning they pretend some zeal; but mere ambition drives them, that so solicitously they snatch all things to themselves. Therefore there ought to be a temper kept; for this disease hath always reigned in princes, to desire to bend religion according to their own pleasure and lust, and for their own profits in the mean time. For they have respect to their profit, because for the most part they are not acted by the Spirit of God, but their ambition carries them." Thus Calvin in Amos vii. 13. Oh what exclamations

would this holy man have poured out, had he lived to see the passages of our days! *Quis talia fando temperet a lachrymis!*25

II. Subordinate ministerial power, which is either,

1. Indirectly, improperly, and only objectively ecclesiastical or spiritual, (so called, because it is exercised about spiritual or ecclesiastical objects, though formally in its own nature it be properly a mere civil or political power.) This is that power which is allowed to the civil magistrate about religion; he is *an overseer of things without the Church*, having an external care of religion as a *nurse-father*, Isa. xlix. 23; as had Hezekiah, Josiah, Asa, Jehoshaphat, &c.; so as, by the law, to restore religion decayed, reform the Church corrupted, protect the Church reformed, &c.

2. Directly, properly, and formally ecclesiastical or spiritual, having respect properly to matters within the Church. This power only belongs to church officers, who are overseers of things within, 1 Cor. iv. 20, 21; 2 Cor. x. 8, and xiii. 10; and this is either, 1. More special and peculiar to the office of some church governors only, as the power of preaching the gospel, dispensing the sacraments, &c., which is only committed to the ministers of the gospel, and which they, as ministers, may execute, in virtue of their office. This is called by some the key of doctrine, or key of knowledge; by others, the power of order, or of special office. See Matt, xxviii. 18-20; Rom. x. 15; 1 Tim. v. 17. 2. More general and common to the office of all church governors, as the power of censures, &c., wherein ruling elders act with ministers, admonishing the unruly, excommunicating the incorrigible, remitting and receiving again of the penitent into church communion. Compare Matt, xviii. 17, 18; 1 Cor. v. 2, 4, 5, 7, 11-13; 2 Cor. ii. 6-12, with Rom. xii. 8; 1 Cor. xii. 28; and 1 Tim. v. 17. This is called the key of discipline, or power of jurisdiction.

CHAPTER IV.
Of the special difference of Church Government from other Governments. And first of the Special Rule of Church Government, viz. the Holy Scriptures.

Touching the special difference, whereby church government is in this description distinguished from all other governments whatsoever, it consists of many branches, which will require more large explication and confirmation; and shall be handled, not according to that order, as they are first named in the description, but according to the order of nature, as they most conduce to the clearing of one another, every branch being distinctly laid down, as followeth:

The rule or standard of church government is only the holy Scriptures. Thus in the description, church government is styled a power or authority revealed in the holy Scriptures. For clearing hereof, take this proposition, viz:

Jesus Christ our Mediator hath laid down in his word a perfect and sufficient rule for the government of his visible Church under the New Testament, which all the members of his Church ought to observe and submit unto until the end of the world. For clearing this, weigh these considerations:

1. The government of the visible Church under the New Testament is as needful as ever it was under the Old Testament. What necessity of government could be pleaded then, which may not as strongly be pleaded now? Is not the visible Church of Christ a mixed body of sound and unsound members, of fruitful and barren branches, of tares and wheat, of good and bad, of sincere believers and hypocrites, of sheep and goats, &c., now as well as it was then? Is there not as great cause to separate and distinguish by church power, between the precious and the vile, the clean and the unclean, (who are apt to defile, infect, and leaven one another,) now as well as then? Ought there not to be as great care over the holy ordinances of God, to preserve and guard them from contempt and pollution, by a hedge and fence of government, now as well as then? Is it not as necessary that by government sin be suppressed, piety promoted, and the Church edified, now as well as then? But under the Old Testament the Church visible had a perfect rule of church government, (as is granted on all sides:) and hath Jesus Christ left his Church now under the New Testament in a worse condition?

2. The Lord Jesus Christ (upon whose shoulder God hath laid the government, Isa. ix. 6, and unto whom *all power both in heaven and in earth is given* by the Father to that end, Matt. xxviii. 18) *is most faithful in all his house*, the Church, fully to discharge all the trust committed to him, and completely to supply his Church with all necessaries both to her being, and well-being ecclesiastical. Moses was faithful in the Old Testament; for, as God gave him a pattern of church government in the ceremonial law, so he did all things according to the pattern; and shall the Lord Jesus be less faithful as *a son over his own house*, than was Moses as a servant over another's house? "Consider the Apostle and High Priest of our profession, Christ Jesus, who was faithful to him that appointed him, as also Moses was faithful in all his house—and Moses verily was faithful in all his house as a servant—but Christ as a son over his own house, whose house are we," Heb. iii. 1, 2, 5, 6. Yea, "Jesus Christ, the same yesterday, and to-day, and forever," Heb. xiii. 8, giving a pattern of church government to Moses, and the church officers of the Old Testament, (the Church being then as a child in nonage and minority, Gal, iv. 1, &c.,) can we imagine he hath not as carefully left a pattern of church government to his apostles, and the church officers of the New Testament, the Church being now as a man come to full age and maturity?

3. The holy Scriptures are now completely and unalterably perfect, containing such exact rules for the churches of God in all states and ages, both under the Old and New Testament, that not only the people of God, of all sorts and degrees, but also the men of God, and officers of the Church, of all sorts and ages, may thereby be made perfect, thoroughly furnished unto all good works. "The law of the Lord is perfect," Psal. xix. 7. "All Scripture is given by inspiration of God, and is profitable for doctrine, for reproof, for correction, for instruction in righteousness, that the man of God may be perfect, thoroughly furnished to every good work," 2 Tim. iii. 16, 17. And in his first epistle to Timothy, (which is the Church's directory for divine worship, discipline, and government,) he saith, "These things write I unto thee—that thou mightest know how thou oughtest to behave thyself in the house of God, which is the Church of the living God," (this is spoken in reference to matters of church government peculiarly,) 1 Tim. iii. 14, 15. And the apostle, having respect to the former matters in his epistle, saith to Timothy, and to all Timothies after him, "I give thee charge in the sight of God—that thou keep this commandment without spot, unrebukable, until the appearing of our Lord Jesus Christ," (therefore, this charge is intended for all ministers after Timothy to the world's end,) 1 Tim. vi. 13, 14, compared with 1 Tim. v. 21, observe *these things*. And the perfection of the whole scripture canon is sealed up with that testimony in the close of the last book, "If any man shall add unto these things, God shall add unto him the plagues that are written in this book: and if any man shall take away from the words of the book of this prophecy, God shall take away his part out of the book of life, and out of the holy city, and from the things which are written in this book," Rev. xxii. 18, 19. Now, if the Scriptures be thus accurately perfect and complete, they must needs contain a sufficient pattern, and rules of church government now under the New Testament; which rules are scattered here and there in several books of the word, (as flowers grow scattered in the field, as silver is mingled in the mine, or as gold is mixed with the sand,) that so God may exercise his Church, in sifting and searching them out.

4. All the substantials of church government under the New Testament are laid down in the word in particular rules, whether they be touching officers, ordinances, censures, assemblies, and the compass of their power, as after will appear; and all the circumstantials are laid down in the word, under general rules of order, decency, and edification, 1 Cor, xiv. 40, and ver. 5,12, 26.

Consequently, there is a perfect and sufficient rule for church government laid down in the Scriptures, which is obligatory upon all.

CHAPTER V.
Of the Proper Author or Fountain, whence Church Government and the authority thereof is derived by Divine Right, viz. Jesus Christ our Mediator.

As the Scripture is the rule of church government, so Christ is the sole root and fountain whence it originally flows; therefore, it is said in the description, church government is a power or authority, derived from Jesus Christ our Mediator. Take it in this proposition, viz:

Jesus Christ our Mediator hath all authority and power in heaven and in earth, for the government of his Church, committed unto him from God the Father. This is clearly evident,

1. By plain testimonies of Scripture, declaring that the government of the Church is laid upon his shoulder, to which end the Father hath invested him with all authority and power. "The government shall be upon his shoulder," &c., Isa. ix. 6,7. "All power is given me in heaven and in earth: go, disciple ye all nations," &c., Matt, xxviii. 18, 19. "He shall be great, and shall be called the Son of the Highest, and the Lord God shall give unto him the throne of his father David; and he shall reign over the house of Jacob forever, and of his kingdom there shall be no end," Luke i. 32, 33. "The Father judgeth no man, but hath committed all judgment to the Son; and hath given him authority to execute judgment also, because he is the Son of man," John v. 22, 27. "The Father loveth the Son, and hath given all things into his hand," John iii. 35. "It is he that hath the key of David, that openeth and no man shutteth, and shutteth and no man openeth," Rev. iii. 7. "God raised him from the dead, and set him at his own right hand in the heavenly places, far above all principality, and power, and might, and dominion, and every name that is named, not only in this world, but also in that which is to come: and hath put all things under his feet, and gave him to be the head over all things to the Church, which is his body," Eph. i. 20-23.

2. By eminent princely titles, attributed unto Jesus Christ our Mediator, having such authority, power, rule, and government legibly engraven upon their foreheads, in reference to his Church.

"A Governor which shall feed" (or rule) "my people Israel," Matt. ii. 6. "That great Shepherd of the sheep," Heb. xiii. 20. "That Shepherd and Bishop of our souls," 1 Pet. ii. ult. "One is your master, Christ," Matt, xxiii. 8, 10. "Christ as a son over his own house," Heb. iii. 6. "The Head of the body the Church," Col. i. 18; Eph. v. 23. "Head over all things to the Church," Eph. i. 22. "To us but one Lord Jesus Christ," 1 Cor. viii. 6. "Made of God both Lord and Christ," Acts ii. 36. "Lord of lords," Rev. xix. 16. "He is Lord of all," Acts x. 36. "God's King set on his holy hill of Zion," Psal. ii. 6. "David their king," Jer. xxx. 9; Ezek. xxxiv. 23, and xxxvii. 24; Hos. iii. 5. "King of kings," Rev. xix. 16.

3. By those primitive, fundamental, imperial acts of power, and supreme authority in the government of the Church, which are peculiarly ascribed to Jesus Christ our Mediator, as appropriate to him alone, above all creatures, e.g.

1. The giving of laws to his Church. "The law of Christ," Gal. vi. 2. "Gave commandments to the apostles," Acts i. 2. "There is one Lawgiver, who is able to save and to destroy," James iv. 12. "The Lord is our judge, the Lord is our lawgiver," (or statute-maker,) "the Lord is our king," Isa. xxxiii. 22.

2. The constituting of ordinances, whereby his Church shall be edified: as *preaching the word*, Matt. x. 7; 1 Cor. i. 17; Matt, xxviii. 18-20; Mark xvi. 15. *Administering of the sacraments. Baptism*, John i. 33, with Matt. iii. 13, &c., and xxviii. 18, 19. *The Lord's supper*, 1 Cor. xi. 20, 23, &c.; Matt. xxvi. 26, &c.; Mark xiv. 22, &c.; Luke xxii. 19, 20. *Dispensing of censures*, Matt. xvi. 10, with xviii. 15-18, &c.

3. The ordaining and appointing of his own church officers, by whom his ordinances shall be dispensed and managed in his Church. "He gave gifts to men; and he gave some, apostles; and some, prophets; and some, evangelists; and some, pastors and teachers," Eph. iv. 7, 8, 11; compare 1 Cor. xii. 28; 1 Thess. v. 12; Acts xx. 28.

4. The dispensing of Christ's ordinances, not in the name of magistrates, ministers, churches, councils, &c., but in Christ's own name. The apostles did "speak and teach in the name of Jesus," Acts iv. 17, 18. "Whatsoever ye ask in my name," John xiv. 13, 14, and xvi. 23. "Baptizing them in the name of the Father, and of the Son," Matt, xxviii. 18, 19. "They were baptized in the name of the Lord Jesus," Acts xix. 5. "In the name—with the power of our Lord Jesus Christ, to deliver such a one to Satan," 1 Cor. v. 4. Yea, assemblies of the

Church are to be in Christ's name: "Where two or three are gathered together in my name," Matt. xviii. 20.

CHAPTER VI.
Of the Special Kind, or Peculiar Nature of this Power and Authority.

Having viewed what is the rule of this authority, viz. the holy Scriptures, and what is the fountain of this authority, viz. Jesus Christ our Mediator; now consider the special kind or peculiar nature of this authority, which the description lays down in two several expressions, viz: 1. It is a spiritual power or authority. 2. It is a derived power, &c.

1. The power or authority of church government is a spiritual power. Spiritual, not so perfectly and completely as Christ's supreme government is spiritual, who alone hath absolute and immediate power and authority over the very spirits and consciences of men; ruling them by the invisible influence of his Spirit and grace as he pleaseth, John iii. 8; Rom. viii. 14; Gal. ii. 20: but so purely, properly, and merely spiritual is this power, that it really, essentially, and specifically differs, and is contradistinct from that power which is properly civil, worldly, and political, in the hand of the political magistrate. Now, that this power of church government is in this sense properly, purely, merely spiritual: and that by divine right may be evidenced many ways according to Scripture; forasmuch as the rule, fountain, matter, form, subject, object, end, and the all of this power, is only spiritual.

1. Spiritual in the rule, revealing and regulating it, viz. not any principles of state policy, parliament rolls, any human statutes, laws, ordinances, edicts, decrees, traditions, or precepts of men whatsoever, according to which cities, provinces, kingdoms, empires, may be happily governed: but the holy Scriptures, that perfect divine canon, wherein the Lord Christ hath revealed sufficiently how his own house, his Church, shall be ruled, 1 Tim. iii. 14, 15; and all his ordinances, word, sacraments, censures, &c., shall therein be dispensed, 2 Tim. iii. 16, 17. (See chap. IV.) Now this Scripture is divinely breathed, or inspired of God—holy men writing not according to the fallible will of man, but the infallible acting of the Holy Ghost, 2 Tim. iii. 16, with 2 Pet. i. 20, 21.

2. Spiritual in the fountain or author of this power, whence it originally flows; it being derived, not from any magistrate, prince, or potentate in the world, not from any man on earth, or the will of man; but only from Jesus Christ our Mediator, himself being the sole or first receptacle of all power from the Father, Matt. xxviii. 18; John v. 22: and consequently, the very fountain of all power and authority to his Church, Matt. xxviii. 18-20, with John xx. 21, 23; Matt. xvi. 19, and xviii. 18-20; 2 Cor. x. 8. See this formerly cleared, chap. III. and V.

3. Spiritual in the matter of it, and the several parts of this power: therefore called the *keys of the kingdom of heaven*, not the keys of the kingdoms of earth, Matt. xvi. 19, (as Christ professed his *kingdom was not of this world*, John xviii. 36; and when one requested of Christ, that by his authority he would speak to his brother to divide the inheritance with him, Christ disclaimed utterly all such worldly, earthly power, saying, "Man, who made me a judge or a divider over you?" Luke xii. 13, 14.) Consider these heavenly spiritual keys in the kinds of them, whether of doctrine or discipline; or in the acts of them, whether of binding or loosing, in all which they are spiritual: e.g. the doctrine which is preached is not human but divine, revealed in the Scriptures by the Spirit of God, and handling most sublime spiritual mysteries of religion, 2 Pet. i.; 2 Tim. iii. 16,17. The seals administered are not worldly seals, confirming and ratifying any carnal privileges, liberties, interests, authority, &c., but spiritual, *sealing the righteousness of faith*, Rom. iv. 11; the death and blood of Jesus Christ, with all the spiritual virtue and efficacy thereof unto his members, Rom. v. 6; Gal. iii.; 1 Cor. x. 16, 17, and xi. 23, 24, &c. The censures dispensed are not pecuniary, corporal, or capital, by fines, confiscations, imprisonments, whippings, stocking, stigmatizing, or taking away of limb or life, (all such things this government meddles not withal, but leaves them to such as bear the civil sword,) but spiritual, that only concern the soul and conscience; as *admonishing* of the unruly and disorderly, Matt. xviii. 18, 19; *casting out the incorrigible* and obstinate from the spiritual fellowship of the saints, Matt. xviii. 18, 19; 2 Cor. v. ult.: *receiving again into spiritual communion* of the faithful, such as are penitent, 2 Cor. ii. 6. Thus the binding

and loosing, which are counted the chief acts of the keys, are spiritually by our Saviour interpreted to be the *remitting and retaining of sins*; compare Matt. xviii. 18, 19, with John xx. 21, 23.

4. Spiritual in the form and manner, as well as in the matter. For this power is to be exercised, not in a natural manner, or in any carnal name, of earthly magistrate, court, parliament, prince, or potentate whatsoever, as all secular civil power is; no, nor in the name of saints, ministers, or the churches: but in a spiritual manner, in the name of the Lord Jesus, from whom alone all his officers receive their commissions. The word is to be *preached in his name*, Acts xvii. 18: seals dispensed in his name, Matt. xxviii. 19; Acts xix. 5: censures inflicted in his name, 1 Cor. v. 4, &c. (See chap. V.)

5. Spiritual in the subject intrusted with this power; which is not any civil, political, or secular magistrate, (as after will more fully appear, in chap. IX.) but spiritual officers, which Christ himself hath instituted and bestowed upon his Church, *apostles*, &c., *pastors, teachers, elders*, Eph. iv. 7, 8, 10, 11. To these only he hath given the *keys of the kingdom of heaven*, Matt. xvi. 19, and xviii. 18,19, and xxviii. 18, 19; John xx. 21-23; 2 Cor. x. 8, *authority which the Lord hath given us*. These he hath made *governments in his Church*, 1 Cor. xii. 28. To these he will have *obedience and subjection* performed, Heb. xiii. 17, and *double honor* allowed, 1 Tim. v. 17.

6. Spiritual in respect of the object about which this power is to be put forth and exercised, viz. not about things, actions, or persons civil, as such; but spiritual and ecclesiastical, as such. Thus injurious actions, not as trespasses against any statute or law political; but as scandalous to our brethren, or the Church of God, Matt. xviii. 18, 19; are considered and punished by this power. Thus the incestuous person was cast out, because a wicked person in himself, and likely to leaven others by his bad example, 1 Cor. v. 6. Thus the persons whom the Church may judge are not the men of the world without the Church, but those that are in some sense spiritual, and within the Church, 1 Cor. v. 12.

7. Spiritual also is this power in the scope and end of it. This the Scripture frequently inculcates: e.g. a brother is to be admonished privately, publicly, &c., not for the gaining of our private interests, advantages, &c., but for *the gaining of our brother*, that his soul and conscience may be gained to God and to his duty, and he be reformed, Matt. xviii. 15. The incestuous person is to be "delivered to Satan, for the destruction of the flesh, that the spirit may be saved in the day of our Lord Jesus," 1 Cor. v. 5; yea, the whole authority given to church guides from the Lord was given to this end, *for the edification, not the destruction* of the Church, 2 Cor. x. 8, and xiii. 10; all which, and such like, are spiritual ends. Thus the power of church government here described is wholly and entirely a spiritual power, whether we respect the rule, root, matter, form, subject, object, or end thereof. So that in this respect it is really and specifically distinct from all civil power, and in no respect encroacheth upon, or can be prejudicial unto the magistrate's authority, which is properly and only political.

2. The power or authority of church government is a derived power. For clearing this, observe, there is a magisterial primitive supreme power, which is peculiar to Jesus Christ our Mediator, (as hath been proved, chap. III. and V:) and there is a ministerial, derivative, subordinate power, which the Scripture declares to be in church guides, Matt. xvi. 19, and xviii. 18; John xx. 21, 23; Matt. xxviii. 19, 20; 2 Cor. x. 8, and xiii. 10, and often elsewhere this is abundantly testified. But whence is this power originally derived to them? Here we are carefully to consider and distinguish three things, touching this power or authority from one another, viz: 1st. The donation of the authority itself, and of the offices whereunto this power doth properly belong. 2d. The designation of particular persons to such offices as are vested with such power. 3d. The public protection, countenancing, authorizing, defending, and maintaining of such officers in the public exercise of such power within such and such realms or dominions. This being premised, we may clearly thus resolve, according to scripture warrant, viz. the designation or setting apart of particular individual persons to those offices in the Church that have power and authority engraven upon them, is from the church nominating, electing, and ordaining of such persons thereunto, see Acts iii. 1-3; 1 Tim. iv. 14, and v. 22; Tit. i. 5; Acts iv. 22. The public protection, defence, maintenance, &c., of such officers in the public exercise of the power and authority of their office in such or such dominions, is from the civil magistrate, as the *nursing-father* of the Church, Isa. xlix. 23; for it is by his authority and sanction that such public places shall be set apart for the public

ministry, that such maintenance and reward shall be legally performed for such a ministry, that all such persons of such and such congregations shall be (in case they neglect their duty to such a ministry) punished with such political penalties, &c. But the donation of the office and spiritual authority annexed thereunto, is only derived from Jesus Christ our Mediator. He alone gives all church officers, and therefore none may devise or superadd any new officers, Eph. iv. 7, 8, 10, 11; 1 Cor. xii. 28. And he alone commits all authority and power spiritual to those officers, for dispensing of word, sacraments, censures, and all ordinances, Matt. xvi. 19, and xxviii. 18-20; John xx. 21-23; 2 Cor. x. 8, and xiii. 10: and therefore it is not safe for any creature to intrude upon this prerogative royal of Christ to give any power to any officer of the Church. None can give what he has not.

CHAPTER VII.
Of the several Parts or Acts of this power of Church Government, wherein it puts forth itself in the Church.

Thus far of the special kind or peculiar nature of this authority; now to the several parts or acts of this power which the description comprehends in these expressions, (in dispensing the word, seals, censures, and all other ordinances of Christ.) The evangelical ordinances which Christ has set up in his church are many; and all of them by divine right that Christ sets up. Take both the enumeration of ordinances and the divine right thereof severally, as followeth.

Jesus Christ our Mediator hath instituted and appointed these ensuing administrations to be standing and perpetual ordinances in his church: which ordinances for method sake may be reduced into two heads, according to the distribution of the keys formerly laid down, (chap. III.,) viz., ordinances appertaining, 1st, To the key of order or of doctrine; 2d, To the key of jurisdiction or of discipline.

1. Ordinances appertaining to the key of order or doctrine, viz:

1. Public prayer and thanksgiving are divine ordinances: for 1st, Paul writing his first epistle to Timothy, "that he might know how to behave himself in the house of God," 1 Tim. iii. 14, 15, among other directions in that epistle, gives this for one, "I exhort therefore that first of all supplications, prayers, intercessions, and giving of thanks be made for all men," 1 Tim. ii. 1, 2, "for this is good and acceptable in the sight of God our Saviour," verse 3. 2. The apostle, regulating public prayers in the congregation, directing that they should be performed with the understanding, takes it for granted that public prayer was an ordinance of Christ. "If I pray in an unknown tongue, my spirit prayeth, but my understanding is unfruitful. What is it then? I will pray with the spirit, and will pray with the understanding also. Else when thou shalt bless with the spirit, how shall he that occupieth the room of the unlearned, say amen at thy giving of thanks, seeing he understandeth not what thou sayest? for thou verily givest thanks well, but the other is not edified." 1 Cor. xiv. 14-17. 3. Further, the apostles did account public prayer to be of more concern than serving of tables, and providing for the necessities of the poor, yea, to be a principal part of their ministerial office, and therefore resolve to addict and "give themselves to the ministry of the word and to prayer," Acts vi. 4; and this was the church's practice in the purest times, Acts i. 13, 14, whose pious action is for our imitation. 4. And Jesus Christ hath made gracious promises to public prayer, viz., of his presence with those who assemble in his name; and of audience of their prayers, Matt, xviii. 19, 20. Would Christ so crown public prayer were it not his own ordinance?

2. Singing of psalms is a divine ordinance, being,

1. Prescribed; "be filled with the spirit: speaking to yourselves in psalms, and hymns, and spiritual songs," Eph. v. 18, 19. "Let the word of Christ dwell in you richly in all wisdom, teaching and admonishing one another in psalms, and hymns, and spiritual songs," Col. iii. 16.

2. Regulated; the right performance thereof being laid down, "I will sing with the spirit, and I will sing with the understanding also," 1 Cor. xiv. 15, 16. "Singing with grace in

your hearts to the Lord," Col. iii. 16. "Singing and making melody in your hearts to the Lord," Eph. v. 19.

3. The public ministry of the word of God in the congregation is a divine ordinance. "We will give ourselves," said the apostles, "to the ministry of the word and prayer," Acts vi. 4. The ministry of the word is a sacred ordinance, whether read, preached, or catechetically propounded.

1. The public reading of the word is a divine ordinance, (though exposition of what is read do not always immediately follow.) For, 1. God commanded the reading of the word publicly, and never since repealed that command, Deut. xxxi. 11-13; Jer. xxxvi. 6; Col. iii. 16. 2. Public reading of the scriptures hath been the practice of God's church, both before Christ, Exod. xxiv. 7; Neh. viii. 18, and ix. 3, and xiii. 1; and after Christ, Acts xiii. 15, 27, and xv. 21; 2 Cor. iii. 14. 3. Public reading of the scriptures is as necessary and profitable now as ever it was. See Deut. xxxi. 11-13.

2. The public preaching of the word is an eminent ordinance of Christ. This is evident many ways, viz:

1. Christ hath commanded that the word shall be preached. "Go ye into all the world, and preach the gospel to every creature," Mark xvi. 15. "Go ye, therefore, and disciple ye all nations; teaching them to observe all things whatsoever I have commanded you," Matt, xxviii. 19, 20. "As ye go, preach, saying, The kingdom of heaven is at hand," Matt. x. 7. See also Mark iii. 14. "I charge thee," &c. "Preach the word," 2 Tim. iv. 1, 2. "Necessity is laid upon me, yea, wo is unto me if I preach not the gospel," 1 Cor. ix. 16, 17. "Christ sent me—to preach the gospel," 1 Cor. i. 17; with which compare also Acts xx. 28, and 1 Pet. v. 1-4.

2. Christ hath appointed who shall preach the word. "How shall they preach except they be sent?" Rom. x. 15. The qualifications of preaching elders see in 1 Tim. iii. 2-8, and Tit. i. 5-9.

3. Christ hath appointed how the word shall be preached. "Be instant, in season, out of season, reprove, rebuke, exhort with all long-suffering and doctrine," 2 Tim. iv. 2. "That he may be able by sound doctrine both to exhort and convince gainsayers," Tit. i. 9. "He that hath my word, let him speak my word faithfully: what is the chaff to the wheat, saith the Lord?" Jer. xxiii. 28.

4. Christ hath made many encouraging promises to the preaching of his word, which he would not have done, were it not his own ordinance. "Teaching them to observe all things whatsoever I have commanded you, and lo I am with you every day to the end of the world," Matt, xxviii. 20. "Whatsoever ye shall bind on earth, shall be bound in heaven; and whatsoever ye shall loose on earth shall be loosed in heaven," Matt. xvi. 19, and xviii. 18. "Whose soever sins ye remit, they are remitted unto them: and whose soever sins ye retain, they are retained," John xx. 23. Both these are partly meant of doctrinal binding and loosing, remitting and retaining. "Be not afraid, but speak, and hold not thy peace: for I am with thee, and no man shall set on thee to hurt thee, for I have much people in this city," Acts xviii. 9, 10.

3. The catechetical propounding or expounding of the word, viz. a plain, familiar laying down of the first principles of the oracles of God, is an ordinance of Christ also. For, 1. This was the apostolical way of teaching the churches at the first plantation thereof. "When for the time ye ought to be teachers, ye have need that one teach you again which be the first principles of the oracles of God, and are become such as have need of milk and not of strong meat," Heb. v. 12. "Therefore, leaving the word of the beginning of Christ, let us go on unto perfection, not laying again the foundation of repentance from dead works, and of faith towards God," &c., Heb. vi. 1,2. "And I, brethren, could not speak unto you as unto spiritual, but as unto carnal, as unto babes in Christ. I have fed you with milk, and not with meat, for hitherto ye were not able to bear it, neither yet now are ye able," 1 Cor. iii. 1, 2. 2. And this is the sense of pastor and people which the Holy Ghost useth, setting forth the reciprocal relation and office between them, with his own approbation. "Let him that is catechized in the word, communicate to him that catechizeth him, in all good things," Gal. vi. 6.

4. The administration of the sacraments is of divine institution.

1. Of baptism. "He that sent me to baptize with water," John i. 33. "Go ye therefore, disciple ye all nations, baptizing them into the name of the Father, and of the Son, and of the Holy Ghost," Matt, xxviii. 18-20.

2. Of the Lord's supper, which Christ ordained *the same night in which he was betrayed*: which institution is at large described, 1 Cor. xi. 20, 23, &c.; Matt. xxvi. 26-31; Mark xiv. 22-27; Luke xxii. 19, 20.

2. Ordinances appertaining to the key of jurisdiction or of discipline, viz:

1. The ordination of presbyters with imposition of the hands of the presbytery, after praying and fasting, is a divine ordinance. "Neglect not the gift that is in thee, which was given thee by prophecy with the laying on of the hands of the presbytery," 1 Tim. iv. 14. Titus was left in Crete for this end, "To set in order things that were wanting, and ordain presbyters" (or elders) "in every city, as Paul had appointed him," Tit. i. 5. Timothy is charged, "Lay hands suddenly on no man, neither be partaker of other men's sins; keep thyself pure," 1 Tim. v. 22. Paul and Barnabas came to Lystra, Iconium, and Antioch, and "when they had ordained them presbyters in every church, and had prayed with fasting, they commended them to the Lord," &c., Acts xiv. 21, 23.

2. Authoritative discerning, and judging of doctrine according to the word of God, is a divine ordinance. As that council at Jerusalem, authoritatively (viz. by ministerial authority) judged of both the false doctrine and manners of false teachers, branding them for "troublers of the Church, subverters of souls," &c. "Forasmuch as we have heard that certain, coming forth from u, have troubled you with words, subverting your souls, saying, ye ought to be circumcised, and keep the law, to whom we gave no such commandment," Acts xv. 24; "it seemed good to the Holy Ghost, and to us, to impose upon you no greater burden than these necessary things," v. 28; and this was done upon debates from scripture grounds, "and to this the words of the prophets agree," Acts xv. 15: and afterwards their results and determinations are called "decrees ordained by the apostles and elders," Acts xvi. 4.

3. Admonition and public rebuke of sinners is a divine ordinance of Christ. "If thy brother trespass against thee, go and tell him his fault between thee and him alone: if he will not hear thee, then take with thee one or two more—and if he shall neglect to hear them, tell it unto the Church," Matt, xviii. 15-17. "Whose soever sins ye bind on earth shall be bound in heaven," John xx. 23. One way and degree of binding is by authoritative, convincing reproof. "Admonish the unruly," 1 Thess. v. 14. "An heretic, after the first and second admonition, reject," Tit. iii. 1. "Them that sin, convincingly reprove before all, that the rest also may fear," 1 Tim. v. 20. "Rebuke them sharply," (or convince them cuttingly,) Tit. iii. 13. "Sufficient to such an one is that rebuke, which was from many," 2 Cor. ii. 6.

4. Rejecting, and purging out, or putting away from the communion of the Church, wicked and incorrigible persons, is an ordinance of Christ. "And if he will not hear them, tell the Church; but if he will not hear the Church, let him be unto thee even as a heathen and a publican." "Verily, I say unto you, what things soever ye shall bind on earth, they shall be bound in heaven," Matt, xviii. 17, 18, compared with Matt. xvi. 19, and John xx. 21, 23. "An heretic, after once or twice admonition, reject," Tit. iii. 10; i.e. excommunicate, till he repent—*Pisc. in loc.* By the lawful judgment of the Church, to deliver the impenitent to Satan.—*Beza in loc.* "Of whom is Hymeneus and Alexander, whom I have delivered to Satan, that they may learn not to blaspheme," 1 Tim. i. 20. The apostle's scope in 1 Cor. v. is to press the church of Corinth to excommunicate the incestuous person. "Ye are puffed up, and have not rather mourned, that he that hath done this deed may be taken from the midst of you. For I verily, as absent in body, but present in spirit, have already as present judged him that thus wrought this thing. In the name of our Lord Jesus Christ, you being gathered together, and my spirit with the power of our Lord Jesus Christ, to deliver such an one to Satan for the destruction of the flesh, that the spirit may be saved in the day of our Lord Jesus," 1 Cor. v. 2-5. "Know ye not that a little leaven leaveneth the whole lump? Purge out therefore the old leaven," ver. 7. "I wrote to you in an epistle, not to be mingled together with fornicators," ver. 9, 11; and explaining what he meant by not being *mingled together*, saith, "If any named a brother be a fornicator, or covetous, or an idolater, or a reviler, or drunkard,

or rapacious, with such an one not to eat together," ver. 11. "Therefore take away from among yourselves that wicked person," ver. 13.

5. Seasonable remitting, receiving, comforting, and authoritative confirming again in the communion of the Church those that are penitent. "What things soever ye shall loose on earth shall be loosed in heaven," Matt. xvi. 19, and xviii. 18. "Whose soever sins ye remit, they are remitted unto them," John xx. 23. This loosing and remitting is not only doctrinal and declarative in the preaching of the word, but also juridical and authoritative in the administration of censures. This is called, for distinction's sake, absolution. After the church of Corinth had excommunicated the incestuous person, and he thereupon had given sufficient testimony of his repentance, the apostle directs them to receive him into church communion again, saying, "Sufficient to such an one is that rebuke inflicted of many; so that contrariwise you should rather forgive and comfort him, lest such an one should be swallowed up of abundant sorrow. Wherefore I beseech authoritatively to confirm love unto him: for to this purpose also I have written unto you, that I may know the proof of you, if ye be obedient in all things," 2 Cor. ii. 6-9.

CHAPTER VIII.
Of the End and Scope of this Government of the Church.

The end or scope intended by Christ in instituting, and to be aimed at by Christ's officers in executing of church government in dispensing the word, sacrament, censures, and all ordinances of Christ, is (as the description expresseth) *the edifying of the Church of Christ.* This end is very comprehensive. For the fuller evidencing whereof these two things are to be proved:1st, That Jesus Christ our Mediator hath under the New Testament one general visible Church on earth. 2d. That the edification of this Church of Christ is that eminent scope and end why Christ gave the power of church government and other ordinances unto the Church.

I. For the first, that Jesus Christ our Mediator hath under the New Testament a general visible Church on earth, made up of all particular churches, may be cleared by considering well these particulars.

1st. That it is evident by the Scriptures that Jesus Christ hath on earth many particular visible churches: (whether churches congregational, presbyterial, provincial, or national, needs not here be determined.) "Unto the churches of Galatia," Gal. i. 2. "The churches of Judea," Gal. i. 22. "Through Syria and Cilicia, confirming the churches," Acts xv. 41. "To the seven churches in Asia," Rev. i. 4, 20. "The church of Ephesus," Rev. ii. 1. "The church in Smyrna," ver. 8. "The church in Pergamus," ver. 12. "The church in Thyatira," ver. 18. "The church in Sardis," Rev. iii. 1. "The church in Philadelphia," ver. 7. And "the church in Laodicea," ver. 14. "The church that is in their house," Rom. xvi. 5; and Philem. 2. "Let your women keep silence in the church," 1 Cor. xiv. 34. "All the churches of the Gentiles," Rom. xvi. 4. "So ordain I in all churches," 1 Cor. vii. 17. "As in all churches of the saints," 1 Cor. xiv. 33. "The care of all the churches," 2 Cor. xi. 28. The New Testament hath many such like expressions.

2d. That how many particular visible churches soever Christ hath on earth, yet Scripture counts them all to be but one general visible Church of Christ. This is manifest,

1. By divers Scriptures, using the word church in such a full latitude and extensive completeness, as properly to signify, not any one single congregation, or particular church, but one general visible Church: as, "Upon this rock I will build my Church," Matt. xvi. 18. "Give none offence, neither to the Jews, nor to the Greeks, nor to the Church of God," 1 Cor. x. 32. "God hath set some in the Church, first, apostles; secondarily, prophets; thirdly, teachers," &c., 1 Cor. xii. 28. "I persecuted the Church of God," 1 Cor. xv. 9; Gal. i. 13. "The Church of the living God, the pillar and ground of the truth," 1 Tim. iii. 15. "Might be known by the Church the manifold wisdom of God," Eph. iii. 10. "In the midst of the Church will I sing praise unto thee," Heb. ii. 12. In which, and such like places, we must needs understand, that one general visible Church of Christ.

34

2. By such passages of scripture as evidently compare all visible professors and members of Christ throughout the world to one organical body, having eyes, ears, hands, feet, &c., viz., several organs, instruments, officers, &c., in it, for the benefit of the whole body; as, "He gave some apostles, and some prophets, and some evangelists, and some pastors and teachers, for the perfecting of the saints, for the work of the ministry, for the edifying of the body of Christ," Eph. iv. 11, 12. "There is one body," Eph. iv. 4. "As we have many members in one body, and all members have not the same office; so we being many are one body in Christ, and every one members one of another," &c., Rom. xii. 4-9. "As the body is one, and hath many members, and all the members of that one body being many, are one body; so also is Christ," (i.e., Christ considered mystically, not personally,) "for by one Spirit are we all baptized into one body, whether we be Jews or Gentiles, whether we be bond or free," &c., 1 Cor. xii. 12, to the end of the chapter, which context plainly demonstrates all Christ's visible members in the world, Jews or Gentiles, &c., to be members of one and the same organical body of Christ, which organical body of Christ is the general visible Church of Christ; for the invisible church is not organical.

II. That the edification of the Church of Christ is that eminent scope and end, why Christ gave church government and all other ordinances of the New Testament to his Church. This is frequently testified in scripture. 1. The apostle, speaking of this power generally, saith, "Our authority which the Lord hath given to us for edification, and not for the destruction of you," 2 Cor. x. 8. The like passage he hath again, saying, "according to the authority," or power, "which the Lord hath given to me for edification, and not for destruction," 2 Cor. xiii. 10; in both which places he speaks of the authority of church government in a general comprehensive way, declaring the grand and general immediate end thereof to be, affirmatively, edification of the church; negatively, not the subversion or destruction thereof. 2. In like manner, when particular acts of government, and particular ordinances are mentioned, the edification of the Church, at least in her members, is propounded as the great end of all: e.g. 1. Admonition is for edification, that an erring *brother may be gained*, Matt. xviii. 15, 16, that wavering minds may be sound in the faith. "Rebuke them cuttingly, that they may be sound in the faith," Tit. i. 13, that beholders and bystanders may fear to fall into like sins. "Them that sin rebuke before all, that others also may fear," 1 Tim. v. 20. 2. Excommunication is for edification; particularly of the delinquent member himself; thus the incestuous person was "delivered to Satan for the destruction of the flesh, that the spirit might be saved in the day of the Lord Jesus," 1 Cor. v. 4, 5. "Hymeneus and Alexander were delivered to Satan, that they might learn not to blaspheme," 1 Tim. i. 20: more generally of the Church; thus the incestuous person was to be put away from among them lest the whole lump of the church should be leavened by him, 1 Cor. v. 3. Absolution also is for edification, lest the penitent party "should be swallowed up of too much sorrow," 2 Cor. ii. 7. 4. All the officers of his Church are for edification of the Church, (Eph. iv. 7, 8, 11, 12, 16,) together with all the gifts and endowments in these officers, whether of prayer, prophecy, tongues, &c., all must be managed to edification. This is the scope of the whole chapter. 1 Cor. xii. 7, &c., and 1 Cor. xiv. 3-5, 9, 12, &c., 26; read the whole chapter. That passage of Paul is remarkable, "I thank my God, I speak with tongues more than you all; yet in the church I had rather speak five words with my understanding, that by my voice I might teach others also, than ten thousand words in an unknown tongue," verses 18, 19. Thus church government, and all sorts of ordinances, with the particular acts thereof, are to be levelled at this mark of edification. Edification is an elegant metaphor from material buildings (perhaps of the material and typical temple) to the spiritual; for explanation's sake briefly thus take the accommodation: The *architects*, or builders, are the *ministers*, 1 Cor. iii. 10. The *foundation* and *corner-stone* that bears up, binds together, and gives strength to the building, is Jesus Christ, 1 Cor. iii. 11; 1 Pet. ii. 4, 6. The *stones* or *materials* are the *faithful* or *saints*, 2 Cor. i. 1. The *building*, or house itself, is the *Church*, that spiritual house, and *temple of the living God*, Eph. ii. 21, and iv. 12; 1 Cor. iii. 9, 16, 17. The edification of this house is gradually to be perfected more and more till the coming of Christ, by laying the foundation of Christianity, in bringing men still unto Christ, and carrying on the superstruction in perfecting them in Christ in all spiritual growth, till at last the top-stone be laid on, the Church completed, and translated *to the house not made with hands, eternal in the heavens.*

35

CHAPTER IX.

Of the proper receptacle and distinct subject of all this power and authority of Church Government, which Christ hath peculiarly intrusted with the execution thereof according to the Scriptures. And 1. Negatively, That the political magistrate is not the proper subject of this power.

Thus we have taken a brief survey of church government, both in the rule, root, kind, branches, and end thereof, all which are comprised in the former description, and being less controverted, have been more briefly handled. Now, the last thing in the description which comes under our consideration, is the proper receptacle of all this power from Christ, or the peculiar subject intrusted by Christ with this power and the execution thereof, viz. only Christ's own officers. For church government is a spiritual power or authority, derived from Jesus Christ our Mediator, only to his own officers, and by them exercised in dispensing of the word, &c. Now about this subject of the power will be the great knot of the controversy, forasmuch as there are many different claims thereof made, and urged with vehement importunity: (to omit the Romish claim for the pope, and the prelatical claim for the bishop,) the politic Erastian pretends that the only proper subject of all church government is the political or civil magistrate; the gross Brownists or rigid Separatists, that it is the body of the people, or community of the faithful in an equal even level; they that are more refined, (who style themselves for distinction's sake26 Independents,) that it is the single congregation, or the company of the faithful with their presbytery, or church officers; the Presbyterians hold that the proper subject wherein Christ hath seated and intrusted all church power, and the exercise thereof, is only his own church officers, (as is in the description expressed.) Here, therefore, the way will be deeper, and the travelling slower; the opposition is much, and therefore the disquisition of this matter will unavoidably be the more.

For perspicuity herein, seeing it is said that this power is derived from Christ only to his own officers; and by this word (only) all other subjects are excluded; the subject of church power may be considered, 1. Negatively, what it is not. 2. Affirmatively, what it is.

Negatively, the proper subject unto whom Christ hath committed the power of church government, and the exercise thereof, is not, 1. The political magistrate, as the Erastians imagine. 2. Nor the body of the people, either with their presbytery or without it, as the Separatists and Independents pretend. Let these negatives first be evinced, and then the affirmative will be more clearly evidenced.

Touching the first of these—that the political magistrate is not the proper subject unto whom Jesus Christ our Mediator hath committed the power of church government, and the exercise of that power; it will be cleared by declaring these two things distinctly and severally, viz: 1. What power about ecclesiasticals is granted to the civil magistrate. 2. What power therein is denied unto him, and why.

SECTION I.

Such power is granted by the reformed churches and orthodox writers to the political magistrate, in reference to church affairs. Take it in these particulars.

A defensive, protecting, patronizing power to the church, and all the members thereof. "Kings shall be thy nursing-fathers," &c., Isa. xlix. 23. "The magistrate is the minister of God for good to well-doers, as well as the avenger, executing wrath upon evil-doers; a terror not to good works, but to the evil," Rom. xiii. 3, 4; he is called *an heir, or, possessor of restraint, to put men to shame,* Judges xviii. 7. And as the church ought to pray for kings and all in authority, so consequently all in authority should endeavor to defend it, that the church and people of God should lead a quiet and peaceable life, (under the wing of their protection,) "in all godliness and honesty," 1 Tim. ii. 2; and this is evident from the end and scope of these prayers here prescribed, as interpreters unanimously agree. And hereupon are those promises to the church, "The sons of strangers shall build up thy walls, and their kings shall minister unto thee," Isa. lx. 10; "and thou shalt suck the breast of kings," Isa. lx.

36

16. Now, this nursing, protecting care of magistrates towards the church, puts forth itself in these or like acts, viz: He,

1. Removes all external impediments of true religion, worship of God, &c., by his civil power, whether persons or things, whether persecutions, profaneness, heresy, idolatry, superstition, &c., that truth and godliness may purely flourish: as did Jehoshaphat, Asa, Hezekiah, Josiah. And hereupon it is that God so oft condemns the not removing and demolishing of the high places and monuments of idolatry, 1 Kings xv. 14, with 2 Chron. xv. 17; 1 Kings xxii. 44; 2 Kings xii. 3: and highly commends the contrary in Asa, 2 Chron. xv. 8, 16: in Jehoshaphat, 2 Chron. xvii. 3, 4, 6-10: in Hezekiah, 2 Chron. xxxi. 1; 2 Kings xviii. 4: in Manasseh, 2 Chron. xxxiii. 15: in Josiah, 2 Kings xxiii. 8, 13, 19, 20, 24: whereupon the Holy Ghost gives him that superlative commendation above all kings before and after him, ver. 25.

2. Countenanceth, advanceth, and encourageth by his authority and example the public exercise of all God's ordinances, and duties of religion within his dominions, whether in matter of divine worship, discipline, and government, maintaining for the Church the fulness of spiritual liberties and privileges communicated to her from Christ: as did Asa, 2 Chron. xv. 9-16: Jehoshaphat, 2 Chron. xx. 7-9: Hezekiah, 2 Chron. xxix., xxx., and xxxi. chapters throughout: Josiah, 2 Chron. xxxiv. and xxxv. chapters. And to this end God prescribed in the law that the king should still have a copy of the law of God by him, therein to read continually, Deut. xvii. 18-20; because he was to be not only a practiser, but also a protector thereof, a keeper of both tables.

3. Supplies the Church with all external necessaries, provisions, means, and worldly helps in matters of religion: as convenient public places to worship in, sufficient maintenance for ministers, (as the Scripture requireth, 1 Tim. v. 17, 18; 1 Cor. ix. 6-15; Gal. vi. 6:) schools and colleges, for promoting of literature, as nurseries to the prophets, &c.; together with the peaceable and effectual enjoyment of all these worldly necessaries, for comfortably carrying on of all public ordinances of Christ. Thus David prepared materials, but Solomon built the temple, 1 Chron. xxii. Hezekiah commanded the people that dwelt in Jerusalem, to give the portion of the priests and the Levites, that they might be encouraged in the law of the Lord; and Hezekiah himself and his princes came and saw it performed, 2 Chron. xxxi. 4, &c., 8: Josiah repaired the house of God, 2 Chron. xxxiv.

Nor need the magistrate think scorn, but rather count it his honor to be an earthly protector of the Church, which is the *body of Christ, the Lamb's wife*, for redeeming of which Christ died, and for gathering and perfecting of which the very world is continued.

An ordering, regulating power is also allowed to the magistrate about ecclesiastical matters in a political way, so that he warrantably,

1. Reforms the Church, when corrupted in divine worship, discipline, or government: as did Moses, Exod. xxxii.; Joshua, Josh. xxiv.; Asa, 2 Chron. xv.; Jehoshaphat, 2 Chron. xvii.; Hezekiah, 2 Kings xviii.; Josiah, 2 Kings xxiii.; 2 Chron. xxxiv.

2. Convenes or convocates synods and councils, made up of ecclesiastical persons, to consult, advise, and conclude determinatively, according to the word, how the church is to be reformed and refined from corruptions, and how to be guided and governed when reformed, &c. For, 1. Pious magistrates under the Old Testament called the Church together, convened councils. David, about bringing back the ark, 1 Chron. xiii. 1, 2, and another council when he was old, 1 Chron. xiii. 1; Solomon, 1 Kings viii. 1; Hezekiah, 2 Chron. xxix. 4; and Josiah, 2 Kings xxiii. 1, 2. 2. All ought to be subject to superior powers, who ought to procure the public peace and prosperity of the Church, Rom. xiii. 1, 2, &c.; 1 Pet. ii. 13, &c., 17; 1 Tim. ii. 2. Therefore superior powers may convocate councils. 3. Christian magistrates called the four general councils: Constantine the first Nicene council; Theodosius, senior, the first council of Constantinople; Theodosius, junior, the first Ephesian council; Marcian Emperor, the Chalcedon council; and, 4. Hereunto antiquity subscribes, as Dr. Whitaker observes.

3. Supports the laws of God with his secular authority, as a keeper of the tables, enjoining and commanding, under civil penalties, all under his dominion, strictly and inviolably to observe the same: as "Josiah made all that were present in Israel to serve the Lord their God," 2 Chron. xxxiv. 33. Nehemiah made the sabbath to be sanctified, and

strange wives to be put away, Neh. xii. 13, &c. Yea, Nebuchadnezzar, a heathen king, decreed, that "Whosoever should speak amiss of the God of Shadrach," &c., "should be cut in pieces, and their houses made a dunghill," Dan. iii. 28, 29. And Darius decreed, "That in every dominion of his kingdom men tremble and fear before the God of Daniel," &c., Dan. vi. 26, 27.

And as he strengthens the laws and ordinances of God by his civil authority, so he ratifies and establishes within his dominions the just and necessary decrees of the Church in synods and councils (which are agreeable to God's word) by his civil sanction.

4. Judges and determines definitively with a consequent political judgment, or judgment of political discretion, concerning the things judged and determined antecedently by the Church, in reference to his own act. Whether he will approve such ecclesiasticals or not; and in what manner he will so approve, or do otherwise by his public authority; for he is not a brutish agent, (as papists would have him,) to do whatsoever the Church enjoins him unto blind obedience, but is to act prudently and knowingly in all his office; and therefore the judgment of discerning (which belongs to every Christian, for the well-ordering of his own act) cannot be denied to the Christian magistrate, in respect of his office.

5. Takes care politically, that even matters and ordinances merely and formally ecclesiastical, be duly managed by ecclesiastical persons orderly called thereto. Thus Hezekiah commanded the priests and Levites to do their duties, 2 Chron. xxix. 5, 24, and the people to do theirs, 2 Chron. xxx. 1; and for this he is commended, that therein he did cleave unto the Lord, and observed his precepts which he had commanded Moses, 2 Kings xviii. 6. Thus when the king is commanded to observe and do all the precepts of the law, the Lord (as orthodox divines do judge) intended that he should keep them, not only as a private man, but as a king, by using all care and endeavor that all his subjects with him perform all duties to God and man, Deut. xvii. 18-20.

6. A compulsive, coactive, punitive, or corrective power, formally political, is also granted to the political magistrate in matters of religion, in reference to all sorts of persons and things under his jurisdiction. He may politically compel the outward man of all persons, church officers, or others under his dominions, unto external performance of their respective duties, and offices in matters of religion, punishing them, if either they neglect to do their duty at all, or do it corruptly, not only against equity and sobriety, contrary to the second table, but against truth and piety, contrary to the first table of the decalogue. We have sufficient intimation of the magistrate's punitive power in cases against the second table; as the stubborn and rebellious, incorrigible son, that was a glutton and a drunkard, sinning against the fifth commandment, was to be stoned to death, Deut. xxi. 18-21. The murderer, sinning against the sixth commandment, was to be punished with death, Gen. ix. 6; Numb. xxxv. 30-34; Deut. x. 11-13. The unclean person, sinning against the seventh commandment, was to be punished with death, Lev. xx. 11, 12, 14, 17, 19-25; and before that, see Gen. xxxviii. 24. Yea, Job, who is thought to live before Moses, and before this law was made, intimates that adultery is a heinous crime, yea, it is an iniquity to be punished by the judges, Job xxxi. 9,11. The thief, sinning against the eighth commandment, was to be punished by restitution, Exod. xxii. 1, 15, &c. The false witness, sinning against the ninth commandment, was to be dealt withal as he would have had his brother dealt with, by the law of retaliation, Deut. xix. 16, to the end of the chapter, &c. Yea, the magistrate's punitive power is extended also to offences against the first table; whether these offences be against the first commandment, by false prophets teaching lies, errors, and heresies in the name of the Lord, endeavoring to seduce people from the true God. "If there arise among you a prophet, or a dreamer of dreams, that prophet, or that dreamer of dreams shall be put to death, because he hath spoken to turn you away from the Lord your God, which brought you out of the land of Egypt," &c., Deut. xiii. 1-6. From which place Calvin notably asserts the punitive power of magistrates against false prophets and impostors that would draw God's people to a defection from the true God, showing that this power also belongs to the Christian magistrate in like cases now under the gospel.

Yea, in case of such seducement from God, though by nearest allies, severe punishment was to be inflicted upon the seducer, Deut. xiii. 6-12. See also ver. 12, to the end of the chapter, how a city is to be punished in the like case. And Mr. Burroughs,27 in his Irenicum, shows that this place of Deut. xiii. 6, &c., belongs even to us under the gospel.

Or whether these offences be against the second commandment, the magistrate's punitive power reaches them, Deut. xvii. 1-8; Lev. xvii. 2-8; 2 Chron. xvi. 13, 16. "Maachah, the mother of Asa the king, he removed from being queen, because she had made an idol in a grove." Job xxxi. 26-28, herewith compare Exod. viii. 25, 26. Or whether the offences be against the third commandment, "And thou shalt speak unto the children of Israel, saying, Whosoever curseth God shall bear his sin: and he that blasphemeth the name of the Lord he shall surely be put to death, and all the congregation shall certainly stone him, as well the stranger as he that is born in the land, when he blasphemeth the name of the Lord shall be put to death," Lev. xxiv. 15, 16. Yea, the heathen king Nebuchadnezzar made a notable decree to this purpose, against blaspheming God, saying, "I make a decree, that every people, nation, and language, who speak any thing amiss against the God of Shadrach, Meshech, and Abednego, shall be cut in pieces, and their houses shall be made a dunghill," Dan. iii. 29: and the pagan magistrate, king Artaxerxes, made a more full decree against all contempt of the law of God: "And whosoever will not do the law of thy God," saith he to Ezra, "and the law of the king, let judgment be executed speedily upon him, whether it be unto death, or to banishment, or to confiscation of goods, or to imprisonment:" and Ezra blesses God for this, Ezra vii. 26, 27.

Besides all this light of nature, and evidence of the Old Testament, for the ruler's political punitive power for offences against God, there are divers places in the New Testament showing that a civil punitive power rests still in the civil magistrate: witness those general expressions in those texts—Rom. xiii. 3, 4: "Rulers are not a terror to good works, but to the evil. If thou do that which is evil, be afraid, for he beareth not the sword in vain: for he is the minister of God, a revenger *to execute* wrath upon him that doeth evil." 1 Pet. ii. 13, 14: "Submit yourselves unto every ordinance of man for the Lord's sake, whether it be to the king as to the supreme, or unto governors which are sent for the *punishment* of evil-doers,28 and the praise of them that do well." Now, (as Mr. Burroughs29 notes,) seeing the Scripture speaks thus generally, except the nature of the thing require, why should we distinguish where the Scripture doth not? so that these expressions may be extended to those sorts of evil-doing against the first as well as against the second table; against murdering of souls by heresy, as well as murdering of men's bodies with the sword; against the blaspheming of the God of heaven, as well as against blaspheming of kings and rulers, that are counted gods on earth. That place seems to have much force in it to this purpose, Heb. x. 28, 29: "He that despised Moses' law, died without mercy under two or three witnesses. Of how much sorer punishment, suppose ye, shall he be thought worthy who hath trodden under foot the Son of God, and hath counted the blood of the covenant, wherewith he was sanctified, an unholy thing, and hath done despite unto the Spirit of grace?" Yea, what deserve such as deny the Spirit to be of God? Papists exempt their clergy from the judgment of the civil power, though they be delinquents against it; and their states, both civil and spiritual, from civil taxes, tributes, and penalties, both which we deny to ours: for, 1st, This is repugnant to the law of nature, that church officers and members, as parts and members of the commonwealth, should not be subject to the government of that commonwealth whereof they are parts. 2d, Repugnant to the laws and practices of the Old Testament, under which we read of no such exemptions. Yea, we have instance of Abiathar the high-priest, who, for his partnership with Adonijah in his rebellion, was exiled by king Solomon, and so consequently deprived of the exercise of his office, 1 Kings ii. 26, 27. 3d, Inconsistent with our Saviour's example, who, as subject to the law, held himself obliged to pay tribute to avoid offence, (Matt. xvii. 26,) which was an active scandal; and he confesses Pilate's power to condemn or release him was *given him from above*, John xix. 11. 4th, And finally, contrary to the apostolical precepts, *enjoining all to be subject to superior powers*, Rom. xiii. 1-4; 1 Pet. ii. 13-15.

Now, all the former power that is granted, or may be granted to the magistrate about religion, is only cumulative and objective, as divines used to express it; thus understand them:—

Cumulative, not privative; adding to, not detracting from any liberties or privileges granted her from Christ. The heathen magistrate may be a *nurse-father*, Isa. xlix. 23; 1 Tim. ii.

2, may not be a *step-father*: may protect the Church, religion, &c., and order many things in a political way about religion; may not extirpate or persecute the Church; may help her in reformation; may not hinder her in reforming herself, convening synods in herself, as in Acts xv., &c., if he will not help her therein; otherwise her condition were better without than with a magistrate. The Christian magistrate much less ought to hinder her therein, otherwise her state were worse under the Christian than under the pagan magistrate.

Objective or objectively ecclesiastical, as being exercised about objects ecclesiastical, but politically, not ecclesiastically. His proper power is *about*, not *in* religious matters. He may politically, outwardly exercise his power about objects or matters spiritual; but not spiritually, inwardly, formally act any power in the Church. He may act in church affairs as did Asa, Jehoshaphat, Hezekiah, Josiah; not as did Corah, Saul, Uzzah, or Uzziah. He is an overseer of things without, not of things within. And in a word, his whole power about church offices and religion is merely, properly, and formally civil or political.30

Nor is this only our private judgment, or the opinion of some few particular persons touching the granting or bounding of the magistrate's power about matters of religion; but with us we have the suffrage of many reformed churches, who, in their Confessions of Faith published to the world, do fully and clearly express themselves to the same effect.

The Helvetian church thus: Since every magistrate is of God, it is (unless he would exercise tyranny) his chief duty, all blasphemy being repressed, to defend and provide for religion, and to execute this to his utmost strength, as the prophet teacheth out of the word; in which respect the pure and free preaching of God's word, a right, diligent, and well-instituted discipline of youth, citizens and scholars; a just and liberal maintenance of the ministers of the church, and a solicitous care of the poor, (whereunto all ecclesiastical means belong,) have the first place. After this, &c.

The French churches thus: He also therefore committed the sword into the magistrates' hands, that they might repress faults committed not only against the second table, but also against the first; therefore we affirm, that their laws and statutes ought to be obeyed, tribute and tribute to be paid, and other burdens to be borne, the yoke of subjection voluntarily to be undergone, yea, though the magistrates should be infidels, so long as the supreme government of God remains perfect and untouched, Matt. xxiv.; Acts iv. 17, and v. 19; Jude verse 8.

The church of Scotland thus: Moreover we affirm, that the purging and conserving of religion is the first and most especial duty of kings, princes, governors, and magistrates. So that they are ordained of God not only for civil polity, but also for the conservation of true religion, and that all idolatry and superstition may be suppressed: as is evident in David, Jehoshaphat, Josiah, Hezekiah, and others, adorned with high praises for their singular zeal.

The Belgic church thus: Therefore he hath armed the magistrates with a sword, that they may punish the bad and defend the good. Furthermore, it is their duty not only to be solicitous about preserving of civil polity, but also to give diligence that the sacred ministry may be preserved, all idolatry and adulterate worship of God may be taken out of the way, the kingdom of antichrist may be pulled down, but Christ's kingdom propagated. Finally, it is their part to take course, that the holy word of the gospel be preached on every side, that all may freely and purely serve and worship God according to the prescript of his word. And all men, of whatsoever dignity, condition, or state they be, ought to be subject to lawful magistrates, to pay them tribute and subsidies, to obey them in all things which are not repugnant to the word of God; to pour out prayers for them, that God would vouchsafe to direct them in all their actions, *and that we may under them lead a quiet and peaceable life in all godliness and honesty.* Wherefore we detest the Anabaptists and all turbulent men who cast off superior dominions and magistrates, pervert laws and judgments, make all goods common, and finally abolish or confound all orders and degrees which God hath constituted for honesty's sake among men.

The church in Bohemia thus: They teach also that it is commanded in the word of God that *all should be subject to the higher powers* in all things, yet in those things only which are not repugnant to God and his word. But as touching those things which concern men's souls, faith, and salvation, they teach that men should hearken only to God's word, &c., his ministers, as Christ himself saith, *Render to Cæsar the things that are Cæsar's, and to God those things that are God's.* But if any would compel them to those things which are against God, and fight and strive against his word, which abideth forever; they teach them to make use of the apostle's example, who thus answered the magistrate at Jerusalem: *It is meet* (say they) *to obey God rather than men.*

Finally, the church in Saxony hath expressed herself notably in this point, saying, among many other passages, God will have all men, yea, even unregenerate men, to be ruled and restrained by political government. And in this government the wisdom, justice, and goodness of God to mankind do shine forth. His wisdom, order declares, which is the difference of virtues and vices, and the consociation of men by lawful governments and contracts ordained in wonderful wisdom. God's justice also is seen in political government, who will have manifest wickednesses to be punished by magistrates; and when they that rule punish not the guilty, God himself wonderfully draws them to punishment, and regularly punishes heinous faults with heinous penalties in this life, as it is said, *He that takes the sword shall perish by the sword;* and, *Whoremongers and adulterers God will judge.* God will have in these punishments the difference of vices and virtues to be seen; and will have us learn that God is wise, just, true, chaste. God's goodness also to mankind is beheld, because by this means he preserves the society of men, and therefore he preserves it that thence the Church may be gathered, and will have polities to be the Church's inns. Of these divine and immoveable laws, which are testimonies of God, and the chief rule of manners, the magistrate is to be keeper in punishing all that violate them. For the voice of the law, without punishment and execution, is of small avail to bridle and restrain men; therefore it is said by Paul, *The power should be a terror to evil works, and an honor to the good.* And antiquity rightly said, *The magistrate is the keeper of the law, both of the first and second table,* so far as appertains to *good order.* And though many in their governments neglect the glory of God, yet this ought to be their chief care, to hear and embrace the true doctrine touching the Son of God, and to foster the churches, as the psalm saith, *And now understand, ye kings, and be instructed, ye judges of the earth.* Again, *Open your gates, ye princes,* i.e., Open your empires to the gospel, and afford harbor to the Son of God. And Isa. xlix.: *And kings shall be thy nursing-fathers, and queens,* i.e., commonwealths, *shall be thy nursing-mothers,* i.e., of the Church, they shall afford lodgings to churches and pious studies. And kings and princes themselves shall be members of the Church, and shall rightly understand doctrine, shall not help those that establish false doctrine, and exercise unjust cruelty, but shall be mindful of this saying, "I will glorify them that glorify me." And Daniel exhorteth the king of Babylon unto the acknowledgment of God's wrath, and to clemency towards the exiled Church, when he saith, "Break off thy sins by righteousness, and thine iniquities by showing mercy to the poor." And since they are among the chief members of the Church, they should see that judgment be rightly exercised in the Church, as Constantine, Theodosius, Arcadius, Marcianus, Charles the Great, and many pious kings, took care that the judgments of the Church should be rightly exercised, &c.

Thus those of the presbyterian judgment are willing to give to Cæsar those things that are Cæsar's, even about matters of religion, that the magistrate may see, it is far from their intention in the least degree to intrench upon his just power, by asserting the spiritual power, which Christ hath seated in his church officers, distinct from the magistratical power: but as for them of the independent judgment, and their adherents, they divest the magistrate of such power.31

SECTION II.

II. Some power on the other hand touching religion and church affairs, is utterly denied to the civil magistrate, as no way belonging to him at all by virtue of his office of magistracy. Take it thus:

Jesus Christ, our Mediator, now under the New Testament, hath committed no spiritual power at all, magisterial or ministerial, properly, internally, formally, or virtually ecclesiastical, nor any exercise thereof, for the government of his Church, to the political magistrate, heathen or Christian, as the subject or receptacle thereof by virtue of his magistratical office.

For explication hereof briefly thus: 1. What is meant by spiritual power, magisterial and ministerial, is laid down in the general nature of the government, Chap. III. And, That all magisterial lordly power over the Church, belongs peculiarly and only to Jesus Christ our Mediator, Lord of all, is proved, Chap. V. Consequently, the civil magistrate can challenge no such power, without usurpation upon Christ's prerogative. We hence condemn the Pope as Antichrist, while he claims to be Christ's vicar-general over Christ's visible Church on earth. So that all the question here will be about the ministerial power, whether any such belong to the civil magistrate. 2. What is meant by power, properly, internally, formally, or virtually ecclesiastical? Thus conceive: These several terms are purposely used, the more clearly and fully to distinguish power purely ecclesiastical, which is denied to the magistrate, from power purely political about ecclesiastical objects, which is granted to him; which is called ecclesiastical, not properly, but improperly; not internally, but externally; not formally, but only objectively, as conversant about ecclesiastical objects. Nor hath he any such ecclesiastical power in him virtually, i.e. so as to convey and give it to any other under him. He may grant and protect the public exercise of that power within his dominions; but designation of particular persons to the office and power, is from the Church; the donation of the office and power only from Christ himself. So that magistracy doth not formally nor virtually comprehend in it ecclesiastical power for church government; for a magistrate, as a magistrate, hath no inward ecclesiastical power at all belonging to him.

For confirmation of this proposition, consider these ensuing arguments.

Argum. 1st. The keys of the kingdom of heaven were never given by Christ to the civil magistrate, as such: therefore he cannot be the proper subject of church government as a magistrate. We may thus reason:

Major. No power of the keys of the kingdom of heaven was ever given by Christ to the civil magistrate, as a magistrate.

Minor. But all formal power of church government is at least part of the power of the keys of the kingdom of heaven.

Conclusion. Therefore no formal power of church government was ever given by Christ to the civil magistrate, as a magistrate.

The major proposition is evident.

1. Because when Christ gave the keys of the kingdom of heaven, he makes no mention at all of the civil magistrate directly or indirectly, expressly or implicitly, as the recipient subject thereof. Compare Matt. xvi. 19, and xviii. 18, John ii. 21-23, with Matt. xxvii. 18-20. 2. Because, in Christ's giving the keys of the kingdom of heaven, he makes express mention of church officers,[32] which are really and essentially different from the civil magistrate, viz. of Peter, in name of all the rest, Matt. xvi. 18, 19, and of the rest of the apostles as the receptacle of the keys with him, Matt. xviii. 18, all the disciples save Thomas being together, he gave them the same commission in other words, John xx. 20-24, and Matt. xxviii. 18-20. Now if Christ should have given the keys, or any power thereof to the magistrate, as a magistrate, he must consequently have given them only to the magistrate, and then how could he have given them to his apostles, being officers in the Church really distinct from the magistrate?

3. Because Jesus Christ, in giving the keys of the kingdom, gave not any one sort, act, part, or piece of the keys severally, but the whole power of the keys, all the sorts and acts thereof jointly. Therefore it is said, *I give the keys of the kingdom*—and *whatsoever thou shalt bind*—*whatsoever thou shalt loose*—*whose soever sins ye remit*—*whose soever sins ye retain*—Matt. xvi. 19, John xx. 23. So that here is not only key, but keys given at once, viz. key of doctrine, and the key of discipline; or the key of order, and the key of jurisdiction; not only binding or retaining, but loosing or remitting of sins, viz. all acts together conferred in the keys. Now if Christ gave the keys to the magistrate, then he gave all the sorts of keys and all the acts thereof to him: if so, the magistrate may as well preach the word, and dispense the sacraments, &c., (as Erastus would have him,) as dispense the censures, &c., (for Christ joined all together in the same commission, and by what warrant are they disjoined?) and if so, what need of pastors, teachers, &c.,, in the Church? Let the civil magistrate do all. It is true, the ruling elder (which was after added) is limited only to one of the keys, viz. the *key of discipline*, 1 Tim. v. 17; but this limitation is by the same authority that ordained his office.

4. Because if Christ gave the keys to the civil magistrate as such, then to every magistrate, whether Jewish, heathenish, or Christian: but not to the Jewish magistrate; for the

sceptre was to depart from him, and the Jewish polity to be dissolved, and even then was almost extinct. Not to the heathenish magistrate, for then those might be properly and formally church governors which were not church members; and if the heathen magistrate refused to govern the Church, (when there was no other magistrate on earth,) she must be utterly destitute of all government, which are grossly absurd. Nor, finally, to the Christian magistrate, for Christ gave the keys to officers then in being; but at that time no Christian magistrate was in being in the world. Therefore the keys were given by Christ to no civil magistrate, as such, at all.

The minor, viz. But all formal power of church government is at least part of the power of the keys of the kingdom of heaven is clear. If we take church government largely, as containing both doctrine, worship, and discipline, it is the whole power of the keys; if strictly, as restrained only to discipline, it is at least part of the power. For, 1st, Not only the power of order, but also the power of jurisdiction, is contained under the word keys; otherwise it should have been said key, not keys; church government therefore is at least part of the power of the keys. 2d, The word key, noting a stewardly power, as appears, Isa. xxii. 22, (as Erastians themselves will easily grant,) may as justly be extended in the nature of it to signify the ruling power by jurisdiction, as the teaching power by doctrine; in that the office of a steward in the household, who bears the keys, consists in governing, ordering, and ruling the household, as well as in feeding it, as that passage in Luke xii. 41-49, being well considered, doth very notably evidence. For, Christ applying his speech to his disciples, saith, "Who then is that faithful and wise steward, whom his Lord shall make ruler of his household?—he will make him ruler over all that he hath," &c. 3d, Nothing in the text or context appears why we should limit keys and the acts thereof only to doctrine, and exclude discipline; and where the text restrains not, we are not to restrain. 4th, The most of sound interpreters extend the keys and the acts thereof as well to discipline as to doctrine; to matters of jurisdiction, as well as to matters of order. From all we may conclude,

Therefore no formal power of church government was ever given by Christ to the civil magistrate, as a magistrate.

Argum. 2d. There was full power of church government in the church when no magistrate was Christian, yea, when all magistrates were persecutors of the Church, so far from being her *nursing fathers*, that they were her *cruel butchers*; therefore the magistrate is not the proper subject of this power. Thus we may argue:

Major. No proper power of church government, which was fully exercised in the Church of Christ, before any magistrate became Christian, yea, when magistrates were persecutors of the Church, was derived from Christ to the magistrate as a magistrate.

Minor. But all proper power of church government was fully exercised in the Church before any magistrate became Christian, yea, when magistrates were cruel persecutors of the Church of Christ.

Conclusion. Therefore no proper power of church government was derived from Christ to the civil magistrate as a magistrate.

The *major* proposition must be granted. For, 1st, Either then the Church, in exercising such full power of church government, should have usurped that power which belonged not at all to her, but only to the magistrate; for what power belongs to a magistrate, as a magistrate, belongs to him only; but dare we think that the apostles, or the primitive purest apostolical churches did or durst exercise all their power of church government which they exercised, merely by usurpation without any right thereunto themselves? 2d, Or if the Church usurped not, &c., but exercised the power which Christ gave her, let the magistrate show wherein Christ made void the Church's charter, retracted this power, and gave it unto him.

The minor proposition cannot be denied. For,

1st. It was about 300 years after Christ before any of the Roman emperors (who had subdued the whole world, Luke ii. 1, under their sole dominion) became Christian. For Constantine the Great was the first emperor that received the faith, procured peace to the Church, and gave her respite from her cruel persecutions, which was in Anno 309 (or thereabouts) after Christ; before which time the Church was miserably wasted and butchered with those ten bloody persecutions, by the tyranny of Nero, and other cruel emperors before Constantine.

2d. Yet within the space of this first 309 or 311 years, all proper power of church government was fully exercised in the Church of Christ; not only the word preached, Acts iv. 2; 1 Tim. iii. 16; and sacraments dispensed, Acts xx. 7; 1 Cor. xi. 17, &c.; Acts ii. 4, and viii. 12: but also *deacons* set apart for that office of *deaconship*, Acts vi.: *elders* ordained and sent forth, Acts xiii. 1-3, and xiv. 23; 1 Tim. iv.; Tit. i. 5: public *admonition in use*, Tit. iii. 10; 1 Tim. v. 20: *excommunication*, 1 Cor. v.; and 1 Tim. i. 20: *absolution* of the penitent, 2 Cor. ii. 6, 7, &c.: synodical conventions and decrees, Acts xv. with xvi. 4. So that we may conclude,

Therefore no proper power of church government was derived from Christ to the civil magistrate, as a magistrate.

Argum. 3d. The magistratical power really, specifically, and essentially differs from the ecclesiastical power; therefore the civil magistrate, as a magistrate, cannot be the proper subject of this ecclesiastical power. Hence we may thus argue:

Major. No power essentially, specifically, and really differing from magistratical power, was ever given by Christ to the magistrate as a magistrate.

Minor. But all proper ecclesiastical power essentially, specifically, and really differs from the magistratical power.

Conclusion. Therefore no proper ecclesiastical power was ever given by Jesus Christ to the civil magistrate as a magistrate.

The major is evident: for how can the magistrate, as a magistrate, receive such a power as is really and essentially distinct and different from magistracy? Were not that to make the magistratical power both really the same with itself, and yet really and essentially different from itself? A flat contradiction.

The minor may be clearly evinced many ways: as, 1st, From the real and formal distinction between the two societies, viz. the Church and commonwealth, wherein ecclesiastical and political power are peculiarly seated. 2d. From the co-ordination of the power ecclesiastical and political, in reference to one another. 3d. From the different causes of these two powers, viz. efficient, material, formal, and final; in all which they are truly distinguished from one another.

1st. From the real and formal distinction between the two societies, viz. church and commonwealth: for, 1. The society of the Church is only Christ's, and not the civil magistrate's: it is his *house*, his *spouse*, his *body*, &c., and Christ hath no vicar33 under him. 2. The officers ecclesiastical are Christ's officers, not the magistrate's, 1 Cor. iv. 1: *Christ gave* them, Eph. iv. 8, 10, 11: *God set them in the Church*, 1 Cor. xii. 28. 3. These ecclesiastical officers are both elected and ordained by the Church, without commission from the civil magistrate, by virtue of Christ's ordinance, and in his name. Thus the apostles appointed officers: *Whom we may appoint*, Acts vi. 3, 4. The power of ordination and mission is in the hands of Christ's officers; compare Acts xiv. 23; 1 Tim. iv. 14, with Acts xiii. 1-4: and this is confessed by the parliament to be an ordinance of Jesus Christ, in their ordinance for ordaining of preaching presbyters. 4. The Church, and the several presbyteries ecclesiastical, meet not as civil judicatories, for civil acts of government, as making civil statutes, inflicting civil punishments, &c., but as spiritual assemblies, for spiritual acts of government and discipline: as preaching, baptizing, receiving the Lord's supper, prayer, admonition of the disorderly, &c. 5. What gross absurdities would follow, should not these two societies, viz. church and commonwealth, be acknowledged to be really and essentially distinct from one another! For then, 1. There can be no commonwealth where there is not a Church; but this is contrary to all experience. Heathens have commonwealths, yet no Church. 2. Then there may be church officers elected where there is no church, seeing there are magistrates where there is no church. 3. Then those magistrates, where there is no church, are no magistrates; but that is repugnant to Scripture, which accounts heathen rulers the servants of God, Isa. xlv. 1; Jer. xxv. 9: and calls them kings, Exod. vi. 13; Isa. xxxi. 35. And further, if there be no magistrates where there is no church, then the church is the formal constituting cause of magistrates. 4. Then the commonwealth, as the commonwealth, is the church; and the church, as the church, is the commonwealth: then the church and the commonwealth are the same. 5. Then all that are members of the commonwealth are, on that account, because members of the commonwealth, members of the church. 6. Then the commonwealth, being formally the same with the church, is, as a commonwealth, the mystical body of Christ. 7. Then the officers of the church are the officers of the commonwealth; the power of the keys gives them right to the civil sword: and consequently, the ministers of the gospel, as ministers, are justices of the peace, judges, parliament-men, &c., all which how absurd, let the world judge.

2d. From the co-ordination of the power ecclesiastical and political, in reference to one another: (this being a received maxim, that subordinate powers are of the same kind; co-ordinate powers are of distinct kinds.) Now, that the power of the Church is co-ordinate with the civil power, may be evidenced as followeth: 1. The officers of Christ, as officers, are not directly and properly subordinate to the civil power, though in their persons they are subject thereto: the apostles and pastors may preach, and cast out of the church, against the will of the magistrate, and yet not truly offend magistracy; thus, in doing the duty they have immediately received from God, they must "obey God rather than men," Acts iv. 19, 20. And the apostles and pastors must exercise their office (having received a command from Christ) without attending to the command or consent of the civil magistrate for the same; *as in casting out the incestuous person,* 1 Cor. v. 5: telling the Church, Matt. xviii. 17: *rejecting a heretic,* Tit. iii. 10. And, 2. Those acts of power are not directly and formally subordinate to the magistrate, which he himself cannot do, or which belong not to him. Thus the kings of Israel could not burn incense: "It appertaineth not unto thee," 2 Chron. xxvi. 18, 19. Likewise, none have the power of the keys, but they to whom Christ saith, "Go ye into all the world and preach the gospel," Matt. xxviii. 19: but Christ spake not this to magistrates: so only those that are *sent,* Rom. x. 15, and those that are governors, are by Christ placed in the Church. 3. The officers of the Church can ecclesiastically censure the officers of the state, though not as such, as well as the officers of the state can punish civilly the officers of the Church, though not as such: the church guides may admonish, excommunicate, &c., the officers of the state as members of the Church, and the officers of the state may punish the officers of the Church as the members of the state. 4. Those that are not sent of the magistrate as his deputies, they are not subordinate in their mission to his power, but the ministers are not sent as the magistrate's deputies, but are *set over the flock by the Holy Ghost,* Acts xx. 28: they are likewise the *ministry of Christ,* 1 Cor. iv. 1, 2: they are *over you in the Lord,* 1 Thess. v. 12: and in his name they exercise their jurisdiction, 1 Cor. v. 4, 5. 5. If the last appeal in matters purely ecclesiastical be not to the civil power, then there is no subordination; but the last appeal properly so taken is not to the magistrate. This appears from these considerations: 1. Nothing is appealable to the magistrate but what is under the power of the sword; but admonition, excommunication, &c., are not under the power of the sword: they are neither matters of dominion nor coercion. 2. If it were so, then it follows that the having of the sword gives a man a power to the keys. 3. Then it follows that the officers of the kingdom of heaven are to be judged as such by the officers of the kingdom of this world as such, and then there is no difference between the things of Cæsar and the things of God. 4. The church of Antioch sent to Jerusalem, Acts xv. 2, and the synod there, without the magistrate, came together, ver. 6; and determined the controversy, ver. 28, 29. And we read, "The spirits of the prophets are subject to the prophets," 1 Cor. xiv. 32; not to the civil power as prophets. So we must seek knowledge at the priest's lips, not at the civil magistrate's, Mal. ii. 7. And we read, that the people came to the priests in hard controversies, but never that the priests went to the civil power, Deut. xvii. 8-10. 5. It makes the magistrate Christ's vicar, and so Christ to have a visible head on earth, and so to be an ecclesiastico-civil pope, and consequently there should be as many visible heads of Christ's Church as there are magistrates. 6. These powers are both immediate; one from God the Father, as *Creator,* Rom. xiii. 1, 2; the other from Jesus Christ, as *Mediator,* Matt. xxviii. 18. Now lay all these together, and there cannot be a subordination of powers; and therefore there must be a real distinction.

3d. From the different causes of these two powers, viz. efficient, material, formal, and final; in all which they are truly distinguished from one another, as may plainly appear by this ensuing parallel:

1. They differ in their efficient cause or author, whence they are derived. Magistratical power is from God, the Creator and Governor of the world, Rom. xiii. 1, 2, 4, and so belongs to all mankind, heathen or Christian; ecclesiastical power is peculiarly from Jesus Christ our Mediator, Lord of the Church, (who hath all power given him, and the government of the Church laid upon his shoulder, as Eph. i. 22; Matt. xxviii. 18, compared with Isa. ix. 16.) See Matt. vi. 19, and xviii. 18, and xxviii. 19, 20; John xx. 21-23; 2 Cor. x. 8: and consequently belongs properly to the Church, and to them that are within the Church, 1 Cor. v. 12, 13. Magistratical power in general is the ordinance of God, Rom. xiii. 1, 2, 4; but magistratical power in particular, whether it should be monarchical in a king, aristocratical in states, democratical in the people, &c., is of men, called, therefore, a human creature, or creation, 1 Pet. ii. 13; but ecclesiastical power, and officers in particular, as well as general, are from Christ, Matt. xvi. 19, and xxviii. 18-20; Tit. iii. 10; 1 Cor. v. 13; 2 Cor. ii. For officers, see Eph. iv. 11, 12; 1 Cor. xii. 28.

2. They differ in their material cause; whether it be the matter of which they consist, in which they are seated, or about which they are exercised. 1. In respect of the matter of which they consist, they much differ. Ecclesiastical power consists of the keys of the kingdom of heaven, which are exercised in the preaching of the word, dispensing the sacraments, executing the censures, admonition, excommunication, absolution, ordination of presbyters, &c.; but magistratical power consists in the secular sword, which puts forth itself in making statutes, inflicting fines, imprisonments, confiscations, banishments, torments, death. 2. In respect of the matter or object about which they are exercised, they much differ: for, the magistratical power is exercised politically, about persons and things without the Church, as well as within the church; but the ecclesiastical power is exercised only upon them that are within the Church, 1 Cor. v. 13. The magistratical power in some cases of treason, &c., banishes or otherwise punishes even penitent persons: ecclesiastical power punishes no penitent persons. The magistratical power punishes not all sorts of scandal, but some: the ecclesiastical power punishes (if rightly managed) all sorts of scandal.

3. They differ in their formal cause, as doth clearly appear by their way or manner of acting: magistratical power takes cognizance of crimes, and passes sentence thereupon according to statutes and laws made by man: ecclesiastical power takes cognizance of, and passes judgment upon crimes according to the word of God, the Holy Scriptures. Magistratical power punishes merely with political punishments, as fines, imprisonments, &c. Ecclesiastical merely with spiritual punishments, as church censures. Magistratical power makes all decrees and laws, and executes all authority, commanding or punishing only in its own name, in name of the supreme magistrate, as of the king, &c., but ecclesiastical power is wholly exercised, not in the name of churches, or officers, but only in Christ's name, Matt. xxviii. 19; Acts iv. 17; 1 Cor. v. 4. The magistrate can delegate his power to another: church-governors cannot delegate their power to others, but must exercise it by themselves. The magistrate about ecclesiasticals hath power to command and compel politically the church officers to do their duty, as formerly was evidenced; but cannot discharge lawfully those duties themselves, but in attempting the same, procure divine wrath upon themselves: as Korah, Numb. xvi.; King Saul, 1 Sam. xiii. 9-15; King Uzziah, 2 Chron. xxvi. 16-22: but church-guides can properly discharge the duties of doctrine, worship, and discipline themselves, and ecclesiastically command and compel others to do their duty also.

4. Lastly, They differ in their final cause or ends. The magistratical power levels at the temporal, corporal, external, political peace, tranquillity, order, and good of human society, and of all persons within his jurisdiction, &c. The ecclesiastical power intends properly the spiritual good and edification of the Church and all the members thereof, Matt. xviii. 15; 1 Cor. v. 5, &c.; 2 Cor. x. 8, and xiii. 10.34 May we not from all clearly conclude, Therefore no proper ecclesiastical power was ever given by Jesus Christ to the magistrate as a magistrate?

Argum. 4th. The civil magistrate is no proper church officer, and therefore cannot be the proper subject of church power, Hence we may argue:

Major. All formal power of church government was derived from Jesus Christ to his own proper church officers only. To them he gave the *keys of the kingdom of heaven*, Matt. xvi. 19, and xviii. 18; John xx. 21, 28: to them he gave the *authority for edification of the church*, 2 Cor. x. 8, and xiii. 10: but this will after more fully appear in Chap. XI. following.

46

Minor. But no civil magistrate, as a magistrate, is any of Christ's proper church officers. For, 1. The civil magistrate is never reckoned up in the catalogue, list, or roll of Christ's church officers in Scripture, Eph. iv. 10-12; 1 Cor. xii. 28, &c.; Rom. xii. 6-8; if here, or anywhere else, let the magistrate or the Erastians show it. 2. A magistrate, as a magistrate, is not a church member, (much less a church governor;) for then all magistrates, heathen as well as Christian, should be church members and church officers, but this is contrary to the very nature of Christ's kingdom, which admits no heathen into it.

Conclusion. Therefore no formal power of church government was derived from Jesus Christ to the magistrate as a magistrate.

Argum. 5th. The civil magistrate, as such, is not properly subordinate to Christ's mediatory kingdom; therefore is not the receptacle of church power from Christ. Hence thus:

Major. Whatsoever formal power of church government Christ committed to any, he committed it only to those that were properly subordinate to his mediatory kingdom. For whatsoever ecclesiastical ordinance, office, power, or authority, Christ gave to men, he gave it as Mediator and Head of the Church, by virtue of his mediatory office; and for the gathering, edifying, and perfecting of his mediatory kingdom, which is his Church, Eph. iv. 7, 10-12. Therefore such as are not properly subordinate to Christ in this his office, and for this end, can have no formal church power from Christ.

Minor. But no magistrate, as a magistrate, is subordinate properly to Christ's mediatory kingdom. For, 1. Not Christ the Mediator, but God the Creator authorizeth the magistrate's office, Rom. xiii. 1, 2, 6. 2. Magistracy is never styled a ministry of Christ in Scripture, nor dispensed in his name. 3. Christ's kingdom is not of this world, John xviii. 36; the magistrate's is.

Conclusion. Therefore no formal power of Church government is committed by Christ to the magistrate as a magistrate.

6th. Finally, divers absurdities unavoidably follow upon the granting of a proper formal power of Church government to the civil magistrate: therefore he cannot be the proper subject of such power. Hence it may be thus argued:

Major. No grant of ecclesiastical power, which plainly introduceth many absurdities, can be allowed to the political magistrate, as the proper subject thereof. For though in matters of religion there be many things mysterious, sublime, and above the reach of reason; yet there is nothing to be found that is absurd, irrational, &c.

Minor. But to grant to the political magistrate, as a magistrate, a proper formal power of church government, introduceth plainly many absurdities, e.g.: 1. This brings confusion betwixt the office of the magistracy and ministry. 2. Confounds the church and commonwealth together. 3. Church government may be monarchical in one man; and so, not only prelatical but papal; and consequently, antichristian. Which absurdities, with many others, were formerly intimated, and neither by religion nor reason can be endured. We conclude:

Conclusion. Therefore the grant of a proper formal power of church government cannot be allowed to the political magistrate as the proper subject thereof, because he is a magistrate.

CHAPTER X.

That the community of the faithful, or body of the people, are not the immediate subject of the power of Church government.

Thus we see, that Jesus Christ our Mediator did not commit any proper formal ecclesiastical power for church government to the political magistrate, as such, as the Erastians conceive. Now, in the next place (to come more close) let us consider that Jesus Christ our Mediator hath not committed the spiritual power of church government to the body of the people, presbyterated, or unpresbyterated (to use their own terms) as the first subject thereof, according to the opinion of the Separatists or Independents. Take it in this proposition:

Jesus Christ our Mediator hath not committed the proper formal power or authority spiritual, for government of his Church,35 unto the community of the faithful, whole church, or body of the people, as the proper immediate receptacle, or first subject thereof.

SECTION I.

Some things herein need a little explanation, before we come to the confirmation.

1. By *fraternity, community of the faithful, whole church or body of the people*, understand a particular company of people, meeting together in one assembly or single congregation, to partake of Christ's ordinances. This single congregation may be considered as presbyterated, i.e., furnished with an eldership; or as unpresbyterated, i.e., destitute of an eldership, having yet no elders or officers erected among them. Rigid Brownists or Separatists say, that the fraternity or community of the faithful unpresbyterated is the first receptacle of proper ecclesiastical power from Christ: unto whom some of independent judgment subscribe. Independents thus resolve: First, That the apostles of Christ are the first subject of apostolical power. Secondly, That a particular congregation of saints, professing the faith, taken indefinitely for any church, (one as well as another,) is the first subject of all church offices with all their spiritual gifts and power. Thirdly, That when the church of a particular congregation walketh together in the truth and peace, the brethren of the church are the first subjects of church liberty; the elders thereof of church authority; and both of them together are the first subject of all church power.36 Which assertions of Brownists and Independents (except the first) are denied by them of presbyterian judgment, as being obvious to divers material and just exceptions.37:

2. By *proper formal power or authority spiritual, for church government*, thus conceive. To omit what hath been already laid down about the natures and sorts of spiritual power and authority, (part 2, chap. III. and VI.,) which are to be remembered, here it may be further observed, that there is a proper public, official, authoritative power, though but stewardly and ministerial, which is derived from Jesus Christ to his church officers, Matt. xvi. 19, and xviii. 18; John xx. 21-23; Matt, xxviii. 18-20; of which power the apostle speaking, saith, "If I should somewhat boast of our power which the Lord hath given us to edification," 2 Cor. x. 8; so 2 Cor. xiii. 10. The people are indeed allowed certain liberties or privileges; as, *To try the spirits*, &c., 1 John iv. 1. To prove all doctrines by the word, 1 Thess. v. 21. To nominate and elect their own church officers, as their deacons, which they did, Acts vi. 3, 5, 6; but this is not a proper power of the keys. But the proper, public, official, authoritative power, is quite denied to the body of the people, furnished with an eldership or destitute thereof.

3. By *proper immediate receptacle, or first subject of power*, understand, that subject, seat, or receptacle of power, which first and immediately received this power from Jesus Christ; and consequently was intrusted and authorized by him, to put forth and exercise that power in his Church for the government thereof. And here two things must be carefully remembered: 1. That we distinguish betwixt the object and subject of this power. The object for which, for whose good and benefit all this power is given, is primarily the general visible Church, Ephes. iv. 7, 10-12; 1 Cor. xii. 28; Rom. xii. 5,6, &c. Secondarily, particular churches, as they are parts and members of the general. But the subject receiving to which the power is derived, is not the Church general or particular, but the officers or governors of the Church. 2. That we distinguish also betwixt the donation of the power, and the designation of particular persons to offices ecclesiastical. This designation of persons to the offices of key bearing or ruling may be done first and immediately by the Church, in nominating or electing her individual officers which is allowed to her; yet is no proper authoritative act of power. But the donation of the power itself is not from the Church as the fountain, but immediately from Christ himself, 2 Cor. xi. 8, and xiii. 10. Nor is it to the Church as the subject, but immediately to the individual church officers themselves, who consequently, in all the exercise of their power, act as the *ministers and stewards of Christ*, 1 Cor. iv. 1, putting forth their power immediately received from Christ, not as the substitutes or delegates of the Church putting forth her power, which from Christ she mediately conveys to them, as Independents do imagine, but by us is utterly denied.

SECTION II.

For confirmation of this proposition thus explained and stated; consider these few arguments:

Argum. I. The community of the faithful, or body of the people, have no authentic commission or grant of proper spiritual power for church government; and therefore they cannot possibly be the first subject or the proper immediate receptacle of such power from Christ. We may thus argue:

Major. Whomsoever Jesus Christ hath made the immediate receptacle or first subject of proper formal power for governing of his Church, to them this power is conveyed by some authentic grant or commission.

Minor. But the community of the faithful, or body of the people, have not this power conveyed unto them by any authentic grant or commission.

Conclusion. Therefore Jesus Christ our Mediator hath not made the community of the faithful, or body of the people, the immediate receptacle or first subject of proper formal power for governing of his Church.

The major proposition is evident in itself: For, 1. The power of church government in this or that subject is not natural, but positive; and cast upon man, not by natural, but by positive law, positive grant: men are not bred, but made the first subject of such power; therefore all such power claimed or exercised, without such positive grant, is merely without any due title, imaginary, usurped, unwarrantable, in very fact null and void. 2. All power of church government is radically and fundamentally in Christ, Isa. ix. 6; Matt, xxviii. 18; John v. 22. And how shall any part of it be derived from Christ to man, but by some fit intervening mean betwixt Christ and man? And what mean of conveyance betwixt Christ and man can suffice, if it do not amount to an authentic grant or commission for such power? 3. This is evidently Christ's way to confer power by authentic commission immediately upon his church officers, the apostles and their successors, to the world's end. "Thou art Peter; and I give to thee the keys of the kingdom of heaven," &c., Matt. xvi. 18, 19. "Whatsoever ye shall bind on earth," &c., Matt, xviii. 19, 20. "As my Father sent me, so send I you; go, disciple ye all nations; whose sins ye remit, they are remitted—and lo, I am with you always to the end of the world," John xx. 21, 23; Matt, xxviii. 19, 20. "Our power, which the Lord hath given us for edification," 2 Cor. x. 8, and xiii. 10: so that we may conclude them that have such commission to be the first subject and immediate receptacle of power from Christ, as will after more fully appear. 4. If no such commission be needful to distinguish those that have such power from those that have none, why may not all without exception, young and old, wise and foolish, men and women, Christian and heathen, &c., equally lay claim to this power of church government? If not, what hinders? If so, how absurd!

The minor proposition, viz: But the community of the faithful, or body of the people, have not this power conveyed to them by any authentic grant or commission, is firm. For whence had they it? When was it given to them? What is the power committed to them? Or in what sense is such power committed to them?

1. Whence had they it? *From heaven or of men?* If from men, then it is a human ordinance and invention; *a plant which the heavenly Father hath not planted*; and therefore *shall be plucked up.* Matt. xv. 13. If from heaven, then from Christ; for *all power is given to him,* Matt, xxviii. 18, &c.; Isa. ix. 6. If it be derived from Christ, then it is derived from him by some positive law of Christ as his grant or charter. A positive grant of such power to select persons, viz. church officers, the Scripture mentions, as was evidenced in the proof of the major proposition. But touching any such grant or commission to the community of the faithful, the Scripture is silent. And let those that are for the popular power produce, if they can, any clear scripture that expressly, or by infallible consequence, contains any such commission.

2. When was any such power committed by Christ to the multitude of the faithful, either in the first planting and beginning of the Church, or in the after establishment and growth of the Church under the apostles' ministry? Not the first; for then the apostles themselves should have derived their power from the community of the faithful: now this is palpably inconsistent with the Scriptures, Which tell us that the apostles had both their apostleship itself, and their qualifications with gifts and graces for it, yea, and the very

designation of all their particular persons unto that calling, all of them immediately from Christ himself. For the first, see Gal. i. 1: "Paul, an apostle, not of men, nor by man, but by Jesus Christ," Matt. xxviii. 18-20. For the second, see John xx. 22, 23: "And when he had said this, he breathed on them, and saith unto them, Receive ye the Holy Ghost; whose soever sins ye remit, they are remitted unto them," &c. For the third, see Luke vi. 13, &c.: "And when it was day he called to him his disciples: and of them he chose twelve, whom also he named apostles; Simon—" Matt. x. 5-7, &c.: "These twelve Jesus sent forth, and commanded them, saying." And after his resurrection he enlarges their commission, Mark xvi. 15, 16: "Go ye into all the world;" and, "As my Father hath sent me, so send I you," John xx. 21. See also how the Lord cast the lot upon Matthias, Acts i. 24-26. Nor the second; for if such power be committed to the community of the faithful after the apostles had established the churches, then let those that so think show where Christ committed this power first to the apostles, and after to the community of the faithful, and by them or with them to their ordinary officers, for execution thereof. But no such thing hath any foundation in Scripture; for the ordinary Church guides, though they may have a designation to their office by the church, yet they have the donation, or derivation of their office and its authority only from Christ: their office is from Christ, Ephes. iv. 8, 11; 1 Cor. xii. 28; Acts xx. 28, 29. Their power from Christ, Matt. xvi. 19, and xxviii. 18, 19; John xx. 21, 23. "Our power which the Lord hath given us," 2 Cor. viii. 10. They are *Christ's ministers, stewards, ambassadors*, 1 Cor. iv. 1; 2 Cor. v. 19, 20. They are to act and officiate *in his name*, Matt, xviii. 19; 1 Cor. v. 4, 5; and to Christ they *must give an account*. Heb. xiii. 17, 18; Luke xii. 41, 42. Now if the ordinary officers have (as well as the apostles their apostleship) their offices of pastor, teacher, &c., from Christ, and are therein the successors of the apostles to continue to the world's end, (Matt. xxviii. 18-20,) then they have their power and authority in their offices immediately from Christ, as the first receptacles thereof themselves, and not from the Church as the first receptacle of it herself. A successor hath jurisdiction from him from whom the predecessor had his; otherwise he doth not truly succeed him. Consequently the Church or community of the faithful cannot possibly be the first receptacle of the power of church government from Christ.

3. What power is it that is committed to the body of the Church or multitude of the faithful? Either it must be the power of order, or the power of jurisdiction. But neither of these is allowed to the multitude of the faithful by the Scriptures, (but appointed and appropriated to select persons.) Not the power of order; for the whole multitude, and everyone therein, neither can nor ought to intermeddle with any branches of that power. 1. Not with preaching; all are not *apt to teach*, 1 Tim. iii. 2, nor able to exhort and convince gainsayers, Tit. i. 9; all are not gifted and duly qualified. Some are expressly prohibited *speaking in the church*, 1 Cor. xiv. 34, 35, 1 Tim. ii. 12, Rev. ii. 20, and none are *to preach, unless they be sent*, Rom. x. 15, nor *to take such honor unto themselves unless they be called*, &c., Heb. v. 4, 5. Are all and every one of the multitude of the faithful able to teach, exhort, and convince? are they all sent to preach? are they all called of God? &c. Nay, hath not Christ laid this task of authoritative preaching only upon his own officers? Matt, xxviii. 18, 19. 2. Not with administration of the sacraments; this and preaching are by one and the same commission given to officers only, Matt, xxviii. 18-20; 1 Cor. xi. 23. 3. Nor to ordain presbyters, or other officers. They may choose; but extraordinary officers, or the presbytery of ordinary officers, ordain. Acts vi. 3, 5, 6: "Look ye out men—whom we may appoint." Compare also Acts xiv. 23; 1 Tim. iv. 14, and v. 22; Tit. iii. 5. So that the people's bare election and approbation is no sufficient Scripture ordination of officers. Nor is there one often thousand among the people that is in all points able to try and judge of the sufficiency of preaching presbyters, for tongues, arts, and soundness of judgment in divinity. Nor is the power of jurisdiction in public admonition, excommunication, and absolution, &c., allowed to the multitude. For all and every one of the multitude of the faithful, 1. Never had any such power given to them from Christ; this key as well as the key of knowledge being given to the officers of the Church only, Matt. xvi. 19, and xviii. 18-20. *Tell the church*, there, must needs be meant of the ruling church only.38 2 Cor. viii. 10; John xx. 21-23. 2. Never acted or executed any such power, that we can find in Scripture. As for that which is primarily urged of the church of Corinth, that the whole church did excommunicate the *incestuous person*, 1

Cor. v. 4, &c., many things may be answered to evince the contrary. 1st, The whole multitude could not do it; for children could not judge, and women must not speak in the Church. 2d, It is not said, *Sufficient to such an one is the rebuke inflicted of all*, but *of many*, 2 Cor. ii. 6, viz. of the presbytery, which consisted of many officers. 3d, The church of Corinth, wherein this censure was inflicted, was not a congregational, but a presbyterial church, having divers particular congregations in it, (as is hereafter cleared in Chap. XXIII.,) and therefore the whole multitude of the church of Corinth could not meet together in one place for this censure, but only the presbytery of that great church. Again, never did the whole multitude receive from Christ due gifts and qualifications for the exercise of church government and jurisdiction; nor any promise from Christ to be with them therein, as officers have, Matt, xxviii. 18-20. And the absurdities of such popular government are intolerable, as after will appear.

4. Finally, in what sense can it be imagined that any such power should be committed from Christ to the community of the faithful, the whole body of the Church? For this power is given them equally with the church-guides, or unequally. If equally, then,.1. The church-guides have power and authority, as primarily and immediately committed to them, as the Church herself hath; and then they need not derive or borrow any power from the body of the faithful, having a power equal to theirs. 2. How vainly is that power equally given as to the officers, so to the whole multitude, when the whole multitude have no equal gifts and abilities to execute the same! If unequally, then this power is derived to the church-guides, either more or less than to the multitude of the faithful. If less, then how improperly were all those names of rule and government imposed upon officers, which nowhere are given by Scripture to the multitude! as*Pastors*, Eph. iv. 8, 11. *Elders*, 1 Tim. v. 17. *Overseers*, Acts xx. 28. *Guides*, Heb. xiii. 7, 17, 22. In this last verse they are contradistinguished from the saints; church-guides, and saints guided, make up a visible organical church. *Rulers in the Lord*, 1 Thes. v. 12; Rom. xii. 8: and*well-ruling Elders*, 1 Tim. v. 17. *Governments*, 1 Cor. xii. 28. *Stewards*, 1 Cor. iv. 1,2; Luke xii. 42, &c. And all these titles have power and rule engraven in their very foreheads; and they of right belonged rather to the multitude than to the officers, if the officers derive their power from the multitude of the people. If more, then church-guides, having more power than the Church, need not derive any from the Church, being themselves better furnished.

Thus, what way soever we look, it cannot be evinced, that the multitude and body of the people, with or without eldership, are the first subject of power, or have any authoritative public official power at all, from any grant, mandate, or commission of Christ. From all which we may strongly conclude,

Therefore Jesus Christ our Mediator hath not made the community of the faithful, or body of the people, the immediate receptacle, or first subject of proper formal power for governing of his church.

Argum. II. As the multitude of the faithful have no authentic grant or commission of such power of the keys in the Church; so they have no divine warrant for the actual execution of the power of the said keys therein: and therefore cannot be the first receptacle of the power of the keys from Christ. For thus we may reason:

Major. Whosoever are the first subject, or immediate receptacle of the power of the keys from Christ, they have divine warrant actually to exercise and put in execution the said power.*Minor.* But the multitude or community of the faithful have no divine warrant actually to exercise and put in execution the power of the keys.

Conclusion. Therefore the community of the faithful are not the first subject, or immediate receptacle of the power of the keys from Jesus Christ.

The major proposition must necessarily be yielded. For, 1. The power of the keys contains both authority and exercise; power being given to that end that it may be exercised for the benefit of the Church. It is called the *power given us for edification*, 2 Cor. viii. 10. Where there is no exercise of power there can be no edification by power. 2. Both the authority and complete exercise of all that authority, were at once and together communicated from Christ to the receptacle of power. "I give unto thee the keys of the kingdom of heaven; and whatsoever thou shalt bind on earth," &c., Matt. xvi. 19, and xviii. 18. "As my Father sent me, so send I you—whose soever sins ye remit, they are remitted," John xx. 21, 23. Here is both power and the exercise thereof joined together in the same commission. Yea, so individual and inseparable are power and exercise, that under exercise, power and authority is derived: as, "Go, disciple ye all nations, baptizing them," &c., Matt. xxviii. 18, 19. 3. How vain, idle, impertinent, and ridiculous is it to fancy and dream of such a power as shall never be drawn into act by them that have it!

The minor proposition, viz. But the multitude or communion of the faithful have no divine warrant, actually to exercise and put in execution the power of the keys, is clear also:

1. By reason: for, the actual execution of this power belongs to them by divine warrant, either when they have church officers, or when they want church officers. Not while they have officers; for, that were to slight Christ's officers: that were to take officers' work out of their hands by them that are no officers, and when there were no urgent necessity; contrary whereunto, see the proofs, Chap. XI. Section 2, that were to prejudice the church, in depriving her of the greater gifts, and undoubtedly authorized labors of her officers, &c. Not when they want officers in a constituted church: as in case where there are three or four elders, the pastor dies, two of the ruling elders fall sick, or the like; in such cases the community cannot by divine warrant supply the defects of these officers themselves, by exercising their power, or executing their offices. For where doth Scripture allow such power to the community in such cases? What one church without its eldership can be instanced in the New Testament, that in such cases once presumed to exercise such power, which might be precedent or example for it to other churches? How needless are church officers, if the multitude of the faithful may, as members of the church, take up their office, and actually discharge it in all the parts of it?

2. By induction of particulars, it is evident, that the community cannot execute the power of the keys by any divine warrant. 1. *They may not preach*: for, "how shall they preach, except they be sent?" Rom. x. 15; but the community cannot be sent, many of them being incapable of the office, either by reason of their *sex*, 1 Cor. xiv. 34, 35; 1 Tim. ii. 11, 12: or by reason of their *age*; as children, and all or most of them by reason of their deficiency in gifts and in scripture qualifications, Tit. i. and 1 Tim. iii. For not one member of a thousand is so completely furnished, as to be "apt to teach, able to convince gainsayers, and to divide the word of truth aright." Besides, they may not send themselves, were they capable, for, *no man takes this honor to himself*—Yea, *Jesus Christ himself did not glorify himself to be made an high-priest*—Heb. v. 4, 5. Now only officers are sent to preach, Matt. xvi. 19, and xviii. 19, 20; Mark xvi. 15. 2. They may not administer the seals, the sacraments, baptize, &c. under the New Testament; for who gave the people any such authority? hath not Christ conjoined preaching and dispensing of the sacraments in the same commission, that the same persons only that do the one, may do the other? Matt. xxviii. 18, 19. 3. They may not ordain officers in the church, and authoritatively send them abroad: for, ordinarily the community have not sufficient qualifications and abilities for proving and examining of men's gifts for the ministry. The community are nowhere commanded or allowed so to do in the whole New Testament, but other persons distinct from them, 1 Tim. v. 22; 2 Tim. ii. 2; Tit. i. 5, &c. Nor did the community ever exercise or assume to themselves any such power of ordination or mission, but only officers both in the first sending of men to preach, as 1 Tim. iv. 14; 2 Tim. i. 6: and to be deacons, Acts vi. 6, and also in after missions, as Acts xiii. 1-3. 4. The community, without officers, may not exercise any act of jurisdiction authoritatively and properly; may not admonish, excommunicate, or absolve. For we have no precept that they should do it; we have no example in all the New Testament that they ever did do it; we have both precept and example, that select officers both did and ought to do it. "Whatsoever ye bind on earth" (saith Christ to his officers) "shall be bound in heaven," &c. Matt. xviii. 18, and xvi. 19. "Whose soever sins ye remit," &c., John xx. 21, 23. "An heretic, after once or twice admonition, reject," Tit. i. 10. "I have decreed—to deliver such an one to Satan," 1 Cor. v. 4. "The rebuke inflicted by many," not all, 2 Cor. ii. "Whom I have delivered to Satan," 1 Tim. i.*ult*. And the Scriptures nowhere set the community over themselves to be their own church-guides and governors; but appoint over them in the Lord rulers and officers distinct from the community. Compare these places, 1 Thes. v. 12; Acts xx. 28, 29; Heb. xiii. 7, 17, 22. "Salute all them that have the rule over you, and all the saints." From the premises we conclude,

Therefore the community of the faithful are not the first subject, or immediate receptacle of the power of the keys from Jesus Christ.

Argum. III. Jesus Christ hath not given nor promised to the community of the faithful a spirit of ministry, nor those gifts which are necessary for the government of the church: therefore the community was never intended to be the first subject of church government.

Major. Whomsoever Christ makes the first subject of the power of church government, to them he promises and gives a spirit of ministry, and gifts necessary for that government. For, 1. As there is diversity of ecclesiastical administrations (which is the foundation of diversity of officers) and diversity of miraculous operations, and both for the profit of the Church; so there is conveyed from the Spirit of Christ diversity of gifts, free endowments, enabling and qualifying for the actual discharge of those administrations and operations. See 1 Cor. xii. 4-7, &c. 2. What instance can be given throughout the whole New Testament of any persons, whom Christ made the receptacle of church government, but withal he gifted them, and made his promises to them, to qualify them for such government? As the apostles and their successors: "As my Father sent me, even so send I you. And when he had said this, he breathed on them, and saith unto them, Receive ye the Holy Ghost: whose soever sins ye remit, they are remitted unto them; and whose soever sins ye retain, they are retained," John xx. 21-23. And, "Go ye therefore, and disciple ye all nations, &c.— And lo, I am with you alway," (or every day,) "even to the end of the world," Matt. xxviii. 19, 20. 3. Christ being the*wisdom of the Father*, Col. ii. 3, John i. 18, and *faithful as was Moses in all his house*; yea,*more faithful—Moses as a servant* over another's, he *as a son over his own house*, Heb. iii. 2, 5, 6—it cannot stand with his most exact wisdom and fidelity, to commit the grand affairs of church government to such as are not duly gifted, and sufficiently qualified by himself for the due discharge thereof.

Minor. But Christ neither promises, nor gives a spirit of ministry, nor necessary gifts for church government to the community of the faithful. For, 1. The Scriptures teach, that gifts for ministry and government are promised and bestowed not on all, but upon some particular persons only in the visible body of Christ. "To one is given by the Spirit the word of wisdom, to another the word of knowledge," &c., not to all, 1 Cor. xii. 8, 9, &c. "If a man know not how to rule his own house, how shall he take care of the church of God?" 1 Tim. iii. 5. The hypothesis insinuates that all men have not gifts and skill rightly to rule their own houses, much less to govern the church. 2. Experience tells us, that the multitude of the people are generally destitute of such knowledge, wisdom, prudence, learning, and other necessary qualifications for the right carrying on of church government.

Conclusion. Therefore Christ makes not the community of the faithful the first subject of the power of church government.

Argum. IV. The community of the faithful are nowhere in the word called or acknowledged to be church governors: therefore they are not the first subject of church government.

Major. Those persons, who are the first subject and receptacle of proper power for church government from Christ, are in the word called and acknowledged to be church governors. This is evident, 1. By Scripture, which is wont to give to them whom Christ intrusts with his government, such names and titles as have rule, authority, and government engraven upon them: as *overseers*, Acts xx. 28; *governments*, 1 Cor. xii. 28; *rulers*, 1 Tim. v. 17, and Rom. xii. 8; with divers others, as after will appear in Chap. XI. 2. By reason, which tells us that government and governors are relative terms; and therefore to whom government belongs, to them also the denominations of governors, rulers, &c., do belong, and not contrariwise.

Minor. But the community of the faithful are nowhere in the word either called or acknowledged to be church governors. This is clear. For, 1. No titles or names are given them by Scripture which imply any rule or government in the visible Church of Christ. 2. They are plainly set in opposition against, and distinction from, church governors: they are called the*flock*; these, *overseers* set over them by the Holy Ghost, Acts xx. 28: they, *the saints*, these*their rulers*, Heb. xiii. 22: these are *over them in the Lord*; and consequently they are *under them in the Lord*, 1 Thes. v. 12. 3. The community of the faithful are so far from being the subject of church government themselves, that they are expressly charged by the word of

Christ to *know, honor, obey,* and *submit,* to other governors set over them, and distinct from themselves. "Know them who are over you in the Lord," 1 Thes. v. 12. "Let the well ruling elders be counted worthy of double honor; especially," &c., 1 Tim. v. 17. "Obey ye your rulers, and submit, for they watch for your souls," Heb. xiii. 17.

Conclusion. Therefore the community of the faithful are not the first subject and receptacle of proper power for church government.

Argum. V. This opinion of making the body of the Church, or community of the faithful, the first subject and immediate receptacle of the keys for the government of the Church, doth inevitably bring along with it many intolerable absurdities. Therefore it is not to be granted. Thus we may argue:

Major. That doctrine or opinion which draws after it unavoidably divers intolerable absurdities, is an unsound and unwarrantable opinion.

Minor. But this doctrine or opinion that makes the whole community or body of the Church to be the first subject and immediate receptacle of the keys, draws after it unavoidable divers intolerable absurdities.

Conclusion. Therefore this doctrine or opinion that makes the whole community or body of the Church to be the first subject, and immediate receptacle of the keys, is an unsound and unwarrantable opinion.

The *Major* is plain. For, 1. Though matters of religion be above reason, yet are they not unreasonable, absurd, and directly contrary to right reason. 2. The Scriptures condemn it as a great brand upon men, that they are absurd or unreasonable; "Brethren, pray for us— that we may be delivered from absurd and evil men," 2 Thes. iii. 2; and therefore if absurd men be so culpable, absurdity, and unreasonableness itself, which make them such, are much more culpable.

The *Minor,* viz. But this doctrine or opinion that makes the whole community or body of the Church to be the first subject and immediate receptacle of the keys, draws after it unavoidably divers intolerable absurdities, will notably appear by an induction of particulars.

1. Hereby a clear foundation is laid for the rigid Brownist's confused democracy, and abhorred anarchy. For, if the whole body of the people be the first receptacle of the keys, then all church government and every act thereof is in the whole body, and every member of that body a governor, consequently every member of that body an officer. But this is absurd; for if all be officers, where is the organical body? and if all be governors, where are the governed? if all be eyes, where are the feet? and if there be none governed, where is the government? it is wholly resolved at last into mere democratical anarchy and confusion, "but God is not the author of confusion," 1 Cor. xiv. 33. What an absurdity were it, if in the body natural *all were an eye,* or *hand!* for *where* then *were the hearing, smelling,* &c.; *or if all were one member, where were the body?* 1 Cor. xii. 17,19. So if in the family all were masters, where were the household? where were the family government? If in a city all were aldermen, where were the citizens? where were the city government? If in a kingdom all were kings, where were the subjects, the people, the commonalty, the commonwealth, or the political government?

2. Hereby the community or whole body of the faithful, even to the meanest member, are vested from Christ with full power and authority actually to discharge and execute all acts of order and jurisdiction without exception: e.g. To preach the word authoritatively, dispense the sacraments, ordain their officers, admonish offenders, excommunicate the obstinate and incorrigible, and absolve the penitent. For *the keys of the kingdom of heaven* comprehend all these acts jointly, Matt. xvi. 19, and xviii. 18-20, with John xx. 21, 23: and to whom Christ in the New Testament gives power to execute one of these acts, to them he gives power to execute all; they are joined together, Matt, xviii. 19, (except in such cases where himself gives a limitation of the power, as in the case of the ruling elder, who is limited to ruling as contradistinct to *laboring in the word and doctrine,* 1 Tim. v. 17.) Now what gross absurdities ensue hereupon! For, 1. Then the weak as well as the strong, the ignorant as well as the intelligent, the children as well as the parents, yea, and the very women as well as the men, may preach, dispense seals, ordain, admonish, excommunicate, absolve authoritatively; (for they are all equally members of the body, one as well as another, and therefore, as such, have all alike equal share in the keys and exercise thereof:) viz. they that are not gifted for these offices, shall discharge these offices; they that are not called nor sent of God to officiate, (for

God sends not all,) shall yet officiate in the name of Christ without calling or sending, contrary to Rom. x., Heb. v. 4. They that want the common use of reason and discretion (as children) shall have power to join in the highest acts of order and jurisdiction: yea, they that are expressly prohibited *speaking in the churches*, as the *women*, 1 Cor. xiv., 1 Tim. ii., shall yet have the *keys of the kingdom of heaven* hung at their girdles. 2. Then the Church shall be the steward of Christ, and dispenser of the mysteries of God authoritatively and properly. But if the whole Church be the dispenser of the mysteries of God, what shall be the object of this dispensation? Not the Church, for according to this opinion she is the first subject dispensing; therefore it must be something distinct from the Church, unto which the Church dispenseth; what shall this be? shall it be another collateral church? then particular churches collateral may take pastoral care one of another reciprocally, and the same churches be both over and under one another; or shall it be those that are without all churches? then the ordinances of the gospel, and the dispensation of them, were not principally bestowed upon the Church and body of Christ for the good thereof, (which is directly repugnant to the Scriptures, Eph. iv. 8, 11-13;) but rather for them that are without. How shall the men, who maintain the principle's of the Independents, clearly help themselves out of these perplexing absurdities?

3. Hereby the body of the people (as Mr. Bayly well observes in his Dissuasive, chap. ix. page 187) will be extremely unfitted for, and unwarrantably taken off from the several duties that lie upon them in point of conscience to discharge in their general and particular callings, in spiritual and secular matters, on the Lord's days and on their own days. For, if the ecclesiastical power be in all the people, then all the people are judges, and at least have a negative voice in all church matters. They cannot judge in any cause prudently and conscientiously, till they have complete knowledge and information of both the substantials and circumstantials of all those cases that are brought before them; they must not judge blindly, or by an implicit faith, &c., but by their own light. For all the people to have such full information and knowledge of every cause, cannot but take up abundance of time, (many of the people being slow of understanding and extremely disposed to puzzle, distract, and confound one another in any business to be transacted in common by them all.) If these matters of discipline be managed by them on the sabbath day after the dispatch of other public ordinances, ministry of the word, prayer, sacraments, &c., what time can remain for family duties privately, as repeating sermons, and meditating upon the word, searching the Scriptures, whether things preached be so indeed, reading the Scriptures, catechizing their children and servants, &c.? and how will the life of religion in families, yea, and in churches also, languish, if these family exercises be not conscientiously upheld? If they be managed on the week days, how can all the people spare so much time, as still to be present, when perhaps many of them have much ado all the week long to provide food and raiment, and other necessaries for their families? and "if any provide not for his own, and specially for those of his own house, he hath denied the faith, and is worse than an infidel," 1 Tim. v. 8. Let the case of the church of Arnheim39 witness the mischief and absurdity of this popular government once for all.

4. Hereby, finally, the community of the faithful (being accounted the proper subject of the power of the keys) have authority and power not only to elect, but also to ordain their own officers, their pastors and teachers. And this they of the independent judgment plainly confess in these words:40 Though the office of a pastor in general be immediately from Christ, and the authority from him also, yet the application of this office, and of this authority to this elect person, is by the church; and therefore the church hath sufficient and just warrant, as to elect and call a presbyter unto an office, so to ordain him to it by imposition of hands. They that have power to elect a king, have power also to depute some in their name to set the crown upon his head. But for the whole church or community to ordain presbyters by imposition of hands, is very absurd. For, 1. Their women and children, being members of the church and of the community, may join in ordaining presbyters by imposing of hands, and have as great an influence in appointing them that shall actually impose hands, as the rest of the church members have, being as properly members as they. 2. Then the community, that generally are unable to judge of the fitness and sufficiency of presbyters for the pastoral office, in point of necessary gifts of learning, &c., shall, without

judicious satisfaction herein by previous examination, ordain men notwithstanding to the highest ordinary office in the church. How ignorantly, how doubtfully, how irregularly, how unwarrantably, let the reader judge. 3. Then the community of the faithful may assume to themselves power to execute this ordinary act of ordination of officers, without all precept of Christ or his apostles, and without all warrant of the apostolical churches. But how absurd these things be, each moderate capacity may conceive. Further absurdities hereupon are declared by Mr. Bain,41 and after him by Mr. Ball.42

Whence we may justly conclude,

Therefore this doctrine or opinion, that makes the whole community or body of the church to be the first subject and immediate receptacle of the keys, is an unsound and unwarrantable opinion.

The middle-way men, (that profess to go between the authoritative presbyterial, and the rigid Brownistical way,) seeing these and such like absurdities, upon which the Brownists inevitably dash themselves, think to salve all by their new-coined distinction of the keys; viz. 1. There is a key of faith or knowledge, Luke xi. 52. The first subject of this key is every believer, whether joined to any particular church or not. 2. There is a key of order, Col. ii. 5, which is either, 1. A key of interest, power, or liberty, Gal. v. 13, which key is of a more large nature; 2. A key of rule and authority, which is of more strict nature, Matt. xvi. 19, John xx. 23. Hence, upon this distinction premised, they thus infer, 1. A particular congregation of saints is the first subject of all the church offices with all their spiritual gifts and power, 1 Cor. iii. 22. 2. The apostles of Christ were the first subject of apostolical power. 3. The brethren of a particular congregation are the first subjects of church liberty. 4. The elders of a particular church are the first subjects of church authority. 5. Both the elders and brethren, walking and joining together in truth and peace, are the first subjects of all church power needful to be exercised in their own body.

Answer. A rotten foundation, and a tottering superstructure, which tumbles down upon the builders' own heads: for,

1. This distribution of the keys is infirm in divers respects: e.g. 1. In that the key of knowledge (as it stands here distinguished from the key of order, comprehending the key of power and authority) is left utterly devoid of all power. Now no key of the kingdom of heaven is to be left without all power, Independents themselves being judges. 2. In that the key of power is left as utterly void of all authority, (being contradistinguished from the key of authority,) as the key of knowledge is left void of power. Now, power and authority, in matters of government, seem to be both one; and the word in the original signifies the one as well as the other. 3. The key of liberty or interest is a new key, lately forged by some new locksmiths in Separation-shop, to be a pick-lock of the power of church officers, and to open the door for popular government; no ordinance of Christ, but a mere human invention, (as will after appear upon examination of that scripture upon which it is grounded,) and therefore this limb of the distribution is redundant, a superfluous excrescence. 4. The texts of Scripture upon which this distribution of the keys is grounded, are divers of them abused, or at least grossly mistaken; for, Luke xi. 52, key of knowledge is interpreted only the key of saving faith. But knowledge, in strict speaking, is one thing, and faith another; there may be knowledge where there is no faith; and knowledge, in a sort, is a key to faith, as the inlet thereof. And the key of knowledge, viz. true doctrine and pure preaching of the word, is a distinct thing from knowledge itself. This key the lawyers had taken away by not interpreting, or misinterpreting of the law; but they could not take away the people's faith, or knowledge itself. Touching Col. ii. 5, 6, *your order*, it will be hard to prove this was only or chiefly intended of the keys delivered to Peter: doth it not rather denote the people's moral orderly walking, according to the rule of faith and life, as in other duties, so in submitting themselves to Christ's order of government, as is elsewhere required, Heb. xiii. 17? And as for Gal. v. 13, produced to prove the key of liberty, *Brethren, you have been called unto liberty*, there is too much liberty taken in wresting this text; for the apostle here speaks not of liberty as a church power, of choosing officers, joining in censures, &c., but as a gospel privilege, consisting in freedom from the ceremonial law, that yoke of bondage, which false teachers would have imposed upon them, after Christ had broken it off; as will

further appear, if you please with this text to compare Gal. v. 1, 11, 15, 10, and well consider the current of the whole context.

2. The inferences upon this distribution of the keys premised, are very strange and untheological. For it may be accepted in general, that it is a groundless fancy to make several first subjects of the keys, according to the several distributions of the keys; for, had all the members of the distribution been good, yet this inference thereupon is naught, inasmuch as the Scripture tells us plainly, that all the keys together and at once were promised to Peter, Matt. xvi. 19, and given to the apostles, Matt, xviii. 18, 19, with xxviii. 18-20, and John xx. 21-23; so that originally the apostles and their successors were the only first subject and immediate receptacle of all the keys from Christ. And though since, for assistance and ease of the pastor, they are divided into more hands—viz. of the ruling elder, Rom. xii. 8; 1 Cor. xii. 28; 1 Tim. v. 17—yet originally the subject was but one. Further, here is just ground for many particular exceptions: as, 1. That every believer, whether joined to any particular church or not, is made the first subject of the key of knowledge, which seems to be extremely absurd: for then every particular believer, gifted or ungifted, strong or weak, man, woman, or child, hath power to preach, (taking the key of knowledge here for the key of doctrine, as it ought to be taken, or else it is no ecclesiastical key at all,) which is one of the highest offices, and which the great apostle said, "Who is sufficient for these things?" 2 Cor. ii. 16. How unscriptural and irrational this is, all may judge. Then also some of the keys may be committed to such as are without the Church. Then finally, it is possible to be a believer, and yet in no visible church; (for Independents hold there is no church but a particular congregation, which is their only church:) but a man is no sooner a true believer, but he is a member of the invisible Church: he is no sooner a professed believer, but he is a member of the general visible Church, though he be joined to no particular congregation. 2. That a particular congregation of saints is made the first subject of all the church offices, with all their spiritual gifts and power, 1 Cor. iii. 22. But is the word subject used here properly, for the first subject recipient of all church offices, with all their gifts and power? Then the congregation of saints are either officers themselves formally, and can execute the function of all sorts of officers, and have all gifts to that end; what need then is there of any select officers? for they can make officers virtually, and furnish those officers with gifts and power to that end; but who gave them any such authority? Or what apostolical church ever assumed to themselves any such thing? Officers, not churches, are the first subject of such gifts and power. Is the word subject here used improperly, for object, whose good all offices with their gifts and power are given? Then not any particular congregation, but the whole general visible Church is the object for which all offices and officers with their gifts and power are primarily given, 1 Cor. xii. 28; Eph. iv. 8, 11, 12. As for that place, 1 Cor. iii. 22, "All is yours," &c., it points not out the particular privilege of any one single congregation, (nor was the church of Corinth such, but presbyterial, see chap. XIII.,) but the general privilege of all true saints, and of the invisible mystical Church: for were Paul and Cephas apostles given peculiarly to the church of Corinth only? Or was the *world, life, death, things present and to come*, given to the wicked in the church of Corinth? 3. That the apostles are made the first subject of all apostolical power. But then, how doth this contradict the former assertion, that a particular congregation is the first subject of all offices with their gifts and power? Are there two first subjects of the same adjuncts? Or is apostleship no office? Are apostolical gifts no gifts, or power no power? or have apostles all from the Church? Doubtless apostles were before all Christian churches, and had the keys given them before the churches had their being. 4. That the brethren of a particular congregation are made the first subjects of church liberty. But, if that liberty be power and authority, then this evidently contradicts the former, that a particular congregation is the first subject of all offices and power; for brethren here are distinct from elders, and both do but make up a particular congregation. If liberty here be not power, then it is none of Christ's keys, but a new forged pick-lock. 5. That the elders of a particular church are made the first subject of church authority; but then here is a contradiction to the former position, that made the particular congregation the first subject of all power. And though apostles and elders be the first subject of authority, yet, when the keys were first committed to them, they were not in relation to any particular church, but to the general. 6. Finally, that both elders and brethren,

walking and joining together in truth and peace, are the first subjects of all church power, is liable also to exception. For this joins the brethren (who indeed have no authoritative power at all) with the elders, as the joint subject of all power. And this but allowed to them walking and joining together in truth and peace: but what if the major part of the Church prove heretical, and so walk not in truth; or schismatical, and so walk not in peace, shall the elders and the non-offending party lose all their power? Where then shall that independent church find healing? for appeals to presbyteries and synods are counted apocryphal by them. But enough hath been said to detect the vanity of these new dreams and notions; it is a bad sore that must be wrapped in so many clouts.43

CHAPTER XI.
Of the proper Receptacle, or immediate subject of the Power of Church Government: affirmatively, what it is, viz. Christ's own Officers.

Thus the proper receptacle or subject of ecclesiastical power hath been considered negatively, what it is not, viz: not the political magistrate, nor yet the community of the faithful, or body of the people, with or without their eldership. Now this receptacle of power comes to be evidenced affirmatively, what it is, viz. (according to the express words of the description of government,) Christ's own officers. This is the last branch of the description, the divine right whereof remains to be cleared; which may most satisfactorily be done by evidencing these three things, viz: 1. That Jesus Christ our Mediator hath certain peculiar church guides and officers which he hath erected in his Church. 2. That Jesus Christ our Mediator hath especially intrusted his own officers with the government of his Church. 3. How, or in what sense the ruling officers are intrusted with this government, severally or jointly?

SECTION I.

1. *Of the Divine Right of Christ's Church Officers, viz. Pastors and Teachers, with Ruling Elders.*

Touching the first, that Christ hath certain peculiar church guides and officers, which he hath erected in his Church. Take it thus:

Jesus Christ our Mediator hath ordained and set in his Church (besides the apostles and other extraordinary officers that are now ceased) pastors and teachers, as also ruling elders, as the subject of the keys for all ordinary ecclesiastical administrations. The divine right of these ordinary church officers may appear as followeth:

I. Pastors and teachers are the ordinance of Jesus Christ. This is generally granted on all sides; and therefore these few particulars may suffice for the demonstration of it, viz:

1. They are enumerated in the list or catalogue of those church officers which are of divine institution. "God hath set" (or put, constituted) "some in the Church, first, apostles; secondarily, prophets; thirdly, teachers," 1 Cor. xii. 28. These are some of the triumphant gifts and trophies of Christ's ascension: "Ascending up on high, he led captivity captive, and gave gifts to men: and he gave some apostles, and some prophets, and some evangelists, and some pastors and teachers," Eph. iv. 8, 11. Thus in that exact roll of ordinary officers: "Having, therefore, gifts different according to the grace given unto us; whether prophecy, let us prophesy according to the proportion of faith; or ministry, let us wait on our ministry;" (here is the general distribution of all ordinary officers under two heads, *prophecy* and *ministry*:) "or he that teacheth, on teaching; or he that exhorteth, on exhortation," (here is the teacher and the pastor, that come under the first head of prophecy,) Rom. xii. 6-8. "Take heed to yourselves, and to all the flock, over which the Holy Ghost hath made" (or set) "you overseers," Acts xx. 28. Note—God hath set in the Church; Christ hath given for his body; the Holy Ghost hath made overseers over the flock, these pastors and teachers: and are not pastors and teachers church officers by divine right, having the authority of God, Christ, and of the Holy Ghost?

2. They are to be thus and thus qualified according to divine direction. The qualifications of these pastors and teachers, (called presbyters and overseers,) see in 1 Tim. iii. 2-8, "An overseer," or bishop, "must be blameless," &c.; and Tit. i. 5-10, "To ordain presbyters," or elders, "in every city—If any be blameless," &c. Now, where God lays down

qualifications for pastors and teachers, there he approves such officers to be his own ordinance.

3. They have manifold church employments committed to them from Christ, as ministers of Christ and stewards of the mysteries of God, (1 Cor. iv. 1, 2,) they being intrusted in whole or in part with the managing of most if not all the ordinances forementioned in part 2, chap. VII., as there by the texts alleged is evident. Matters of order and special office are committed to them only *divisim:* matters of jurisdiction are committed to them with ruling elders*conjunctim*. If Christ hath intrusted them thus with church ordinances, and the dispensing of them, sure they are Christ's church officers.

4. The very names and titles given them in Scripture proclaim them to be Christ's own ordinance; among many take these: "Ministers of Christ," 1 Cor. iv. 1; "Stewards of the mysteries of God," 1 Cor. iv. 1; "Ambassadors for Christ," 2 Cor. v. 20; "Laborers thrust forth into his harvest by the Lord of the harvest," Matt. ix. 38; "Ruling over you in the Lord,"44 1 Thess. v. 12.

5. The Lord Christ charges their flock and people with many duties to be performed to their pastors and teachers, because of their office; as to know them, love them, obey them, submit unto them, honor them, maintain them, &c., which he would not do were they not his own ordinance. "But we beseech you, brethren, to know them that labor among you, and rule over you in the Lord, and esteem them very highly in love for their work's sake," 1 Thess. v. 12, 13. "Obey your rulers, and submit; for they watch for your souls as those that must give an account," Heb. xiii. 17. "The elders that rule well count worthy of double honor; especially them that labor in the word and doctrine; *for the Scripture saith,* Thou shalt not muzzle the mouth of the ox that treadeth out the corn, and the laborer is worthy of his hire," 1 Tim. v. 17, 18; compared With 1 Cor. ix. 6-15. "Let him that is catechized, communicate to him that catechizeth him in all good things," Gal. vi. 6-8.

Thus much for the present may suffice to have been spoken touching the divine right of pastors and teachers, the ordinary standing ministers of Christ under the New Testament. But forasmuch as we observe that in these days some rigid Erastians and Seekers oppose and deny the very office of the ministry now under the gospel, and others profess that the ministry of the church of England is false and antichristian; we intend, (by God's assistance,) as soon as we can rid our hands from other pressing employments, to endeavor the asserting and vindicating of the divine right of the ministers of the New Testament in general, and of the truth of the ministry of the church of England in particular.

II. Ruling elders, distinct from all preaching elders and deacons, are a divine ordinance in the Church of God now under the New Testament.

The divine right of this church officer, the mere ruling elder, is much questioned and doubted by some, because they find not the Scriptures speaking so fully and clearly of the ruling elder as of the preaching elder and of the deacon. By others it is flatly denied and opposed, as by divers that adhere too tenaciously to the Erastian and prelatical principles: who yet are willing to account the assistance of the ruling elder in matter of church government to be a very prudential way. But if mere prudence be counted once a sufficient foundation for a distinct kind of church officer, we shall open a door for invention of church officers at pleasure; then welcome commissioners and committee men, &c.; yea, then let us return to the vomit, and resume prelates, deans, archdeacons, chancellors, officials, &c., for church officers. And where shall we stop? who but Christ Jesus himself can establish new officers in his church? Is it not the fruit of his ascension, &c.? Eph. iv. 7, 11, 12. Certainly if the Scriptures lay not before us grounds more than prudential for the ruling elder, it were better never to have mere ruling elders in the church. Both the Presbyterians and Independents45acknowledge the divine right of the ruling elder. For satisfaction of doubting unprejudiced minds, (to omit divers considerations that might be produced,) the divine right of the ruling elder may be evinced by these ensuing arguments.

Argum. I. The first argument for the divine right of the ruling elder in the Church of Christ, shall be drawn from Rom. xii. 6-8: "Having, then, gifts differing according to the grace that is given to us, whether prophecy, let us prophesy according to the proportion of faith; or ministry, *let us wait* on our ministering; or he that teacheth, on teaching; or he that exhorteth, on exhortation; he that giveth, *let him do it* with simplicity; he that ruleth, with diligence," &c. Let the scope and context of this chapter be a little viewed, and it will make way for the more clear arguing from this place. Briefly thus: The apostle having finished the principal part of his epistle, which was problematical, wherein he disputed—1. About justification, chap. i.-vi.; 2. Sanctification, chap. vi. 7, 8; and, 3. Predestination, chap. ix. 10, 11, he comes to the next branch, which is more practical, about good works, chap. xii.-xvi. This twelfth chapter is wholly in the way of exhortation, and he herein exhorts to divers duties. 1. More generally that we should even consecrate ourselves wholly to the service of God, ver. 1; that we should not conform to the world, ver. 2. More specially he descends to particular duties, which are of two sorts, viz: 1. Such as concern ecclesiastical officers as officers, ver. 3-9; 2. Such as concern all Christians in common as Christians, both towards one another and towards their very enemies, verse 9, to the end of the chapter. Touching ecclesiastical officers, the apostle's evident scope is to urge them not to be proud of their spiritual gifts, (which in those days abounded,) but to think soberly, self-denyingly of themselves, and to use all their gifts well. This he presseth upon them, 1. From the nature of the Church, which is as a natural organical body, wherein are many members, having their several offices for the good of the whole body; so the members of Christ's body being many, have their several gifts and offices for the good of the whole, that the superior should not despise the inferior, nor the inferior envy their superior, ver. 3-5. 2. From the distribution or enumeration of the several kinds of ordinary standing officers in this organical body, the Church, who are severally exhorted duly to discharge those duties that are specially required of them in their several functions, ver. 6-8. These officers are reduced first to two general heads, viz: Prophecy (understand not the extraordinary gift of foretelling future things, &c., but the ordinary, in the right understanding and interpreting of Scripture) and ministry; and the general duties thereof are annexed, ver. 6, 7. Then these generals are subdivided into the special offices contained under them, the special duty of every officer being severally pressed upon them. Under prophecy are contained, 1. *He that teacheth*, i.e., the doctor or teacher; 2. *He that exhorteth*, i.e., the pastor, ver. 7, 8. Under ministry are comprised, 1. *He that giveth*, i.e., the deacon; 2. *He that ruleth*, i.e., the ruling elder. The current of our best interpreters to this effect resolve this context. So that here we have a very excellent and perfect enumeration of all the ordinary standing officers in the Church of Christ distinctly laid down. This premised, the argument for the divine right of the ruling elder may be thus propounded:

Major. Whatsoever members of Christ's organical body have an ordinary office of ruling therein given them of God, distinct from all other ordinary standing officers in the church, together with directions from God how they are to rule; they are the ruling elders we seek, and that by divine right.

Minor. But *he that ruleth*, mentioned in Rom. xii. 8, is a member of Christ's organical body, having an ordinary office of ruling therein given him of God, distinct from all other standing officers in the church, together with direction how he is to rule.

Conclusion. Therefore he that ruleth, mentioned in Rom. xii. 8, is the ruling elder we seek, and that by divine right.

The major proposition is clear. For in the particulars of it, well compared together, are observable both a plain delineation or description of the ruling elder's office; and also a firm foundation for the divine right of that office. The ruling elder's office is described and delineated by these several clauses, which set out so many requisites for the making up of a ruling elder, viz: 1. He must be a member of Christ's organical body. Such as are without, pagans, heathens, infidels, &c., out of the Church, they are not fit objects for church government, to have it exercised by the Church upon them; the Church only judges them that are within, (1 Cor. v. 12, 13,) much less can they be fit subjects of church government to exercise it themselves within the Church. How shall they be officers in the Church that are not so much as members of the Church? Besides, such as are only members of the invisible body of Christ, as the glorified saints in heaven, they cannot be officers in the Church; for not the Church invisible, but only the Church or body of Christ visible is organical. So that every church officer must first be a Church member, a member of the visible organical body: consequently a ruling elder must be such a member. 2. He must have an office of ruling in this body of Christ. Membership is not enough, unless that power of rule be superadded thereto; for the whole office of the ruling elder is contained in the matter of rule; take away rule, you destroy the very office. Now, rule belongs not to every member: "Salute all them that have the rule over you, and all the saints," Heb. xiii. 24, where rulers and saints are made contradistinct to one another. In the body natural all the members are not eyes, hands, &c., governing the body, some are rather governed; so in the body of Christ, 1 Cor. xii. 3. This his office of ruling must be an ordinary office; apostles had some power that was extraordinary, as their apostleship was extraordinary; but when we seek for this ruling elder, we seek for a fixed, standing, ordinary officer ruling in the church. 4. All that is not enough, that he be a member of the church, that he have an office of rule in the church, and that office also be ordinary; but besides all these it is necessary that he be also distinct from all other standing officers in the church, viz. from pastors, teachers, deacons; else all the former will not make up a peculiar kind of officer, if in all points he fully agree with any of the said three. But if there can be found such an officer in whom all these four requisites do meet, viz: That, 1. Is a member of Christ's organical body; 2. Hath an office of rule therein; 3, That office is ordinary; and, 4. That ordinary office is distinct from all other ordinary standing offices in the church; this must unavoidably be that very ruling elder which we inquire after. By this it is evident, that in this proposition here is a plain and clear delineation of the ruling elder's office. Now, in the next place, touching the foundation for the divine right of this office; it also is notably expressed in the same proposition, while it presupposeth, 1. That God is the giver of this office; 2. That God is the guider of this office. For whatsoever office or officer God gives for his Church, and having given it, guides and directs to the right discharge thereof, that must needs be of divine right beyond all contradiction. Thus this proposition is firm and cogent. Now let us assume:

Minor. But *he that ruleth*, mentioned in Rom. xii. 8, is a member of Christ's organical body, having an ordinary office of ruling therein, given him of God, distinct from all other ordinary standing officers in the church, together with direction from God how he is to rule.

This assumption or minor proposition (whereon the main stress of the argument doth lie) may be thus evidenced by parts, from this context:

He that ruleth is a member of Christ's organical body. For, 1. The Church of Christ is here compared to a body, *We being many are one body in Christ*, ver. 5. 2. This body is declared to be organical, i.e. consisting of several members, that have their several offices in the body, some of teaching, some of exhorting, and some of ruling, &c. "For as we have many members in one body, and all members have not the same office, so we being many are one body in Christ, and every one members one of another," &c., ver. 4-6, &c. 3. Among the rest of the members of this body, *he that ruleth* is reckoned up for one, ver. 5-8; this is palpably evident.

He that ruleth hath an office of ruling in this body of Christ. For, 1. This word (translated)*he that ruleth*, in the proper signification and use of it, both in the Scriptures and in other Greek authors, doth signify one that ruleth authoritatively over another, (as hereafter is manifested in the 3d argument, § 2.) 2. Our best interpreters and commentators do render and expound the word generally to this effect: e.g. He that is over46—one set over47—he that stands in the head or front48—as a captain or commander in the army, to which this phrase seems to allude—*he that ruleth*. 3. This word, wherever it is used in a genuine proper sense, in all the New Testament, notes rule, or government. It is used metaphorically for taking care (as one set over any business) of good works, only in two places, Tit. iii. 8, and iii. 14. Properly for government which superiors have over inferiors; and that either domestical, in private families, so it is used in 1 Tim. iii. 4, 5, 12, or ecclesiastical, in the church, which is the public family of God; in this sense it is used, 1 Thes. v. 12, 1 Tim. v. 17, and here, Rom. xii. 8, and these are all the places where this word is found used in all the New Testament.

3. *He that ruleth* here, hath an ordinary, not an extraordinary office of rule in the church. For he is ranked and reckoned up in the list of Christ's ordinary standing officers, that are constantly to continue in the church, viz. pastors, teachers, deacons. Commonly this place is interpreted to speak of the ordinary church officers, and none other; consequently he that ruleth is such a one.

4. *He that ruleth* here, is an officer distinct from all other ordinary officers in the Church of Christ. For in this place we have a full enumeration of all Christ's ordinary

officers, and he that ruleth is a distinct officer among them all. 1. Distinct in name, he only is called *he that ruleth*, the rest have every one of them their several distinct name, ver. 7, 8. 2. Distinct in his work here appropriated to him; the doctor teacheth; the pastor exhorteth; the deacon giveth; this elder *ruleth*, as the very name signifieth, ver. 8. Compare 1 Tim. v. 17, 1 Cor. xii. 28. As the elder ruleth, so he is distinct from the deacon that hath no rule in the church; and as he only rules, so he is distinct from both pastor and teacher, that both teach, exhort, and rule; they both have power of order and jurisdiction, the ruling elder hath only power of jurisdiction. 3. Finally, he is distinct among and from them all in the particular direction here given these officers about the right discharge of their functions. The teacher must be exercised *in teaching*; the pastor *in exhortation*; the deacon must *give with singleness*; and the elder, he must *rule with diligence, studiousness*, &c. Now what other solid reason can be imagined, why *he that ruleth* should here have a distinct name, distinct work and employment, and distinct direction how to manage this work, than this, that the Holy Ghost might set him out unto us as an ordinary officer in the church, distinct from all the other standing officers here enumerated?

5. God himself is the author and giver of this office of him that ruleth, as well as of all the other offices here mentioned. For, 1. All gifts and endowments in the church in general, and in every member in particular; they are from God, it is he that gives and divides them as he will,*as God hath dealt to every one the measure of faith*, Rom. xii. 3. 2. All the special offices, and gifts for these offices in special, are also from the same God, *we having therefore gifts according to the grace given unto us, differing; whether prophecy*, &c., Rom, xii. 6, 7, &c. Here it is plain that he distinguished betwixt grace and gifts. By grace here we are to understand that holy office or charge in the church, which is given to any man by the grace and favor of God. And in this sense the apostle in this very chapter, ver. 3, useth the word*grace: For I say through the grace given to me*, i.e. through the authority of my apostleship, which by grace I have received, &c. By gifts, we are to understand those endowments wherewith God hath freely furnished his officers in the church for their several offices. Now both these gifts and this grace, both the endowments and the office, are originally from God, his grace is the fountain of them; and both the grace of each office, and the gifts for such office, relate to all these ordinary offices here enumerated, as is evident by the current and connection of the whole context, see ver. 6-8; consequently the grace, i.e. the office of ruling, which is of divine grace, and the gifts for that office, arise from the same fountain, God himself.

6. Finally, God himself is the guider and director of him that ruleth, here prescribing to him how he is to rule, viz. *with diligence, with studiousness*, &c., ver. 8. Now we may receive this as a maxim, That of divine right may be done, for which God gives his divine rule how it is to be done: and that office must needs be of divine right, which God himself so far approves as to direct in his word how it shall be discharged.

Now, to sum up all, he that ruleth here, 1. Is a member of Christ's organical body. 2. Hath an office of ruling in this body. 3. This his office is not extraordinary but ordinary, standing, and perpetual. 4. He is an officer distinct from all other ordinary officers in the Church. 5. God himself is the giver and author of this office. 6. And God himself is the guider and director of this office: and then see if we may not clearly conclude,

Conclusion. Therefore, he that ruleth, mentioned in Rom. xii. 8, is the ruling elder we seek, and that by divine right.

The adversaries of ruling elders muster up divers exceptions against the alleging of Rom. xii. 8, for proof of the divine right of their office, the weakness of which is to be discovered ere we pass to another argument. *Except*. 1. This is an arguing from a general to a special affirmatively. It doth not follow, because the apostle here in general mentioneth him that ruleth, therefore in special it must be the ruling elder.49

Ans. This exception is the same with first exception against the second argument hereafter laid down. There see. For the same answer appositely and satisfactorily is applicable to both.

Except. 2. But the apostle here speaks of them that rule, but we have nowhere received that such elders have rule over the church—and he speaks of all that rule in the church, who therefore would wrest this place only to elders? One cannot rightly attribute that word translated *he that ruleth* to elders only, which is common unto more. If these elders he here meant, neither pastors nor teachers ought to rule, for this word agrees no otherwise to him that ruleth, than the word of exhorting to him that exhorteth.50

Ans. 1. That such elders rule in the church is evident, both by Rom. xii. 8, where this word implies rule as hath been showed, and he that ruleth is reckoned up amongst ordinary church officers, as hath been said, therefore he rules in the church: these the apostle also calls ruling elders, 1 Tim. v. 17, viz. officers in the church, and distinct from them that labor in the word and doctrine; as in the third argument will appear: yea, they are governments set of God in the church, distinct from other officers, 1 Cor. xii. 28, as in the second argument shall be evidenced: there see; therefore these elders have rule.

2. Though in this term the apostle speaks of him that ruleth, yet he speaks not of every one that ruleth. For, 1. He speaks singularly, he that ruleth, as of one kind of ruling officer; not plurally, they that rule, as if he had indefinitely or universally meant all the ruling officers in the church. 2. He reckons up here distinct kinds of ordinary officers, pastors, teachers, elders, and deacons; and pastors and teachers, besides laboring in the word, have power of rule, 1 Thes. v. 12, Heb. xiii. 7-17, and he that ruleth, here, is distinct from them both; and therefore this term cannot mean all church rulers, but only one kind, viz. the ruling elder.

3. Though this name, *he that ruleth*, be common unto more rulers in the church, than to the mere ruling elder; yet it doth not therefore necessarily follow, that it cannot here particularly point out only the mere ruling elder, inasmuch, as *he that ruleth*, is not here set alone, (for then this objection might have had some color,) but is enumerated with other officers as distinct from them.

4. Though the ruling elder here be called *he that ruleth*, yet this doth not exclude the pastor from ruling, no more than when the ordinary ministers are called pastors and teachers, the apostles and evangelists are excluded from feeding and teaching, in Eph. iv. 11, 12; 1 Cor. xii. 28. This elder is called, *he that ruleth*, not that there is no other ruler than he, but because he doth no other thing but rule, others rule and preach also.

Except. 3. If this were meant of such elders, then these elders were as necessary to the church as pastors, being given to the church by the like reason. Consequently where these elders are not, there is no church; as there is no church where the word and sacraments are not.51

Ans. 1. According to this argument deacons are as necessary as either pastors, teachers, or elders, and without deacons there should be no church; for they are all enumerated here alike, Rom. xii. 7, 8, and in 1 Cor. xii. 28; but this would be absurd, and against experience. 2. Though both pastors and ruling elders belong to the church by divine right, yet doth it not follow that the ruling elder is equally as necessary as the pastor. The ruling elder only rules, the pastor both rules and preaches, therefore he is more necessary to the church. There are degrees of necessity; some things are absolutely necessary to the being of a church, as matter and form, viz. visible saints, and a due profession of faith, and obedience to Christ, according to the gospel. Thus it is possible a church may be, and yet want both deacons, elders, and pastors too, yea, and word and sacraments for a time: some things are only respectively necessary to the well-being of a church; thus officers are necessary, yet some more than others, without which the church is lame, defective, and miserably imperfect.

Except. 4. Should ruling elders here be meant, then deacons that obey, should be preferred before the elders that rule.52

Ans. Priority of order is no infallible argument of priority of worth and dignity; as is evidenced in answer to the third exception against Arg. II.—there see; we find Priscilla a woman named before Aquila a man, and her husband, Acts xviii. 18; Rom. xvi. 3; 1 Tim. iv. 19; is therefore the woman preferred before the man? the wife before the husband? And again, Aquila is set before Priscilla, Acts xviii. 2, 26, 1 Cor. xvi. 19, to let us see that the Holy Ghost indifferently speaks of superior and inferior before one another.

Except. 5. But here the apostle speaketh of divers gifts and graces, for so *differing gifts* do import, not of divers offices: for then they might not concur in one man, and consequently neither might the prophet teach, nor exhort, nor the deacon distribute, nor show mercy. Many gifts may be common in one man, many offices cannot;—which of these gifts in the apostles' times was not common as well to the people as to the pastors; and to women as well as to men? &c.53

Ans. Divers considerations may be propounded to discover the vanity of this exception: chiefly take these three.

1. There is no sufficient reason in this exception, proving the apostle here to speak only of divers gifts and graces, and not of divers offices also. For, 1. This is not proved by that expression, *differing gifts*, ver. 6, for these differing gifts are not here spoken of abstractly and absolutely, without reference to their subjects, but relatively with reference to their subjects wherein they are, viz. in the several officers, ver. 7, 8, and therefore, as the apostle mentions the *differing gifts*, so here he tells us in the same sixth verse, that we have these "different gifts, according to the grace given unto us," i.e. according to the office given unto us of God's grace, (as hath been manifested,) after which immediately is subjoined an enumeration of offices. 2. Nor is this proved by the inference made, upon the granting that divers offices are here meant, viz. [Then they might not concur in one man, the prophet might not teach nor exhort, &c.; many gifts may be common in one man, many offices cannot.] For who is so little versed in the Scriptures, but he knows that apostles, pastors, elders, deacons, are distinct officers one from another; yet all the inferior offices are virtually comprehended in the superior, and may be discharged by them: elders may distribute as well as deacons; and beyond them, rule: pastors may distribute and rule as well as deacons and elders, and beyond both preach, dispense sacraments, and ordain ministers. Apostles may do there all, and many things besides extraordinary. Much more may the prophet teach and exhort, and the deacon distribute and show mercy; these being the proper acts of their office. 3. Nor, finally, is this proved by that suggestion, that all these gifts in the apostles' times were common to all sorts and sexes, women as well as men; as he after takes much pains to prove, but to very little purpose. For not only in the apostles' times, but in our times also, all Christians may teach, exhort, distribute, show mercy, &c., privately, occasionally, by bond of charity, and law of fraternity towards one another mutually: but may not teach, exhort, rule, distribute, &c., authoritatively by virtue of their office, so as to give themselves wholly to such employments, which is the thing here intended; yet it is worth observing how far Bilson was transported against ruling elders, that rather than yield to their office, he will make all these gifts common to all sorts and sexes, men and women. This is new divinity; all sorts and sexes may both preach and rule. Let Bilson have the credit of symbolizing with the Separatists, if not of transcending them.

2. Here is good ground in the context to make us think that the apostle here spoke of distinct church officers, and not only of distinct gifts. For, 1. In the similitude of a natural body (whereunto here the church is compared) he speaks of distinct members, having distinct offices, ver. 4. "For as we have many members in one body, and all members have not the same office." 2. In his accommodation of this similitude, he speaks not only of gifts, but also of offices according to which these gifts are given, which he calls *grace*, ver. 6, (as was noted.). This grace given, or this office given of grace, is branched out, first, into two general heads, viz. *prophecy* and *ministry*, ver. 6, 7. Then these generals are subdivided into the special offices contained under them, viz.: Under prophecy the teacher, *he that teacheth*; and the pastor, *he that exhorteth*; under ministry the deacon, *he that distributeth*; and the ruling elder, *he that ruleth*. Now there is in the text just ground for this resolution of the text, in making prophecy and ministry generals, and all the rest special kinds of officers; forasmuch as prophecy and ministry are expressed abstractly, *whether prophecy*, (not, whether we are prophets;) *whether ministry*, (not, whether we are deacons, ministers:) and both prophecy and ministry are put in the accusative case; and both of them have relation, and are joined unto the participle of the plural number *having*, intimating that divers do share in prophecy, pastor and teacher; divers in ministry, deacon and ruling elder. But all the other are expressed concretely, and in the nominative case, and in the singular number, and to every of them the single article is prefixed, translated He—*He that teacheth*—*He that exhorteth*—*He that giveth*—*He that ruleth.* Hence we have great cause to count prophecy and ministry as generals; all the rest as special offices under them.

Argum. II. The second argument for the divine right of the ruling elder shall be grounded upon 1 Cor. xii. 28: "And God hath set some in the church, first, apostles, secondly, prophets, thirdly, teachers, afterwards powers, then gifts of healing, helps, governments, kinds of tongue." God, in the first founding of Christianity and of the primitive churches, bestowed many eminent gifts upon divers Christians; the church of Corinth greatly excelled in such gifts, 1 Cor. i. 5, 7. Hence their members gifted, grew spiritually proud, and despised their brethren; to correct which abuse of gifts, and direct them to the right use thereof for the common profit of all, is the chief scope of this chapter, see verse 7, "The manifestation of the Spirit is given to every man to profit withal." For, 1. All their gifts flow from one and the same fountain, the Spirit of God, therefore should be improved for the common good of all, especially considering no one man hath all gifts, but several men have several gifts, that all might be beholden to one another, ver. 8-11. 2. The whole Church of Christ throughout all the world is but one body, and that body organical, having several members therein placed for several uses, as eyes, hands, &c., wherein the meanest members are useful and necessary to the highest: therefore all members should harmoniously lay out their gifts for the good of the whole body, without jars or divisions, ver. 12-28. 3. All the several officers, whether extraordinary or ordinary, though furnished with several gifts and several administrations, yet are placed by one and the same God, in one and the same general Church; and therefore should all level at the benefit of the whole church, without pride, animosities, divisions, &c., ver. 28, to the end. These things being briefly premised for the clearing the context and scope of the chapter, we may thus argue from ver. 28:

Major. Whatsoever officers God himself, now under the New Testament, hath set in the Church as governors therein, distinct from all other church governors, whether extraordinary or ordinary; they are the ruling elders we inquire after, and that by divine right.

This proposition is so clear and evident of itself, that much needs not to be said for any further demonstration of it. For what can be further desired for proof that there are such distinct officers as ruling elders in the Church of Christ, and that of divine right, than to evince, 1. That there are certain officers set of God in the Church as governors therein. 2. That those officers so set of God in the Church, are set in the Church under the New Testament, which immediately concerns us, and not under the Old Testament. 3. That these officers set of God as governors in the Church of the New Testament, are distinct from all other church governors, whether extraordinary or ordinary? For, by the third of these, we have a distinct church officer delineated and particularized: by the second we have this distinct church officer limited to the time and state of the Church only under the New Testament, which is our case: and by the first of these, we have this distinct New Testament officer's ruling power in the Church, and the divine right thereof evidently demonstrated, by God's act in setting him there in this capacity; (see Part 1. Chap. VI.;) so that by all put together, the consequence of this major proposition seems to be strong and unquestionable.

Minor. But the governments named in 1 Cor. xii. 28, are officers which God himself now under the New Testament hath set in the Church as governors therein, distinct from all other church governors, whether extraordinary or ordinary.

This minor or assumption is wholly grounded upon, and plainly contained in this text, and may thus be evidenced by parts.

1. The church here spoken of [*in the church*] is the Church of Christ now under the New Testament: for, 1. The church here mentioned, ver. 28, is the same with that ONE BODY mentioned, ver. 12, 13, of this chapter, as the whole context and coherence of the chapter evinceth; but that ONE BODY denotes not the Church of God under the Old Testament, but only the Church of Christ under the New Testament; partly, inasmuch as it is counted the Church of God in Christ, yea, (so intimate is the union between head and members,) it is called CHRIST, *so also is* CHRIST, ver. 12, (viz. not Christ personally considered, but Christ mystically considered, as comprehending head and body;) now this denomination of the Church, viz. Christ, or the Church of Christ, &c., is peculiar to the Church under the New Testament: for where in all the Scripture is the Church of God under the Old Testament called the Church of Christ, &c.? and partly, inasmuch as all, both Jews and Gentiles, are incorporated jointly into this ONE BODY, and coalesce into one Church: "For by one Spirit are we all baptized into one body, whether Jews or Gentiles, whether bond or free," 1 Cor. xii. 13. Now this union or conjunction of Jews and Gentiles into one body, one

Church, is only done under the New Testament; see Eph. ii. 11, to the end of the chapter. 2. The officers here mentioned to be set in this Church, are only the New Testament officers, ver. 28. 3. The scope of the whole chapter is to redress abuses of spiritual gifts in the church of Corinth, which was a church under the New Testament; and therefore it would have been too remote for the apostle to have argued from the several distributions of gifts peculiar to the officers or members of the Church under the Old Testament.

2. The governments here mentioned are officers set in this church as governors, or rulers therein: "Hath set some in the Church, first, apostles—governments." For clearing of this, consider the enumeration here made; the denomination of these officers, governments; and the constitution or placing of these governments in the Church. 1. The enumeration here made is evidently an enumeration of several sorts of church officers, some extraordinary, to endure but for a time, some ordinary, to continue constantly in the Church; to this the current of interpreters doth easily subscribe: and this the text itself plainly speaks; partly, if we look at the matter, viz. the several officers enumerated, which are either extraordinary, these five, viz. apostles, prophets, powers, or miracles, gifts of healing, and kinds of tongues: these continued but for a season, during the first founding of Christian churches: (the proper and peculiar work of these extraordinary officers, what it was, is not here to be disputed.) Or ordinary, these three, viz. *teachers*, (there is the preaching elder,) *governments*, (there is the ruling elder,)*helps*, (there is the deacon;) these are the officers enumerated; and however there be some other officers elsewhere mentioned, whence some conceive this enumeration not to be so absolutely perfect, yet this is undoubtedly evident, that it is an enumeration of officers in the church: partly, this is evident, if we look at the manner of the apostle's speech, which is in an enumerating form, viz. first, secondly, thirdly, afterwards, then: and partly, it is evident that he intended to reckon up those officers that were distinct from all other parts of the mystical body of Christ, by his recapitulation, "Are all apostles, are all prophets?" &c., ver. 29, 30, i.e. not all, but only some members of the body are set apart by God to bear these offices in the church. Now, if there be here a distinct enumeration of distinct officers in the church, as is evident; then consequently *governments* must needs be one of these distinct church officers, being reckoned up among the rest; and this is one step, that governments are in the roll of church officers enumerated. 2. The denomination of these officers, *governments*, evidenceth that they are governing officers, vested with rule in the Church. This word (as hath been noted in chap. II.) is a metaphor from pilots or shipmasters governing of their ships by their compass, helm, &c., James iii. 4, (who is hence called *governor*, viz. of the ship, Acts xxvii. 11; Rev. xviii. 17,) and it notes such officers as sit at the stern of the vessel of the Church, to govern and guide it in spirituals according to the will and mind of Christ: governments—the abstract is put for governors, the concrete: this name of governments hath engraven upon it an evident character of power for governing. But this will be easily granted by all. All the doubt will be, whom the apostle intended by these governments? Thus conceive, negatively, these cannot be meant, viz. not governors in general, for, besides that a general exists not but in the particular kinds or individuals thereof, a member of a body in general exists not but in this or that particular member, eye, hand, foot, &c.: besides this, it is evident that Christ hath not only in general appointed governors in his Church, and left particulars to the church or magistrate's determination, but hath himself descended to the particular determination of the several kinds of officers which he will have in his Church; compare these places together, Eph. iv. 7, 11, 12; 1 Cor. xii. 28; Rom. xii. 7, 8: though in the ordinance of magistracy God hath only settled the general, but for the particular kinds of it, whether it should be monarchical, &c., that is left to the prudence of the several commonwealths to determine what is fittest for themselves. (See Part 2, chap. IX.) 2. Not masters of families: for all families are not in the Church, pagan families are without. No family as a family is either a church or any part of a church, (in the notion that church is here spoken of;) and though masters of families be governors in their own houses, yet their power is not ecclesiastical but economical or domestical, common to heathens as well as Christians. Not the political magistrate,54 for the reasons hinted, (Part 1, chap. I.; see also Part 2, chap. IX.,) and for divers other arguments that might be propounded. 4. Not the prelatical bishops, pretending to be an order above preaching presbyters, and to have the reins of all church government in

their hands only; for, in Scripture language, bishop and presbyter are all one order, (these words being only names of the same officer;) this is evident by comparing Tit. i. 5, with ver. 7. Hereunto also the judgment of antiquity evidently subscribeth, accounting a bishop and a presbyter to be one and the same officer in the church; as appears particularly in Ambrose, Theodoret, Hierom, and others. Now, if there be no such order as prelatical bishops, consequently they cannot be governments in the church. 5. Not the same with *helps*, as the former corrupt impressions of our Bibles seemed to intimate, which had it thus, *helps in governments*, which some moderns seem to favor; but this is contrary to the original Greek, which signifies *helps, governments*; contrary to the ancient Syriac version, which hath it thus, (as Tremel. renders it,) *and helpers, and governments*: and therefore this gross corruption is well amended in our late printed Bible. *Helps, governments*, are here generally taken by interpreters for two distinct officers. 6. Nor, finally, can the teaching elder here be meant; for that were to make a needless and absurd tautology, the teacher being formerly mentioned in this same verse. Consequently, by *governments* here, what can be intended, but such a kind of officer in the church as hath rule and government therein, distinct from all governors forementioned? And doth not this lead us plainly to the ruling elder?

3. These governments thus set in the Church, as rulers therein, are set therein by God himself; God hath set some in the Church, *first, apostles—governments—God hath set, put, made, constituted*, &c., (as the word imports,) *in the Church*. What hath God set in the Church? viz. apostles and—governments, as well as apostles themselves. The verb, *hath set*, equally relates to all the sorts of officers enumerated. And is not that officer IA the Church of divine right, which God himself, by his own act and authority, sets therein? Then doubtless these governments are of divine right.

4. Finally, these governments set in the Church under the New Testament as governors therein, and that by God himself, are distinct from not only all governing officers without the Church, (as hath been showed,) but also from all other governing officers within the church. For here the apostles make a notable enumeration of the several sorts of church officers, both extraordinary and ordinary, viz. eight in all. Five of these being extraordinary, and to continue but for a season, for the more effectual spreading and propagating of the gospel of Christ at first, and planting of Christian churches, viz. apostles, prophets, powers, gifts of healings, kinds of tongues: three of these being ordinary, and to be perpetuated in the Church, as of continual use and necessity therein, viz. teachers, governments, [i.e. ruling elders,] and helps, [i.e. deacons, who are to help and relieve the poor and afflicted.] This is the enumeration. It is not contended, that it is absolutely and completely perfect, for that some officers seem to be omitted and left out, which elsewhere are reckoned up, Eph. iv. 11; Rom. xii. 7, 8. Evangelists are omitted in the list of extraordinary officers, and pastors are left out of the roll of the ordinary officers; and yet some conceive that pastors and teachers point not out two distinct sorts of officers, but rather two distinct acts of the same officers; and if this will hold, then pastors are sufficiently comprised under the word teachers; yea, some think that both evangelists and pastors are comprehended under the word teacher.55 But, however, be that as it will, these two things are evident, 1. That this enumeration (though evangelists and pastors be left out) is the fullest and completest enumeration of church officers which in any place is to be found throughout all the New Testament. 2. That though we should grant this defect in the enumeration, yet this is no way prejudicial to the present argument, that governments here mentioned are ruling officers in the Church, distinct from all other church officers that have rule; for they are plainly and distinctly recited as distinct kinds of officers, distinct from apostles, from prophets, from teachers, from all here mentioned. And thus interpreters56commonly expound this place, taking governments for a distinct kind of church officer from all the rest here enumerated.

Now to sum up all that hath been said for the proof of the assumption; it is evident, 1. That the church here spoken of is the Church of Christ now under the New Testament. 2. That the governments here mentioned, are officers set in this church, (not out of the church,) as rulers governing therein. 3. That these governments set as rulers or governors in this church, are set there not by man, but by God himself; *God hath set in the Church—governments*. 4. And, finally, That these governments thus set in the Church, are distinct, not only from all governors out of the Church, but also from all governing officers within the

Church. And if all this laid together will not clearly evince the divine right of the ruling elder, what will? Hence we may strongly conclude,

Conclusion. Therefore these governments in 1 Cor. xii. 28, are the ruling elders we inquire after, and that of divine right.

Now against the urging of 1 Cor. xii. 28, for the proof of the divine right of the ruling elders, divers exceptions are made, which are to be answered before we pass to the third argument.

Except. 1. The allegation of this place is too weak to prove the thing in question. For will any man that knoweth what it is to reason, reason from the general to the particular and special affirmatively? or will ever any man of common sense be persuaded that this consequence is good: There were governors in the primitive church mentioned by the Apostles—therefore they were lay governors? Surely I think not.57

Ans. This exception hath a confident flourish of words, but they are but words. It may be replied, 1. By way of concession, that to argue indeed from a general to a special, is no solid reasoning; as, This is a kingdom, therefore it is England; this is a city, therefore it is London; the apostle mentions government in the primitive Church, therefore they are ruling elders: this were an absurd kind of reasoning. 2. By way of negation. Our reasoning from this text for the ruling elder, is not from the general to a special affirmatively—there are governments in the Church, therefore ruling elders: but this is our arguing—these governments here mentioned in 1 Cor. xii. 28, are a special kind of governing officers, set of God in the Church of Christ now under the New Testament, and distinct from all other church officers, whether extraordinary or ordinary: and therefore they are the ruling elders which we seek after, and that by divine right. So that we argue from the enumeration of several kinds of church officers affirmatively: here is an enumeration or roll of divers kinds of church officers of divine right; governments are one kind in the roll, distinct from the rest; therefore governments are of divine right, consequently ruling elders; for none but they can be these governments, as hath been proved in the assumption. If the apostle had here mentioned governments only, and none other kind of officers with them, there had been some color for this exception, and some probability that the apostle had meant governors in general and not in special: but when the apostle sets himself to enumerate so many special kinds of officers, apostles, prophets, teachers, &c., how far from reason is it to think that in the midst of all these specials, governments only should be a general. 3. As for Dr. Field's scoffing term of lay governors or lay elders, which he seems in scorn to give to ruling elders; it seems to be grounded upon that groundless distinction of the ministry and people into clergy and laity; which is justly rejected by sound orthodox writers58, as not only without but against the warrant of Scripture, clergy being nowhere appropriated to the ministry only, but commonly attributed to the whole church, 1 Pet. v. 2, 3. The Scripture term given to these officers is *ruling elders*, 1 Tim. v. 17; and so far as such, (though they be elected from among the people,) they are ecclesiastical officers.

Except. 2. But it is not said here governors in the concrete, as apostles, prophets, teachers are mentioned concretely, which are distinct officers: but it is said governments, in the abstract, to note faculties, not persons. The text may be thus resolved: The apostle first sets down three distinct orders, apostles, prophets, and teachers: then he reckons up those common gifts of the Holy Ghost (and among the rest the gift of governing) which were common to all three. So that we need not here make distinct orders in the Church, but only distinct gifts which might be in one man.59

Ans. 1. As the apostles, prophets, and teachers are here set down concretely, and not abstractly, and are confessed to be three distinct orders enumerated: so all the other five, though set down abstractly, are (by a metonymy of the adjunct for the subject) to be understood concretely, helps for helpers; governments for governors, &c.; otherwise we shall here charge the apostle with a needless impertinent tautology in this chapter, for he had formerly spoken of these gifts abstractly, ver. 8-10, as being *all given to profit* the Church*withal*, ver. 7; but here, ver. 28-30, he speaks of these gifts as they are in several distinct subjects, for the benefit of the organical body the church; else what saith he here, more than he said before? 2. That all these eight here enumerated, one as well as another, do denote, not distinct offices or acts of the same officer, but distinct officers, having distinct administrations, and distinct gifts for those administrations, is evident, partly by the apostle's form of enumeration, *first, secondly, thirdly, afterwards, then* or *furthermore*: if he had intended only three sorts of officers, he would have stopped at thirdly, but he goes on in an enumerating way, to show us those that follow are distinct officers as well as those that go before; partly, by the apostle's recapitulation, ver. 29, 30, which plainly points out different officers, persons not gifts, besides those three: *Are all apostles? are all prophets? are all teachers?* (and here he stops not, but reckons on) *are all workers of miracles? have all the gifts of healing?* &c. If it should be replied, But he doth not add, Are all helps? are all governments? therefore these are not to be accounted distinct officers from the rest; otherwise why should the apostle thus have omitted them, had there been any such distinct officers in the Church in his time? It may be replied, These two officers, helps and governments, are omitted in the recapitulation, ver. 29, 30, not that the Church then had no such officers, for why then should they have been distinctly mentioned in the enumeration of church officers, ver. 28? But either, 1. For that helps and governments were more inferior ordinary officers, and not furnished with such extraordinary, or at least, eminent gifts, as the other had, (which they abused greatly to pride, contention, schism, and contempt of one another, the evils which the apostle here labors so much to cure,) and so there was no such danger that these helps and governments should run into the same distempers that the other did. Or, 2. For that he would instruct these helps and governments to be content with their own stations and offices, (without strife and emulation,) though they be neither apostles, nor prophets, nor teachers, nor any of the other enumerated, which were so ambitiously coveted after; and the last verse seems much to favor this consideration, *but covet earnestly the best gifts*, viz. which made most for edification, not for ostentation.60

Except. 3. But helps here are placed before governments, therefore it is not likely that governments were the ruling elders; Helps, i.e. deacons, which is an inferior office, seeming here to be preferred before them.61

Ans. This follows not. Priority of order is not always an argument of priority of worth, dignity, or authority. Scripture doth not always observe exactness of order, to put that first which is of most excellency: sometimes the pastor is put before the teacher, as Ephes. iv. 11, sometimes the teacher before the pastor, as Rom. xii. 7, 8. Peter is first named of all the apostles, both in Matt. x. 2, and in Acts i. 13, but we shall hardly grant the Papist's arguing thence to be solid—Peter is first named, therefore he is the chief and head of all the apostles; no more can we account this any good consequence—helps are set before governments, therefore governments are officers inferior to helps, consequently they cannot be ruling elders: this were bad logic.

Except. 4. But the word governments is general, and may signify either Christian magistrates, or ecclesiastical officers, as archbishops, bishops, or whatsoever other by lawful authority are appointed in the Church.62 And some of the semi-Erastians of our times, by governments understand the Christian magistracy, holding the Christian magistracy to be an ecclesiastical administration.63

Ans. 1. Governments, i.e. governors, (though in itself and singly mentioned, it be a general, yet) here being enumerated among so many specials, is special, and notes the special kind of ruling elders, as hath been proved. 2. As for archbishops and diocesan bishops, they are notoriously known to be, as such, no officers set in the Church by God, but merely by the invention of man; therefore they have no part nor lot in this business, nor can here be meant. And if by others, by lawful authority appointed in the Church, they mean those officers that God appoints well: if those whom man sets there without God, as chancellors, commissioners, &c., such have as much power of government in the Church, as they are such, as archbishops and bishops, viz. just none at all by any divine warrant. 3. Nor can the civil Christian magistrate here be implied. 1. Partly, because this is quite beside the whole intent and scope of this chapter, treating merely upon spiritual church-matters, not at all of secular civil matters, viz: of spiritual gifts for the Church's profit, ver. 1 to 12; of the Church herself as one organical body, ver. 12 to 28; and of the officers which God hath set in this organical body, ver. 28, &c. Now here to crowd in the Christian magistrate, which is a mere political governor, into the midst of these spiritual matters, and into the roll of these merely ecclesiastical officers, how absurd is it! 2. Partly, because the magistrate, as such, is not set of

God in the Church either as a church officer, or as a church member, (as hath been demonstrated formerly, chap. IX.;) and though he become a Christian, that adds nothing to the authority of his magistracy, being the privilege only of his person, not of his office. 3. Partly, because when this was written to the Corinthians, the apostle writes of such governments as had at that time their present actual being and existence in the Church: and neither then, nor divers hundreds of years after, were there any magistrates Christian, as hath been evidenced, chap. IX.64

Except. 5. Teachers are here expressed, but pastors omitted; and therefore well might governors be mentioned instead of pastors.65

Answ. 1. Then, according to his judgment, pastors were a distinct kind of officers from teachers; otherwise the naming of teachers would have sufficiently implied pastors, without the addition of the word governors, one act or function of the office being put for the whole office. But prelates did not love to hear of such a distinction. However, it is the judgment of many others no less learned or pious than they, that in the same congregation where there are several ministers, he that excels in exposition of scriptures, teaching sound doctrine, and convincing gainsayers, may be designed hereunto, and called a teacher or doctor: he that excels in application, and designed thereunto, may be called a pastor; but where there is only one minister in one particular congregation, he is to perform, as far as he is able, the whole work of the ministry. 2. If pastors are to be understood by this term governors, as contradistinct from teachers, formerly enumerated in the text; doth not this seem to devolve the matter of government so wholly upon the pastor, as that the teacher hath nothing to do with it? and hereby both pastor and teacher are wronged at once: the teacher, while power of governing is denied him, which belongs to him as well as to the pastor; the teacher being a minister of the word, hath power of administration of the sacraments and discipline, as well as the pastor: the pastor, while he consequently is deprived of the necessary and comfortable assistance of the teacher in point of government. Therefore the pastor cannot here be intended by governors. 3. Bilson himself was not very confident of this gloss, and therefore he immediately adds, "If this content you not, I then deny they are all ecclesiastical functions that are there specified," &c. What then doth he make them? viz. he makes divers of them, and governments among the rest, to be but several gifts, whereof one and the same officer might be capable. And a little after he ingenuously confesses he cannot tell what these governors were, saying, "I could easily presume, I cannot easily prove what they were. The manner and order of those wonderful gifts of' God's Spirit, after so many hundreds may be conjectured, cannot be demonstrated—governors they were, (for so the apostle speaketh,) or rather governments, i.e. gifts of wisdom, discretion, and judgment, to direct and govern the whole church, and every particular member thereof, in the manifold dangers and distresses which those days did not want. Governors also they might be called, that were appointed in every congregation to hear and appease the private strifes and quarrels that grew betwixt man and man, lest the Christians, to the shame of themselves, and slander of the gospel, should pursue each other for things of this life before the magistrates, who then were infidels; of these St. Paul speaketh, 1 Cor. vi. 1-7. These governors and moderators of their brethren's quarrels and contentions I find, others I find not in the apostle's writings, but such as withal were watchmen and feeders of the flock." Thus inconsistent he is with himself: one while these governors must be pastors; another while arbitrators or daysmen about private differences; another while gifts, not officers; another while he cannot easily prove what they were. But they have been proved to be ruling elders, and the proof still stands good, notwithstanding all his or others' exceptions.

Argum. III. The third argument for the divine right of the mere ruling elder shall be drawn from 1 Tim. v. 17, "Let the elders that rule well, be counted worthy of double honor, especially they that labor in the word and doctrine." From which words we may thus argue for the divine right of the ruling elder:

Major. Whatsoever officers in the Church are, according to the word of Christ, styled elders, invested with rule in the Church, approved of God in their rule, and yet distinct from all them that labor in the word and doctrine; they are the ruling elders in the Church which we inquire after, and that by divine right.

70

This proposition seems clear and unquestionable. For, 1. If there be a certain kind of church officer which Christ in his word calls an elder, 2. Declares to have rule in his church, 3. Approves in this his rule, and, 4. Distinguished from him that labors in the word and doctrine; this is plainly the ruling elder, and here is evidently the divine right of his office. Such a divine approbation of his office, testified in Scripture, implies no less than a divine institution thereof.

Minor. But the officers mentioned in 1 Tim. v. 17, are, according to the word of Christ, styled elders, invested with rule in the church: approved of God in their rule, and yet distinct from all them that labor in the word and doctrine. This assumption may be thus evidenced by parts.

1. The officers mentioned here in this word of Christ, are styled elders. This Greek word translated *elder*, is used in the New Testament chiefly in three several senses: 1. For men of ancient time, not now living; and so it is opposed to modern: Tradition of elders, Matt. xv. 2, i.e. of them of old time, see Matt. v. 21. 2. For elders in age now living; so it is opposed to younger, 1 Tim. v. 1; 1 Pet. v. 5. 3. For elders in function or office, opposed to private men not in office, as Acts xiv. 23; and in this last sense it is to be taken in this place, an office of ruling being here ascribed to these elders. They are called elders, say some, because for the most part they were chosen out of the elder sort of men: others better, from the maturity of knowledge, wisdom, gifts, gravity, piety, &c., which ought to be in them. This name elder seems to have rule and authority written upon it, when applied to any church officer; and it is by the Septuagint often ascribed to rulers political, *elders in the gate*, Judges viii. 14; Ruth iv. 2, 3; 1 Sam. v. 3; 1 Chron. xi. 3. In this place (as it is well noted by some[66]) the word elders is a genus, a general attribute, agreeing both to them that rule well, and also to those that labor in the word and doctrine: the one sort only rule; the other sort both rule and preach; but both sorts are elders.

2. The officers here mentioned are not only styled elders, but invested with rule in the church. For it is plain both by the text and context duly considered, and the apostle's scope in writing of this epistle, 1 Tim. iii. 15, that these elders are officers in the Church. And that in the church they are vested with rule appears not only by their name of elders, which when applied to officers, imports rule, authority, &c., as hath been said; but also by the adjunct participle *that rule*, or *ruling*, annexed to elders—*Let the elders ruling well*. So that here we have not only the office, the thing, but the very name of ruling elders. The word seems to be a military term, for captains and commanders in an army, *foremost standers*, (as the word imports,) that lead on and command all the rest that follow them: hence metaphorically used for the foremost-standers, rulers, governors in the church. It noteth not only those that go before others by doctrine, or good example: but that govern and rule others by authority. For, 1. Thus the word is used in Scripture: "One that ruleth well his own house, having his children in subjection with all gravity," 1 Tim. iii. 4: where it plainly notes an authoritative ruling. Again, "If a man know not how to rule his own house," 1 Tim. iii. 5. And again, "Ruling their children and their own houses well," 1 Tim. iii. 12. And can any man be so absurd as to think that a master of a family hath not a proper authoritative rule over his own children and family, but rules them only by doctrine and example?

2. Thus learned divines[67] and accurate Grecians[68] use the word to denote authority: so that the Holy Ghost here calling them ruling elders, implies they are vested with rule: and those that deny this place to hold out two sorts of elders, yet confess it holds out two sorts of acts, ruling and preaching.

3. These ruling elders are here approved of God in their rule; and that two ways, viz: 1. In that God's Spirit here commends their ruling, being duly discharged, *ruling well, excellently*, &c. Did no rule in the Church belong to them for matter, God would never command or approve them for the matter. He cannot be accounted with God to do any thing well, that hath no right to do it at all. 2. In that God's Spirit here commands their well ruling to be honorably rewarded. *Let them be counted worthy of double honor*: or, *Let them be dignified with double honor*. Here is not only reward, but an eminent reward appointed them, and that urged from Scripture, ver. 18. Where God thus appoints rewards, he approves that for which he rewards; and what God thus approves is of divine right. See part 1, chap. V.

4. Yet, finally, These elders, vested with rule in the Church, and divinely approved in their rule, are distinct from all them that labor in the word and doctrine. This may thus be evidenced from the text, as some[69] have well observed: For, 1. Here is a general, under which the several kinds of officers here spoken of are comprehended, *elders*; all here mentioned are elders. 2. Here are two distinct kinds of elders, viz: *those that rule well*, there is one kind; and *they that labor in the word* (as the pastors) *and doctrine*, (as the doctors and teachers,) here is the other kind. 3. Here are two participles expressing these two species or kinds of elders—*ruling*, and *laboring*: those only rule, that is all their work, and therefore here are called ruling elders; not because *they* alone rule, but because their only work is to rule: but these not only rule, but, over and besides, *they* labor in the word and doctrine. 4. Here are two distinct articles distinctly annexed to these two participles—*they that rule; they that labor.* 5. Finally, here is an eminent disjunctive particle set betwixt these two kinds of elders, these two participles, these two articles, evidently distinguishing one from the other, viz. especially *they that labor in the word*, &c., intimating, that as there were some ruling elders that did labor in the word and doctrine, so there were others that did rule, and not labor in the word: both were worthy of double honor, but especially they that both ruled and labored in the word also. And wheresoever this word, here translated *especially*, is used in all the New Testament, it is used to distinguish thing from thing, person from person, that are spoken of; as, "Let us do good to all, but especially to those of the household of faith," Gal. vi. 10: therefore there were some of the household of faith, and some that were not; and accordingly we must put a difference in doing good to them. "All the saints salute you, especially those of Cæsar's household;" some saints not of his household: all saluted them, but especially those of Cæsar's household. "He that provides not for his own, especially for them of his own house, he hath denied the faith," 1 Tim. v. 8. A believer is to provide for his friends and kindred, but especially *for those of his own house*, wife and children. See also 1 Tim. iv. 10; Tit. i. 11; 2 Tim. iv. 13; 2 Pet. ii. 10; Acts xx. 38, and xxvi. 3; in all which places the word *especially* is used as a disjunctive particle, to distinguish one thing from another, without which distinction we shall but make nonsense in interpreting those places. And generally the best interpreters[70] do from this text conclude, that there were two sorts of elders, viz: the ruling elder, that only ruled; the preaching elder, that besides his ruling, labored in the word and doctrine also.

Now, therefore, seeing the officers here mentioned are, 1. According to the word of Christ, (for this is the word of Christ,) styled elders; 2. Vested with rule; 3. Approved of God in their rule; and yet, 4. Distinct from all that labor in the word and doctrine, as hath been particularly proved; we may conclude, that,

Conclusion. Therefore the officers here mentioned are the ruling elders in the Church which we inquire after, and that by divine right.

But against this place of 1 Tim. i. 17, and the argument from it, divers cavils and exceptions are made; let them have a brief solution.

Except. 1. There were two sorts of elders, some laboring in the word and doctrine, some taking care of the poor, viz. deacons; both were worthy of double honor, especially they that labored in the word, &c.[71]

Ans. 1. This is a new distinction of elders without warrant of Scripture. Deacons are nowhere in all the New Testament styled elders;[72] nay, they are contradistinguished from elders, both teaching and ruling. "He that giveth *let him do it* with simplicity: he that ruleth, with diligence," Rom. xii. 8. "Helps, governments," 1 Cor. xii. 28. Compare also Tit. i. 5, 6, &c., 1 Tim. iii. 2, &c., with 1 Tim. iii. 8, &c. 2. As deacons are not elders, so deacons have no rule in the church. It is true, they are to "rule their children and their own houses well," 1 Tim. iii. 12; this is only family rule: but as for the church, their office therein is to be *helps*, 1 Cor. xii. 28; *to distribute*, Rom. xii. 8; *to serve tables*, Acts vi. 2, 3; but no rule is ascribed to them.

Except. 2. But by ruling well, some understand living well, leading a holy, exemplary life. The apostle would have ministers not only to live well themselves, but also to feed others by the word and doctrine; they that live well are to be double honored, especially they who labor in the word, &c., as 1 Thess. v. 12, 13.[73]

Ans. 1. The apostle here speaks rather of officers than of acts of office: of persons rather than of duties, if his phrase be observed. 2. Living well is not ruling well here in the apostle's sense, who intends the rule of elders over others; he that lives well rules well over himself; not over others: else all that live well were church rulers; they conduct by example, do not govern by authority, Altar. Damasc. c. xii. 8. If well ruling be well living, then double honor, double maintenance from the church is due for well living, (1 Tim. v. 17, 18,) consequently all that live well deserve this double honor. 4. This seems to intimate that ministers deserve double honor for living well, though they preach not. *How absurd!* 5. D. Downham, once pleased with this gloss, after confessed it was not safe.

Except. 3. Those that rule well may be meant of aged, infirm, superannuated bishops, who cannot labor in the word and doctrine.[74]

Ans. 1. Here is no speech of prelatical bishops, but of ruling and preaching elders in this text. 2. How shall old, decrepit bishops rule well, when they cannot labor in the word and doctrine? 3. By this gloss, the preaching elders that labor in the word and doctrine, should be preferred before the most ancient bishop in double honor; such doctrine would not long since have been very odious and apocryphal to our late prelates. 4. Those preachers that have faithfully and constantly spent their strength, and worn out themselves with ministerial labor, that they cannot rule nor preach any longer, are yet worthy of double honor for all their former travels in the service of Christ and his Church.

Except. 4. Among ministers some did preach, others only administered the sacraments; so Paul showeth that he preached and "labored more than all the apostles," 1 Cor. xv. 10; but baptized few or none, 1 Cor i. 14, leaving that to be performed by others; and when Paul and Barnabas were companions, and their travels were equal, yet Paul is noted to have been the chief speaker, (Acts xiv. 12:) all were worthy of double honor, but especially they who labored in the word and doctrine.[75]

Ans. 1. This gloss imagineth such a ministry in the apostles' times as the prelates had erected of late in their days, viz: many dumb dogs that could not bark nor preach at all, yet could administer the sacraments by the old service-book. But the apostles, as Cartwright[76]observes, allowed no such ministers, will have every bishop or preaching elder to be both "apt to teach, *and* able to convince," 1 Tim. iii. 2; Tit. i. 9. So that it was far from Paul to countenance a non-preaching or seldom-preaching ministry, by allowing any honor at all, much less a double honor, to such. Sure, preaching is one part, yea, a most principal part or duty of the minister's office, (as hath been evidenced before, Part 2, Chap. VII.,) and shall he be counted worthy of double honor that neglects a principal duty of his office? Nay, he deserves not the very name of such an officer in the church: why should he be called a pastor that doth not feed? or a teacher, that doth not teach his flock? &c., saith Chrysost. Hom. xv. in 1 Timothy. 2. Why should Paul's laboring be restrained here to his preaching only? when Paul speaks of his own labor elsewhere, he speaks of it in another sense, 2 Cor. xi. 17, "in labor and weariness"—compare it with the context; and in this place judicious Calvin seems rather to interpret it of other manner of labor, and Pareus extends it, besides preaching, to divers other labors which Paul did undergo. 3. What warrant doth this exception hold out for two sorts of ministers here pretended, some *preaching*, others *only administering the sacraments?* Thus,*Paul preached much, baptised but few.* therefore, *there were some that only administered the sacraments.* well concluded. Yet Paul baptized some, 1 Cor. i. 14, 16, distributed the Lord's supper to some, Acts xx. 7, 11; so that he both preached and dispensed the sacraments. Let any show where any person dispensed the sacraments that was not a preacher. Again, *Paul and Barnabas equally travelled together, but Paul was chief speaker.* what then? therefore*some labored in the word, others in the sacraments only.* This is woful logic. 4. To whomsoever the power of dispensing the sacraments was given by Christ, to them also the power of preaching was given; dispensing the word and sacraments are joined in the same commission, Matt, xxviii. 18-20: what Christ joins together let not man put asunder. 5. Touching the preaching elder there is mentioned only one act peculiar to his office, viz.*laboring in the word,* &c.; but, taking a part for the whole, we may understand his dispensing the sacraments also, and what else is peculiar to the preaching elder's office, though for brevity's sake it be not here named.[77]

Except. 5. By elders that rule well may be meant certain governors, or inferior magistrates, chosen to compose controversies or civil strifes. Suitable hereunto is the late

Erastian gloss, that by elders ruling well may be meant kings, parliament-men, and all civil governors.<u>78</u>

Ans. 1. It is well known that in the primitive times there was no Christian magistrate in the Church, and for the Church to choose heathen judges or magistrates to be arbitrators or daysmen in civil controversies, is a thing utterly condemned by the apostle, 1 Cor. vi. 1, &c. 2. The apostle speaks here of ecclesiastical, not of civil officers, as the latter phrase intimates. The main scope of this epistle was to instruct Timothy how to behave himself, not in the commonwealth, but in the Church of God, (1 Tim. iii. 15,) and here he speaks of such officers as were in being in the Church at that time. 3. If kings, parliament-men, and all civil governors be these ruling elders, then ministers have not only an equal share with them in government by this text, which the Erastians will not like well; but also are to have a superior honor or maintenance to kings, parliament-men, and all civil governors. Certainly the magistrates will never triumph in this gloss, nor thank them that devised it. 4. Sutlive seems to be against this opinion, (though no great friend to ruling elders,) saying Beza bestows many words to prove that the judges in 1 Cor. vi. were not of the number of presbyters: which truly I myself should easily grant him. For there were none such ever constituted. 5. This is a novel interpretation, as some observe,<u>79</u> unknown among ancient writers.

Except. 6. Those words [*especially they who labor in the word and doctrine*] are added to the former explanatively, to teach us who they are that rule well, viz. *they who labor much in the word and doctrine*, and not to distinguish them that labor in the word, from elders ruling well; as if Paul had said, "Let the elders that rule well be counted worthy of double honor, greatly laboring in the word," &c. For the word translated *especially* here more aptly signifies *much, greatly*, than especially. For though with the adversative *but* along with it, it signifieth especially, yet alone (as it is here) it signifies *much, greatly*.<u>80</u>

Ans. 1. If this sentence [*especially they who labor*, &c.] were added only to explain who are well-ruling elders, viz. such as greatly labor in the word, &c., then few of the prelatical bishops were to be counted well-ruling elders, for very few, if any of them, were guilty of laboring greatly in the word and doctrine. 2. Then also the apostle would have said, either who especially labor, or simply without the article, especially laboring; then especially, they who labor, as here he doth, carrying his speech rather to distinct persons and officers, than to distinct duties or actions. 3. This word translated *especially*, hath been already in the minor proposition proved to be rather disjunctive, than explanatory; a term of distinction to point out a several sort of elders from only ruling elders, rather than a term of explication, signifying who are to be reputed these well-ruling elders. 4. The word *especially* is used for a term of distinction, even in those places where the adversative *but* is not joined to it, as in Tit. i. 10, "For there are many unruly and vain talkers and deceivers, especially they of the circumcision:" where *especially* distinguishes *them of the circumcision*, from all other *vain talkers, and deceivers*; and in 1 Tim. iv. 10, "Who is the Saviour of all men, especially of them that believe;" here *especially* without *but* distinguishes them that believe from all other men, as capable of a special salvation from God; if here it were not a note of distinction, according to this gloss, we should thus read the place, "Who is the Saviour of all men, greatly believing;" but this were cold comfort to weak Christians of little faith. So here *especially*, though *but* be wanting, distinguished them that labor in the word and doctrine, from them that labor not therein, and yet rule well.

Except. 7. It is one thing to preach, another thing to labor in the word and doctrine. If there be here any distinction of elders it is between those that labor more abundantly and painfully, and between those that labor not so much. This objection takes much with some.<u>81</u> B. Bilson much presses this objection from the emphasis of the word *laboring*, signifying endeavoring any thing with greater striving and contention, &c., to this sense, "Let the elders that rule well be counted worthy of double honor, especially they who labor and sweat, &c., in the word—who give themselves even to be tired and broken with labors;" and this, saith he, is the genuine signification of the word translated laboring, when it is borrowed from the labor of the body, to denote the contention or striving of the mind, &c.<u>82</u>

Ans. 1. This gloss takes it for granted, that this text speaks only of preaching, or the ministry of the word, and therein of the lesser or greater pains taken: which (besides that it begs the thing in question) makes the ministry of the word common to both sorts here distinctly spoken of, whereas rather the plain current of the text makes ruling common to both, over and beyond which the preaching elder *labors in the word*. 2. Doth not this interpretation allow a double honor to ministers that labor not so much as others in the word? And can we think that the laborious Paul intended to dignify, patronize, or encourage idle drones, lazy, sluggish, seldom preachers? Ministers must be exceeding instant and laborious in their ministry, 2 Tim. iv. 1-3. If this were the sense only to prefer the greater before the less labor in the ministry, the apostle would have used this order of words, "Let the elders that rule well be counted worthy of double honor, especially they who labor," &c., take upon themselves more weighty cares. For those words (in the word and doctrine) should either have been quite omitted, as now was expressed, or should have been inserted immediately after them that rule well, and before the word especially, to this effect, "Let the elders that rule well and preach the word and doctrine well, be counted worthy of double honor; but especially those who labor much in well ruling and in well preaching:" in such an expression the case had been very clear and evident. 4. Should this comment stand, that they who labor more in the ministry than others should have more honor, more maintenance, than others, how many emulations and contentions were this likely to procure? Who shall undertake to proportion the honor and reward, according to the proportion of every minister's labor? 5. As for the criticism of the word *laboring*, which Bilson lays so much stress upon, these things are evident, 1. That here *laboring*, signifies emphatically nothing else but that labor, care, diligence, solicitude, &c., which the nature of the pastoral office requires in every faithful pastor; as is implied 1 Thess. v., 12, 13, "Know them which labor among you, and are over you in the Lord;" and the apostle saith that every minister "shall receive a reward according to his own labor," 1 Cor. iii. 8. Such labor and diligence also is required in them that rule, whilst they are charged to rule *with diligence*, Rom. xii. 8, which is as much as *with labor*: yea, the common charity of Christians hath its labor; and this very word *labor* is ascribed thereunto, *labor of love*, 1 Thess. i. 3; Heb. vi. 10. 2. That if the apostle had here intended the extraordinary labor of some ministers above others, not ordinarily required of all, he would have taken a more emphatical word to have set it out, as he is wont to do in some other cases, as in 2 Cor. xi. 27, "In labor and weariness." 1 Thess. ii. 9, "For ye remembered, brethren, our labor and weariness." 6. Finally, "If there be but one kind of church officers here designed, then," as saith the learned Cartwright, "the words (*especially those that labor*) do not cause the apostle's speech to rise, but to fall; not to go forward, but to go backward; for to teach worthily and singularly is more than to teach painfully; for the first doth set forth all that which may be required in a worthy teacher, where the latter noteth one virtue only of pains taking."

Except. 8. Though it could be evinced, that here the apostle speaks of some other elders, besides the ministers of the word, yet what advantage can this be for the proof of ruling elders? For the apostle being to prove that the ministers of the word ought to be honored, i.e. maintained; why might he not use this general proposition, that all rulers, whether public or domestic, whether civil or ecclesiastical, are to be honored? And when the apostle speaketh of the qualifications of deacons, he requires them to be such as have ruled their own houses well.[83]

Ans. 1. This slight gloss might have appeared more tolerable and plausible, were it not, partly, that the grand scope of the apostle in this chapter and epistle is to direct about church officers and church affairs, as both the context, and 1 Tim. iii. 14, 15, clearly evidence; and partly, had the word rulers been expressed alone in the text, and the word elders left out: but seeing that the apostle speaks not generally of them that rule well, but particularly of the elders that rule well in the Church; here is no place for this poor faint gloss. 2. Had the apostle here intended such a lax and general proposition for all sorts of rulers, then had he also meant that an honorable maintenance is due from the Church to domestic as well as public, yea, to civil as well as ecclesiastical rulers: then the Church should have charge enough: yea, and then should ministers of the word (according to this interpretation) have more honor and maintenance than any other rulers, domestic or public, civil or ecclesiastical. Magistrates will never thank him for this gloss. 3. Though some kind of skill to rule and govern be required in deacons, yet that is no public rule in the Church, but a private rule in their own houses only, which the apostle mentions, 1 Tim. iii. 12.

Except. 9. But these Well-ruling presbyters may be referred to these pastors and teachers which were resident in every church, who therefore are properly said to have care and inspection of the faithful, as being affixed to that place for that end; but the word *laboring,* or *they that labor,* may be referred to them who travelled up and down for the visiting and confirming of the churches.[84] "There were some ministers that remained in some certain places, for the guiding and governing of such as were already won by the preaching of the gospel: others that travelled with great labor and pains from place to place to spread the knowledge of God into all parts, and to preach Christ crucified to such as never heard of him before. Both these were worthy of double honor, but the latter that builded not upon another man's foundation, more especially than the former, that did but keep that which others had gotten, and govern those that others have gained."[85]

Ans. 1. If this be the sense, that there were some ministers fixed, and limited to particular places and churches; others unfixed, having an unlimited commission, and these are to be especially honored: then the meaning is, that the apostles and evangelists who were unfixed, and had unlimited commissions, and laid the foundation, were to be especially honored above pastors and teachers that were fixed and limited, and only built upon their foundation. But how should this be the meaning? For this seems a needless exhortation; what church would not readily yield an especial honor to apostles and evangelists above pastors and teachers? This would savor too much of self-seeking in the apostle, and providing for his own honor. This implies that the text hath reference to apostles and evangelists, whereas it evidently speaks only of ordinary ruling and preaching presbyters.

2. If this be the sense of Dr. Field and Bilson, that some mere ordinary presbyters travelled laboriously to lay the foundation of Christianity, others were fixed to certain places to build upon that foundation: this seems to be false; for we read that mere ordinary presbyters were ordained for several cities and places as their peculiar charges, whom they were to feed, and with whom they were to remain, as Acts xiv. 23; Tit. i. 5; herewith compare Acts xx. 28; 1 Pet. v. 2; 1 Thess. v. 12. But that mere ordinary presbyters were ordained and employed in the Church without limitation of commission, where can it be evidenced in all the Scriptures? Wandering presbyters are nowhere commended; wandering stars are condemned, Jude, ver. 13.

3. To refer the word *laboring* to them that travelled from place to place for visiting and confirming of the churches, is very weak and unjustifiable in this place; for this clashes with Dr. Field's former gloss, (mentioned Except. 4, limiting *laboring* to preaching.) But any thing for a present shift. This word is sometimes given to the apostle, as 1 Cor. xv. 10; 2 Cor. xi. 27: but where are apostles and evangelists called *laboring,* merely in respect of their travelling from place to place, to lay the foundation of Christianity, thereby to distinguish them from ordinary pastors and teachers? Nay, the apostle himself makes *them that rule,* and *them that labor,* the same, 1 Thess. v. 12, 13. So here in 1 Tim. v. 17, *they that rule—and they that labor—* are the same, i.e. both of them ordinary presbyters, both of them ruling, only to one of them the office of *laboring* in the word and doctrine is superadded; yea, the very women that *were* godly were said *to labor in the Lord,* Rom. xvi. 6, 12, not for their far travels up and down several countries to propagate the gospel, for where are Mary and Persis reported to have done this? Yet doubtless such good women privately labored much to bring in others, especially of their own sex, to hear the apostles, and entertain the gospel; and if the women may be said to *labor much in the Lord,* in respect of their private endeavors, how much more may labor be ascribed to presbyters in respect of both their private and public employments! So that this word *laboring,* which is applied in Scripture not only to ordinary presbyters, but also to women, cannot (without violence) be drawn peculiarly to signify apostles and evangelists, as this exception intends.

Except. 10. Seeing in every minister of the word three things are requisite, unblamableness of life, dexterity of governing, and integrity of doctrine; the two first are commended here, but especially the labor in doctrine above them both; therefore here are set down not a two-fold order of presbyters, but only two parts of the pastoral office, preaching and governing; both which the apostle joins in the office of pastors, 1 Thes. v. 2-

13.<u>86</u> "The guides of the church are worthy of double honor, both in respect of governing and teaching, but especially for their pains in teaching; so noting two parts or duties of presbyterial offices, not two sorts of presbyters."<u>87</u>

Ans. 1. It is true, pastors have the power both of ruling and preaching belonging to their office, as is intimated, 1 Thes. v. 12, 13, and Heb. xiii. 7, and in other places; but doth it therefore follow, that none have the power of ruling, but those that have the power of preaching? or that this text, or 1 Tim. v. 17, intends only those rulers that preach? 2. Bilson, in this exception, confesseth that *laboring* belongs to ordinary fixed pastors, and therefore contradicts himself in his former objection, wherein he would have appropriated it to unfixed apostles and evangelists; yea, by this gloss it is granted, that preaching presbyters are to be more honored than non-preaching ruling prelates. These are miserable shifts and evasions, whereby they are necessitated thus to wound their own friends, and to cross their own principles. 3. According to this gloss, this should be the sense, "Let the ministers that rule well by good life, and skilful government, be counted worthy of double honor, especially they who labor in the word and doctrine." Now doth not this tacitly insinuate, that some ministers may rule well, and be worthy of double honor, though they labor not in the word and doctrine? and how absurd were this? But if the text be interpreted not of several acts of the same office, but of several sorts of officers, this absurdity is prevented, *Let ruling elders be doubly honored, especially those that both rule and preach.* 4. The text evidently speaks not of duties, but of persons; not of acts, but of agents; not of offices, but of officers; for it is not said, "Let the elders be counted worthy of double honor, for well ruling; especially for laboring"—but, *Let the elders that rule well, especially they that labor in the word, &c.* So that this gloss is vain, and against the plain letter of the text.

Except. 11. Though the emphasis of the word, *they that labor,* be not to be neglected, yet the difference betwixt presbyters is not put by that word, but by those (*in the word and doctrine.*) This does not signify two kinds of presbyters, but two offices of ministers and pastors; one general, to *rule well;* another special, *to labor in the word and doctrine.* To rule well, saith Hierom, is to fulfil his office; or, as the Syriac interpreter expounds it, "to behave themselves well in their place;" or as the Scripture speaks, *To go in and out before God's people as becomes them, going before them in good works in their private conversations, and also in their public administrations;* whence the apostle makes here a comparison betwixt the duties of ministers thus, "All presbyters that generally discharge their office well are worthy of double honor; especially they who labor in the word, which is a primary part of their office."<u>88</u>

Ans. 1. For substance this objection is the same with objection 10, already answered, therefore much more needs not to be added. 2. It is to be noted, that the apostle saith not, "Let the presbyters that rule well be counted worthy of double honor, especially because they labor in the word—for then he should have pointed at the distinct offices of ministers;" but he saith,*especially they that labor,* which clearly carries the sense to the distinction of elders themselves, who have distinct employments. 3. If preaching presbyters only should here be meant, and under that phrase (*that rule well*) their whole office in general, and the right managing thereof, should be contained, whereas *laboring in the word and doctrine* (as this exception implies) is but one part thereof, then hence it would inevitably follow, that a minister deserves more honor for the well administration of one part of his office only, than for the well managing of the whole, which is absurd! Here therefore the apostle doth not compare one primary part of the pastor's office, with the whole office and all the parts thereof; but one sort of presbyters with another, distinguishing the mere ruling presbyter from the ruling and preaching presbyter, as the acute and learned Whitaker hath well observed.

Except. 12. It is evident in the text itself, that all these elders here meant were worthy of double honor, whether they labored or governed; which by St. Paul's proofs, presently following, and by the consent of all old and new writers, is meant of their maintenance at the charges of the Church.<u>89</u> Now that lay-judges and censors of manners were in the apostle's time found at the expense of the Church, or by God's law ought to have their maintenance at the people's hands, till I see it justly proved, I cannot believe it: which yet must be proved before this construction can be admitted.<u>90</u>

77

Ans. 1. This word *honor* signifies (after the custom of the Hebrews, Exod. xx. 12) all pious offices and relief. This phrase (*double honor*) interpreters expound either absolutely or comparatively. Absolutely thus: *double honor*, i.e. great honor, so some; maintenance in this life, happiness in the life to come, so others; honor of reverence to their persons, and of maintenance for their labors, so Chrysostom, of which saith Calvin, "That Chrysostom interprets double honor to be maintenance and reverence, I impugn not." Comparatively thus:*double honor* here seems to relate to what was before spoken, ver. 3, "Honor widows that are widows indeed." Now here he intimates, that though widows are to be honored, yet these should be much more honored; they should have single, these double honor. In this last sense, which seems most genuine, it seems most likely that the apostle here intended principally, if not only, the honor of maintenance; partly because the honor appointed for widows, ver. 3, &c., was only maintenance; partly because the reason of this charge to honor, &c., refers only to maintenance, ver. 18. Thus far we grant, that the text speaks of maintenance. 2. It may be further yielded that all the presbyters here spoken of are to be counted worthy of double honor, of honorable, liberal maintenance; even they that rule well (if need require) are to be thus honored, but the principal care of maintenance ought to be of them that labor in the word and doctrine, because the apostle saith *especially they that labor, &c.*: the like injunction, see Gal. vi. 6, "Let him that is catechized, communicate to him that catechizeth him in all good things;" and thus much this text plainly evidenceth. 3. What then can be inferred hereupon by the adversaries of ruling elders? "Therefore the ruling elders (in the reformed churches) that take no maintenance of the church, are not the elders that rule well here mentioned?" This follows not: the apostle Paul took no wages of the church of Corinth, 2 Cor. xi. 7-9, and xii. 12, 13, &c., was he therefore not an apostle to them, as to other churches of whom he took maintenance? Divers among us in these days labor in the word and doctrine, and are not sufficiently maintained by their churches, but forced to spend of their own estates to do others service; are they therefore no ministers? *Forgive them this wrong.* Most churches are not able (or at least not willing) to maintain their very preaching presbyters and their families comfortably and sufficiently, as the gospel requireth: if therefore in prudence, that the Church be not needlessly burdened, those ruling elders are chosen generally that need no maintenance, doth their not taking maintenance of the church make their office null and void? Or if the church do not give them maintenance (when they neither need it, nor desire it, nor is the church able to do it) is the church therefore defective in her duty, or an ill observer of the apostolical precepts? Sure maintenance is not essentially and inseparably necessary to the calling of either ruling or preaching elder. There may be cases when not only the preaching, but the ruling elders ought to be maintained, and there may be cases when not only the ruling but also the preaching presbyter (as it was with Paul) should not expect to be maintained by the church. 4. It is as observable that the apostle here saith, let them be counted worthy of double honor, though the reformed churches do not actually give double maintenance to elders that rule well, yet they count them worthy of double maintenance, though the elders do not take it, though the churches cannot give it.

Finally, unto these testimonies and arguments from Scripture, many testimonies of ancient and modern writers (of no small repute in the Church of God) may be usefully annexed, speaking for ruling elders in the Church of Christ from time to time: some speaking of such sort of elders, presbyters, or church-governors, as that ruling elders may very well be implied in their expressions; some plainly declaring that the Church of Christ *in fact* had such officers for government thereof; and some testifying that of right such officers ought to be in the Church of Christ now under the New Testament for the well guiding thereof; by which it may notably appear, that in asserting the office of the ruling elder in the Church, we take not upon us to maintain any singular paradox of our own devising, or to hold forth some new light in this old opinionative age: and that the ruling elder is not a church officer first coined at Geneva, and a stranger to the Church of Christ for the first 1500 years, (as the adversaries of ruling elders scornfully pretend,) but hath been owned by the Church of Christ as well in former as in later times.[91]

An Appendix touching the Divine Right of Deacons.

Though we cannot find in Scripture that the power of the keys is committed by Christ unto deacons, with the other church governors, but conceive that deacons, as other members of the church, are to be governed, and are not to govern; yet forasmuch as deacons are ordinary officers in the Church of God, of which she will have constant use in all ages, and which at first were divinely appointed, and after frequently mentioned in the New Testament; it will not be thought unfit, before we conclude this section, touching the divine right of Christ's church-officers, briefly to assert the divine right of deacons, as followeth.

Deacons in the church are an ordinance of Jesus Christ. For,

1. They are found in Christ's catalogue of church officers, distinct from all other officers, both extraordinary and ordinary. *Helps*, 1 Cor. xii. 28. The Greek word in the natural acceptation properly signifies, to lift over against one in taking up some burden or weight; metaphorically, it here is used for deacons, whose office it is to *help* and *succor the poor and sick, to lend them a hand to lift them up*, &c., and this office is here distinctly laid down from all other ordinary and extraordinary offices in the text. So they are distinguished from all ordinary officers reckoned up, Rom. xii. 7, 8: under *prophecy*, there is the *teacher* and *pastor*; under *ministry*, the *ruling elder*, and the *deacon*, verse 8. This officer was so well known, and usual in the primitive churches, that when the apostle writes to the church at Philippi, he directs his epistle not only to the saints, but to the officers, viz. *to the overseers, and deacons*, Philip, i. 1. The occasion of the first institution of this office, see in Acts vi. 1, 2, &c. At the first planting of the Christian Church, the apostles themselves took care to receive the churches' goods, and to distribute to every one of their members *as they had need*, Acts iv. 34, 35; but in the increase of the church, the burden of this care of distributing alms increasing also, upon some complaints of the Greeks, *that their widows were neglected*, the office of deacons was erected, for better provision for the poor, Acts vi. 1-7; and because the churches are never like to want poor and afflicted persons, there will be constant need of this officer. The pastor and deacon under the New Testament seem to answer the priests and Levites under the Old Testament.

2. The qualifications of deacons are laid down by Christ in the New Testament, at large: 1 Tim. iii. 8-14, *Deacons also must be grave, not double-tongued*, &c., and Acts vi. 3, 5.

3. The manner also of deacons' vocation or calling unto their office is delineated, viz: 1. They must be chosen by the church; "Look ye out among you seven men of honest report," &c., "and they chose Stephen," &c., Acts vi. 3, 5. 2. They must first be proved and tried by the officers of the church, before they may officiate as deacons; "and let these also first be proved, then let them use the office of a deacon, being blameless," 1 Tim. iii. 10. 3. They must be appointed by the officers of the church to their office, and set apart with prayer, Acts vi. 3, 6: "Look ye out men—whom we may appoint over this business—whom they set before the apostles, and when they had prayed, they laid their hands on them."

4. Deacons have by Scripture their work and employment appointed them. Their work is, *to serve tables*, (hence the name deacon seems derived,) Acts vi. 2, 3. To be an help, no hinderance in the church; called *helps*, 1 Cor. xii. 18.

5. Deacons have a divine approbation and commendation in Scripture, if they execute their office well. "For they that have used the office of a deacon well, purchase to themselves a good degree, and great boldness in the faith which is in Christ Jesus," 1 Tim. iii. 13. Here the well administration of deaconship is commended as producing two good effects to such deacons, viz: 1. *A good degree*, i.e. great honor, dignity, and reputation, both to themselves and to their office; they adorn, grace, and credit their office in the church; not that they purchase to themselves by desert a higher office in the church, that from deacons they should be advanced to be presbyters, as some would interpret this text. 2. *Much boldness in the faith which is in Christ Jesus*. For nothing makes a man more bold than a good conscience in the upright and faithful discharge of our duties in our callings; innocency and integrity make brave spirits; such with great confidence and boldness serve Christ and the church, being men that may be trusted to the uttermost. Now where God thus approves or commends the well managing of an office, he also divinely approves and allows the office itself, and the officer that executes the same.92

SECTION II.

2. *Of the first receptacle, or subject of the power of church government from Christ, viz. Christ's own officers.*

Touching the second, that Jesus Christ our Mediator hath peculiarly intrusted his own officers with the power of church government: take it thus—

Jesus Christ our Mediator did immediately commit the proper, formal, ministerial, or stewardly authority and power for governing of his church to his own church guides as the proper immediate receptacle or first subject thereof.

For explication of this proposition, four things are to be opened.

1. What is meant by proper, formal, ministerial or stewardly authority and power for church government? See this already discussed, Part 2, chapters III., V., and IX., in the beginning of Section 2, so that here there needs no further addition, as to this point.

2. What is meant by church guides? By church guides here understand, negatively, 1. Not the political magistrate. For though he be the *nurse-father* of the church, Isa. xlix. 23, *the keeper and avenger of both the tables*, and *have an outward care of religion*, and *may exercise a political power about sacred things*, as did Asa, Jehoshaphat, Hezekiah, Josiah, &c., yet hath he no proper, inward, formal power in sacred things, nor is it lawful for him to exercise the same; as Korah, Num. xvi.; King Saul, 1 Sam. xiii. 9-15; Uzzah, 2 Sam. vi. 6-8, 1 Chron. xiii. 9, 10; and King Uzziah, 2 Chron. xxvi. 16-22, did to the provoking of God, and to their own destruction. (But see what power is granted, and what denied to the civil magistrate in matters of religion, and why, Part 2, Chap. IX. Sect. 1.) 2. Not any officer of man's mere invention and setting up in the church, whether papal, as cardinals, &c., prelatical, as deans, archdeacons, chancellors, officials, &c., or political, as committees, commissioners, &c. For who can create and institute a new kind of offices in the church, but Jesus Christ only, who alone hath the lordly magisterial power as Mediator appropriated to him? Eph. iv. 8, 11; Rom. xii. 5-8; 1 Cor. xii. 28; and therefore how can such acts be sufficiently excused from bold usurpation upon Christ's own prerogative? 3. Nor the deacons themselves, (though officers of Christ's appointment, as was formerly proved;) for their office is not to rule and govern, but *to serve tables*, &c., Acts vi. 2, 3. None of these are the church guides which Christ hath committed his proper power unto. But affirmatively understand all these church guides extraordinary and ordinary, which Christ hath erected in his Church, vesting them with power and authority therein, viz. apostles, prophets, evangelists, pastors and teachers, governments, or ruling elders, mentioned together in Eph. iv. 8, 11; 1 Cor. xii. 28; 1 Tim. v. 17; Rom. xii. 6-8. These are Christ's own church officers, these Christ hath made the immediate receptacle and first subject of the keys, or of ecclesiastical power derived from himself.

3. What is meant by Christ's committing this stewardly power first and immediately to the church guides? *Ans.* There is, 1. A priority and immediateness of the donation of the power of the keys: thus Christ first and immediately gave keys to his own officers, whom Scripture, therefore, calls *the ministers of Christ*, (not of the Church,) 1 Cor. iv. 1, not first and immediately to the community of the faithful, or Church, and then by the Church secondarily and mediately to the officers, as her substitutes and delegates, acting for her, and not in virtue of their own power from Christ. 2. A priority and immediateness of designation of particular individual persons to the office of key-bearing, and this is done by the mediate intervening act of the church officers in separating of particular persons to the office which Christ instituted; though it is not denied but that the church or company of the faithful may lawfully nominate or elect individual persons to be officers in the congregation, which yet is no act of authority or power.

4. How hath Christ committed this power of the keys to his church guides, that thereby they become the most proper receptacle thereof? *Ans.* Thus briefly. All absolute lordly power is in God originally: all lordly magisterial mediatory power is in Christ dispensatorily: all official, stewardly power is by delegation from Christ only in the church guides93 ministerially, as the only proper subject thereof that may exercise the same lawfully in Christ's name: yet all power, both magisterial in Christ, and ministerial in Christ's officers, is for the Church of Christ and her edification objectively and finally.

These things thus explained and stated, we come now to the confirmation of the proposition. Consider these arguments:

1. Jesus Christ committed immediately ecclesiastical power and the exercise thereof to his church guides. Thus we may argue:

Major. All those that have ecclesiastical power, and the exercise thereof, immediately committed to them from Jesus Christ, are the immediate subject or receptacle of that power.

For what makes any persons the immediate subject of power, but the immediate derivation and commission of power to them from Jesus Christ, who is the fountain of all power?

Minor. But the church guides have the ecclesiastical power and the exercise thereof immediately committed to them from Jesus Christ. This may be evinced many ways by Scriptures. 1. It is said expressly, "Of our authority which the Lord hath given us for your edification," 2 Cor. 10, 8: by *us* here we are to understand church guides, for here they are set in opposition to the church members (*for edification,*) not destruction of (you.) Here are edifiers and edified. Now these church guides have authority given them, and that from the Lord, i.e. Christ; here is their commission or power, not from the Church or any creature, but from Christ; hence the apostle calls church guides, "Your rulers or guides in the Lord," 1 Thes. v. 12; *in the Lord,* i.e. by the Lord's authority and commission. So that church officers are *rulers in the Lord,* and the churches ruled by them; yea, ruling elders being one sort of church guides, have such an undoubted power of governing in the Church divinely committed to them, that of them it is said, "God hath set in the church governments", 1 Cor. xii. 28, i.e. governors, the abstract being put for the concrete. If *God have set governors in the Church,* then God vested those governors with a power of governing, whence they have their name of governments.

2. The keys of the kingdom of heaven, with all their acts, were immediately committed to the church guides, viz. to the apostles and their successors to the end of the world; compare these testimonies, Matt. xvi. 16, 19, and xviii. 18-20; John xx. 21-23; with Matt, xxviii. 18-20: therefore consequently ecclesiastical power was committed immediately unto them as the subject thereof. For, *By the kingdom of heaven* here we are to understand (according to the full latitude of the phrase) both the kingdom of grace in this world, and of glory in the world to come; *binding and loosing both in earth and in heaven,* upon the right use of the keys, being here the privileges promised to church guides; and *by kingdom of heaven*—on earth, understand the whole visible Church of Christ in the earth, not only some single congregation. By *keys of the kingdom of heaven,* thus apprehend, Christ promiseth and giveth not the sword *of the kingdom,* any secular power; nor the sceptre *of the kingdom,* any sovereign, lordly, magisterial power over the Church. But the *keys,* &c. i.e. a stewardly, ministerial power, and their acts, *binding and loosing,* i.e. *retaining and remitting sins on earth,* (as in John it is explained;) opening and shutting are proper acts of keys; binding and loosing but metaphorical, viz. a speech borrowed from bonds or chains wherewith men's bodies are bound in prison or in captivity, or from which the body is loosed: we are naturally all under sin, Rom. v. 12, and therefore liable to death, Rom. vi. 23. Now sins are to the soul as bonds and cords, Prov. v. 22. *The bond of iniquity,* Acts viii. 23; and death with the pains thereof, are as chains, 2 Pet. ii. 4, Jude 6; in hell as in a prison, 1 Pet. iii. 10: the remission or retaining of these sins, is the loosing or the binding of the soul under these cords and chains. So that the keys themselves are not material but metaphorical; a metaphor from stewards in great men's houses, kings' houses, &c., into whose hands the whole trust and ordering of household affairs is committed, who take in and cast out servants, open and shut doors, &c., do all without control of any in the family save the master of the family. Such, in the Hebrew phrase, are said to be *over the house,* Gen. xliii. 18; Isa. xxii. 15; 2 Kings xviii. 18: and the keys of the house are committed to them as a badge of their power. So that when God threatens to put Shebna out of his office in the king's house, and to place Eliakim, son of Hilkiah, in his room, he saith, "I will commit thy government into his hand—and the key of the house of David will I lay upon his shoulder," Isa. xxii. 21, 22, parallel of that phrase, "and the government shall be upon his shoulder," Isa. ix. 6. Hence, as key is in the Old Testament used for stewardly power and government, Isa. xxii. 21, 22; (only twice properly, Judges iii. 25; 1 Chron. ix. 27;) so in the New Testament, *key* is always used, metaphorically, to denote power, and that about ecclesiasticals or spirituals, viz. in Matt. xvi. 19; Luke xi. 52; Rev. i. 18, and iii. 7, and ix. 1, and xx. 1. So that *keys,* &c., are metaphorically the ordinances which Christ hath instituted, to be dispensed in his church, preaching the word, administrations of the seals and censures: for it is not said *key,* but *keys,* which comprehendeth them all: by the

right use of which both the gates of the Church here, and of heaven hereafter, are opened or shut to believers or unbelievers; and Christ promising or giving these *keys* to Peter and the apostles, and their successors *to the end of the world*, Matt. xxviii. 20, doth intrust and invest them with power and authority of dispensing these ordinances for this end, and so makes them *stewards* in his house *of the mysteries of God*, 1 Cor. iv. 1, so that we may conclude:

Conclusion. Therefore the church guides are the immediate subject and receptacle of that ecclesiastical power, and of the exercise thereof.

Argum. II. Jesus Christ our Mediator did institute ecclesiastical offices for church government under the New Testament before any Christian Church under the New Testament was gathered or constituted. Therefore those persons that were intrusted with those offices must needs be the first and immediate receptacle or subject of the power of the keys. Thus we may argue:

Major. All those whose ecclesiastical offices for church government, under the New Testament, were instituted by Christ, before any formal visible Christian Church was gathered or constituted, are the first and immediate receptacle or subject of the power of the keys from Jesus Christ.

Minor. But the ecclesiastical offices of Christ's own officers for governing of the Church, now under the New Testament, were instituted by Christ before any formal visible Christian Church was gathered or constituted.

Conclusion. Therefore Christ's own officers for governing of the Church now under the New Testament are the first and immediate receptacle or subject of the keys from Jesus Christ.

The major proposition cannot reasonably be denied, and may be further cleared by these considerations, viz: 1. That the Church offices for church government under the New Testament are in their own nature intrinsically offices of power. The apostle styles it *power*, or *authority*, which is *given* to these officers by *the Lord*, 2 Cor. x. 8, and xiii. 10. *The keys of the kingdom of heaven* are committed to them, Matt. xvi. 19, and *keys* import a stewardly power: compare Matt. xvi. 19, and xviii. 18, John xx. 21, 23, with Isa. xxii. 21, 22. Materially, the acts and exercise of these officers are acts of power, as *binding, loosing*, &c., Matt, xviii. 18; not only *preaching*, &c., but *excommunicating*, is an act of power, 1 Cor. v. 4. Absolving the penitent, and confirming him again in the Church's love, is an act of power:—*to confirm love unto him*, i.e. authoritatively to confirm, &c., as the word signifies, 2 Cor. ii. 8. Formally, these acts are to be done as acts of power, in Christ's name, and by his authority, Matt. xxviii. 19; 1 Cor. v. 4. Now if these offices be in their own nature offices of power, consequently they that have such offices conferred upon them by Christ, before the Christian Church had being or existence, they must needs be the first and immediate recipient subject of the power of the keys from Christ. 2. Either those church officers, whose offices were instituted before the Christian Church was constituted, must be the first subject of the power, &c., or some others. If any other, then, 1. Either heathens, or heathen magistrates, who are out of the Church: but both these were absurd to grant; for then they that are not so much as church members should be church governors, and the Church be ecclesiastically judged by them that are without. 2. Or the first subject of this power was the Christian Church itself before it had existence; but that were notoriously absurd; and besides these, no other can be imagined, but the church officers; therefore they must needs be the first subject of the power of the keys.

The minor proposition (viz. But the ecclesiastical offices of Christ's own officers for governing of the Church now under the New Testament, were instituted by Christ before any formal visible Christian Church was gathered or constituted) is so evident in the current of the New Testament, that it needs little confirmation. For, 1. The church offices under the New Testament, as apostleship, pastorship, &c., were instituted by Christ either before his death—compare these places together, Mark iii. 13, 14, &c.; Luke ix. 1, &c., and x. 1, 2, &c.; John xx. 21-23; Matt, xxviii. 18-20—or presently upon his ascension, Eph. iv. 8, 11, 12, &c.; Acts ii.; 1 Cor. xiii. 28. Now no formal Christian Church was constituted and gathered till the feast of Pentecost and afterwards. Then, after the apostles had received the gifts of the Holy Ghost, &c., Acts ii., great multitudes of Jews and Gentiles were converted to Christ, and being converted, incorporated and associated themselves into churches, as the history of the

Acts, chap. ii., and forward, evidenceth abundantly. 2. Church officers, under the New Testament, are for the calling and gathering men unto Christ, and to his body mystical; and for admitting of those that believe into that one body, Matt. xxviii. 18, 19; 1 Cor. xii. 28. And is not he that calleth, before them that are called by them; they that baptize, before the baptized; and they that gather the churches, before those churches which they gather? May we not hence conclude, *Therefore*, &c.

Argum. III. The names, titles, and other denominations purposely and peculiarly given to the church guides in Scripture, generally do bear power and authority engraven upon their foreheads. *Therefore*, they are the proper, immediate, and only subjects of ecclesiastical power. Thus we may argue:

Major. All those persons in the Church, that have such names, titles, or denominations given to them peculiarly in the Scriptures by the Spirit of Christ, as generally have authority and power engraven upon them in reference to the Church, are the immediate and only proper subjects of ecclesiastical power.

Minor. But Christ's officers in the Church have such names, titles, or denominations given to them peculiarly in the Scriptures by the Spirit of Christ, as generally have authority and power engraven upon them in reference to the Church.

Conclusion. Therefore Christ's own officers in the Church are the proper, immediate, and only subjects or receptacles of ecclesiastical power.

This major proposition must be granted. For, 1. Is not this the Holy Ghost's familiar and ordinary manner in Scripture, to give titles and denominations, which are apt, pertinent, significative and instructing both to others and themselves that have such denominations conferred upon them? As in the family, the husband is called *the head of the wife*, 1 Cor. xi., because he is to govern, she is to be subject: the wife is called *an help-meet*, &c., Gen. ii.: to teach the wife her duty, to help his good and comfort every way, to hinder it no way. So in the commonwealth, magistrates are called *heirs of restraint, to put men to shame*, Judges xviii. 7, because they are to restrain disorders, shame evil-doers: higher powers, to teach others subjection to them, Rom. xiii. 1. "An ordinance of man or human creation," 1 Pet. ii. 13: because, though magistracy in general be an ordinance of God, yet this or that special kind of magistracy, whether monarchical, aristocratical, &c., is of man. Thus in the Church: the Church is called *Christ's body*, Ephes. iv. 12, to show Christ's headship, the Church's subjection to Christ, and their near union to one another. Christians are called *members*, Rom. xii.; 1 Cor. xii., to teach them mutual love, care, and serviceableness to one another. Ministers are called *ambassadors of Christ*, 2 Cor. v. *Angels of the churches*, Rev. ii., to teach them to be faithful in their offices, and others to respect them for their offices. *Salt of the earth*, Matt. v. 13, because they are to season others spiritually. *Stars*, Rev. i., because they are to shine forth for the enlightening and guiding of others, &c. 2. If this proposition be denied, then to what end are such names and denominations, importing authority, generally given by the Spirit of God to some sort of persons only, and not to others? Is it for no end? That would be a dangerous charge upon the Spirit of Christ. Is it for any end? Then what other can be imagined, than to signify, hold forth, and instruct both themselves and others in their duties, and to distinguish them that are vested with authority in the Church, from them that are not?

The *major proposition* (viz. But Christ's own officers in the Church have such names, titles, or denominations given to them peculiarly in the Scriptures by the Spirit of Christ, as generally have authority and power engraven upon them in reference to the Church) may be evinced, 1. By induction of particular names attributed to Christ's officers. 2. By a denial of them, or the like, to any other members of the Church.

1. By induction of particular titles or denominations attributed to Christ's officers, which generally have power and authority palpably engraven upon them: (yea, the self-same names are given to them, by which not only heathen writers, but also the Greek version of the Old Testament by the Septuagint, and the very original of the New Testament are wont to give to political officers, to express their political authority, power, and government,) as, for instance:

1. *Presbyter or elder*, is ascribed often to Christ's church officers, as in Acts xiv. 23, and xv. 2, 4, and xx. 17; 1 Tim. v. 17; Tit. v.; 1 Pet. v. 1. This same word is ascribed to *rulers*

political, to *elders in the gate*, by the Septuagint, in Judges viii. 14; Ruth iv. 2, 3; 2 Sam. v. 3; 1 Chron. vi. 3.

2. *Overseer* or *bishop*, noting authority and power in having the charge and oversight of the flock, is ascribed to church officers in Acts xx. 28; Phil. i. 1; 1 Tim. iii. 2; Tit. i. 7. This same word is used by the Septuagint, to denote the power of the civil magistrate, to whom the care and oversight of the commonwealth is committed, Numb. xxxi. 14; Judges ix. 28; 2 Kings xi. 15.

3. *Guide, leader, conductor, captain, governor*, signifies them all, and is given to church officers, as contradistinct from the *church* and *saints*, Heb. xiii. 7, 17, 24. It is also attributed to civil rulers to set forth their power, in Deut. i. 13; Micah iii. 9, 11; 2 Chron. v. 1; Ezek. xliv. 3, and xlv. 7; Dan. iii. 2; Acts vii. 10. This very word *governor*, is attributed to Christ himself,*out of thee shall come forth a governor, that shall rule* (or *feed*) *my people Israel*, Matt. ii. 6.

4. *Steward, dispenser.* "Stewards of the mysteries of God," is the title given to ministers, 1 Cor. iv. 1, 2. "Steward of God," Tit. i. 7. "That faithful and wise steward, whom his Lord shall make ruler over his household," &c., Luke xii. 42. This also is a title of power given to them that are set over families, as Gal. iv. 2, "he is under tutors and stewards." And to them that are set over cities—as Rom. xvi. 23, "Erastus the steward" (or as we render it, *the chamberlain*) "of the city saluteth you."

5. *Pastor* is ascribed to Christ's officers; Eph. iv. 11, "and some pastors and teachers." They govern the Church as the shepherd his flock, feeding, ruling them as well with the shepherd's staff, as with food. This term is sometimes given to civil magistrates, Isa. xliv. 28; Micah v. 5: sometimes to Christ the great shepherd of the sheep, 1 Pet. v. 4; noting his authority, Matt. xxvi. 31; John x. 2, 11, 14, 16; Heb. xiii. 20; 1 Pet. ii. 25: sometimes to God himself the supreme Ruler of the world, Ps. lxxx. 1.

6. *Governments*, a denomination given to *ruling elders*, 1 Cor. xii. 28, as hath been proved Sect. 1 of this Chapter. A metaphor from mariners or pilots, that steer and govern the ship: translated thence, to signify the power and authority of church governors, spiritual pilots, steering the ship or ark of Christ's Church. This word is used also by heathen authors, to signify political governors.94

Ruler. 1 Tim. v. 17, "Let the elders that rule well"—and,

"He that ruleth," Rom. xii. 8, and "Your rulers in the Lord," 1 Thes. v. 12, viz. not only in the fear of the Lord,95 nor only in those things that appertain to God's worship,96 but also in the Lord; i.e. who are over you, to rule according to the will of the Lord,97 even by the Lord Christ's power and authority ascribed to them. Now these names are among heathen authors ascribed to rulers of cities, armies, and kingdoms.98

By these among other titles given to Christ's officers in Scripture, he that runs may read a plain authority and power enstamped on them in reference to the Church; and consequently on them that are thus denominated, unless they be applied to them improperly, unfitly, abusively; which we suppose no sober intelligent reader dare affirm.

2. By a denial of these and like titles to the whole Church of Christ, or to any other members of the Church whatsoever, besides church officers. For where can it be showed in all the book of God, that in this sense, either the whole Church or any members thereof besides officers, are ever styled *presbyters, bishops, governors, stewards of God, or of the mysteries of God, pastors, governments, or rulers?* The greatest factors for popular government must let this alone forever. Thus, from all that hath been said, we need not fear to conclude:

Conclusion. Therefore Christ's own officers in the Church are the proper, immediate, and only subjects or receptacles of ecclesiastical power.

Argum. IV. The relations which Christ's officers have unto his Church, imply and comprehend in themselves authority and power in reference to the Church, and therefore they are the proper subjects of ecclesiastical power. Thus we reason:

Major. Whosoever they are that peculiarly stand in such relations to the Church of Christ, as imply and comprehend in themselves authority and power for governing of the Church, they are the only subject of ecclesiastical power.

This proposition is evident; for, otherwise, to what end are those peculiar relations to the Church which comprehend government in them, unless such as are so peculiarly related be the only subjects of government? Shall all those relations be mere names and shadows? or shall others in the church be counted the subject of this authority and power for church government, that have no such relations to the Church at all implying any such power?

Minor. But the officers of Christ peculiarly stand in such relations to the Church of Christ as imply and comprehend in themselves authority and power for the government of the church.

This assumption or minor proposition will be evident by a due induction of some of their particular relations that have such power enstamped on them; as for instance, Christ's officers stand in these relations of power to the Church and people of God.

1. *They are pastors,* Eph. iv. 11. The church is the *flock,* John x. 16; 1 Cor. ix. 7; *flock,* Acts xx. 28, 29; 1 Pet. v. 2, 3. Hath not the *pastor* power to rule and govern his *flock?*

2. They are *stewards.* "Who is that faithful and wise steward?" Luke xii. 42. "Stewards of the mysteries of God," 1 Cor. iv. 1, 2. "Stewards of God," Tit. i. 7. The Church and people of God are the Lord's *household,* over which these stewards are set, &c., Luke xii. 42. *God's house,* 1 Tim. iii. 15; Heb. iii. 6. Have not stewards power to govern and order those *families* over which they are set, and wherewith they are intrusted? Gal. iv. 1.

3. They are *bishops* or *overseers,* Phil. i. 1; 1 Tim. iii. 2; Tit. i. 7. The Church and people of God are that *charge* which the Lord hath committed to their inspection. "Over which the Holy Ghost hath made you overseers," Acts xx. 28. Have not *overseers* power over that which is *committed to their inspection?*

4. They are *catechizers* and *teachers,* Rom. xii. 7, 8; Eph. iv. 11. The Church and people are *catechized,* Gal. vi. 6; *taught.* Hath not he that *catechizeth* power for government of him that is *catechized?* He that *teacheth* of him that is *taught?*

5. They are *co-workers* with God, 1 Cor. iii. 9; 2 Cor. vi. 1. *Architects, builders,* &c., 1 Cor. iii. 10; some of them *laying the foundation, others building thereupon.* The Church and people of God are God's building. "Ye are God's building," 1 Cor. iii. 9. Have not *builders* power of disposing and ordering affairs appertaining to the *building?*

6. Finally, to add no more, the officers of Christ in the Church are not only as *nurses,* "We *were* gentle among you, even as a nurse cherisheth her children," 1 Thess. ii. 7: and as *mothers,* "My little children, of whom I travail in birth again," Gal. iv. 19: but also as *fathers,* 1 Thess. ii. 11; 1 Cor. iv. 15, spiritual fathers in Christ: and the Church and people of God, they are the *sons* and *daughters,* the spiritual *babes* and *children,* begotten, brought forth, and nursed up by them, 1 Thess. ii. 7, 11; Gal. iv. 19: and have fathers no authority nor power of government over their children? See Eph. vi. 1-3; 1 Tim. iii. 4.

Thus Christ's officers stand in such relation to the Church as do evidently carry power of government along with them; but where are any other members of the church besides officers, stated in such relation of *pastors, stewards, overseers, catechizers, builders, husbandmen, nurses, mothers,* and *fathers* to the Church of God and members of Christ, that can be evidenced by the Scriptures? Why may we not then clearly conclude,

Conclusion. Therefore the officers of Christ are the only subjects of ecclesiastical power.

Argum. V. The many divine commands and impositions of duties of obedience, submission, subjection, &c., upon the Church and people of God, to be performed by them to Christ's officers, and that in reference to their office, do plainly proclaim the officers of Christ to be the proper receptacle and subject of authority and power from Christ for the government of his Church. Thus it may be argued:

Major. Whatsoever persons they are to whom the Church and people of God are peculiarly bound by the commands of Christ, to perform duties of obedience and subjection, and that in reference to their office in the church, they are the only subjects of authority from Christ for the government of his Church.

This proposition needs no proof, unless we will be so absurd as to say that the Church and people of God are peculiarly obliged by Christ's command to obey and be subject to them, that yet have no peculiar authority nor power over them, and that in reference to their office in the church.

Minor. But the officers of Christ are those to whom the Church and people of God are peculiarly bound by the commands of Christ to perform duties of obedience and subjection, and that in reference to their office in the church.

85

This assumption or minor proposition may be evidenced, 1. Partly by induction of some particular instances of Christ's commands, whereby the Church and people of God are bound to perform duties of obedience and subjection to the officers of Christ, in reference to their office in the church. 2. Partly by a denial of the like commands in reference to all others in the church, except the officers of the church only.

Touching the first, viz. the instances of such commands, consider these following. The Church and people of God are commanded,

1. To know their rulers. "We beseech you, brethren, to know them that labor among you, and are over you in the Lord," 1 Thess. v. 12. *To know*, i.e., not simply and merely to know, but to acknowledge, accept, and approve of them as such rulers over you in the Lord. This teaches subjection to the office of ruling.

2. To love them exceedingly for their work's sake. "Esteem them superabundantly in love for their work's sake," 1 Thess. v. 13. For what work? viz. both laboring and ruling, mentioned verse 12. If they must love them so exceedingly for ruling over them, must they not much more be obedient to this rule?

3. To count them worthy of double honor in reference to their well-ruling. "Let the elders that rule well be counted worthy of double honor, especially—," 1 Tim. v. 17: whether we take *double honor* here for reverence or maintenance, or both; yet how can we esteem the *elders ruling well worthy of double honor* without some submission to their rule?

4. To obey them that are their rulers and governors. *Obey ye your rulers, or governors*, Heb. xiii. 17; where the words *obey ye* doth not (as some dream) signify a persuasion, but obedience, and in this sense it is commonly used, not only in profane authors, but also in the Holy Scriptures, as James iii. 3, Gal. iii. 1.

5. Finally, to submit and be subordinate unto them. The Church and people of God are charged to submit unto them. "Obey your governors and submit ye," Heb. xiii. 17. The word properly notes a submissive yielding without opposition or resistance; yea, it signifies intense obedience. They must not only yield, but yield with subjection and submission, which relates to authority. They are also charged to be subordinate to them. "Likewise, ye younger, submit yourselves to the elders," 1 Pet. v. 5; i.e., *be ye subordinate*, (it is a military term,) viz: be ordered, ranked, guided, governed, disciplined by them, as soldiers are by their commanders. The word *elders* here is by some taken only for elders in age, and not in office. But it seems better to interpret it of elders in office; and the context well agrees with this; for the apostle having immediately before charged the ruling preaching presbyters with their duties towards their flock, ver. 1-4, here he seems to enjoin the ruled flock (which commonly were younger in age and gifts) to look to their duties of subjection to their elders in office.

Touching the second, viz. the denial of like commands, and upon like grounds to all others in the church, except to the church officers only: where can it be evidenced in all the Scriptures that the people of God are commanded to know, to esteem very highly in love, to count worthy of double honor, to obey, and submit themselves to any persons in the church but to the ruling officers thereof in reference to their office, and the due execution thereof?

Now, seeing the Church and people of God are peculiarly obliged, by so many commands of Christ, to perform such duties of subjection and obedience to the officers of Christ, may it not be concluded,

Therefore the officers of Christ are the only subjects of authority from Christ for the government of his Church?

Argum. VI. Finally, the directions touching rule and government in the Church; the encouragements to well-ruling by commendations, promises, rewards, together with the contrary deterring discouragements from ill-ruling, by discommendations, threats, &c., being specially applied and appropriated by the word of Christ unto Christ's officers, very notably discover to us that Christ's officers are the only subjects of power from Christ for the government of his Church. Thus it may be argued:

Major. Whatsoever persons in the Church have directions for church government, encouragements to well-ruling, and discouragements from ill-ruling, particularly and peculiarly applied unto them by the word of Christ; they are the only subjects of power from Christ for the government of his Church:

This proposition is evident: For, 1. How should it be consistent with the infinite wisdom of God peculiarly to apply unto them directions about ruling and governing the church that are not the only subjects in whom the power of government is intrusted by Jesus Christ? 2. How can it stand with the justice of God to encourage them only unto well-ruling, by commendations, promises, rewards, &c., or to deter them from ill-governing by dispraises, threats, &c., &c., to whom the power of government doth not appertain, as to the only subjects thereof? 3. What strange apprehensions and distractions would this breed in the hearts of Christ's officers and others, should those that have not the power of church government committed to them by Christ, be yet directed by his word how to govern, encouraged in governing well, and deterred from governing ill?

Minor. But the officers of Christ in the church have directions for church government, encouragements to well-ruling, and discouragements from ill-ruling, particularly and peculiarly applied unto them by the word of God.

This assumption or minor proposition may be cleared by divers Scriptures according to the particular branches thereof, viz:

1. Directions for church government are particularly applied by the word of Christ to his own officers: as for instance, they are directed to *bind and loose*—to *remit* and *retain sins on earth*, Matt. xvi. 19, and xviii. 18; John xx. 21, 23. *To judge them that are within the* Church,*not without*, 1 Cor. v. 12. *Not to lord it, domineer,* or *overrule the flock of Christ*, 1 Pet. v. T.o*rule well*, 1 Tim. v. 17. To rule *with diligence*, Rom. xii. 8. To *lay hands suddenly on no man, neither to be partakers of other men's sins, but to keep themselves pure,* 1 Tim. v. 22. *Not to prefer one before another, nor do anything by partiality,* 1 Tim. v. 21. *To rebuke them that sin before all, that others also may fear,* 1 Tim. v. 20. *To reject a heretic after once or twice admonition,* Tit. iii. 10. To use the *authority that is given them from the Lord to the edification, not to the destruction* of the Church, 2 Cor. x. 8, and xiii. 10; with divers such like rules specially directed to Christ's officers.

2. Encouragements to well-ruling are peculiarly directed to Christ's officers. For, 1. They are the persons specially commended in that respect; *well-ruling,* 1 Tim. v. 17. *Good and faithful steward,* Luke xii. 42. The angels of the churches are praised for their good government, Rev. ii. 2, 3, 6, and ver. 18, 19. 2. They are the persons to whom the promises, in reference to good government, are directed, as Matt. xvi. 19, and xviii. 18-20; John xx. 21, 23; Matt. xxviii. 19, 20; Luke xii. 42-44; 1 Pet. v. 4. 3. They are the persons whom the Lord will have peculiarly rewarded, now with *double honor,* 1 Tim. v. 17; hereafter with *endless glory,* 1 Pet. v. 4.

3. Discouragements, deterring from ill-governing, are also specially applied to Christ's officers, whether by way of dispraise or threats, &c., Rev. ii. 12, 14-16, and ver. 18, 20.

Now if, 1. Rules for church government, 2. Encouragements in reference to well ruling, and, 3. Discouragements in reference to ill-ruling, be so peculiarly directed by the word of Christ to his own officers, we may conclude,

Therefore the officers of Christ in the Church are the only subjects of power from Christ for the government of his Church.

Object. But the church99 of a particular congregation fully furnished with officers, and rightly walking in judgment and peace, is the first subject of all church authority, as appears from the example of the church of Corinth in the excommunication of the incestuous Corinthian, 1 Cor. v. 1-5; wherein it appears that the presbytery alone did not put forth this power, but the brethren also concurred in this sentence with some act of power, (viz. a negative power:) for, 1. The reproof, for not proceeding to sentence sooner, is directed to the whole Church, as well as to the presbytery. They are all blamed for not mourning, &c., 1 Cor. v. 2. 2. The command is directed to them all, when they are gathered together, (*and what is that but to a church meeting?*) to proceed against him, 1 Cor. v. 4, 13. 3. He declareth this act of theirs, in putting him out, to be a judicial act, ver. 12. 4. Upon his repentance the apostle speaketh to the brethren, as well as to their elders, to forgive him, 2 Cor. ii. 4-10. Consequently, Christ's church officers are not the peculiar, immediate, or only subject of the power of the keys, as hath been asserted.

Ans. I. As for the main proposition asserted in this objection, something hath been formerly laid down to show the unsoundness of it. (See chap. X. near the end.) Whereunto thus much may be superadded. 1. What necessity is there that a particular congregation should be fully furnished with officers, to make it the subject of all church authority? For deacons are one sort of officers, yet what authority is added to the Church by the addition of deacons, whose office it is only to serve tables, Acts vi., not to rule the Church? or if the Church have no deacons, as once it had not, Acts i. 2, and before that, all the time from Christ, wherein is she maimed or defective in her authority? 2. If the Church, fully furnished with officers, yet walk not in judgment and peace, then in such case it is granted, that a particular congregation is not the first subject of all church authority. Then a congregation that walks in error or heresy, or passion, or profaneness, all which are contrary to judgment; and that walks in divisions, schisms, contentions, &c., which are contrary to peace, loseth her authority. Stick but close to this principle, and you will quickly lay the church authority of most independent congregations in the dust. But who shall determine whether they walk in judgment and peace, or not? Not themselves; for that were to make parties judges in their own case, and would produce a very partial sentence. Not sister churches; for all particular churches, according to them, have equal authority, and none may usurp one over another. Not a presbyterial church, for such they do not acknowledge. Then it must be left undetermined, yea undeterminable, (according to their principles;) consequently, who can tell when they have any authority at all? 3. Suppose the congregation had all her officers, and walked in judgment and peace also, yet is she not the first subject of all authority; for there is a synodal authority, beyond a congregational authority, as confessed by Mr. Cotton.100

II. As for the proofs of this proposition asserted here, they seem extremely invalid and unsatisfying. For,

The instance of the church of Corinth excommunicating the incestuous person, will not prove the congregation to be the first subject of all church authority: 1. Partly, because the church of Corinth was a presbyterial church, having several congregations in it, (as hereafter is evidenced, chap. XIII.;) now to argue from the authority of a presbyterial church, to the authority of a congregational, affirmatively, is not cogent. 2. Partly, because here were but two acts of power mentioned in this instance, viz. casting out and receiving again of the incestuous person: suppose the community had joined the presbytery in these two acts, (which yet is not proved,) will it follow therefore they are the first subject of all church authority? Are not ordination of presbyters, determination in case of appeals, of schism, of heresy, &c., acts of authority above the sphere of a single congregation? What one congregation can be instanced in the New Testament that did ever execute any of these acts of authority?

The reasons brought, prove not that the brethren did concur with the presbytery in this sentence with some act of power, as will appear plainly, if they be considered severally.

1. Not the reproof, 1 Cor. v. 2, "And ye are puffed up, and have not rather mourned, that he that hath done this deed might be taken away from among you." Here they are blamed, that they no more laid to heart so vile a scandal, which should have been matter of mourning to the whole congregation; that they instead of mourning were puffed up, gloried in their shame; and that they sluggishly neglected to endeavor, in their sphere, his casting out. And all this blame might justly be charged upon the whole church, the fraternity as well as the presbytery: the scandal of one member should be the grief of the whole body of the church. What then? Hath therefore the fraternity, as well as the presbytery, power to cast him out? That were a miserable consequence indeed: the people should not only have mourned for the sin, but have urged the presbytery to have proceeded to sentence, and after sentence have withdrawn from him, in obedience to the sentence; but none of all these can amount to a proper act of church authority in them.

2. Nor doth the apostle's command prove the people's concurrence in any act of power with the presbytery, 1 Cor. v. 4, 5, "In the name of our Lord Jesus Christ, when ye are gathered together, to deliver such an one unto Satan," &c.: ver. 7, "Purge out therefore the old leaven," &c.: and ver. 13, "Therefore put away from among yourselves that wicked person." In which passages it is supposed the apostle directs his injunction to them all (as well as to their presbytery) when they come together in their church meeting to proceed to sentence.

But against this reason, well ponder upon these considerations, viz: 1. It is certain beyond all controversy, that the apostle did not direct these commands to the whole church of Corinth absolutely, and universally, without all exception and limitation to any members at all: for by his own rule, "Women must be silent in their churches, it being a shame for a woman to speak in the church," 1 Cor. xiv. 34, 35, and children or fools were not able to judge. Hence it is evident that a church absolutely and universally taken, cannot possibly be the ministerial ruling church which hath the authority. 2. It is evident to any man that is but moderately acquainted with the Scriptures, that God useth to direct his commands, reproofs, and other speeches to a people indifferently, and as it were collectively and generally, which yet he intends should be particularly applied and appropriated; not to all, but to this or that person or persons, only among such a people distributively and respectively; according to their respective callings, interests, relations, &c., as in the Old Testament God directs a command to the people of Israel indefinitely, and as it were collectively, to kill enticers to idolatry, false prophets, Deut. xiii. 9; but intended that the judge should sentence him, finding him guilty by witnesses. The Lord also directs his command to all the people, as it were collectively, to put out of the camp "every one that was a leper, and had an issue, or was defiled by the dead," Numb. v. 2; but intended that the priest should peculiarly take and apply this command to himself, who was to judge in these cases. See Lev. xiii. and elsewhere. So in the New Testament the apostle praised the Corinthians indefinitely, and as it were collectively, for "remembering him in all things, and keeping the ordinances as he delivered them to them," 1 Cor. xi. 2; wherein he intended only to commend the virtuous; and after he discommends them indefinitely for "coming together not for better, but for worse," 1 Cor. xi. 17; intending only their dispraise that were herein particularly delinquent among them. Again, he speaks indefinitely, and as it were collectively and generally, "Ye may all prophesy one by one," 1 Cor. xiv. 31; but he intended it only to the prophets respectively, not to all the members; for he saith elsewhere, "Are all prophets?" 1 Cor. xii. 29. And writing to the churches of Galatia, Gal. i. 2, against false teachers he speaks thus to all those churches collectively, "A little leaven leaveneth the whole lump," Gal. v. 9. And, "I would they were even cut off who trouble you," ver. 12. Now every one of these churches were to apply this to themselves respectively, Independents themselves being judges. So here in this present case of the church of Corinth, the apostle directs his commands to them, as it were collectively, about putting away the incestuous person, which commands were particularly to be put in execution by the presbytery in that church in whose hands the church authority was.[101]

Thus taking these commands, 1 Cor. v. 4, 7, 13, though directed indefinitely, and as it were collectively to the whole church, yet intended respectively to be put in execution by the presbytery in that church, they hold forth no concurrence of the people in any act of power at all with the church officers or presbytery. And it is a good note which Cameron[102] hath upon this place, "These things that are written in this epistle are so to be taken of the presbytery and of the people, that every one both of the presbyters and of the people, should interpret the command according to the reason of his office." 3. When the apostle reciteth the proceedings of the church in this very case of the incestuous person, in his 2d epistle, he saith, "Sufficient to such a man is this punishment" (or censure) "which was inflicted of many," 2 Cor. ii. 6. It is very observable, he saith not, *of all*; nor *of many*, but *of the chief ones*, viz. the church officers, who had the rule and government of the church committed to them: (the article *the*being emphatical;) for this word translated *many* may as well be translated chief, denoting worth, &c., as many, denoting number. And in this sense the Holy Ghost ofttimes useth this word in the New Testament; as for instance, "Is not the life better than meat?" Matt. vi. 25. "Behold, a greater than Jonah is here," Matt. xii. 41. "And behold, a greater than Solomon is here," Matt. xii. 41. "To love him with all the heart," &c., "is more than all whole burnt-offerings and sacrifices," Mark xii. 33. And again, ver. 43, "This poor widow hath cast more than all they," &c. And thus it is frequently used to signify quality, worth, greatness, dignity, eminency, &c., and so it may be conveniently interpreted in this of the Corinthians. 4. Though all proper acts of authority appertain only to the church officers, yet we are not against the people's fraternal concurrence therewith. People may incite the presbytery to the acts of their office; people may be present at the administration of censures, &c., by the elders, as Cyprian of old would dispatch all public acts, the people being present; people may judge with a judgment of discretion, acclamation, and approbation, &c., as the elders judge with a judgment of power; and people afterwards may, yea must, withdraw from delinquents sentenced, that the sentence may attain its proposed end. But none of these are properly any acts of power.

3. Nor doth the apostle's expression, verse 12, "Do you not judge them that are within?" prove that the people concur with any authoritative act in the elders' sentence. For, 1. This being spoken to them indefinitely, was to be applied distributively and respectively, only to them to whom it properly appertained, viz. the elders, as hath been showed. They only have authority to judge. 2. Such a judgment is allowed to the saints in church censures, as shall be allowed to them when the saints shall judge the world, yea angels, 1 Cor. vi. 1-3, viz. in both a judgment of acclamation, approbation, &c., as assessors, as people judge at the assizes; not in either a judgment of authority, which the judge and jury only do pronounce.

4. Nor, finally, doth the apostle's direction to forgive the incestuous, being penitent, 2 Cor. ii. 4-10, which seems to be given to all, prove the people's concurrence with the elders in any act of power. For the authoritative forgiving and receiving him again, belonged only to the elders; the charitable forgiving, receiving, and comforting of him, belonged also to the people. As the judge and jury at an assizes, acquit by judgment of authority, the people only by judgment of discretion and acclamation.

Thus it appears how little strength is in this instance of the church of Corinth, (though supposed to be the strongest ground the Independents have,) for the propping up of their popular government, and authoritative suffrage of the people.

SECTION III.

III. Having thus considered the subject of authority and power for church government: 1. Negatively, what it is not, viz. neither the political magistrate, nor yet the community of the faithful, or whole body of the people, Chap. IX. and X. 2. Positively, what it is, viz. Christ's own officers in his church, as hath been explained and evidenced, Sect. 2, of this Chap. 3. Now, in the third and last place, we are to insist a little further upon this subject of the power, by way of explanation: and to inquire, seeing Christ's officers are found to be the subject of this power, in what sense or notion they are the subject and receptacle of this authority and power from Christ, whether jointly or severally; as solitarily and single from one another, or associated and incorporated into assemblies with one another; or in both respects?

For resolution herein we must remember that distribution of the keys, or of proper ecclesiastical power, (which was briefly mentioned before in Part 2, Chap. III.) into that which is,

1. More special and peculiar to the office of some church governors, which by virtue of their office they are to execute and discharge: thus it is peculiar to the minister's office, 1. To preach the word; compare these places together, Matt. xxviii. 18-20, John xx. 21-23, Rom. x. 15, 1 Tim. v. 17, Heb. xiii. 7, 2 Tim. iv. 1, 2, &c. 2. *To dispense the sacraments*, Matt. xxviii. 18-20, 1 Cor. xi. 24, 25. The word and sacraments were joined together in the same commission to the same officers, viz. the preaching presbyters, &c., as is evident in that of Matt. xxviii. 19.

2. More general and common to the office of all church governors, as the power of censures, viz. admonishing, excommunicating, and absolving, and of such other acts as necessarily depend thereupon; wherein not only the preaching, but also the ruling elders are to join and contribute their best assistance; as may be collected from these several testimonies of Scripture, Matt. xviii. 17, 18, *Tell the Church*,103 1 Cor. v. 2-13, 2 Cor. ii. 6-12, compared with Rom. xii. 8, 1 Cor. xii. 28, and 1 Tim. v. 17.

Now these officers of Christ, viz. they that labor in the word and doctrine, and the ruling elders, are the subject of this power of jurisdiction as they are united in one body, hence called a Church, Matth. xviii. 18, viz. the governing or ruling church; for no other can there be meant; and presbytery,104 i.e. a society or assembly of presbyters together, 1 Tim. iv. 14.

The presbyters, elderships, or assemblies wherein these officers are united and associated, are of two sorts, viz: 1. The lesser assemblies, consisting of the ministers and ruling elders in each single congregation; which, for distinction's sake, is styled the congregational eldership. 2. The greater assemblies, consisting of church governors sent from several churches and united into one body, for governing of all these churches within their own bounds, whence their members were sent. These greater assemblies are either presbyterial or synodal. 1. Presbyterial, consisting of the ministers and elders of several adjacent or neighboring single congregations, or parish churches, ruling those several congregations in common; this kind of assembly is commonly called the presbytery, or, for distinction's sake, the classical presbytery, i.e. the presbytery of such a rank of churches. 2. Synodal, consisting of ministers and elders, sent from presbyterial assemblies, to consult and conclude about matters of common and great concernment to the church within their limits. Such was that assembly mentioned, Acts xv. These synodal assemblies are either, 1. Of ministers and elders from several presbyteries within one province, called provincial. 2. Or of ministers and elders from several provinces within one nation, called therefore national. Or, 3. Of ministers and elders from the several nations within the whole Christian world, therefore called ecumenical: for all which assemblies, congregational, presbyterial, and synodal, and the subordination of the lesser to the greater assemblies respectively, there seems to be good ground and divine warrant in the word of God, as (God willing) shall be evinced in the xii., xiii., xiv., and xv. chapters following.

CHAPTER XII.
Of the Divine Right of Congregational Elderships or Kirk Sessions, for the government of the Church.

Touching congregational elderships, consisting of the ministers and ruling elders of the several single congregations, which are called the lesser assemblies, or smaller presbyteries, and which are to manage and order all ecclesiastical matters within themselves, which are of more immediate, private, particular concernment to their own congregations respectively; and consequently, of more easy dispatch, and of more daily use and necessity. Concerning these congregational presbyteries, we shall not now take into consideration either, 1. What are the members constituting and making up these elderships; whether ruling elders by divine warrant may be superadded to the pastors and teachers, and so be associated for the government of the congregation. For the divine right of the ruling elders, distinct from the preaching elder for the government of the church, hath been evidenced at large, Chapter XI., Section 1, foregoing. And if any acts of government in the church belong to the ruling elder at all, sure those acts of common jurisdiction, to be dispatched in these least assemblies, cannot of all other be denied unto him. 2. Nor shall it here be discussed, what the power of congregational elderships is, whether it be universally extensive to all acts of government ecclesiastical whatsoever, without exception or limitation; and that independently, without subordination to the greater assemblies, and without all liberty of appeal thereunto in any cases whatsoever, though of greatest and most common concernment. Which things are well stated and handled by others;105 and will in some measure be considered afterwards in Chapter XV.

3. But the thing for the present to be insisted upon, against the Erastian and prelatical party, is, the divine right of authority and power for church government, which is in congregational presbyteries or elderships, in reference to their respective congregations. Take it thus:

Elderships of single congregations vested and furnished with ecclesiastical authority and power to exercise and dispense acts of government in and over those respective congregations whereunto they do belong, are by divine right warrantable.

For confirmation hereof the light of nature, the institution of Christ, the apostolical practice, and the law of necessity, seem to speak sufficiently unto us.

1. The common light of nature thus far directeth all sorts of smaller societies, whether political or ecclesiastical, to compose all particular and more private differences and offences within themselves; and to decide and determine small, common, easy causes and matters, by smaller courts and judicatories appointed for that end: a vain thing to trouble more and greater assemblies with those matters, that may as well be determined by the lesser. It was

wise and grave counsel which Jethro, Moses' father-in-law, gave to Moses, that he should set up over the people certain judges inferior to himself, who themselves might judge all smaller matters, but all *great and hard matters to be brought to Moses*, Exod. xviii. 22, 26. And our Saviour seems to insinuate, that the Jews had their inferior courts for inferior causes, superior judicatories for greater, in that gradation of his, Matt. v. 22. Likewise they had lesser and greater ecclesiastical assemblies, (as after will appear.) Now, to what use are greater and lesser judicatories, civil or ecclesiastical, but that the lesser and lighter causes may be judged in the inferior, harder and greater in the superior?

2. The institution of Christ recorded Matt. xviii. 15-21, seems to hold forth notably both single congregational elderships, and their power. And this, whether we consider the Jewish form, unto which our Saviour seems to refer; or whether we observe the matter of his discourse.

1. As for the Jewish form of church government (unto which our Saviour here seems to allude) we may observe it was managed by two, if not three sorts of ecclesiastical courts, viz: By the Sanhedrin, presbytery, and synagogue, (much like to the evangelical synod, presbytery, and congregational eldership since Christ.) 1. They had their ecclesiastical,106 as well as their civil Sanhedrin, for high and difficult affairs of the church; which seems first to be constituted, Exod. xxiv. 1, and after decay thereof, it was restored by King Jehoshaphat, 2 Chron. xix. 8; and from this court that national church's reformation proceeded, Neh. vi. 13. 2. Again, it is very probable they had between their Sanhedrin and their synagogue a middle ecclesiastical court called *The Presbytery*, Luke xxii. 66, and Acts xxii. 5, *and the whole presbytery.* Let such as are expert in Jewish antiquities and their polity, consider and judge. 3. Finally, they had their lesser judicatories in their synagogues, or congregational meetings: for, their synagogues were not only for prayer, and the ministry of the word, in reading and expounding the Scriptures, but also for public censures, correcting of offences, &c., as that phrase seems to import, "And I punished them oft in every synagogue," Acts xxvi. 11. His facts and proceedings, it is true, were cruel, unjust, impious. But why inflicted *in every synagogue*, rather than in other places, and that by virtue of the *high priest's letters*, Acts ix. 1, 2; but there the Jews had judicatories, that inflicted public punishments upon persons ecclesiastically offending? Besides, we read often in the New Testament of the *rulers of the synagogue*, as Mark v. 35, 36, 38; Luke viii. 41, and xiii. 14; and of Crispus and Sosthenes the chief *rulers of the synagogue*, Acts xviii. 8, 17; whence is intimated to us, that these synagogues had their rule and government in themselves; and that this rule was not in one person, but in divers together; for if there were chief rulers, there were also inferiors subordinate unto them: but this is put out of doubt, in Acts xiii. 15, where after the lecture of the law and the prophets, *the rulers of the synagogue sent unto them—synagogue* in the singular number, and rulers in the plural. Thus analogically there should be ecclesiastical rulers and governors in every single congregation, for the well guiding thereof. But if this satisfy not, add hereunto the material passages in our Saviour's speech.

2. Now touching the matter of our Saviour's discourse, it makes this very clear to us; for by a gradation he leadeth us from admonition private and personal, to admonition before two or three witnesses, and from admonition before two or three witnesses, to the representative body of one church, (as the phrase *tell the church* must here necessarily be interpreted,) if there the difference can be composed, the offence removed, or the cause ended; rather than unnecessarily render the offence, and so our brother's shame, more public and notorious. And that the presbytery or eldership of a particular congregation, vested with power to hear and determine such cases as shall be brought before them, is partly, though not only here intended, seems evident in the words following, which are added for the strengthening and confirming of what went before in ver. 17: "Verily, I say unto you, whatsoever ye shall bind on earth shall be bound in heaven; and whatsoever ye shall loose on earth shall be loosed in heaven. Again, I say unto you, that if two of you shall agree on earth as touching any thing that they shall ask, it shall be done for them of my Father which is in heaven. For where two or three are gathered together in my name, there am I in the midst of them," Matt. xviii. 18-20. In which passages these things are to be noted: 1. That this church to which the complaint is to be made, is invested with power of *binding* and *loosing*, and that so authoritatively that what by this church shall be bound or loosed on earth shall also be

bound or loosed in heaven, according to Christ's promise. 2. That these acts of *binding* or *loosing*, may be the acts but of two or three, and therefore consequently of the eldership of a particular congregation; for where such a juridical act was dispatched by a classical presbytery, it is said to be done of *many*, 2 Cor. ii. 6, because that in such greater presbyteries there are always more than *two or three*. And though some do pretend, that the faults here spoken of by our Saviour in this place, were injuries, not scandals; and that the church here mentioned was not any ecclesiastical consistory, or court, but the civil Sanhedrin, a court of civil judicature; and yet most absurdly they interpret the binding and loosing here spoken of, to be doctrinal and declarative; not juridical and authoritative; as if the doctrinal binding and loosing were in the power of the civil Sanhedrin:107 yet all these are but vain, groundless pretences and subterfuges, without substance or solidity, as the learned and diligent reader may easily find demonstrated by consulting these judicious authors mentioned in the foot note,108 to whom for brevity's sake he is referred for satisfaction in these and divers such like particulars.

3. The consideration of the apostolical practice, and state of the Church of God in those times, may serve further to clear this matter to us. For, 1. We sometimes read of single congregations; and as the Holy Ghost doth call the whole body of Christ *the Church*, Matt. xvi. 18, 1 Cor. xii. 28, and often elsewhere; and the larger particular members of that body of Christ (partaking the nature of the whole, as a drop of water is as true water as the whole ocean) churches; as, *the church of Jerusalem*, Acts viii. 1; *the church of Antioch*, Acts xiii. 1; *the church of Ephesus*, Rev. ii. 1; *the church of Corinth*, 2 Cor. i. 1; (these being the greater presbyterial churches, as after will appear, Chap. XIII.;) so the same holy Spirit of Christ is pleased to style single congregations, *churches*, "Let women keep silence in the churches," 1 Cor. xiv. 34, i.e. in the single congregations of this one church of Corinth: and often mention is made of the church that is in such or such an *house*, as Rom. xvi. 5; 1 Cor. xvi. 19; Col. iv. 15; Philem. 2; whether this be interpreted of the church made up only of the members of that family, or of the church that ordinarily did meet in such houses, it implies a single congregation. Now shall single congregations have the name and nature of churches, and shall we imagine they had not in them the ordinary standing church officers, viz. pastors and teachers, governments, or elders *ruling well*, and helps or deacons? or is it probable they were furnished with these officers, and yet the officers furnished with no power for the government of these single congregations at all? 2. We find that the apostles being crowned with such success in their ministry, as to be instruments of converting such multitudes to the faith as were sufficient to make up many several churches from time to time, did diligently take care to ordain them presbyters, or elders *in every church*, Acts xiv. 23; Tit. i. 5. Now can it be clearly evidenced by any, that these were not ruling as well as preaching presbyters; especially when it appears by other places that the primitive churches had both? Rom. xii. 8; 1 Cor. xii. 28;

1 Tim. v. 17. Or can we think that the apostles were not as careful to erect elderships in several congregations, as to appoint elders? otherwise how could the apostles have answered it to their Lord and Master Jesus Christ, in leaving them without that necessary provision of government, which Christ himself had allowed to them, at least, in some cases, as hath been evidenced?

4. Finally, necessity (which is a strong and cogent law) plainly and forcibly pleads for elderships in particular congregations endowed with authority and power from Christ for government within themselves. For, 1. How wearisome a thing would it be to all congregations, should every one of their members be bound to attend upon synods and greater presbyteries, (which in the country are at a great distance from them,) in all ecclesiastical matters of judicature, if they had no relief in their own congregations? How impossible would it be for the greater presbyteries, not only to hear and determine all hard and weighty, but also all small and easy causes that would be brought before them? And what should become of such a congregation as either voluntarily transplants itself, or is accidentally cast among heathens or pagans in far countries, where there are no Christians or churches to join and associate withal, if they be denied an authoritative presbytery within themselves, for preventing and healing of scandals, and preserving themselves from destruction and ruin, which anarchy would unavoidably bring upon them?

CHAPTER XIII.

Of the Divine Right of Presbyteries, (for distinction's sake called Classical Presbyteries,) for the government of the Church.

Having spoken of the lesser, viz. congregational elderships, we come now to the greater ruling assemblies, which are either presbyterial or synodal. And first, of the presbyterial assembly, or classical presbytery, viz. an assembly made up of the presbyters of divers neighboring single congregations, for governing of all those respective congregations in common, whereunto they belong, in all matters of common concernment and greater difficulty in the Church. The divine warrant and right of this presbytery, and of the power thereof for church government, may principally be evidenced, 1. By the light of nature. 2. By the light of Scripture, which light of Scripture was followed by the Church in the ages after the apostolical times.

I. The light of nature and right reason may discover to us (though more dimly) the divine warrant of the greater presbyteries, and of their power for the governing of the church. For,

1. There are many ecclesiastical matters which are of common concernment to many single congregations, as trial of church officers, ordination and deposition of ministers, dispensation of censures, judicial determination of controversies, resolution in difficult cases of conscience, ordering of things indifferent, &c.; here the rule holds well, that which concerns many congregations, is not to be considered and determined upon only by one, but those many concerned and interested therein.

2. Single congregational elderships stand in need of all mutual help and assistance one of another in the Lord, being, 1. Inwardly weak in themselves; too prone to be turned out of the way, Heb. xii. 13, Gal. v. 15, and too feeble for divers great tasks: as examination and ordination of ministers, &c., which weakness is healed by association with others assisting them. 2. Outwardly opposed by many dangerous and subtle adversaries: men as grievous wolves, &c., Acts xx. 28-30; 2 Pet. ii. 1; Phil. iii. 2; 1 Tim. iv. 1-7; Eph. iv. 14; devils, 1 Pet. v. 8. In such cases two are better than one: "Wo to them that are alone; if they fall, who shall take them up?"

3. Such intricate cases may fall out as cannot be determined and settled by the eldership of a single congregation. As for instance, some member in the congregation may conceive himself so wronged by the eldership thereof, that he cannot submit to their unjust sentence; shall he not in such case have liberty of appeal from them? If not, then he is left without a remedy, (which is the calamity of the Independent government.) If he may, whether shall he appeal regularly but to an associated presbytery? therefore there must be such a presbytery to appeal unto. Again, there may be a controversy betwixt the whole congregation, and their presbytery; yea, the presbytery itself may be equally divided against itself; yea, one single congregation may have a great and weighty contest with another sister congregation, (all single congregations being equal in power and authority, none superior, none inferior to others.) Now, in these and such like cases, suppose both parties be resolute and wilful, and will not yield to any bare moral suasion or advice without some superior authority, what healing is left in such cases, without the assistance of an authoritative presbytery, wherein the whole hath power to regulate all the parts?

4. Single congregations, joined in vicinity and neighborhood to one another, should avoid divisions, (which are destructive to all societies, as well ecclesiastical as civil,) and maintain peace and unity among themselves, (which is conservative to all societies;) neither of which, without associated presbyteries, can be firmly and durably effected. Both which ought with all diligence to be endeavored. For, 1. Peace and unity in the Church are in themselves amiable, and ought to be promoted, Psal. cxxxiii. 1, &c.; Eph. iv. 3, 13; 1 Cor. i. 10. 2. Schisms and divisions are simply evil, and all appearance, cause, and occasion thereof, ought carefully to be avoided, 1 Cor. xii. 25; Rom. xvi. 17; 1 Thes. iv. 22. 3. All congregations are but as so many branches, members, parts of that one church, one body, one family, one commonwealth, one kingdom, whereof Christ is Head, Lord, and King; and therefore they

should communicate together, and harmoniously incorporate and associate with one another, (so far as may be,) for the common good, peace, unity, and edification of all. See 1 Cor. xii. 12-29; Eph. ii. 12-16, and iv. 12-14, and v. 23-25.

II. The light of Scripture will hold forth the divine warrant of greater presbyteries and their power for church government, far more clearly than the light of nature. Forasmuch as we find in the Scriptures a pattern of these greater presbyteries, and of their presbyterial government over divers single congregations in common in the primitive apostolical churches. For the greater evidence and perspicuity hereof, take this proposition:

Jesus Christ our Mediator hath laid down in his word a pattern of presbyterial government in common over divers single congregations in one Church, for a rule to his Church in all after ages. For confirmation hereof, there are chiefly these three positions to make good, which are comprised in this proposition, viz: 1. That there is in the word a pattern of divers single congregations in one church. 2. That there is in the word a pattern of one presbyterial government in common over divers single congregations in one church. 3. Finally, that the pattern of the said presbyterial government, is for a rule to the churches of Christ in all after ages.

POSITION I.

That there is in the word a pattern of divers single congregations in one church, may be plentifully evinced by four instances of churches, (to mention no more,) viz. the churches of Jerusalem, Antioch, Ephesus, and Corinth. Touching which four these two things are clear in the Scripture, viz: 1. That every of them was one church. 2. That in every one of these churches there were more congregations than one. Both which will fully evince a pattern of divers single congregations in one church held forth in the word.

1. The former of these, viz. That every one of these was one church, may be proved by induction of particulars. 1. All the believers in Jerusalem were one church; hence they are often comprised under the word church, of the singular number:—"Against the church which was at Jerusalem," Acts viii. 1. "Then tidings of these things came unto the ears of the church which was in Jerusalem," Acts ii. 22. "And when they were come to Jerusalem, they were received of the church, and of the apostles and elders," Acts xv. 4. 2. All the believers in Antioch were one church. "Now there were in the church that was at Antioch, certain prophets," Acts xiii. 1. "And when he had found him, he brought him to Antioch. And it came to pass, that a whole year they assembled themselves with the church, and taught much people, and the disciples were first called Christians in Antioch," Acts xi. 26. 3. All the believers in Ephesus were one church: "And from Miletus he sent to Ephesus, and called the elders of the church," Acts xx. 17. And after he gives them this charge, "Take heed therefore to yourselves, and to all the flock, over which the Holy Ghost hath made you overseers, to feed the church of God," ver. 28; all were but *one flock, one church.* "Unto the angel of the church of Ephesus, write," Rev. ii. 1. 4. All the believers in Corinth were one church, and comprised under that singular word, church: "Unto the church of God which is at Corinth," 1 Cor. i. 2. "Paul, an apostle of Jesus Christ, by the will of God, and Timothy our brother, unto the church of God which is at Corinth," 2 Cor. i. 1. Thus in all these four instances it is clear beyond all contradiction, that they were every of them respectively one church.

The latter of these, viz. that these primitive apostolical churches of Jerusalem, Antioch, Ephesus, and Corinth, were not every of them severally and respectively only one single congregation, (as some imagine,) but consisted every of them of more congregations than one. This shall be manifested in these four churches severally, as followeth:

The church of Jerusalem in Judea contained in it more congregations than one. This may be convincingly evidenced divers ways, particularly from, 1. The multitude of believers in that church. 2. The multitude of church officers there. 3. The variety of languages there. 4. The manner of the Christians' public meetings in those primitive times, both in the church of Jerusalem, and in other churches.

1. From the multitude of believers in the church of Jerusalem. For it is palpably evident to any impartial reader that will not wilfully shut his eyes, and subject his reason unto the groundless dictates of men, against the clear light of the Scripture, that there were more believers in the church of Jerusalem, than could ordinarily meet in one congregation, to partake of all the ordinances of Christ.

95

And this may fully appear by these many instances following. 1. Christ after his resurrection, and before his ascension, "was seen of above five hundred brethren at once," 1 Cor. xv. 6. 2. "After that of James, then of all the apostles," ver. 7. 3. At the election of Matthias, and before Christ's ascension, there were disciples together, the "company of their names together was as it were one hundred and twenty," Acts i. 15. 4. At Peter's sermon, "they that gladly received his word, were baptized. And that day were added about three thousand souls," Acts ii. 1, 4. 5. And "The Lord added to the Church daily such as should be saved," ver. 27. 6. Afterwards at another of Peter's sermons, "Many of them that heard the word believed; and the number of the men was about five thousand," Acts iv. 4. 7. After that, "Believers were the more added to the Lord, multitudes both of men and women," Acts v. 14. 8. Furthermore, the disciples multiplying, and the work of the ministry thereupon much increasing, the apostles were necessitated to appoint seven deacons for serving of tables, that they might wholly "give themselves to the ministry of the word and prayer," Acts vi. 1 to 7; whence some have thought, that there were seven congregations in Jerusalem, a deacon for every one. Certainly there were rather more than fewer, (saith the author of the Assertion of the Government of the Church of Scotland,109) though we cannot determine how many. However this, the Holy Ghost clearly testifieth that "The word of God increased, and the number of the disciples in Jerusalem multiplied greatly." 9. "And a great company of the priests became obedient to the faith," Acts vi. 7; and probably the example of the priests drew on multitudes to the Gospel. All these forementioned were in a short time converted, and became members of this one church of Jerusalem, and that before the dispersion occasioned by the persecution of the Church, Acts viii. 1. Now should we put all these together, viz. both the number of believers expressed in particular, which is 8,620, and the multitudes so often expressed in the general, (which, for aught we know, might be many more than the former,) what a vast multitude of believers was there in Jerusalem! and how impossible was it for them to meet all together in one congregation, to partake of all the ordinances of Jesus Christ! 10. In like manner, after the dispersion forementioned, the word so prospered, and the disciples brought into the faith by it, so multiplied, that it was still far more impossible for all the believers in the church of Jerusalem to meet in one congregation to partake of all the ordinances of Christ, than before. For it is said, "Then had the churches rest throughout all Judea" (and the church of Jerusalem in Judea was doubtless one of those churches) "and Galilee and Samaria, and were edified; and walking in the fear of the Lord, and comfort of the Holy Ghost, were multiplied." 11. Again, "the word of the Lord increased and multiplied," Acts xii. 24. 12. Furthermore, when Paul, with other disciples, his fellow-travellers, came to Jerusalem, and "declared to James and the elders, what things God had wrought by his ministry among the Gentiles—They glorified the Lord, and said unto him, Thou seest, brother, how many" myriads (or ten thousands) "of believing Jews there are, and they are all zealous of the law"—Acts xxi. 20. Our translation seems herein very defective, rendering it how many thousands; whereas it should be, according to the Greek, how many ten thousands: and these myriads seem to be in the church of Jerusalem, seeing it is said of them, ver. 22, "The multitude must needs come together, for they will hear that thou art come." Now considering this emphatical expression, not only *thousands*, but *ten thousand*: not *only ten thousand* in the singular number, but *ten thousands, myriads*, in the plural number: nor only *myriads, ten thousands*, in the plural number, but *how many ten thousands*; we cannot in reason imagine but there were at least three ten thousands, viz: thirty thousand believers, and how all they should meet together in one congregation for all ordinances, let the reader judge. Thus far of the proof, from the multitude of believers in the church of Jerusalem.

Except. But the five thousand mentioned Acts iv. 4, are no new number added to the three thousand, but the three thousand included in the five thousand, as Calvin and Beza think.

Ans. 1. Then it is granted that five thousand one hundred and twenty, besides an innumerable addition of converts, were in Jerusalem; which if such a number, and multitudes besides, could for edification meet in one place, to partake of all the ordinances, let the reader judge.

2. Though Calvin and Beza think the three thousand formerly converted to be included in this number of five thousand, Acts iv. 4, yet divers both ancient and modern interpreters are of another mind, as Augustine. There came unto the body of the Lord in number three thousand faithful men; also by another miracle wrought, there came other five thousand.110 These five thousand are altogether diverse from the three thousand converted at the first sermon: so Lorinus, Aretius, and divers others.

3. Besides a great number of testimonies, there are reasons to induce us to believe, that the three thousand are not included in the five thousand, viz: 1. As the three thousand mentioned in Acts ii. 41, did not comprehend the one hundred and twenty mentioned Acts i. 15, so it holds in proportion that the three thousand mentioned there, are not comprehended here in Acts iv. 4. Besides, 2. This sermon was not by intention to the church, or numbers already converted, but by occasion of the multitude flocking together to behold the miracle Peter and John wrought on the "man that was lame from his mother's womb;" as Acts iii. 10-12; so that 'tis more than probable that the five thousand mentioned Acts iv. 4, are a number superadded besides the three thousand already converted.

Except. But suppose such a number as three thousand, and afterwards five thousand were converted in Jerusalem, yet these remained not constant members of that Church, for the three thousand were not dwellers at Jerusalem, but strangers who came out of all countries to keep the feast of Pentecost: yea, Acts ii. 9, they are said expressly to be "dwellers of Mesopotamia, Cappadocia," &c., and so might erect churches where they came.

Ans. 1. 'Tis said, Acts ii. 14, "Peter standing" (when he began to preach this sermon wherein the three thousand were converted) "said, Ye men of Judea, and all ye that dwell at Jerusalem, hearken to my voice;" intimating that these he preached to dwelt at Jerusalem.

But grant that some of these men that heard Peter's sermon were formerly dwellers in Mesopotamia and Cappadocia, what hinders but that they might be now dwellers at Jerusalem?

3. The occasion of their coming up to Jerusalem at this time was not only the observation of the feast of Pentecost, (which lasted but a day,) but also the great expectation that the people of the Jews then had of the appearance of the Messiah in his kingdom, as we may collect from Luke xix. 11, where it is said, "They thought the kingdom of God should immediately appear;" so that now they might choose to take up their dwellings at Jerusalem, and not return, as they had been wont, at the end of their usual feasts.

4 The Holy Ghost makes mention that in the particular places mentioned, ver. 9, 10, that of all those nations there were some that dwelt at Jerusalem; read Acts ii. 5, "There were dwelling at Jerusalem Jews, devout men out of every nation under heaven;" if out of every nation, then out of those nations there specified; and even there dwelling at Jerusalem. 5. Those who were scattered by reason of persecution into Judea and Samaria, and other parts of the world, did not erect new churches, but were still members of that one church in Jerusalem; so saith the Scripture expressly, that "they" (of the church of Jerusalem) "were all scattered abroad throughout the region of Judea and Samaria," Acts viii. 1.

Except. Although it should be granted that before the dispersion mentioned Acts viii. 1, 2, the number was so great that they could not meet together in one place, yet the persecution so wasted and scattered them all, that there were no more left than might meet in one congregation?

Ans. After the dispersion there were more believers in Jerusalem than could meet together in one place for all acts of worship, as appears by Acts ix. 31, "The churches had rest throughout all Judea," &c., "and were multiplied;" Acts xii. 24, "The word of God grew and multiplied;" and Acts xxi. 20, James saith of the believers of this church, "how many thousands of the Jews there are which believe, and are zealous of the law;" or, as it is in the Greek, thou seest how many *ten thousands* there are of the Jews which believe; this text will evince, that there were many thousands in the church of Jerusalem after the dispersion, as hath been observed: and if this number were not more after the dispersion than could meet together to partake of all ordinances, let the reader judge.

Except. But the text saith expressly, all were scattered except the apostles.

Ans. All must be understood either of all the believers, or all the teachers and church officers in the church of Jerusalem, except believers; but it cannot be understood of all the believers that they were scattered: and therefore it must be understood that all the teachers and church officers were scattered, except the apostles. That all the believers were not scattered will easily appear: For, 1. 'Tis said that Paul broke into houses, "haling men and women, committed them to prison," ver. 3, and this he did in Jerusalem, Acts xxvi. 10; therefore all could not be scattered. 2. "They that were scattered, preached the word," ver. 4, which all the members, men and women, could not do; therefore by all that were scattered must of necessity be meant, not the body of believers in the church, but only the officers of the church. 3. If all the believers were scattered, to what end did the apostles tarry at Jerusalem—to preach to the walls? this we cannot imagine.

Except. But can any think the teachers were scattered, and the ordinary believers were not, except we suppose the people more courageous to stay by it than their teachers?

Ans. It is hard to say, that those that are scattered in a persecution, are less courageous than those that stay and suffer. In the time of the bishops' tyranny, many of the Independent ministers did leave this kingdom, while others of their brethren did abide by it, endured the heat and burden of the day, "had trial of cruel mockings, bonds and imprisonments:" now the Independent ministers that left us, would think we did them wrong, should we say that they were less courageous than those that stayed behind, enduring the hot brunt of persecution.

II. From the multitude of church officers in Jerusalem, it may further appear, that there were more congregations than one in the church of Jerusalem. For there were many apostles, prophets, and elders in this church of Jerusalem, as is plain, if we consider these following passages in the Acts of the Apostles. After Christ's ascension, "the eleven apostles returned to Jerusalem, and continued in prayer and supplication," Acts i. 12-14. Matthias chosen by lot, was also "numbered with the eleven apostles," Acts i. 26. "And when the day of Pentecost was fully come, they were all with one accord in one place," Acts ii. 1. "Peter standing up with the eleven, lift up his voice and said," Acts ii. 14. "They were pricked in their heart, and said to Peter and to the rest of the apostles, Men and brethren, what shall we do?" Acts ii. 37. "And the same day there were added about three thousand souls, and they continued steadfastly in the apostles' doctrine and fellowship, and in breaking of bread, and in prayers," Acts ii. 42. "And with great power gave the apostles witness of the resurrection of the Lord Jesus," Acts iv. 33. "As many as were possessors of lands or houses, sold them, and brought the prices of the things that were sold, and laid them down at the apostles' feet," Acts iv. 34, 35, 37. "Then the twelve called the multitude of the disciples to them," Acts vi. 2. "Now, when the apostles which were at Jerusalem," Acts viii. 14. "They determined that Paul and Barnabas and certain other of them should go up to Jerusalem unto the apostles and elders about this question. And when they were come to Jerusalem, they were received of the church, and of the apostles and elders; and the apostles and elders came together," Acts xv. 2, 4, 6, 22, 23; xi. 30. And "in those days came prophets from Jerusalem unto Antioch," Acts xi. 27. In all which places, the multitude of apostles, elders, and prophets in this church of Jerusalem is evident. And it is further observable, that the apostles devolved the serving of tables upon the seven deacons, that they might wholly "give themselves to prayer and the ministry of the word," Acts vi, 2; which needed not, nor would there have been full employment for the apostles, if there had not been divers congregations in that one church of Jerusalem.

Except. 'Tis true, the apostles were for a time in Jerusalem, yet when in Judea or elsewhere any received the gospel, the apostles went abroad to erect other churches.

Ans. Touching the apostles going abroad, there can be given but one instance, Acts viii. 14, where the whole twelve went not forth, but only two were sent, viz. Peter and John: but suppose it were granted, that upon some special occasions the apostles went out from Jerusalem, can it be imagined that the apostles' ordinary abode would be at Jerusalem, to attend only one single congregation, as if that would fill all their hands with work?

Except. The apostles were well employed when they met in an upper room, and had but one hundred and twenty for their flock, and this for forty days together; now if they stayed in Jerusalem when they had but one hundred and twenty, and yet had their hands filled with work, the presence of the apostles argues not more congregations in Jerusalem than could meet in one place for all acts of worship.

Ans. 1. From Christ's ascension (immediately after which they went up to the upper chamber) to the feast of Pentecost, there were but ten days, not forty; so that there is one mistake.

2. During that time betwixt Christ's ascension and the feast of Pentecost, (whether ten or forty days is not very material,) the apostles were especially taken up in prayer and supplication, waiting for the promise of the Spirit to qualify them for the work of the ministry: now, because the twelve apostles, before they had received the extraordinary gifts of the Spirit, did continue for a short time in Jerusalem with a small number in prayer, will it therefore follow that after they had received these extraordinary gifts, that they were bound up within the limits of one single congregation?

Except. The argument that there were many teachers in Jerusalem, proves not that there were more congregations in Jerusalem than one, because there were then many gifted men, which were not officers, which yet occasionally instructed others, as Aquila did Apollos; therefore it seems they were only gifted persons, not officers.

Ans. 1. Grant that in those times there were many gifted men, not in office, which might occasionally instruct others, as Aquila did Apollos; yet it is further to be noted, that,

2. This instructing must be either private, or public; if private only, then the objection is of no force, (because these teachers instructed publicly;) if in public, then if this objection were of force, it would follow, that women might instruct publicly, because Priscilla, as well as Aquila, instructed Apollos.

3. The current of expositors say, that the seventy disciples were at Jerusalem among the one hundred and twenty, Acts i. 16, who were teachers by office.

III. From the variety of languages among the disciples at Jerusalem, it is evident there were more congregations than one in that one church: the diversity of languages among them is plainly mentioned in divers places, "And there were dwelling at Jerusalem, Jews, devout men out of every nation under heaven. Now every man heard them speak in his own language," &c., Acts ii. 5, 8-12. Now, of those that heard this variety of languages, and Peter's sermon thereupon, "They that gladly received his word, were baptized, and the same day there were added about three thousand souls," Acts ii. 41, which diversity of languages necessitated those members of the church of Jerusalem to enjoy the ordinances in divers distinct congregations in their own language. And that they might so do, the Spirit furnished the apostles, &c., with diversity of languages, which diversity of languages were as well for edification of them within the Church, as for a sign to them that were without.

Except. Though the Jews being dispersed were come in from other countries, yet they were all generally learned, and understood the Hebrew tongue, the language of their own nation, so that diversity of tongues proves not, that of necessity there must be distinct places to meet in.

Ans. 1. It is easier said than proved, that the Jews were so generally skilled in the Hebrew tongue, when, while they were scattered in Media and Parthia, and other places, they had no universities or schools of learning. Besides, it is not to be forgotten, that the proper language or dialect in those days in use among the Jews was Syriac; as appears by divers instances of Syriac words in the New Testament, as of the Jews' own terms: Acts i. 19, which "in their proper tongue, is called Aceldama;" John xix. 13. 17, *Gabbatha, Golgotha*, &c.; Mark xv. 34,*Eloi, Eloi, lama-sabachthani*; with divers other pure Syriac terms. Grant they did; yet,

2. There were in Jerusalem proselytes also, Romans, Cappadocians, Cretians, and Arabians, Acts ii. 10, 11; how could they be edified in the faith, if only one congregation, where nothing but Hebrew was spoken, met in Jerusalem; if so be there were not other congregations for men of other languages, that understood not the Hebrew tongue?

IV. From the manner of Christians' public meetings in those primitive times, both in the church of Jerusalem and in other churches. It is plain that the multitudes of Christians in Jerusalem, and other churches, could not possibly meet all together in one single congregation, inasmuch as they had no public temples, or capacious places for worship and partaking of all ordinances, (as we now have,) but private places, *houses, chambers*, or *upper rooms*, (as the unsettled state of the Church and troublesomeness of those times would permit,) which in all probability were of no great extent, nor any way able to contain in them so many thousand believers at once, as there were: "They met from house to house, to break bread," Acts ii. 46. "In an upper room the apostles with the women and brethren continued in prayer and supplication," Acts i. 12-14. We read of their meetings in the *house of Mary*, Acts xii. 12. In the school *of one Tyrannus*, Acts xix. 9. In an *upper chamber at Troas*, Acts xx. 8. In *Paul's own hired house* at Rome, Acts xxviii. 30, 31. In the *house of Aquila and Priscilla*, where the church met, therefore called the *church in his house*, Rom. xvi. 5; 1 Cor. xvi. 19. In the *house of Nimphas*, Col. iv. 15, and in the *house of Archippus*, Philem. 2. This was their manner of public meetings in the apostles' times: which also continued in the next ages, as saith Eusebius,111 till, by indulgence of succeeding emperors, they had large churches, houses of public meeting erected for them.

To sum up all: 1. There were in the church at Jerusalem greater numbers of believers than could possibly meet at once to partake of all Christ's ordinances. 2. There were more church officers than one single congregation could need, or than could be fully employed therein, unless we will say, that they preached but seldom. 3. There was such diversity of languages among them, that they must needs rank themselves into several congregations, according to their languages, else he that spoke in one language to hearers of many several languages, would be a barbarian to them, and they to him. 4. Finally, their places of ordinary meeting were private, of small extent, incapable of containing so many thousands at once as there were believers; and by all these, how evident is it, that there must needs be granted that there were more congregations than one in this one church of Jerusalem!

II. The church of Antioch, in Syria, consisted also of more congregations than one. This appears,

1. From the multitude of believers at Antioch. For, 1. After the dispersion upon Saul's persecution, *the Lord Jesus was preached at Antioch, and a great number believed*, &c., Acts xi. 21. 2. Upon *Barnabas's* preaching there, *much people was added to the Lord*, Acts xi. 24. 3. *Barnabas* and *Saul* for a year together taught much people there, and disciples there so mightily multiplied, that there Christ's disciples first received the eminent and famous denomination of CHRISTIANS, and so were and still are called throughout the whole world, Acts xi. 25, 26.

2. From the multitudes of prophets and preachers that ministered at Antioch. For, 1. Upon the dispersion of the Jews at Jerusalem, *divers of them (being men of Cyprus and Cyrene) preached the Lord Jesus at Antioch*, Acts xi. 20; here must be three or four preachers at least, otherwise they would not be *men of Cyprus and Cyrene*. 2. After this *Barnabas* was sent to preach at Antioch; there is a fifth, Acts xi. 22-24. 3. *Barnabas* finds so much work at *Antioch*, that he goes to Tarsus to bring *Saul* thither to help him; there is a sixth, ver. 25, 26. 4. Besides these, *there came prophets from Jerusalem to Antioch in those days*; there are at least two more, viz. eight in all, Acts xi. 27, 28. 4. Further, besides *Barnabas* and *Saul*, three more teachers are named, viz. *Simon called Niger, Lucius of Cyrene, and Manaen*, Acts xii. 1-3. 6. Yea, "Paul and Barnabas continued in Antioch, teaching and preaching the word of the Lord, with many others also," Acts xv. 35. Now sum up all, what a multitude of believers, and what a college of preachers were here at Antioch! How is it possible that all these preachers should bustle themselves about one congregation (and doubtless they abhorred idleness) in dispensing the ordinances of Christ to them only? or how could so many members meet in one single congregation at once, ordinarily to partake of all ordinances?

III. The church of Ephesus (*in Asia Minor*, Acts xix. 22) had in it more congregations than one: For,

1. The number of prophets and preachers at Ephesus were many. *Paul* continued there *two years and three months*, Acts xix. 8, 10; and *Paul* settled there about twelve *disciples who prophesied*, Acts xix. 1, 6, 7. And how should these thirteen ministers be employed, if there were not many congregations? Compare also Acts xx. 17, 28, 36, 37, where it is said of the bishops of Ephesus, that "Paul kneeled down and prayed with them all, and they all wept sore." Here is a good number implied.

2. The gift of tongues also was given unto all these twelve prophets, Acts xix. 6, 7. To what end, if they had not several congregations of several languages, to speak in these several tongues unto them?

3. The multitude of believers must needs be great at Ephesus: For, 1. Why should *Paul*, who had universal commission to plant churches in all the world, stay *above two*

years together at Ephesus if no more had been converted there than to make up one single congregation? Acts xix. 8, 10. 2. During this space, "all that dwelt in Asia," usually meeting at Ephesus for worship, "heard the word of the Lord, both Jews and Greeks," Acts xix. 10. 3. At the knowledge of *Paul's* miracles, "fear fell upon all the Jews and Greeks dwelling at Ephesus, and the name of the Lord Jesus was magnified," Acts xix. 17. 4. *Many* of the believers *came and confessed, and showed their deeds*, ver. 18, whereby is intimated that more did believe than did thus. 5. "Many also of them that used curious arts brought their books together, and burned them before all men, and they counted the price of them, and found it fifty thousand pieces of silver," (this they would never have done publicly if the major part, or at least a very great and considerable part of the city, had not embraced the faith, that city being so furiously zealous in their superstition and idolatry,) "so mightily grew the word of God, and prevailed," Acts xix. 19, 20. 6. *Paul* testifies that at Ephesus *a great door and effectual was open unto him*, viz. a most advantageous opportunity of bringing in a mighty harvest of souls to Christ, 1 Cor. xvi. 8, 9. Put all together, 1. The number of prophets and preachers; 2. The gifts of tongues conferred upon those prophets; and, 3. The multitude of believers which so abounded at Ephesus: how is it possible to imagine, upon any solid ground, that there was no more but one single congregation in the church of Ephesus?

IV. The church of Corinth in Græcia comprised in it also more congregations than one, as may be justly concluded from, 1. The multitude of believers. 2. The plenty of ministers. 3. The diversity of tongues and languages. 4. And the plurality of churches at Corinth. Let all these be well compared together.

1. From the multitude of believers. There appears to be a greater number of believers at Corinth than could all at once meet together to partake of all the ordinances of Christ: For, 1. At Paul's first coming to Corinth, and at his first sermon preached in the house of Justus, it is said, "And Crispus, the chief ruler of the synagogue, believed on the Lord, and all his house, and many of the Corinthians hearing, believed and were baptized," Acts xviii. 1, 7, 8. Here is Crispus and all his house, (which probably was very great, he being the chief ruler of the synagogue,) and *many of the Corinthians, believing*, an excellent first-fruits; for who can justly say but Paul at his first sermon converted so many as might be sufficient to make up one single congregation? 2. Immediately after this (Paul having shook his raiment against the Jews, who, contrary to his doctrine, opposed themselves and blasphemed; and having said unto them, "Your blood be upon your own heads, I am clean: from henceforth I will go unto the Gentiles," Acts xviii. 6) the Lord comforts Paul against the obstinacy of the Jews by the success his ministry should have among the Gentiles in the city of Corinth: "Then spake the Lord to Paul in the night by a vision, Be not afraid, but speak, and hold not thy peace: for I am with thee, and no man shall set on thee to hurt thee: for I have much people in this city," Acts xviii. 9, 10. *Much people* belonging to God, according to his secret predestination, over and besides those that already were actually his by effectual vocation. And *much people*, in respect of the Jews that opposed and blasphemed, (who were exceeding many,) otherwise it would have been but small comfort to Paul if by *much people* should be meant no more than could meet at once in one small single congregation. 3. Paul himself continued at Corinth "a year and six months teaching the word of God among them," Acts xviii. 11. To what end should Paul the apostle of the Gentiles stay so long in one place, if he had not seen the Lord's blessing upon his ministry, to bring into the faith many more souls than would make up one congregation, having so much work to do far and near? 4. "They that believed at Corinth were baptized," Acts xviii. 8. (Baptism admitted them into that one body of the Church, 1 Cor. xii. 13.) Some were baptized by Paul, (though but few in comparison of the number of believers among them: compare Acts xviii. 8, with 1 Cor. 14-17,) the generality consequently were baptized by other ministers there, and that in other congregations wherein Paul preached not, as well as in such wherein Paul preached; it being unreasonable to deny the being of divers congregations for the word and sacraments to be dispensed in, himself dispensing the sacrament of baptism to so few.

2. From the plenty of ministers and preachers in the church of Corinth, it is evident it was a presbyterial church, and not only a single congregation; for to what end should there be many laborers in a little harvest, many teachers over one single congregation? &c. That there were many preachers at Corinth is plain: For, 1. Paul himself was the master-builder

there that laid the foundation of that church, 1 Cor. iii. 10, their spiritual father; "In Christ Jesus I have begotten you through the gospel," 1 Cor. iv. 15. And he stayed with them *one year and a half*, Acts xviii. 11. 2. While the apostle sharply taxeth them as guilty of schism and division for their carnal crying up of their several teachers: some doting upon one, some upon another, some upon a third, &c. "Every one of you saith, I am of Paul, and I of Apollos, and I of Cephas, and I of Christ," 1 Cor. i. 12. Doth not this intimate that they had plenty of preachers, and these preachers had their several followers, so prizing some of them as to undervalue the rest? and was this likely to be without several congregations into which they were divided? 3. When the apostle saith, "Though ye have ten thousand instructors in Christ, yet have ye not many fathers," 1 Cor. v. 15; though his words be hyperbolical, yet they imply that they had great store of teachers and preachers. 4. We have mention of many prophets in the church of Corinth: "Let the prophets speak two or three, and let the other judge—And the spirits of the prophets are subject to the prophets," 1 Cor. xiv. 20, 31. Here are *prophets* speaking *two or three*, and prophets judging of their doctrine, which sure were more than they that were judged; it being unreasonable for the minor part to pass judgement upon the major part. And though these prophets had extraordinary gifts, (as the church of Corinth excelled all other churches in gifts, 1 Cor. i. 7,) and were able to preach in an extraordinary singular way; yet were they the ordinary pastors and ministers of that church of Corinth, as the whole current of this fourteenth chapter evidenceth, wherein so many rules and directions, aptly agreeing to ordinary pastors, are imposed upon them for the well ordering of their ministerial exercises. Now, where there were so many pastors, were there not several congregations for them to feed? Or were they idle, neglecting the exercise and improvement of their talents?

3. From the diversity of tongues and languages, wherein the church did eminently excel. "In every thing ye are enriched by him, in all utterance, and in all knowledge—So that you come behind in no gift," &c., i.e., ye excel in every gift, more being intended than is expressed, 1 Cor. i. 5, 7. Among other gifts some of them excelled in tongues which they spake, the right use of which gift of tongues the apostle doth at large lay down, 1 Cor. xiv. 2, 4-6, 13, 14, 18, 19, 23, 26, 27. "If any speak in *an unknown* tongue let it be by two, or at the most by three, and that by course, and let one interpret." So that there were many endued with gifts of tongues in that church. To what end? Not only for a *sign to unbelievers*, ver. 22, but also for edification of divers congregations, of divers tongues and languages within that church of Corinth.

4. From the plurality of churches mentioned in reference to this church of Corinth. For the apostle regulating their public assemblies and their worship there, saith to the church of Corinth, "Let your women keep silence in the churches." It is not said, in the *church*, in the singular number; but in the *churches*, in the plural; and this of the *churches in Corinth*, for it is said, *Let your women*, &c., not indefinitely, *Let women*, &c. So that according to the plain letter of the words, here are churches in the church of Corinth, viz. a plurality of single congregations in this one presbyterial church. And this plurality of churches in the church of Corinth is the more confirmed if we take the church of Cenchrea (which is a harbor or seaport to Corinth) to be comprised within the church of Corinth, as some learned authors do conceive it may.112

POSITION II.

That there is in the word of Christ a pattern of one presbyterial government in common over divers single congregations in one church. This may be evidenced by these following considerations: For,

1. Divers single congregations are called one church, as hath at large been proved in the second position immediately foregoing; inasmuch as all the believers in Jerusalem are counted one church: yet those believers are more in number than could meet for all ordinances in any one single congregation. And why are divers congregations styled one church? 1. Not in regard of that oneness of heart and soul which was among them, "having all things common," &c., Acts iv. 32. For these affections and actions of kindness belonged to them by the law of brotherhood and Christian charity to one another, (especially considering the then present condition of believers,) rather than by any special ecclesiastical obligation, because they were members of such a church. 2. Not in regard of any explicit

church covenant, knitting them in one body. For we find neither name nor thing, print nor footstep of any such thing as a church covenant in the church of Jerusalem, nor in any other primitive apostolical church in all the New Testament; and to impose an explicit church covenant upon the saints as a necessary constituting form of a true visible Church of Christ, and without which it is no Church, is a mere human invention, without all solid warrant from the word of God. 3. Not in regard of the ministration of the word, sacraments, prayers, &c. For these ordinances were dispensed in their single congregations severally, it being impossible that such multitudes of believers should meet all in one congregation, to partake of them jointly, (as hath been evidenced.) 4. But in regard of one joint administration of church government among them, by one common presbytery, or college of elders, associated for that end. From this one way of church government, by one presbytery in common, all the believers in Jerusalem, and so in other cities respectively, were counted but one church. 2. In every such presbyterial church made up of divers single congregations, there were ecclesiastical ruling officers, which are counted or called the officers of that church, but never counted or called governors, elders, &c., of any one single congregation therein; as in the church of Jerusalem, Acts xi. 27, 30, and xv. 2: of Antioch, compare Acts xiii. 1-3, with xv. 35: of Ephesus, Acts xx. 17, 28: and of the church of Corinth, 1 Cor. i. 12, and iv. 15, and xiv. 29.

3. The officers of such presbyterial churches met together for acts of church government: as, to take charge of the church's goods, and of the due distribution thereof, Acts iv. 35, 37, and xi. 30: to ordain, appoint, and send forth church officers, Acts vi. 2, 3, 6, and xiii. 1, 3: to excommunicate notorious offenders, 1 Cor. v. 4, 5, 7, 13, compared with 2 Cor. ii. 6: and to restore again penitent persons to church communion, 2 Cor. ii. 7-9.

Except. Receiving of alms is no act of government.

Ans. True, the bare receiving of alms is no act of government, but the ordering and appointing how it shall be best improved and disposed of, cannot be denied to be an act of government, and for this did the elders meet together, Acts xi. 30.

4. The apostles themselves, in their joint acts of government in such churches, acted as ordinary officers, viz. as presbyters or elders. This is much to be observed, and may be evidenced as followeth: for, 1. None of their acts of church government can at all be exemplary or obligatory upon us, if they were not presbyterial, but merely apostolical; if they acted therein not as ordinary presbyters, but as extraordinary apostles. For what acts they dispatched merely as apostles, none may meddle withal but only apostles. 2. As they were apostles, so they were presbyters, and so they style themselves, "The elder to the elect lady," 2 John i. "The elders which are among you I exhort," saith Peter, "who am also an elder," (i.e. who am a fellow-elder, or co-presbyter,) 1 Pet. v. 1; wherein he ranks himself among ordinary presbyters, which had been improper, unless he had discharged the offices and acts of an ordinary presbyter. 3. Their acts were such, for substance, as ordinary presbyters do perform, as preaching and prayer, Acts vi. 4: ordaining of officers, Acts vi. 6, and xiv. 23: dispensing of the sacraments, 1 Cor. i. 14; Acts ii. 42, and xx. 7: and of church censures, 1 Cor. v. 4, 5, compared with 1 Tim. v. ver. 1, ult.: which acts of government, and such like, were committed by Christ to them, and to ordinary presbyters (their successors) to the end of the world; compare Matt. xvi. 19, and xviii. 17, 18, to the end, and John xx. 21, 23, with Matt. xxviii. 18-20. 4. They acted not only as ordinary elders, but also they acted jointly with other elders, being associated with them in the same assembly, as in that eminent synod at Jerusalem, Acts xv. 6, 22, 23, and xvi. 4, "And as they went through cities, they delivered them the decrees for to keep, that were ordained of the apostles and elders which were at Jerusalem." 5. And, finally, they took in the church's consent with themselves, wherein it was needful, as in the election and appointment of deacons, Acts vi. 2, 3. 6. The deacons being specially to be trusted with the church's goods, and the disposal thereof, according to the direction of the presbytery, for the good of the church, &c.

Let all these considerations be impartially balanced in the scales of indifferent unprejudiced judgments; and how plainly do they delineate in the word, a pattern of one presbyterial government in common over divers single congregations within one church!

Except. The apostles' power over many congregations was founded upon their power over all churches; and so cannot be a pattern for the power of elders over many.

103

Ans. 1. The apostles' power over many congregations as one church, to govern them all as one church jointly and in common, was not founded upon their power over all churches, but upon the union of those congregations into one church; which union lays a foundation for the power of elders governing many congregations.

2. Besides, the apostles, though extraordinary officers, are called elders, 1 Pet. v. 1, to intimate to us, that in ordinary acts of church government, they did act as elders for a pattern to us in like administrations.

Except. The apostles, it is true, were elders virtually, that is, their apostleship contained all offices in it, but they were not elders formally.

Ans. 1. If by formally be meant, that they were not elders really, then it is false; for the Scripture saith Peter was an elder, 1 Peter v. 1. If by formally be meant that they were not elders only, that is granted; they were so elders, as they were still apostles, and so apostles as they were yet elders: their eldership did not exclude their apostleship, nor their apostleship swallow up their eldership.

2. Besides, two distinct offices may be formally in one and the same person; as Melchisedec was formally a king and priest, and David formally a king and prophet; and why then might not Peter or John, or any of the twelve, be formally apostles and elders? And ministers are formally pastors and ruling elders.

Except. 'Tis true, the apostles acted together with elders, because it so fell out they met together; but that they should meet jointly to give a pattern for an eldership, is not easy to prove; one apostle might have done that alone, which all here did.

Ans. 1. 'Tis true, the apostles as apostles had power to act singly what they did jointly; yet, when they acted jointly, their acts might have more authority in the Church: upon which ground they of Antioch may be conceived to have sent to the whole college of apostles and elders at Jerusalem, (rather than to any one singly;) why was this, but to add more authority to their acts and determinations?

2. Why should not their meeting together be a pattern of a presbytery, as well as their meeting together when they took in the consent of the people, Acts vi., in the choice of the deacons, to be a pattern or warrant that the people have a power in the choice of their officers? (as those of contrary judgment argue:) if one be taken in as an inimitable practice, why not the other?

3. If the apostles joining with elders, acted nothing as elders, then we can bring nothing of theirs into imitation; and by this we should cut the sinews, and raze the foundation of church government, as if there were no footsteps thereof in the holy Scriptures.

POSITION III.

Finally, That the pattern of the said presbytery and presbyterial government is for a rule to the churches of Christ in all after ages, may appear as followeth:

1. The first churches were immediately planted and governed by Christ's own apostles and disciples; 1. Who immediately received the keys of the kingdom of heaven from Christ himself in person, Matt. xvi. 19, and xviii. 17,18; John xx. 21, 23. 2. Who immediately had the promise of Christ's perpetual presence with them in their ministry, Matt, xxviii. 18-20; and of the plentiful donation of the Spirit of Christ to lead them into all truth, John xiv. 16, and xvi. 13-15; Acts i. 4, 5, 8 3. Who immediately received from Christ, after his resurrection and before his ascension, "commandments by the Holy Ghost,"—"Christ being seen of them forty days, and speaking of the things pertaining to the kingdom of God," Acts i. 2, 3; and, 4. Who were first and immediately *baptized by the Holy Ghost*, extraordinarily, Acts ii. 1-5. Now, who can imagine that the apostles and disciples were not actuated by the Spirit of Christ bestowed upon them? or did not discharge Christ's commandments, touching his kingdom imposed upon them? or did not duly use those keys of Christ's kingdom committed to them in the ordering and governing of the primitive churches? And if so, then the pattern of their practices must be a rule for all the succeeding churches, 1 Cor. xi. 1; Phil, iv. 9.

2. To what end hath the Holy Ghost so carefully recorded a pattern of the state and government of the primitive churches in the first and purest times, but for the imitation of successive churches in after times? "For whatsoever things were written aforetime, were

written for our learning," or instruction. But what do such records instruct us? Only *in fact*, that such things were done by the first churches? or *of right* also, that such things should be done by the after churches? Surely, this is more proper and profitable for us.

3. If such patterns of Christ's apostles, disciples, and primitive churches in matters of the government will not amount to an obligatory rule for all following churches, how shall we justify sundry other acts of religion commonly received in the best reformed churches, and founded only or chiefly upon the foundation of the practice of Christ's apostles and the apostolical churches? As the receiving of the Lord's supper on the Lord's days, Acts xx. 7, &c.; which notwithstanding are generally embraced without any considerable opposition or contradiction, and that most deservedly.

CHAPTER XIV.
Of the Divine Right of Synods, or Synodal Assemblies.

Thus far of the ruling assemblies, which are styled presbyterial; next come into consideration those greater assemblies, which are usually called synodal, or synods, or councils. They are so called from their convening, or coming together: or rather from their calling together. Both names, viz. synod and council, are of such latitude of signification, as that they may be applied to any public convention of people: but in the common ordinary use of these words, they are appropriated to large ecclesiastical assemblies, above classical presbyteries in number and power. These synodal assemblies are made up, (as occasion and the necessity of the church shall require.) 1. Either of presbyters, sent from the several classical presbyteries within a province, hence called provincial synods: 2. Or of presbyters, sent from the several provincial synods within a nation, hence called national synods: 3. Or of presbyters, delegated or sent from the several national churches throughout the Christian world, hence called ecumenical synods, or universal and general councils.

Touching the divine warrant of synods, and their power in church affairs, much need not be said, seeing divers learned authors have so fully stated and handled this matter.[113] Yet, that the reader may have a short view hereof, and not be left wholly unsatisfied, these two things shall briefly be opened and insisted upon, viz: 1. Certain considerations shall be propounded, tending to clear the state of the question about the divine right of synods, and their power. 2. The proposition itself, with some few arguments adduced, for the proof thereof.

For the former, viz: The true stating of this question about the divine right of synods, and of their power, well weigh these few considerations.

1. Synods differ in some respects from classical presbyteries, handled in Chap. XIII., though the nature and kind of their power be the same for substance. For, 1. Synods are more large extensive assemblies than classical presbyteries, the members of presbyteries being sent only from several single congregations, the members of synods being delegated from several presbyteries, and proportionably their power is extended also. 2. The exercise of government by presbyteries, is the common ordinary way of government held forth in Scripture. By synods it is more rare and extraordinary, at least in great part, as in case of extraordinary causes that fall out: as, for choosing an apostle, Acts i., healing of scandals, &c., Acts xv.

2. All synods are of the same nature and kind, whether provincial, national, or ecumenical, though they differ as lesser and greater, in respect of extent, from one another, (the provincial having as full power within their bounds, as the national or ecumenical within theirs.) So that the proving of the divine right of synods indefinitely and in general, doth prove also the divine right of provincial, national, and ecumenical synods in particular: for, greater and lesser do not vary the species or kind. What is true of ecclesiastical synods in general, agrees to every such synod in particular.

Object. But why hath not the Scripture determined these assemblies in particular?

Ans. 1. It is not necessary the Scripture should in every case descend to particulars. In things of one and the same kind, general rules may serve for all particulars; especially seeing particulars are so innumerable, what volumes would have contained all particulars? 2. All

105

churches and seasons are not capable of synods provincial or national: for, in an island there may be no more Christians than to make up one single congregation, or one classical presbytery. Or in a nation, the Christian congregations may be so few, or so dispersed, or so involved in persecution, that they cannot convene in synods, &c.

3. The power of synods contended for, is, 1. Not civil; they have no power to take cognizance of civil causes, as such; not to inflict any civil punishments; as fines, imprisonments, confiscations, banishments, death, (these being proper to the civil magistrate:) but merely spiritual; they judge only in ecclesiastical causes, in a spiritual manner, by spiritual censures, to spiritual ends, as did that synod, Acts xv. 2. Not corruptive, privative, or destructive to the power of classical presbyteries, or single congregations; but rather perfective and conservative thereunto. As suppose a single congregation should elect a minister unsound in judgment, or scandalous in conversation, the synod may annul and make void that election, and direct them to make a better choice, or appoint them a minister themselves; hereby this liberty of election is not at all infringed or violated, but for their own advantage regulated, &c. 3. Not absolute, and infallible; but limited and fallible: any synod or council may err, being constituted of men that are weak, frail, ignorant in part, &c., and therefore all their decrees and determinations are to be examined by the touchstone of the Scriptures, nor are they further to be embraced, or counted obligatory, than they are consonant thereunto, Isa. viii. 20. Hence there is liberty of appeal, as from congregational elderships to the classical presbytery, and from thence to the provincial synod, so from the provincial to the national assembly, &c. 4. Finally, the power of synods is not only persuasive and consultative, (as some think,) able to give grave advice, and to use forcible persuasions in any case, which if accepted and followed, well; if rejected and declined, there is no further remedy, but a new non-communion instead of a divine church censure: but it is a proper authoritative juridical power, which all within their bounds are obliged reverently to esteem, and dutifully to submit unto, so far as agreeable to the word of Christ.

4. Finally, this authoritative juridical power of synods is threefold, viz. *doctrinal, regulating, and censuring*. 1. *Doctrinal*, in reference to matters of faith, and divine worship; not to coin new articles of faith, or devise new acts of divine worship: but to explain and apply those articles of faith and rules of worship which are laid down in the word, and declare the contrary errors, heresies, corruptions. Hence the Church is styled, *the pillar and ground of truth*, 1 Tim. iii. 15. Thus to the Jewish Church *were committed of trust the oracles of God*, Rom. iii. 2. 2. *Regulating*, in reference to external order and polity, in matters prudential and circumstantial, which are determinate according to the true light of nature, and the general rules of Scripture, such as are in 1 Cor. x. 31, 32; Rom. xiv.; 1 Cor. xiv. 26, 40, &c.; not according to any arbitrary power of men. 3. *Censuring* power, in reference to error, heresy, schism, obstinacy, contempt, or scandal, and the repressing thereof; which power is put forth merely in spiritual censures, as admonition, excommunication, deposition, &c. And these censures exercised, not in a lordly, domineering, prelatical way: but in an humble, sober, grave, yet authoritative way, necessary both for preservation of soundness of doctrine, and incorruptness of conversation; and for extirpation of the contrary. This is the power which belongs to synods. Thus much for clearing the right state of this question.

II. For the second thing, viz. the proposition itself, and the confirmation thereof, take it briefly in these terms.

Jesus Christ our Mediator hath laid down in his word sufficient ground and warrant for juridical synods, and their authority, for governing of his Church now under the New Testament. Many arguments might be produced for proof of this proposition: as, 1. From the light of nature. 2. From the words of the law, Deut. xvii. 8, 12, compared with 2 Chron. xix. 8, 11; Ps. cxxii. 4, 5, holding forth an ecclesiastical Sanhedrin in the Church of the Jews, superior to other courts. 3. From the words of Christ, Matt, xviii. 15-21. 4. From the unity of the visible Church of Christ now under the New Testament. 5. From the primitive apostolical pattern laid down, Acts xv., &c., and from divers other considerations; but for brevity's sake, only the two last arguments shall be a little insisted upon.

Argum. I. The unity or oneness of the visible Church of Christ now under the New Testament, laid down in Scripture, gives us a notable foundation for church government by juridical synods. For, 1. That Jesus Christ our Mediator hath one general, visible Church on earth now under the New Testament, hath been already proved, Part 2, Chap. VIII. 2. That in this Church there is a government settled by divine right, is evidenced, Part 1, Chap. I. 3. That all Christ's ordinances, and particularly church government, primarily belong to the whole general Church visible, for her edification, (secondarily to particular churches and single congregations, as parts or members of the whole,) hath been manifested, Part 2, Chap. VIII. Now, there being one general visible Church, having a government set in it of divine right, and that government belonging primarily to the whole body of Christ; secondarily, to the parts or members thereof; must it not necessarily follow, that the more generally and extensively Christ's ordinance of church government is managed in greater and more general assemblies, the more fully the perfection and end of the government, viz. the edification of the whole body of Christ, is attained; and on the contrary, the more particularly and singly church government is exercised, as in presbyteries, or single congregational elderships, the more imperfect it is, and the less it attains to the principal end: consequently, if there be a divine warrant for church government by single congregational elderships, is it not much more for church government by presbyteries, and synods, or councils, wherein more complete provision is made for the edification of the general Church or body of Jesus Christ?

Argum. II. The primitive apostolical practice in the first and purest ages of the Church after Christ, may further evidence with great strength the divine warrant for church government by juridical synods or councils. Let this be the position:

Jesus Christ our Mediator hath laid down in his word a pattern of a juridical synod, consisting of governing officers of divers presbyterial churches, for a rule to the Church of Christ in all succeeding ages.

For proof hereof take these two assertions: 1. That Jesus Christ hath laid down in his word a pattern of a juridical synod. 2. That this juridical synod is for a rule to the churches of Christ in all succeeding ages.

ASSERTION I.

That Jesus Christ hath laid down in his word a pattern of a synod, yea, of a juridical synod, consisting of governing officers of divers presbyterial churches, is manifest, Acts xv. and xvi., where are plainly set forth: 1. The occasion of the synod. 2. The proper members of the synod. 3. The equal power and authority exercised by all those members. 4. The way and method of ordinary synodal proceeding. 5. The juridical acts of power put forth by the synod; with the issue and consequent of all upon the churches.

First, Here was a proper ground and occasion for a juridical synod. For thus the text expressly declareth, that "certain men which came down from Judea, taught the brethren, and said, Except ye be circumcised after the manner of Moses, ye cannot be saved; when therefore Paul and Barnabas had no small dissension and disputation with them, they determined that Paul and Barnabas, and certain other of them, should go up to Jerusalem to the apostles and elders about this question," Acts xv. 1, 2, compared with ver. 5—"But there rose up certain of the sect of the Pharisees, which believed, saying, that it was needful to circumcise them, and to command them to keep the law of Moses;" and with ver. 23, 24—"The apostles, and elders, and brethren send greeting unto the brethren which are of the Gentiles, in Antioch, and Syria, and Cilicia: Forasmuch as we have heard, that certain which went out from us, have troubled you with words, subverting your souls, saying, Ye must be circumcised and keep the law." In which passages these things are evident:

1. That false doctrine, destructive to the doctrine of Christ in his gospel, did arise in the Church, viz: That circumcision and keeping of the ceremonial law of Moses was necessary to salvation, ver. 1, 5, 24; and this false doctrine promoted with lying, as if the apostles and elders of Jerusalem had sent forth the false teachers with directions to preach so, as their apology ("to whom we gave no such commandment," ver. 24) seems to import. Here is corruption both in doctrine and manners fit for a synod to take cognizance of.

2. That this corrupt doctrine was vented by certain that came down from Judea. It is evident, it was by certain of the sect of the Pharisees that believed; as Paul and Barnabas make the narrative to the church at Jerusalem, ver. 5, therefore the false teachers coming from Judea (where the Churches of Christ were first of all planted, and whence the church plantation spread) published their doctrines with more credit to their errors and danger to

the churches; and so both the churches of Judea whence they came, and of Antioch, Syria, and Cilicia, whither they came, were interested in the business.

3. That the said false teachers by the leaven of their doctrine troubled them with words, subverting the souls of the brethren, both at Antioch, Syria, and Cilicia, ver. 23, 24; here was the disturbance and scandal of divers churches: compare ver. 39 with 41.

4. That Paul and Barnabas at Antioch had no small dissension and dispute against the false teachers, ver. 1, 2, that so (if possible) they might be convinced, and the Church's peace preserved, without craving further assistance in a solemn synod.

5. That after these disputes, and for the better settling of all the churches about this matter, (which these disputes could not effect,) *they decreed* (or ordained) *that Paul and Barnabas, and some others of themselves, should go up to the apostles and elders at Jerusalem about this question, ver.* 2. Here was an authoritative mission of delegated officers from the presbyterial church at Antioch, and from other churches of Syria and Cilicia also, ver. 23, 41, to a synodal assembly with the presbyterial church at Jerusalem.

Secondly, Here were proper members of a synod convened to consider of this question, viz. the officers and delegates of divers presbyterial churches: of the presbyterial church at Jerusalem, the apostles and elders, Acts xv. 6: of the presbyterial church at Antioch, Paul, Barnabas, and others; compare verse 2 and 12. And besides these, there were brethren from other churches, present as members of the synod; as may appear by these two considerations, viz:

1. Partly, because it is called "The whole multitude," ver. 12; "The apostles and elders with the whole church," ver. 22; "The apostles, and elders, and brethren," ver. 23. This whole multitude, whole church, and brethren, distinct from the apostles and elders which were at Jerusalem, cannot be *the company of all the faithful at Jerusalem*, for (as hath been evidenced, Chap. XIV., Position 2,) they were too many to meet in one house. But it was the synodal multitude, the synodal church, consisting of apostles, and elders, and brethren; which brethren seem to be such as were sent from several churches, as Judas and Silas, ver. 24, who were assistants to the apostles and evangelists—Judas, Acts xv. 22, 32; Silas, Acts xv. 32, 40, and xvi. 19, and xvii. 4, 14, 15, and xviii. 5. Some think Titus was of this synod also.

2. Partly because the brethren of Antioch, Syria, and Cilicia, were troubled with this question, ver. 23, 24. Therefore it cannot be reasonably imagined, but all those places sought out for a remedy; and to that end, severally and respectively sent their delegates to the synod at Jerusalem: else they had been very regardless of their own church peace and welfare. And the epistle of the synod was directed to them all by name, ver. 23; and so did formally bind them all, having men of their own members of the synod, which decrees did but materially, and from the nature of the thing, bind the other churches at Lystra and Iconium, Acts xvi. 4. Now, if there were delegates but from two presbyterial churches, they were sufficient to constitute a synod; and this justifies delegates from ten or twenty churches, proportionably, when there shall be like just and necessary occasion.

Thirdly, Here all the members of the synod, as they were convened by like ordinary authority, so they acted by like ordinary and equal power in the whole business laid before them; which shows it was an ordinary, not an extraordinary synod. For though apostles and evangelists, who had power over all churches, were members of the synod, as well as ordinary elders; yet they acted not in this synod by a transcendent, infallible, apostolical power, but by an ordinary power, as elders. This is evident,

1. Because the Apostle Paul, and Barnabas his colleague, (called a prophet and teacher, Acts xiii. 1, 2, and an apostle, Acts xiv. 14,) were sent as members to this synod, by order and determination of the church of Antioch, and they submitted themselves to that determination, Acts xv. 2, 3; which they could not have submitted unto as apostles, but as ordinary elders and members of the presbytery at Antioch: they that send, being greater than those that are sent by them. Upon which ground it is a good argument which is urged against Peter's primacy over the rest of the apostles, because the college of apostles at Jerusalem sent Peter and John to Samaria, having received the faith, Acts viii. 14.

2. Because the manner of proceeding in this synod convened, was not extraordinary and apostolical, as when they acted by an immediate infallible inspiration of the Spirit, in

penning the Holy Scriptures, (without all disputing, examining, or judging of the matter that they wrote, so far as we can read,) 2 Tim. iii. 16,17; 2 Pet. i. 20, 21; but ordinary, presbyterial, and synodal; by ordinary helps and means, (as afterwards shall appear more fully;) stating the question, proving and evidencing from Scripture what was *the good and acceptable will of God* concerning the present controversy, and upon evidence of Scripture concluding, *It seemed good to the Holy Ghost, and to us,* Acts xv. 28; which words, any assembly, having like clear evidence of Scripture for their determination, may without presumption use, as well as this synod did.114

3. Because the elders and brethren (who are as authoritatively members of the synod as the apostles) did in all points as authoritatively act as the apostles themselves. For, 1. Certain other of the church of Antioch, as well as *Paul* and *Barnabas*, were sent as delegates from the church of *Antioch*, Acts xv. 2. 2. They were all sent as well to the *elders*, as to the *apostles* at *Jerusalem*, about this matter, ver. 2. 3. They were received at *Jerusalem*, as well by the *elders*, as the *apostles*, and reported their case to them both, ver. 4. 4. The *elders*, as well as the *apostles*, met together to consider thereof, ver. 6. 5. The letters containing the synodal decrees and determinations, were written in the name of the *elders and brethren*, as well as in the name of the *apostles*, ver. 23. 6. The *elders and brethren*, as well as the *apostles*, blame the false teachers for troubling of the Church, *subverting of souls*; declaring, that they gave the false teachers *no such commandment* to preach any such doctrine, ver. 24. 7. The *elders and brethren*, as well as the *apostles*, say, "It seemed good to the Holy Ghost, and to us," ver. 28. 8. The *elders* and *brethren*, as well as the *apostles*, did impose upon the churches "no other burden than these necessary things," ver. 28. 9. The *elders*, as well as the *apostles*, being assembled, "thought good to send chosen men of themselves," viz. *Judas* and *Silas*, with *Paul* and *Barnabas*, to *Antioch*, to deliver the synodal decrees to them, and to tell them the same things by mouth, ver. 22, 25, 27. 10. And the decrees are said to be ordained as well by the *elders*, as by the *apostles at Jerusalem*, Acts xvi. 4. So that through this whole synodal transaction, the elders are declared in the text to go on in a full authoritative course of judgment with the apostles, from point to point. And therefore in this synod, the apostles acted as ordinary elders, not as extraordinary officers.

Fourthly. Here was the ordinary way and method of synodal proceedings by the apostles, elders, and brethren, when they were convened unanimously, ver. 25. For,

1. They proceeded deliberatively, by discourses and disputes, deliberating about the true state of the question, and the remedy of the scandal. This is laid down, 1. More generally, "and when there had been much disputing," ver. 7. 2. More particularly, how they proceeded when they drew towards a synodal determination, Peter speaks of the Gentiles' conversion, and clears the doctrine of justification "by faith without the works of the law," ver. 7-12. Then Barnabas and Paul confirm the conversion of the Gentiles, "declaring the signs and wonders wrought by them among the Gentiles," ver. 12. After them James speaks, approving what Peter had spoken touching the conversion of the Gentiles, confirming it by Scripture; and further adds (which Peter did but hint, ver. 10, and Paul and Barnabas did not so much as touch upon) a remedy against the present scandal, ver. 13-22. Here is now an ordinary way of proceeding by debates, disputes, allegations of Scripture, and mutual suffrages. What needed all this, if this had been a transcendent, extraordinary, and not an ordinary synod?

2. They proceeded after all their deliberative inquiries and disputes decisively to conclude and determine the matter, ver. 20-30. The result of the synod (as there is evident) is threefold. 1. To set down in writing their decrees and determinations. 2. To signify those decrees in an epistle to the brethren at Antioch, Syria, and Cilicia. 3. To send these letters by some from among themselves, viz. Judas and Silas, together with Paul and Barnabas, to all the churches that were offended or endangered, that both by written decrees and word of mouth, the churches might be established in faith and peace.

Fifthly, Here were several authoritative and juridical acts of power, put forth in this synod, according to the exigency of the present distempers of the churches. This appears plainly,

1. By the proceedings of the synod in accommodating a suitable and proportionable remedy to every malady at that time distempering the Church, viz. a triple medicine for a threefold disease.

1. Against the heresy broached, viz. that they must be circumcised and keep the ceremonial "law of Moses, or else they could not be saved," Acts xv. 2. The synod put forth a doctrinal power, in confutation of the heresy, and clear vindication of the truth, about the great point of "justification by faith without the works of the law," Acts xv. 7-23; and (Independents themselves being judges) a doctrinal decision of matters of faith by a lawful synod, far surpasseth the doctrinal determination of any single teacher, or of the presbytery of any single congregation; and is to be reverently received of the churches as a binding ordinance of Christ.

2. Against the schism, occasioned by the doctrine of the false teachers that troubled the Church, Acts xv. 1, 2, the synod put forth a censuring power, stigmatizing the false teachers with the infamous brands of troubling the Church with words, subverting of souls, and (tacitly, as some conceive from that expression, "Unto whom we gave no such commandment," ver. 24) of belying the apostles and elders of Jerusalem, as if they had sent them abroad to preach this doctrine.

Object. But the synod proceeded not properly to censure the false teachers by any ecclesiastical admonition, or excommunication; therefore the power exercised in the synod was only doctrinal, and not properly juridical.

Ans. 1. They censured them in some degree, and that with a mark of infamy, ver. 24, as was manifested. And this was not only a warning and hint to the churches, to note such false teachers, avoid them, and withdraw from them, compare Rom. xvi. 17, 18, with 1 Tim. vi. 3-5; but also was a virtual admonition to the false teachers themselves, while their doctrines and ways were so expressly condemned. 2. They proceeded not to present excommunication, it is granted; nor was it at first dash seasonable, prudent, or needful. But the synod knew well, that if these false teachers, after this synodal mark of disgrace set upon them, should still persist in their course, incurably and incorrigibly obstinate, they might in due time be excommunicated by course; it being a clear case in itself that such heretics or schismatics, as otherwise cannot be reduced, are not to be suffered, but to be cast out of the churches. "An heretic, after once or twice admonition, reject," Tit. iii. 10, 11; see Rev. ii. 2, 14, 20.

3. Against the scandal of the weak Jews, and their heart-estrangement from the Gentiles, who neglected their ceremonial observances, as also against the scandal of the Gentiles, who were much troubled and offended at the urging of circumcision, and the keeping of the law as necessary to salvation, ver. 1, 2, 19, 24, the synod put forth an ordering or regulating power, framing practical rules or constitutions for the healing of the scandal, and for prevention of the spreading of it, commanding the brethren of the several churches to abstain from divers things that might any way occasion the same: "It seemed good to the Holy Ghost, and to us, to impose" (or lay) "upon you no further burden than these necessary things," Acts xv. 28, 29. Here is *burden* and *necessary things*, (so judged to be necessary for those times, and that state of the Church,) and imposing of these upon the churches: will not this amount to a plain ordering power and authority? Especially considering that the word *to impose*, or *lay on*, when it is used of the judgment, act, or sentence of an assembly, ordinarily signifies an authoritative judgment, or decree, as, "Why tempt ye God, to lay, or impose, a yoke upon the neck of the disciples?" Acts xv. 10. Thus some in the synod endeavored to carry the synod with themselves, authoritatively to have imposed the ceremonies upon the churches; whom Peter thus withstands. So, "They bind heavy burdens, and hard to be borne, and impose them upon men's shoulders," Matt, xxiii. 4: and this laying on of burdens by the Pharisees, was not by a bare doctrinal declaring, but by an authoritative commanding, as seems by that, "teaching for doctrines the commandments of men," Matt. xv. 9.

2. By the title or denomination given to the synodal results contained in their letters sent to the brethren. They are styled, "The decrees ordained, or judged," Acts xvi. 4. Here are plainly juridical authoritative constitutions. For it is very observable,

That wheresoever the words translated *decree* or *decrees* are found in the New Testament, thereby are denoted, laws, statutes, or decrees: as "Decrees of Cæsar," Acts xvii. 7: "A decree from Cæsar," Luke ii. 1: Moses' ceremonial law, "The hand-writing to ordinances," Col. ii. 14: "The law of commandments in ordinances," Eph. ii. 15: and this word is found used only in these five places in the whole New Testament: and the Septuagint interpreters often use the word in the Old Testament to this purpose; for *laws*, Dan. vi. 8; for *decrees*, Dan. ii. 13, and iii. 10, 29, and iv. 3, and vi. 9.

And the other word translated *ordained*, when applied to an assembly by the Septuagint, is used for a judgment of authority, as, "And what was decreed against her," Esth. ii. 1; and so a word derived from it, signifies a *decree*, Dan. iv. 14, 21.

In this sense also the word is sometimes used in the New Testament, when applied to assemblies; as, "Take ye him, and judge him according to your law," John xviii. 31; "Whom we laid hold upon, and would have judged according to our law," Acts xxiv. 6.

Now, if there be so much power and authority engraven upon these two words severally, how strongly do they hold forth authority, when they are applied to any thing jointly, as here to the synodal decisions!

3. By the consequent of these synodal proceedings, viz. the cheerful submission of the churches thereunto. This appears both in the church of Antioch, where the troubles first were raised by the false teachers; where, "when the epistle" of the synod "was read, they rejoiced for the consolation," Acts xv. 30, 31; and Judas and Silas exhorted and confirmed the brethren by word of mouth, according to the synod's direction, ver. 32; and in other churches, to which Paul and Timothy delivered the "decrees ordained by the apostles and elders which were at Jerusalem; and so were the churches confirmed in the faith, and abounded in number daily," Acts xvi. 4, 5; whence we have these evidences of the churches' submission to the synodal decrees: 1. The decrees are counted by the churches a consolation. 2. They were so welcome to them, that they *rejoiced for the consolation.* 3. They were hereby notably *confirmed in the faith*, against the false doctrines broached among them. 4. The churches *abounded in number daily*, the scandal and stumbling-blocks that troubled the Church being removed out of the way. How should such effects so quickly have followed upon the publication of the synodal decrees, in the several churches, had not the churches looked upon that synod as vested with juridical power and authority for composing and imposing of these their determinations?

ASSERTION II.

That this juridical synod is for a rule to the churches of Christ in all succeeding ages, there need no new considerations for proof hereof; only let the reader please to look back to Position iv. of the last chapter, where the substance of those considerations which urge the pattern of presbyteries and presbyterial government for a rule to succeeding churches, is applicable (by change of terms) to the pattern of juridical synods.115

CHAPTER XV.
Of the subordination of particular churches to greater assemblies for their authoritative and judicial determination of causes ecclesiastical, and the divine right thereof.

The divine right of ecclesiastical assemblies, congregational, classical, and synodal, and of their power for church government, being thus evidenced by the Scriptures, now in the last place take a few words briefly touching the subordination of the lesser to the greater assemblies, and the divine warrant thereof. In asserting the subordination of particular churches to higher assemblies, whether classical or synodal,

1. It is not denied, but particular churches have within themselves power of discipline entirely, so far as any cause in debate particularly and peculiarly concerneth themselves, and not others.

2. It is granted, that where there is no consociation, or neighborhood of single churches, whereby they may mutually aid one another, there a single congregation must not be denied entire jurisdiction; but this falls not within the compass of ordinary rules of church

government left us by Christ. If there be but one congregation in a kingdom or province, that particular congregation may do much by itself alone, which it ought not to do where there are neighboring and adjacent churches that might associate therewith for mutual assistance.

3. It is granted, that every single congregation hath equal power, one as much as another, and that there is no subordination of one to another; according to that common and known axiom, An equal hath no power or rule over an equal. Subordination prelatical, which is of one or more parishes to the prelate and his cathedral, is denied; all particular churches being collateral, and of the same authority.

4. It is granted, that classical or synodal authority cannot be by Scripture introduced over a particular church in a privative or destructive way to that power which God hath bestowed upon it; but contrarily it is affirmed, that all the power of assemblies, which are above particular congregations, is cumulative and perfective to the power of those inferior congregations.

5. It is granted, that the highest ecclesiastical assembly in the world cannot require from the lowest a subordination absolute, and at their own mere will and pleasure, but only in some respect; subordination absolute being only to the law of God laid down in Scripture. We detest popish tyranny, which claims a power of giving their will for a law. 'Tis subjection in the Lord that is pleaded for: the straightest rule in the world, unless the holy Scripture, we affirm to be a rule to be regulated; peace being only in walking according to Scripture canon, Gal. vi. ver. 16.

6. Nor is it the question whether friendly, consultative, fraternal, Christian advice or direction, be either to be desired or bestowed by neighboring churches, either apart or in their synodal meetings, for the mutual benefit of one another, by reason of that holy profession in which they are all conjoined and knit together: for this will be granted on all hands, though when it is obtained, it will not amount to a sufficient remedy in many cases.

But this is that which we maintain, viz. that the law of God holdeth forth a subordination of a particular church to greater assemblies, consisting of divers choice members, taken out of several single congregations: which assemblies have authoritative power and ecclesiastical jurisdiction over that particular church, by way of giving sentence in and deciding of causes ecclesiastical. For confirmation of this assertion, thus:

Argum. I. The light of nature may be alleged to prove, that there ought to be this subordination: this is warranted not only by God's positive law, but even by nature's law. The church is a company of people who are not outlawed by nature. The visible church being an ecclesiastical polity, and the perfection of all polity, doth comprehend in it whatsoever is excellent in all other bodies political. The church must resemble the commonwealth's government in things common to both, and which have the same use in both. The law of nature directs unto diversities of courts in the commonwealth, and the greater to have authority over the lesser. The church is not only to be considered as employed in holy services, or as having assemblies exercised in spiritual things, and after a spiritual manner, but it is also to be considered as consisting of companies and societies of men to be regularly ordered, and so far nature agreeth to it, that it should have divers sorts of assemblies, and the lower subordinate to the higher. That particular parts should be subject to the whole for the good of the whole, is found necessary both in bodies natural and politic. Is the foot to be lanced? though it have a particular use of its own, and a peculiar employment, yet it is to be ordered by the eye, the hand, and the rest. Kingdoms have their several cities and towns, which all have their governments apart by themselves; yet for the preservation of the whole, all join together in the Parliament. Armies and navies have their several companies and ships, yet in any danger every particular company and ship is ordered by the counsels and directions of the officers and guides of the whole army or navy. The Church is spiritual, but yet a kingdom, a body, an army, &c. D. Ames himself affirms that the light of nature requires that particular churches ought to combine in synods for things of greater moment. The God of nature and reason hath not left in his word a government against the light of nature and right reason. Appeals are of divine and natural right, and certainly very necessary in every society, because of the iniquity and ignorance of judges. That they are so, the practices of all ages and nations sufficiently testify.

Argum. II. The Jewish church government affords a second argument. If in that they had synagogues in every city, which were subordinate to the supreme ecclesiastical court at Jerusalem, then there ought to be a subordination of particular churches among us to higher assemblies; but so it was among them: therefore,

That the subordination was among them of the particular synagogues to the assembly at Jerusalem, is clear—Deut. xvii. 8, 12; 2 Chron. xix. 8, 11; Exod. xviii. 22, 26.

That therefore it ought to be so among us, is as plain: for the dangers and difficulties that they were involved in without a government, and for which God caused that government to be set up among them, are as great if not greater among us, and therefore why should we want the same means of prevention and cure? Are not we in greater danger of heresies now in the time of the New Testament, the churches therein being thereby to be exercised by way of trial, as the apostle foretells, 1 Cor. xi. 19? Doth not ungodliness in these last times abound, according to the same apostle's prediction? Is there not now a more free and permitted intercourse of society with infidels than in those times?

Nor are the exceptions against this argument of any strength: as, 1. That arguments for the form of church government must yet be fetched from the Jewish Church; the government of the Jews was ceremonial and typical, and Christians must not Judaize, nor use that Judaical compound of subordination of churches: the Mosaical polity is abrogated now under the New Testament. Not to tell those that make this exception, 1. That none argue so much from the Jewish government as themselves for the power of congregations, both in ordination and excommunication, because the people of Israel laid hands on the Levites, and all Israel were to remove the unclean; 2. We answer, the laws of the Jewish church, whether ceremonial or judicial, so far are in force, even at this day, as they were grounded upon common equity, the principles of reason and nature, and were serving to the maintenance of the moral law. 'Tis of especial right, that the party unjustly aggrieved should have redress, that the adverse party should not be sole judge and party too, that judgment ought not to be rashly or partially passed upon any. The Jewish polity is only abrogated in regard of what was in it of particular right, not of common right: so far as there was in their laws either a typicalness proper to their church, or a peculiarness of respect to their state in that land of promise given unto them. Whatsoever was in their laws of moral concernment or general equity, is still obliging; whatsoever the Jewish Church had not as Jewish, but as it was a political church, or an ecclesiastical republic, (among which is the subordination of ecclesiastical courts to be reckoned,) doth belong to the Christian Church: that all judgments were to be determined by an high-priest, was typical of Christ's supremacy in judicature; but that there were gradual judicatories for the ease of an oppressed or grieved party, there can be no ceremony or type in this. This was not learned by Moses in the pattern of the Mount, but was taught by the light of nature to Jethro, Exod. xviii. 22, and by him given in advice to Moses. This did not belong unto the peculiar dispensation of the Jews, but unto the good order of the church.

To conclude our answer to this exception, if the benefit of appeals be not as free to us as to the Jews, the yoke of the gospel should be more intolerable than the yoke of the law; the poor afflicted Christian might groan and cry under an unjust and tyrannical eldership, and no ecclesiastical judicatory to relieve him; whereas the poor oppressed Jew might appeal to the Sanhedrin: certainly this is contrary to that prophecy of Christ, Psal. lxxii. 12, 14.

Argum. III. A third argument to prove the subordination of particular congregations, is taken from the institution of our Saviour Christ, of gradual appeals, Matt. xviii. 17, 18, where our Saviour hath appointed a particular member of a church (if scandalous) to be gradually dealt withal; first to be reproved in private, then to be admonished before two or three witnesses, and last of all to be complained of to the church: whence we thus argue:

If Christ hath instituted that the offence of an obstinate brother should be complained of to the church; then much more is it intended that the obstinacy of a great number, suppose of a whole church, should be brought before a higher assembly: but the former is true, therefore the latter. The consequence, wherein the strength of the argument lies, is proved several ways.

1. From the rule of proportion: by what proportion one or two are subject to a particular church, by the same proportion is that church subject to a provincial or a national

assembly; and by the same proportion that one congregation is governed by the particular eldership representing it, by the same proportion are ten or twelve congregations governed by a classical presbytery representing them all.

2. From the sufficiency of that remedy that Christ here prescribes for those emergent exigencies under which the Church may lie; since, therefore, offences may as well arise between two persons in the same congregation, Christ hath appointed that particular congregations, as well as members, shall have liberty to complain and appeal to a more general judgment for redress: the salve here prescribed by Christ is equal to the sore; if the sore of scandal may overspread whole churches, as well as particular persons, then certainly the salve of appeals and subordination is here also appointed. If a man be scandalized by the neighbor-church, to whom shall he complain? The church offending must not be both judge and party.

3. From that ecclesiastical communion that is between churches and churches in one and the same province or nation, whereby churches are joined and united together in doctrine and discipline into one body, as well as divers particular persons in a particular congregation; since, therefore, scandals may be committed among them that are in that holy communion one with another, most unworthy of and destructive to that sacred league, certainly those scandals should be redressed by a superior judicatory, as well as offences between brother and brother.

4. He that careth for a part of a church must much more care for the whole; he whose love extends itself to regard the conversion of one, is certainly very careful of the spiritual welfare of many, the edification of a whole church; the influence of Christ's love being poured upon the whole body, bride and spouse, by order of nature, before it redound to the benefit of a finger or toe, viz. some one single person or other. Nor are the exceptions against this institution of gradual appeals of any moment.

The grand one, and that makes directly against our position is, that our Saviour would have the controversy between brother and brother to be terminated in a peculiar church, and that its judgment should be ultimately requested, he saith, *Tell the church*, not churches. The subordination here appointed by Christ is of fewer to more, but still within the same church, not without it. To which we answer, our Saviour means not by church only one single particular congregation, but also several, combined in their officers, as appears by these following reasons.

1. A particular church in sundry cases cannot decide the difference, or heal the distemper our Saviour prescribes against; as when a particular church is divided into two parts, both in opposition one to the other; or when one church is at variance with another; if Christ here limits only to a particular church, how shall such distempers be remedied?

2. When Christ bids *tell the church*, he speaks in allusion to the Jewish Church, which was represented not only by parts in the single synagogue or congregation, but wholly in their sanhedrin, consisting of select persons, appointed by God, for deciding controversies incident to their particular congregations, and their members. So that we may thus reason: the subordination here established by Christ is so far to be extended in the Christian Church, as in the Church of the Jews, for Christ alludeth to the Jewish practice; but in the Jewish Church there was a subordination of fewer to more, not only within the same synagogue or congregation, but within the whole nation, for all synagogues were under the great council at Jerusalem. Now that Christ gives here the same rule that was of old given to the Jews for church government, is clear, 1. From the censure of the obstinate, who was to be reputed a heathen and a publican; wherein is a manifest allusion to the present estate of the Church of the Jews; and, 2. From the familiarity and plainness of Christ's speech, *Tell the church*, which church could not have been understood by the disciples had not Christ spoken of the Jewish judicatory; besides which they knew none for such offences as Christ spake of to them, there being no particular church which had given its name to Christ: as also, 3. From his citing the words of that text, Deut. xix. 15, where the witnesses and offenders were, by way of further appeal, to stand before the Lord, before the priests for judgment, ver. 17.

3. It is plain that our Saviour intended a liberty of going beyond a particular congregation for determining cases of controversy, from the reason of that subordination which Christ enjoins, of one to two or three, and of them to the church. The reason of that

gradual progress there set down, was because in the increase of numbers and greatness of assemblies, more wisdom, judgment, and gravity is supposed to be, than in the admonitions of a few and smaller number; now, then, this power of right admonition increaseth with the number of admonishers, as well without as within the same congregation; if ten go beyond two in wisdom and gravity, forty will go beyond ten, and be more likely to win upon the offender, and regain him.

Argum. IV. A fourth argument is taken from the pattern of the apostolical churches, Acts xv.

The church of Antioch (though presbyterial, as was proved Chapter XIII., Position II.) was subordinate to the synod at Jerusalem; therefore a particular church is subordinate to higher assemblies, &c.

If a synodal decree did bind them in those times, then may it bind particular churches now, and these ought even still to be subject to synods.

The consequence is undeniable, unless we hold that what the synod there imposed was unjust, or that we have now less need of those remedies than they had; nay, since the apostles (who were assisted with an extraordinary spirit of inspiration) would nevertheless in a doubtful business have synodal conventions for determining of controversies, much more ought we to do so whose gifts are far inferior to theirs; and unless it had been in their determination to leave us their example of a synodal way of church government for our pattern, they had not wanted the meeting together of so many with them for decision of the doubt, whose doctrine was infallible, and of itself, without an assembly, to be believed.

The exceptions against this pattern of church polity are of no validity, e.g.

1. This was no synod. First, that it was no synod appears, in that we read of no word of a synod. Secondly, no commissioners from Syria and Cilicia, which churches should have sent their delegates, had they been a synod, and had their decrees been to have bound in a synodal way. Thirdly, all the believers had voices here.

2. If it were a synod, yet it is no pattern for us, in regard it was consisting of members guided by an infallible and apostolical spirit.

We answer, 1. Here is the thing synod, though not the word, which is a meeting consisting of the deputies of many single churches.

2. That Jerusalem and Antioch had their commissioners there, is evident; and by consequence many single churches had their commissioners, for there were many single congregations at Jerusalem and Antioch, as hath been proved, Chapter XIII., Position II.; that these met together, the word used, verse 6, *they came together*, evidenceth, and verse 25. For the churches of Syria and Cilicia not sending their commissioners, it follows not that because *they are not named*, therefore *they were not there*; and if *they were not there*, therefore *they ought not to have been*: but it is rather thought Syria and Cilicia had commissioners there, in regard the synodal decrees are directed to them as well as others, and the decrees bound them, which they could not do as formal Scripture; for the words, *it seemeth good to us*, and their submitting the matter to disputation, argue the contrary; therefore as synodal decrees, which inasmuch as they bound those churches, they either were present, or were obliged to be present by their commissioners.

3. To that exception, that the multitude of believers had voices there, and therefore it is not one of our synods, ver. 22—

We answer, it can nowise be proved that every particular believer had a suffrage in the assembly.

Eminent divines116 understand by *multitude* and *church*, the multitude and whole church of apostles and elders, who are said to be *gathered together*, verse 6, *to consider of the matter*; besides which no other multitude is said to be gathered together, while the matter was in debate; yet we shall not deny even to other members the liberty of their consent and approbation, and freedom to examine all determinations by the rule of God's word: but the ordaining and forming those decrees is here evinced to be by the apostles and elders, when as they are called *their decrees*, Acts xvi. 4,6.

3. Those only had definitive votes, who met together synodically to consider of the question; but they were only the apostles and elders, Acts xv. 6. That the epistle is sent in the

name of all, is granted; because it was sent by common consent, and withal thereby was added some more weight to the message.

4. Further, if the believers of Jerusalem voted in that assembly, by what authority was it? How could they *impose a burden* upon, and command decrees unto the churches of Syria and Cilicia, and other churches, who, according to our brethren's opinion, were not only absent in their commissioners, but independent in their power?

To the exception, that other synods may not pretend to the privileges of that, since its decrees were indited by the Holy Ghost; and therefore no pattern for our imitation—

Ans. The decrees of this assembly did oblige, as synodal decrees, not as apostolical and canonical Scripture: this appears several ways:

1. The apostles, in framing these canons, did proceed in a way synodal and ecclesiastical, and far different from that which they used in dictating of Scripture, and publishing divine truths; their decrees were brought forth by much disputation, human disquisition, but divine oracles are published without human reasonings, from the immediate inditing of the Spirit, 2 Pet. i. 2.

2. Besides the apostles, there were here commissioned elders and other brethren, men of ordinary rank, not divinely and infallibly inspired. The apostles in the penning of Scripture consult not with elders and brethren, (as our opposites here say they did:) our brethren make mandates of ordinary believers divine and canonical Scripture.

3. Divine writ is published only in the name of the Lord; but these in the name of man also, "It seemed good to the Holy Ghost and to us," Acts xv. 28.

4. Canonical and apostolical writing of new Scripture shall not continue till Christ's coming, because the canon is complete, Rev. xxii. 18, 19, &c.; but thus to decree through the assistance of the Holy Ghost, who remaineth with the Church to the end, and to be directed by Scripture, shall still continue. Therefore this decreeing is not as the inditing of the Holy Scripture. The minor is clear both from Christ's promise, "Where two or three are met together," Matt. xvii. 18-20; Matt. viii. 20; as also by the Spirit's inspiring those councils of Nice of old, and Dort of late: Therefore the apostles here laid aside their apostolical extraordinary power, descending to the places of ordinary pastors, to give them examples in future ages.

To conclude, it is plain, that all the essentials in this assembly were synodal, as whether we consider: 1. The occasion of the meeting, a controversy; 2. The deputation of commissioners from particular churches, for the deciding of that controversy; or 3. The convention of those that were deputed; or 4. The discussion of the question, they being so convened; or 5. The determination of the question so discussed; or 6. The imposition of the thing so determined; or 7. The subjection to the thing so imposed.

1 Tim. i. 17

TO THE IMMORTAL GOD ALONE BE GLORY FOR EVER AND EVER.

FOOTNOTES:

1 [This truth, that Jesus Christ is a king, and hath a kingdom and government in his Church distinct from the kingdoms of this world, and from the civil government, hath this commendation and character above all other truths, that Christ himself suffered to the death for it, and sealed it with his blood. For it may be observed from the story of his passion, this was the only point of his accusation, which was confessed and avouched by himself, Luke xxiii. 3; John xviii. 33, 36, 37; was most aggravated, prosecuted, and driven home by the Jews, Luke xxiii. 2; John xix. 22, 23; was prevalent with Pilate as the cause of condemning him to die, John xix. 12, 13, and was mentioned also in his superscription upon his cross, John xix. 19; and although in reference to God, and in respect of satisfaction to the Divine justice for our sins, his death was [Greek: lytron] a price of redemption; yet in reference to men who did persecute, accuse, and condemn him, his death was [Greek: martyrion] a martyr's testimony to seal such a truth.—Mr. *G. Gillespie, in his Aaron's Rod Blossoming, &c., Epist. to the Reader.*]

2 [*Cent. I. lib. 2, cap.* 7, *p.* 407 *ad* 418, *Edit. Basil. An.* 1624. De rebus ad Gubernationem Ecclesiae pertinentibus, Apostoli certos quosdam, Canones tradiderunt: quos ordine subjiciemus, &c.]

3 [Directions of the Lords and Commons, &c. Aug. 19, 1645, p. 10]

4 [(1) The ancient discipline of the Bohemian Brethren, published in Latin, in octavo, *Anno*1633, pages 99, 100.

(2) The discipline of Geneva, *Anno* 1576, in *Art.* 1, 22, 57, 86, and 87.

(3) The discipline of the French church at Frankfort, *Edit.* 2, in octavo, *Anno* 1555, *in cap. de Disciplina et Excom.,* p. 75, and the Ecclesiast. Discipline of the reformed churches of France, printed at London, *Anno* 1642, *Art.* 15, 16, and 24, p. 44. (1) The Synodal Constitution of the Dutch churches in England, chap. 4, *Art.* 13, and *Tit.* 1, *Art.* 2; and the Dutch churches in Belgia, (see *Harmonia Synodorum Belgicarum,*) *cap.* 14, *Art.* 7, 11, and 15, p. 160. (5) The reformed churches at Nassau, in Germany, as *Zeoper*testifies, *De Politei Eccles.,* printed *Herborne, Anno* 1607, in octavo, *Tit. de Censuris Ecclesiast., Part* 4, *Art.* 64, p. 813. (6) The discipline in the churches constituted by the labor of *Joannes à Lasco,* entitled *Forma ac ratio tota Ecclesiastici Miniterii, &c.,author Joannes à Lasco Poloniae Barone, Anno* 1555, p. 291. (7) The discipline agreed upon by the English exiles that fled from the *Marian* persecution to Frankfort, thence to Geneva, allowed by *Calvin;* entitled *Ratio ac forma publicè orandi Deum, &c., Genevae,* 1556, *Tit. de Disciplina,* p. 68. (8) The Order of Excommunication and Public Repentance used in the Church of Scotland, *Anno* 1571, *Tit.* The offences that deserve public repentance, &c., pp. 87, 88.]

5 [See more in chap. 10, sect. 1.]

6 [R. Park, de Polit. Eccl. 1. 2, cap. 42.]

7 [Malcolm. Com. in loco.]

8 [Calvin in loco.]

9 [Chrys. wisheth—"But, O that there had not wanted one that would have delivered diligently unto us the history of the apostles, not only what they wrote, or what they spake, but how they behaved themselves throughout their whole life, both what they did eat, and when they did eat, when they sat, and whither they went, and what they did every day, in what parts they lived, and into what house they entered, and whither they sailed, and that would accurately have expounded all things; so full of manifold utility are all things of theirs."—Chrys., Argum. in Epist. ad Philem. And elsewhere he affirmeth,—"Nor hath the grace of the Holy Ghost without cause left unto us these histories written, but that he may stir us up to the imitation and emulation of such unspeakable men. For when we hear of this man's patience, of that man's soberness, of another man's readiness to entertain strangers, and the manifold virtue of every one, and how every one of them did shine and become illustrious, we are stirred up to the like zeal." Chrys. in Gen. xxx. 25. Homil. 57, in initio.]

10 ["For this cause, therefore, the conversation of these most excellent men is accurately related, that by imitation of them our life may be rightly led on to that which is good."—Greg. Nyssen, lib. de Vita Mosis, tom. i. p. 170, vid. tot. lib.]

11 [Perkins on Matth. vi. 16. See him also on Heb. xi. 6, p. 28, in fol. col. 2, B, C, &c., and on Heb. xi. 22, p. 131, col. 2, D, and notably on Heb. xii. 1, p. 200, col. 2, C, D, &c., and on Rev. ii. 19, p. 313, col. 1, B, and his Art of Prophesying, p. 663, col. 1 and 2. Vide Pet. Martyr in lib. Jud. p. 2, col. 1, and in Rom. iv. 23, 24. And Calvin in Heb. xii. 1; and in Rom. iv. 23, 24, and in 1. Pet. i. 21, &c.]

12 [Park. de Pol. Eccl. 1. 2, c. 42.]

13 [2 Cor. x. 8, and xiii. 10.]

14 [Matt. xvi. 19, and xviii. 15-18; 1 Cor. v. 4, 5; 2 Cor. x. 8, and xiii. 10.]

15 [2 Tim. iii. 16, 17; 1 Tim. iii. 14, 15, with all places that mention any thing of government.]

16 [Eph. iv. 8, 11, 12; 1 Cor. xii. 28; Matt. xxviii. 18-20; John xx. 21-23; Matt. xvi. 19; 2 Cor. x. 8.]

17 [Matt. xvi. 19, and xxviii. 19; John xx. 21, 23; 2 Cor. x. 8, and xiii. 10.]

18 [Matt, xxviii. 18-20; Acts vi. 4; 2 Tim. iv. 2.]

19 [Matt, xxviii. 18-20; 1 Cor. xi. 24.]

20 [Matt, xviii. 15-17; Tit. iii. 19; 1 Tim. v. 20; 1 Cor. v. 4, 5, 13; 2 Cor. ii. 6: 1 Tim. i. 20; 2 Cor. ii 7, 8, &c.]

21 [1 Cor. iv. 1.]

22 [2 Cor. x. 8, and xiii. 10.]

23 [[Greek: Ekklaesia], Acts xix. 32, 39, 40; Eph. v. 23; 1 Cor. xii. 98.]

24 [Cameron. Praelect de Eccles. in fol. pp. 296-298.]

25 [Who in relating such things can refrain from weeping?]

26 [See Mr. Edwards's Antapologia, page 201, printed in anno 1644, proving this out of their own books. Especially see a little book in 12mo. printed in anno 1646, styled a collection of certain matters, which almost in every page pleads for Independency and Independents by name: from which most of the Independent principles seem to be derived.]

27 [Let not any man put off this Scripture, saying, This is in the Old Testament, but we find no such thing in the gospel; for we find the same thing, almost the same words used in a prophecy of the times of the gospel, Zech. xiii. 3. In the latter end of the xii. chapter, it is prophesied that those who pierced Christ, should *look upon him and mourn*, &c., having a *spirit of grace and supplication* poured upon them, chap. xiii. 1. "There shall now be opened a fountain for sin, and for uncleanness," ver. 3. "It shall come to pass that he that takes upon him to prophesy, that his father and mother that begat him, shall say unto him, Thou shalt not live, for thou speakest lies in the name of the Lord: and his father and his mother that begat him, shall thrust him through, when he prophesieth." You must understand this by that in Deuteronomy. The meaning is not that his father or mother should presently run a knife into him, but that though they begat him, yet they should be the means to bring him to condign punishment, even the taking away his life; these who were the instruments of his life, should now be the instruments of his death.—Mr. Jer. Burroughs in ills Irenicum, chap. v., Pages 19, 20, printed 1646.]

28 [But schismatics and heretics are called evil-workers, Phil. iii. 2; and heresy is classed among the works of the flesh, Gal. v. 20.]

29 [Mr. Burroughs in his *Irenicum*, c.v. page 25; printed 1646.]

30 [See this evidenced upon divers grounds in *Appollon. jus Majest.*, pp. 25, 26.]

31 [See M.S. to A.S., pages 55-60.]

32 [The civil magistrate is no proper church officer, as was intimated, Part 1 c. 1., and will be further evidenced in this chapter.]

33 [That the civil magistrate is not the vicar of Christ our Mediator, see abundantly proved by Mr. S. Rutherford, in his Divine Right of Church Government, &c., Ch. 27, Quest. 23, pages 595 to 647.]

34 [The formal difference or distinction betwixt these two powers, is fully and clearly asserted by that learned bishop, Usher, in these words: "God, for the better settling of piety and honesty among men, and the repressing of profaneness and other vices, hath established two distinct powers upon earth: the one of the keys, committed to the Church; the other of the sword, committed to the civil magistrate. That of the keys, is ordained to work upon the inward man; having immediate relation to the remitting or retaining of sins, John xx. 23. That of the sword is appointed to work upon the outward man; yielding protection to the obedient, and inflicting external punishment upon the rebellious and disobedient. By the former, the spiritual officers of the Church of Christ are inclinable to govern well, 1 Tim. v. 17. To *speak*, and *exhort*, and *rebuke* with all *authority*, Tit. ii. 15. To loose such as are penitent, Matt. xvi. 19, and xviii. 18. To commit others to the Lord's prison, until their amendment, or to bind them over to the judgment of the great day, if they shall persist in their wilfulness and obstinacy. By the other, princes have an imperious power assigned by God unto them, for the defence of such as do well, and executing revenge and wrath, Rom. xiii. 4, upon such as do evil, whether by death, or banishment, or confiscation of goods, or imprisonment, Ezra vii. 26, according to the quality of the offence.

"When St. Peter, that had the keys committed unto him, made bold to draw the sword, he was commanded to put it up, Matt. xxvi. 52, as a weapon that he had no authority to meddle withal. And on the other side, when Uzziah the king would venture upon the execution of the priest's office, it was said unto him, 'It pertaineth not unto thee, Uzziah, to burn incense unto the Lord, but to the priests, the sons of Aaron, that are consecrated to burn incense,' 2 Chron. xxvi. 18. Let this therefore be our second conclusion: That the power of the sword, and of the keys, are two distinct ordinances of God; and that the prince hath no more authority to enter upon the execution of any part of the priest's function, than the priest hath to intrude upon any part of the office of the prince." In his speech delivered in the Castle-chamber at Dublin, &c., concerning the oath of supremacy, pages 3, 4, 5. Further differences betwixt these two powers, see in Gillespie's Aaron's Rod, Book 2, Chap. 4.]

35 [See this proposition for substance fully and clearly asserted by that acute and pious author, Mr. P. Bains, in his Diocesan's Trial, quest. 3, pages 83, 84, conclus. 3.]

36 [See Cotton's Keys, &c., pp. 31-33, and Mr. Thomas Goodwin, and Mr. Philip Nye, in their epistle prefixed thereunto, do own this book as being for substance their own judgment.]

37 [See that judicious treatise, Vindiciae Clavium, chap. III. IV. V., pp. 33-52.]

38 [John Cameron, Praelect. in Matt, xviii. 15, p. 149-151, in fol, and Baine's Diocesan's Trial, the third quest, pp. 79, 80, and D. Parcus in Matt. xviii. 15. This is fully discussed and proved by Mr. Rutherford in his Peaceable Plea, Chap. viii. p. 85, &c.]

39 [A difference arose betwixt two gentlemen in that church about singing of hymns: the second gentleman was complained of to the church by the first, and upon hearing of the whole business, and all the words that passed between them, this second gentleman was censured by the church, and Mr. Nye *charged sin upon him* (that was the phrase) in many particulars, and still at the end of every charge Mr. Nye repeated, "this was your sin." After this censure, so solemnly done, the gentleman censured brings in accusations against Mr. Nye, in several articles, charging him with pride, want of charity, &c., in the manner of the censure; and this being brought before the church, continued in debate about half a year, three or four days in a week, and sometimes more, before all the congregation. Divers of the members having callings to follow, they desired to have leave to be absent. Mr. Goodwin oft professed publicly upon these differences, If this were their church fellowship, he would lay down his eldership; and nothing was more commonly spoke among the members, than that certainly for matter of discipline they were not in the right way, for that there was no way of bringing things to an end. At last, after more than half a year's debate, not being able to bring these differences to an end, and being come into England, they had their last meeting about it, to agree not to publish it abroad when they came into England, &c. Mr. Edwards's Antapolog., pp. 36, 37.]

40 [Mr. J. Cotton, in his Way of the Churches of Christ in New England, chap, ii. sect. 7, p. 43.]

41 [Were the power in the church, the church should not only call them, but make them out of virtue and power received into herself; then should the church have a true lordlike power in regard of her ministers. Besides, there are many in the community of Christians incapable of this power regularly, as women and children. Mr. P. Bain in his Diocesan's Trial, quest. 3, conclus. 3, page 84, printed 1621.]

42 [If spiritual and ecclesiastical power be in the church or community of the faithful, the church doth not only call, but make officers out of virtue and power received into herself, and then should the church have a true lordlike power in regard of her ministers. For, as he that will derive authority to the church, maketh himself lord of the church, so, if the church derive authority to the ministers of Christ, she maketh herself lady or mistress over them, in the exercise of that lordlike authority; for, as all men know, it is the property of the lord and master to impart authority. Did the church give power to the pastors and teachers, she might make the sacrament and preaching which one doth in order, no sacrament, no preaching; for it is the order instituted of God that giveth being and efficacy to these ordinances; and if the power of ruling, feeding, and dispensing the holy things of God do reside in the faithful, the word and sacrament, in respect of dispensation and efficacy, shall depend upon the order and institution of the society. If the power of the keys be derived from the community of the faithful, then are all officers immediately and formally servants to the church, and must do every thing in the name of the church, rule, feed, bind, loose, remit, and retain sins, preach and administer the sacraments; then they must perform their office according to the direction of the church, more or less, seldom or frequent, remiss

or diligent; for from whom are they to receive direction how to carry themselves in their offices, but from him or them of whom they receive their office, whose work they are to do, and from whom they must expect reward? If their office and power be of God immediately, they must do the duties of their place according to his designment, and unto him they must give account; but if their power and function be from the church, the church must give account to God, and the officers to the church, whom she doth take to be her helpers, &c. Mr. John Ball, in his Trial of the grounds tending to separation, chap. xii. pages 252, 253, &c.]

43 [See Vindiciae Clavium, judiciously unmasking these new notions.]

44 [Here understand by this phrase, (*over you in the Lord,*) viz: Not only in the fear of the Lord, nor only in those things that appertain to God's worship, but also according to the will, and by the authority of the Lord Christ derived to them.]

45 [See the Apologetical narration by the five Independents, page 8; and Mr. Jo. Cotton, at large, asserts the divine institution of the ruling elder. Way of the Churches of Christ, &c., chap. 2, sect. 2, page 13-35.]

46 [Calvin, Beza, Pareus, Pagnin.]

47 [Arias Montan.]

48 [Tremel. out of the Syriac; so the old Geneva translation, and our new translation.]

49 [Field, of the Church, book 5, chap. 26.]

50 [Sutlive, who afterwards declared, that he was sorry with all his heart, that ever he put pen to paper to write against Beza as he had done, in behalf of the proud domineering prelates; and he spoke this with great indignation.]

51 [Mat. Sutliv. de Presbyterio, cap. 12, p. 87, edit. 1591.]

52 [Ibid. pages 72 and 87, edit. 1591.]

53 [Bilson's perpetual Government of Christ's Church, c. 10, p. 136, 137, 138, printed in Ann. 1610.]

54 [That the magistrate cannot be here meant, see fully evidenced in Mr. Gillespie's Aaron's Rod, &c., book ii. chap. 6, pages 218-224, and also chap. 9, p. 284.]

55 [Pareas in 1 Cor. xii. 28.]

56 [D. Field, Of the Church, book v. chap. xxvi.]

57 [Peter Martyr, Beza, Piscator, and Calvin.]

58 [Calvin in 1 Pet. v. 2, 3. *Vid. etiam Jacob. Laurent. Comment. in* 1 Pet. v. 2, 3, *ubi fusius de hac distinctione disserit,* p. 322, ad. 325.]

59 [Mat. Sutliv. De Presbyterio, cap. 12, page 72 and 87: edit. Lond., an. 1591. Bilson's Perpetual Government of Christ's Church, chap. 10, page 141; in 4to. printed in anno 1610.]

60 [*Vide* Calv. in loc.]

61 [Sutlive.]

62 [Whitgift.]

63 [Coleman.]

64 [Who desire more full satisfaction touching this poor and empty gloss, that the civil magistrate should be meant by these governments, let them consult Mr. Gillespie's elaborate treatise, called Aaron's Rod Blossoming, book 2, chap, 6, pp. 218 to 224.]

65 [Bilson.]

66 [Mr. Rutherford in his Due Right of Presbyteries, p. 145.]

67 [Calvin, Beza, &c. on this place.]

68 [See Gillespie's Aaron's Rod, book 2, chap. 9.]

69 [Mr. Rutherford in his Due Rights of Presbyteries, chap. 7, sec. 7, pages 145-147.]

70 [Beza, Piscata, Calvin, on this verse.]

71 [Bilson's Perpetual Government of Christ's Church, chap. x. pages 130, 131.]

72 [Altar. Damas. cap. xii., page 918 and page 920.]

73 [B. King, in his Sermon on Cant. viii., Bilson in his Perpetual Government of Christ's Church, c. x. page 132, &c.]

74 [B. King, in his Sermon on Cant. viii., page 40.]

75 [B. Whitgift in his Defence against Cartwright's first Reply. This is one of D. Field's three glosses. Field, Of the Church, lib v., chap. 26.]

76 [Bishops that have no tolerable gift of teaching, are like idols, their cases, or rather coffins, set up in the church's choice. Cartwright Testam. *Annot.*, in 1 Tim. v. 17.]

77 [Altar. Damasc. chap, xii., page 919.]

78 [Bridge, Hussey.]

79 [Altar. Damasc. chap, xii., page 919.]

80 [Sutlive.]

81 [Sutlive, De Presbyterio, cap. 12, pages 72, 73.]

82 [Bilson's Government of the Church, page 133.]

83 [Sutlive, De Presbyterio, c. 12, pages 72, 73.]

84 [Bilson, page 135.]

85 [Field, Book v.]

86 [Bilson, page 133.]

87 [Field, book v.]

88 [D. Downham. See Altar. Damasc. c. xii. page 924.]

89 [Chrysost. Homil. 15, in 1 Tim. 5, Hier. in 1 Tim. cap. 5, Ambr. in 1 Tim. cap., Calv. in 1 Tim. cap. 5, Bullinger in 1 Tim. cap. 5, Beza in 1 Tim. 5.]

90 [Bilson, Sutlive, and Downham.]

91 [The London ministers have here inserted the testimonies of these ancient writers in favor of the divine right of the office of the ruling elder, viz. Ignatius, Purpurius, Tertullian, Origen, Cyprian, Optatus, Ambrose, Augustine, and Isidorus; and of these three late ones, viz. Whitaker, Thorndike, and Rivet. The amount of their testimony, when taken together, appears to be simply this, that there have been ruling elders, as distinct from preaching elders, in the Church of Christ from the beginning. It is therefore judged unnecessary to give the quotations from these authors at large.—*Editor.*]

92 [Against the office of deacons, and the divine right thereof, fourteen objections are answered by Mr. S. Rutherford in his Due Right of Presbyteries, chap. 7, pages 159 to 175. To which the reader that shall make any scruple about the deacon's office, is referred for his further satisfaction.]

93 [Some of our brethren in New England, observing what confusion necessarily depends upon the government which hath been practised there, have been forced much to search into it within this four years, and incline to acknowledge the presbyters to be the subject of the power without dependence upon the people. "We judge, upon mature deliberation, that the ordinary exercise of government must be so in the presbyters, as not to depend upon the express votes and suffrages of the people. There hath been a convent or meeting of the ministers of these parts, about this question at Cambridge in the Bay, and there we have proposed our arguments, and answered theirs, and they proposed theirs, and answered ours; and so the point is left to consideration." Mr. Thomas Parker in his letter written from Newbury in New England, December 17, 1643, printed 1644.]

94 [Vid. Hen. Steph. Thes. L. Graec. in verb.]

95 [Piscator.]

96 [Beza.]

97 [Zanch. in loco.]

98 [Vid. Hen. Steph. Thes. ad verb.]

99 [Mr. Jo. Cotton's Keys of the Kingdom of Heaven, chap. vii. in propos. 3, pages 44-46.]

100 [See Mr. Cotton's own words in chap. XIV. at the end, in the margin.]

101 [See John Calvin, in 1 Cor. v. 4.]

102 [Cameron, in Matt. xviii. 15.]

103 [Thus Mr. Bayne remarkably expounds this text, Matt. xviii., saying: Where first mark, that Christ doth presuppose the authority of every particular church taken indistinctly. For it is such a church as any brother offended may presently complain to. Therefore no universal, or provincial, or diocesan church gathered in a council. 2. It is not any particular church that he doth send all Christians to, for then all Christians in the world should come to one particular church, were it possible. He doth therefore presuppose indistinctly the very

particular church where the brother offending and offended are members. And if they be not both of one church, the plaintiff must make his denunciation to the church where the defendant is. 3. As Christ doth speak it of any ordinary particular church indistinctly, so he doth by the name of church not understand essentially all the congregation. For then Christ should give not some, but all the members of the church to be governors of it. 4. Christ speaketh it of such a church to whom we may ordinarily and orderly complain; now this we cannot to the whole multitude. 5. This church he speaketh of then doth presuppose it, as the ordinary executioner of all discipline and censure. But the multitude have not this execution ordinary, as all but Morelius, and such democratical spirits, do affirm. And the reason ratifying the sentence of the church, doth show that often the number of it is but small, "For where two or three are gathered together in my name;" whereas the church or congregations essentially taken for teachers and people, are incomparably great. Neither doth Christ mean by church the chief pastor, who is virtually as the whole church.—Mr. Bayne's Diocesan's Trial.]

104 [Timothy received grace by the laying on of the hands of the presbytery. For that persons must be understood here, is apparent by the like place, when it is said, by the laying on of my hands, he noteth a person, and so here a presbytery. 2. To take presbytery to signify the order of priesthood, is against all lexicons, and the nature of the Greek termination. 3. Timothy never received that order of a presbyter, as before we have proved. 4. It cannot signify, as Greek expositors take it, a company of bishops; for neither was that canon of three bishops and the Metropolitan, or all the bishops in a province, in the apostle's time; neither were these who were now called bishops, then called presbyters, as they say, but apostles, men that had received apostolic grace, angels, &c. Finally, it is very absurd to think of companies of other presbyters in churches that Paul planted, but presbyteries of such presbyters as are now distinguished from bishops, which is the grant of our adversaries.—Bayne's Diocesan's Trial, page 82.]

105 [See Assertion of the Government of the Church of Scotland, Part I. Chap. 2, p. 122, &c.]

106 [Mr. Gillespie's Aaron's Rod Blossoming, book i. chap. iii. pages 8-38.]

107 [Vid. Joannis Seldeni de Anno Civili, and Calendario, &c. Dissertationem in Praefat., page 8. See also Mr. John Lightfoot's Commentary upon the Acts, c. x. 28, pages 235-239.]

108 [John Cameron, Praelect. in Matt. xviii. 15, page 143 ad 162, and Mr. G. Gillespie's Aaron's Rod Blossoming, &c., book i., chap. 3, page 8, &c., and book ii., chap. 9, page 294-297; and book iii., chapters 2-6, handling this elaborately, pages 350-423.]

109 [Assertion, &c., part 2, chap. 3, p. 139.]

110 [Basilius in Psal. cxv. Oecumenius in loc. Jerom. Chrysostome, hom. 33, in Matt. Irenaeus, lib. 1, chap. 11. Salmeron.]

111 [Euseb. Hist. Eccles. 1. 8 c. 1.]

112 [If Cenchrea be comprehended under the church of Corinth in this epistle, and the apostle writing to the Corinthians, wrote also to this church, called, Rom. xvi. 1, *the church of Cenchrea*, then have we more congregations than one at Corinth. Now, Cenchrea was a seaport or harbor of the Corinthians. It was a place near to Corinth, on the east of the Egean Sea. Rutherford, in his Due Right of Presbyteries, page 462.]

113 [Paget, Gillespie, and the four Leyden professors, unto whose judicious and elaborate treatises, the reader is referred for more full satisfaction against the usual cavils and exceptions that are made against synods, and their power.]

114 [This is the judgment of the learned Whitaker upon these words: other lawful councils may in like manner assert "their decrees to be the decrees of the Holy Ghost, if they shall be like to this council, and shall keep the same rule, which in this council the apostles did keep and follow. For if they shall decree and determine nothing but from Scripture, (which was done in this council.) and if they shall examine all questions by the Scripture, and shall follow the voice of the Scriptures in all their decrees, then they may assert, that the Holy Ghost so decreed," &c. Whitaker, Cont. page 610.]

115 | That there is an authoritative, juridical synod; and that this synod, Acts xv., was such a one; and that this synod is a pattern to us;—all this is most ingenuously acknowledged and asserted by that learned Independent, Mr. John Cotton, in these words, viz:

"IV. Proposition, in case a particular church be disturbed with errors of scandal, and the same maintained by a faction among them. Now a synod of churches, or of their messengers, is the first subject of that power and authority, whereby error is judicially convinced and condemned, the truth searched out and determined; and the way of truth and peace declared and imposed upon the churches.

"The truth of this proposition may appear by two arguments

"*Argum.* 1. From the want of power in such a particular church, to pass a binding sentence where error or scandal is maintained by a faction; for the promise of binding and loosing which is made to a particular church, Matt, xviii. 18, is not given to the church when it is leavened with error and variance. And the ground——If then the church, or a considerable part of it, fall into error through ignorance, or into faction; by variance, they cannot expect the presence of Christ with them according to his promise, to pass a blind sentence. And then as they fall under the conviction and admonition of any other sister church, in a way of brotherly love, by virtue of communion of churches; so their errors and variance, and whatsoever scandals else do accompany the same, they are justly subject to the condemnation of a synod of churches.

"2. A second argument to prove that a synod is the first subject of power, to determine and judge errors and variances in particular churches, is taken from the pattern set before us in that case, Acts xv. 1-28: when certain false teachers having taught in the church of Antioch a necessity of circumcision to salvation, and having gotten a faction to take part with them, (as appeareth by the dissension and disputation of Paul and Barnabas against them,) the church did not determine the case themselves, but referred the whole matter to the *apostles and elders at Jerusalem*, Acts xv. 1, 2. Not to the apostles alone, but to the apostles and elders. The apostles were as the elders and rulers of all churches; and the elders there were not a few, the believers in Jerusalem being many thousands. Neither did the apostles determine the matter (as hath been said) by apostolical authority from immediate revelation: but they assembled together with the elders, *to consider of the matter*, ver. 6, and a *multitude of brethren* together with them, ver. 12, 22, 23; and after searching out the cause by an ordinary means of disputation, ver. 7, Peter cleared it by the witness Of the Spirit to his ministry in Cornelius's family; Paul and Barnabas by the like effect of their ministry among the Gentiles: James confirmed the same by the testimony of the prophets, wherewith the whole synod being satisfied, they determine of a JUDICIAL SENTENCE, and of a way to publish it by letters and messengers; in which they CENSURE the false teachers as troublers of their church, and subverters of their souls; they reject the imposition of circumcision as a yoke which neither they nor their fathers were able to bear; they IMPOSE upon the Church none but some necessary observations, and them by way of THAT AUTHORITY which the Lord had given them, ver. 28: which PATTERN clearly showeth us to whom the key of authority is committed, when there groweth offence and difference in a church. Look as in the case of the offence of a faithful brother persisted in, the matter is at last judged and determined in a church: so in the offence of the church or congregation, the matter is at last judged in a congregation of churches, a church of churches; for what is a synod else but a church of churches?"—Keys of the Kingdom of Heaven, pages 47-49.]

116 | Junius, Beza, Calvin, and Piscator.]

APPENDIX.
NO. 1.117
Of the Scriptural Qualifications and Duties of Church Members.

Quest. What persons have a right in the sight of God to be actual members of the Church of Christ?

Ans. Only regenerated and converted persons, such as are married to, and have put on Christ; such as are savingly and powerfully enlightened, quickened, and convinced of sin, righteousness, and judgment;[118] such as have chosen Christ for their Lord and Saviour, and resigned and made over themselves to him, and received him upon his own terms;[119] such only as are reconciled unto, and are in favor with God; as are justified by faith, sanctified by the Spirit, and set apart for holiness, and unto a living to God, and no more unto themselves:[120] such as are the beloved of God, called effectually to be saints, and have really and sincerely taken upon them the yoke of Christ Jesus, I say such persons, and only such, doth Jesus Christ account worthy of this privilege and dignity.[121] Although men do not certainly know those that are such, and by reason of their darkness and fallible judgments they may and do admit others into the Church, and unto her privileges, yet in truth these have no right unto them, and ought not to be there; for these spiritual holy things are for, and only for, spiritual and holy persons. Christ prepares men by his grace, word, and Spirit to make them fit materials, and then he calls them to join together and become a spiritual house, for his delight, service, and glory.[F] And therefore holy persons, and such only, ought to be full members of the Church of Christ.

This will appear by these following particulars:

1. Because God often declares his detestation and abhorrence of others being there, and manifests his indignation against them. As to the man that came to the marriage supper without the wedding-garment, Matt. xxii. 11-13; and the five foolish virgins, chap. xxv.; and the dreadful end of the tares, chap. xiii. 38-44, which were the hypocrites, that by the devil's instigation had crept into the Church. It is true that such were, and will be, in the best of churches, although their guides may do all they can to prevent it, because they cannot make an infallible judgment of persons' states; yet it is as certain these are usurpers and ought not to be there. For, although they are in God's providence permitted to creep in, yet we may be sure they are not there with his approbation:—they are not all Israel that are of Israel; for, saith God to all uncircumcised, What have you to do to take my covenant into your mouth, seeing you hate instruction and cast my words behind your back, (as all hypocrites do,) Ps. l. 16, 17. And Christ says, that such as will not have him to reign over him (and to be sure hypocrites will not) shall be destroyed, Luke xix. 27. Now, as hypocrites are most loathsome and abominable persons in the sight of God, as may be seen at large in Matt, xxiii. 13-35, they have no right unto the spiritual privileges of the Church of Christ, because, in the sight of God, the gospel Church should consist only of new creatures and real members of Jesus Christ.

II. That all church members ought to be sincere-hearted believers appears by the high titles which the Lord Jesus gives unto them in Scripture: they are described to be like the king's daughter, all glorious within. They are called saints, holy brethren, and beloved, elect, dear children of God, the spouse of Christ, a holy temple of God, lively stones, built up a spiritual house, a holy priesthood, and the Lord's sealed ones. Now such honorable titles belong not unto mere formal professors, but only unto the real members of Christ: not unto those that have a name only; but to such as are so indeed and in truth.

III. A third reason is taken from the ends of God in instituting and appointing churches. They are said to be built by the Spirit for God, i.e. for God to dwell and walk in them, to repose himself in them, as in his holy garden, house, and temple. They are designed for promoting his glory in the world, to distinguish his people from others; that they should be to the praise of his glorious grace, and be the living witnesses to his name, truths, and ways; that they should be the habitations of beauty and glory, of fame and renown in the world, and be the light thereof; and that with one heart and mouth they should glorify God. Believers are united into a church capacity for their spiritual profit and advantage, that God may there give them his love, and communicate his grace, truths, and counsels to them, as to his avowed household and family Christ walks there, and God the Father dwells there, and the Holy Spirit speaks to them in a special and frequent manner to distribute liberally of their love and fulness. They are formed and set up by Jesus Christ to be the only seats and subjects of his laws, ordinances, power, and authority, that they might receive, obey, and observe his laws, declare before the world their owning of him for their Lord, by their open and public profession of, and subjection unto him, as such; and that, by their regular and distinct following of him in their united church state, they might manifest to all men, that they are his subjects and disciples, that they have chosen him for their Lord and King, and his law for the rule of their faith and obedience; that they are not their own, but his; and that they have reposed themselves in him, as their happiness and eternal blessedness; that they are called out of the world and set apart by his grace for himself, to live unto him; and that they have taken upon themselves his holy yoke, and the observation of all his laws. God has united believers into churches, that by his Spirit and ministers he may feed and nourish them there as his flock, water them as his garden, support them as his house, and order and govern them as his family and household.

IV. The Church of Christ should consist of new creatures and sincere-hearted believers, because they only can and will answer and prosecute the foresaid, and such like holy ends of God, in and by his Church. They are fitted and framed, moulded and polished, by the Holy Ghost, for their growing up into a holy temple in the Lord; and so, by the constant and promised guidance and conduct of their living head Jesus Christ, with their spiritual qualifications, they are enabled to answer and perform the great ends of God, in erecting and building them up in a church state. But unregenerate persons cannot do this, because they are strangers in heart to Jesus Christ, and to the power of godliness; nor would they if they could, because they have not the saving knowledge of Christ in them, but are full of obstinacy against God.

V. Because all the laws, ordinances, and works of church members are holy, spiritual, and heavenly. They are such as the natural man understands not, and cannot discern what they are, because they are spiritual and holy; and therefore they that are not taught of God savingly to form a proper judgment of them, do think and judge of them carnally and vainly. But believers have them written in their hearts beforehand. Yet they have them not without book, I mean they have the same laws of Christ written in the books of their hearts which they find in the Bible, by which they are in some measure enabled to understand, receive, love, and rightly to obey, the laws and ordinances of Christ without. Their laws are holy and spiritual, and their works in a church state are so likewise. They have a holy God, who is a Spirit, to serve and worship; a spiritual Head to believe in and obey; holy and spiritual work to do; and therefore they need to be holy and spiritual persons, not only externally in profession, but also internally, in truth. Almost all the laws and ordinances of Christ are committed unto them, and God expects his principal and choicest worship from his Church; and these are all above and beyond the reach of carnal minds.

VI. The Church ought to be composed of believers and regenerated persons, because they are called to continue and stand fast in all storms and tempests; and to hold out unto the end, as being built upon the rock Jesus Christ. For whatever church is built upon the sand, and not upon the Lord Jesus, and by the authority of his word and Spirit, will not stand long, because it wants a foundation to bear up its weight. They must all be built upon the rock and chief corner-stone, the sure foundation that God hath laid. The Lord Jesus tells us, Matt. xvi. 18, that upon this rock (i.e. himself and the truths that Peter had confessed) will I build my Church, and the gates of hell shall not prevail against it. But it is certain that hypocrites are not built upon Christ by faith, but fix their vain hopes on a sandy foundation. Therefore, if their persons are not built upon Christ, their church state cannot; but upon the sand. Hence then it follows that only true believers are built on Christ, and so they are the only persons that Christ wishes to have built up into holy temples; because the churches that Christ builds shall be built upon himself, that they may stand impregnable against all opposition: and therefore they should only be composed of such as are united to him by faith, and have chosen him for their only rock and foundation, and not of such as do secretly reject him.

Quest. What qualifications should believers find in themselves for their own satisfaction, before they enter into full communion with the visible Church of Christ?

Ans. They should be able to answer the following questions in the affirmative.

I. Can you say indeed that you do seriously and heartily desire to see, and to be more deeply and powerfully convinced of your own vileness and sinfulness, of your own weakness and wretchedness, and of your wants and unworthiness? and that, in order to your deep and spiritual humiliation and self-debasing, that you may be more vile in your own eyes, and Jesus Christ and free grace more precious and excellent, more high and honorable, and more

125

sweet and desirable, that your hearts may be melted into godly sorrow, and that you may be moved thereby to abhor yourselves, and to repent in dust and ashes? Job xlii. 5, 6.

II. Can you say that you do seriously and heartily desire and endeavor to believe in Christ, and to receive and accept of him in the gospel way, such as you find in Mark viii. 34; Luke xiv. 26-28, and elsewhere? Do you thus desire and choose to have him with his yoke and cross? Matt. xi. 28, 29. And do you so deny yourselves, and your sinful self, righteous self, worldly self, supposed able, powerful self, and every other carnal and spiritual self, that Christ only may be exalted, that you may be nothing in your justification and salvation, but that Jesus Christ and free grace may be all, and in all things? Col. iii. 11; Phil. iii. 7, 8. Do you desire, choose, and endeavor to have Christ on the hardest terms; and do you desire, that all may go for Christ's person, blood, and righteousness, his grace, love, life, and Spirit, for the pardon of your sins, and the justification of your persons, that you may be found in him, not having your own righteousness, but the righteousness of Christ by faith? Phil. iii. 9. And do you go and present yourselves as destitute condemned sinners to him, and to God the Father in and by him, that you may be clothed with the righteousness of Christ, and that God may pardon, justify, and accept you for his sake only?

III. Do you seriously and heartily desire and choose to have Christ Jesus for your Lord and Ruler too, Col. ii. 6; that he may rule in you, and over you, and that your lusts and yourselves, your interests, and your all, may be subject unto him, and be wholly at his command and disposal continually? Is Christ the Lord as acceptable to you as Christ Jesus the Saviour? and are you willing to obey him, and to be subject to his authority and dominion, as well as to be saved by him? Would you have him to destroy your lusts, to make an end of sin, and to bring all under his obedience?

IV. Do you seriously and heartily desire and endeavor never to sin more; but to walk with God unto all well-pleasing continually? Col. i. 10. And do you pray earnestly that God would work in you that which is well-pleasing in his sight, Heb. xiii. 21, that you may in all your ways honor and glorify him, as the end of your living in this world? 2 Cor. v. 15. Would you indeed live to the praise of his glorious grace, be an ornament unto his name and gospel, and be fruitful in every good word and work? Are these things the scope, aim, and intent of your hearts and souls (in some good measure and degree) daily, in duties and ordinances, and at other times?

V. Do you seriously and heartily choose and desire communion with Christ, and in truth endeavor to obtain and keep it? Do you so seek for it in the way of gospel obedience, and in observing your duty in keeping Christ's commandments? And do you prefer it to all earthly, carnal things? Do your hearts breathe and pant after it, and are you willing to deny self, and all self-interests to get it? Are you glad when you find it, and sad when by your own carelessness you lose it? Doth it when obtained quicken your love to and zeal for Christ? Doth it warm your hearts, and cause them for a time to run your race in gospel obedience cheerfully? Doth it lead you unto, and cause your hearts to centre in Christ? and doth it oblige and bind them faster unto him and stir you up to thankfulness?

VI. Do you sincerely and heartily desire, seriously choose, and earnestly endeavor, to be filled with gospel sincerity towards God and man, and would you rather be true-hearted towards God than seem to be so towards man? Would you much rather have the praise of God, and be approved of by him, than the praise of men, and be extolled by them? Is it the great thing you aim at, in your profession and practice, to attain sincerity and uprightness in heart? Is all hypocrisy hateful and abominable unto you? Are you afraid of it, and do you watch and strive against it, as against an enemy to God and your own souls, and are you grieved indeed when you find it in you?

VII. Do you desire and choose Jesus Christ for the great object of your love, delight, and joy? and do you find him to be so in some measure? Do you desire and endeavor to make him the object of your warmest affections, and to love him sincerely, heartily, spiritually, fervently, and constantly; and do you express your love to him by keeping his commandments? Are you grieved in spirit, because you can love him no more? and do you earnestly pray unto him to shed abroad his love into your hearts by the Holy Ghost, that you may love him as ye ought? Rom. v. 5. Doth his love and loveliness attract your hearts to him, and cause you to yield the obedience of faith to his holy laws?

VIII. Is it the desire, choice, and endeavor of your souls to have all sins purged out of them, and to have them filled with Christ's grace, truth, and holiness; and do you hate your sin, watch and fight against it, and endeavor to keep it under? Do you indeed aim at, desire, labor, and strive, to be holy in heart and life, and conformable unto Jesus Christ in all things possible? Are your lusts your heaviest burdens and your greatest afflictions, and do you intend and endeavor their utter ruin and destruction? Will no degree of grace satisfy you until you be perfect to the utmost as Christ is? Are you so much concerned for Christ's honor, and your soul's holiness and happiness, that you dare not knowingly sin against them for a world; or do, in word or deed, by omission or commission, that which may dishonor, grieve, or wound them? Are these things so indeed?

IX. Have you a measure of spiritual knowledge and discerning of spiritual things? Do you understand the nature and concerns of the house of God, and the work and duties, the privileges and enjoyments thereof, and what you have to do there; together with the ends of God in instituting and erecting gospel churches?

X. Do you intend and resolve, in the light, life, and power of Christ, to seek for, and endeavor unfeignedly to obtain, and prosecute the ends of church fellowship, when you shall be accepted among them? and do you desire and aim at the holy ends appointed by God in desiring communion with them? as, 1. To enjoy God and communion with him in all his ordinances. 2. To worship God there in spirit and truth, and to give him your homage and service in his house. 3. To show your subjection and obedience to him, and to make a public and open profession of him, and of his truths before men. 4. To receive of his grace, to enrich your souls with his fulness, and to be sealed by his Spirit unto the day of your redemption. 5. That you may walk orderly and beautifully, and shine as lights in the Church, and in the world, before saints and sinners. 6. That you may be established in the truth, live under the watch and care of Christ's ministers, and of fellow-members; that by their inspection and faithful dealings with you you may be kept, or brought back from sin to God, by their wise reproofs and holy instructions. 7. That you may yield up yourselves in holy obedience to Christ, and do all things whatsoever he commands you, that you may have the right use and enjoyment of all your purchased privileges, and be secured against the gates of hell. Are these and such like ends in your hearts and minds, in your walk and in church fellowship, and can you find the forementioned signs of grace in you in some suitable measure, though not so clearly and fully as you would wish? Then I may venture to assure you, that you are qualified for being actual members of the Church of Christ, that you are called and invited into his house, and that you are indispensably bound to answer to the call of God, and to enter into his holy temple.

I say that church privileges are yours, the doors of God's house stand open for you, Christ stands at the door and waits for you, he invites you to come in and to sit down at his table, and you shall be most freely and heartily welcome to your Lord, and to his people.

Quest. What are those qualifications, which the rulers of a church, for their own satisfaction, should look for, and find in such persons, as they admit into full communion with the Church of Christ?

Ans. It is certain that all that profess the name of Christ and his ways, ought not, and may not be admitted into the Lord's holy temple, because many, if not the most of them, are very ignorant of Christ and his ways, and notoriously scandalous in their lives, as sad and woful experience shows. If church rulers should admit known hypocrites, they betray their trust, and defile Christ's holy temple, by taking in such persons as they know, or ought to know, he would not have there: and that they ought to try and prove persons, that they may know their fitness, before they admit them in, is clear in Acts ix. 26, 27, and because Christ hath committed the keys of his house to take in and exclude according to his will and appointment.

As to satisfying qualifications in persons desiring admission into the church, when they appear to be real sound-hearted believers, according to the judgment of charity, by the rules of the word, the church ought to receive them in the Lord.

I. If they can satisfy the church, by giving Scripture evidence of their regeneration, conversion, repentance, and faith in Christ; of their knowledge of Christ, his laws and

127

ordinances; of their lost and perishing state by reason of sin, and of their sincere desires and resolutions to become the Lord's, and to walk with him unto all well-pleasing in all his ways.

II. If they are sound in the faith of the gospel; I mean in the chief and principal doctrines thereof, although they may be ignorant of, or mistaken in matters of less importance. If they have some distinct knowledge and faith concerning these, and other such truths and matters contained in the word of God; as of the state and condition in which man was at first created; how he lost that holy and blessed estate, and the misery into which he brought himself and all his posterity thereby. Concerning themselves, that they are by nature children of wrath, dead in trespasses and sins, and condemned to eternal death; that they are enemies to, and at enmity with, God; that they have neither will nor power by nature to will and to do that which they ought, and which is well-pleasing to God; that they have forsaken God, and are under the curse of the law; and that they are the children, subjects, and servants of the devil, the world, and their own lusts; that God left not all men in this lost state and condition, but provided an all-sufficient remedy, namely, Jesus Christ, and that by an everlasting covenant, entered into with him, in the behalf of men, before the foundation of the world, Tit. i. 2; 2 Tim. i. 9; Prov. viii.: and that, in pursuance thereof, he elected and gave some to Christ, that he might save them out of his mere grace and love. John vi. 37, 40:—That God the Father gave and sent his Son, the second person of the Trinity, to mediate peace between God and man, and to reconcile them to God, by his active and passive obedience;—that Jesus Christ gave himself, and became a propitiation for their sins;—that he assumed our nature into a personal union with himself, whereby there are two natures in one person, by which he was made capable of his mediatorship;—that he, being God and man in one person, took upon himself our guilt and punishment, obeyed the whole law of God, that men had broke, and did always the things that pleased God;—that, when he had finished his active obedience, he became obedient unto the death of the cross, to the wrath of God, and to the curse of the law, Gal. iii. 13; Phil. ii. 8;—that he really died and was buried, lay in the grave, and rose again the third day; and after forty days he ascended into heaven, and sat down at the right hand of God; and that he will come again to judge the quick and the dead;—that he is king, priest, and prophet; a king to give laws unto men, and to command their obedience to him, to rule and govern his subjects, and to reward the obedient, and to punish the disobedient;—that all power in heaven and earth is committed unto him; and that he is coequally and coeternally God with the Father and Holy Spirit;—that as a High Priest he died and made atonement for the sins of his people, and sits in heaven to make intercession, and to appear in the presence of God for them, Heb. vii. 25, and ix. 24;—that there are three persons in the Godhead, yet but one God;—that the Holy Ghost is eternally God, was sent into the world, and came from the Father and Son, for the elect's sake;—that it is he that regenerates persons, works effectually in their hearts, applies Jesus Christ and all his benefits to men, and savingly convinces his elect of sin, righteousness, and judgment. That all that rightly believe in Christ shall be saved, but those that believe not shall be damned; and that all that believe in him must be careful to perform good works. That believers are made righteous, through the righteousness of Jesus Christ, and that they have none of their own to commend them unto God. That God hath made Jesus Christ unto his chosen, wisdom, righteousness, sanctification, and redemption; and that they are made the righteousness of God in him. That God imputed their sins to Christ, and imputes the blood and righteousness of Christ to them; and that they are justified thereby, and not by inherent holiness and righteousness. That God loves, pardons, justifies, and saves men *freely*, without any respect unto their good works, as any cause thereof; but that all the moving cause (without himself) is Jesus Christ in his mediation. That the ground and reason of their obedience, in performing good works, is the revealed will and pleasure of Christ commanding them, and the ends of them are to express their thankfulness to God for his grace and love, to please and honor him, to meet with God, and to enjoy communion with him, to receive of his grace and the good of many promises; to shine as lights in the world, and to be useful unto men; to declare whose and what they are, and to lay up a reward in another world; to keep their lusts under, and their graces in use and exercise; and to manifest their respect and subjection to Jesus Christ, his authority, and law. That the law, for the matter of it, as in the hand of Christ, is the rule of all obedience; and that all are bound to yield subjection to it. That there shall be a resurrection of the just and unjust. That regeneration is absolutely necessary to salvation, and that without it none can enter into the kingdom of heaven. That the Scriptures of the Old and New Testaments contain, and exhibit unto men, the whole revealed will of God, and are sufficient to make the man of God perfect, thoroughly furnished unto every good work; and that whatsoever they are to believe and do is contained therein; and that it is the ground of their faith, hope, and practice. That Jesus Christ hath instituted and appointed many ordinances of worship, for his own glory and his people's good, and that all are bound to observe and to wait on God in them. That all persons are indispensably bound to mind, and carefully to observe the principal manner and end of all their duties, and to see that they be right, holy, and spiritual indeed, and not to please themselves with the matter of them alone. That no man can serve God, or do any work acceptable unto him, until he be regenerated, and brought into a state of grace.

These are some of the matters of faith that they should in some measure be acquainted with and believe, that are admitted into full communion with the Church of Christ. And these and other truths must not be known and believed in a general, notional, light, and speculative manner; but heartily, powerfully, and particularly: not for others, but for themselves; otherwise their faith and knowledge will no way profit their souls to salvation.

III. They must be qualified also with a blameless conversation. Their conversation must be as becometh the gospel, otherwise they are not meet for communion with the gospel church. Carnal walking will not suit spiritual temples: for they will greatly pollute and defile them, and stain and obscure their beauty and glory. Therefore they must not be brawlers and contentious persons, covetous and worldly-minded, vain and frothy. They must not be froward and peevish, nor defraud others of their right. Nor must they neglect the worship of God in their families, nor be careless in governing and educating them in good manners, and in the things of God. They must not be such as are known to omit the duties and ordinances of religion in their proper seasons, or to have vicious families through their neglect: nor to have any other kind of conversation hateful to God and to his people. And therefore, whatever their profession be, they may not be admitted into the Church of God, until they have repented of these, or any other scandal in their life and conduct.

IV. They ought to be such as have chosen the Lord Jesus Christ for their king and head, and dedicated and devoted themselves to him, to live in him and for him: such as have singled him out, and set him apart, (as it were,) to be the object of their love, trust, and delight, of their service and obedience. They must have chosen and closed with him upon his own terms, (i.e. *freely*,) renouncing and rejecting all their own righteousness, worthiness, interest, and sufficiency, and choosing and appropriating him to themselves, for their righteousness, worthiness, portion, and sufficiency, under a sight and conviction of their own emptiness and deformity; and with a heart-satisfied persuasion of the loveliness and fulness of Christ.

V. All this must be done seriously, humbly, and heartily, so far as men can judge. If persons declare their knowledge of God and faith in Christ in such a manner, and apparently by such a spirit as evidences some sense and feeling of what they do declare, church rulers may be much helped in forming a right judgment of them, that they are fitted by God for church-membership. If they do seriously profess, that what they do is in obedience to the will, and, as they judge, to the call of Christ as their indispensable duty;—that they join in church fellowship to meet with and enjoy God, to receive out of his fulness to enable them to perform all duties, and to conform their hearts and lives in his will to all things;—such persons may undoubtedly be accounted worthy members, and admitted as such.

Quest. What are the duties of church members towards one another?

Ans. I. The greatest is love; love and spiritual affections are the holy cords which tie the hearts, souls, and judgments of believers together. This is that which, together with the fear of God, makes them avoid all things that may give just offence or grief to one another, and that which provokes them to follow after the things that make for peace and edification. Love is the bond of peace. It is that which, together with divine light and truth, causes church members to draw together as in one yoke, and unanimously as with one heart and soul to design, aim at, and carry on mutual and common good in the church. Without this they cannot, they will not cement, nor long abide and live together as a church, in peace and unity, nor promote any good work among themselves. Without heart-uniting love they will receive and entertain jealousies and suspicions one of another, and put the worst construction on whatever is said or done; and they cannot walk together comfortably and profitably when these are entertained. Therefore it is absolutely necessary for all church members to be firmly united in cordial love and charity, which is the bond of perfectness to and in all other duties. God highly commends and strictly commands this love one to another, and puts it into the heart of his peculiar people, that they may do what he commands.

1. God highly commends it wherever he finds it in act and exercise; 1 Thess. iv. 10, "and indeed," says he, "ye do it towards all the brethren." To this duty, and to manifest his high approbation of it, God hath promised a great reward, Heb. vi. 10.

2. God commands it and vehemently exhorts to it often in the gospel. Oh how importunately did the Lord Jesus enjoin it, and frequently press it on his disciples when he was on earth! John xiii. 34, "A new commandment give I unto you." What is that new commandment? Why, "That ye love one another, as I have loved you, that ye also love one another." And in John xv. 12, 17, "This is my commandment, that ye love one another, as I have loved you;" i.e. Take the pattern of my love to you for your pattern in loving one another. I have loved and will love you—1. With *great* love, John xv. 13: so do you likewise. 2. My love to you is *free*, without any desert in you: let yours be free, without carnal respects one to another also. 3. My love to you is *real, hearty*, and *unfeigned*: so let yours be one to another, 1 Pet. i. 22. 4. My love to you is an exceeding *fruitful love*. I loved you so, as to labor, toil, sweat, and die for you: so must you love one another with a fruitful, profiting love. 5. My love to you is a *pitying, sparing, and forgiving love; a forbearing and tender-hearted love*: so must you be to one another, Col. iii. 12, 13. 6. I love you with a *warm and fervent love*: so do you love one another. 7. I love with a *holy, spiritual love*, as new men who have my image stamped on, and my holy nature in you, and as you are made perfect by the comeliness and beauty I have put on you: so do you love one another, because you are a lovely and holy people unto me. 8. I love you with a *constant and unchangeable love*; notwithstanding of all your weaknesses, yea, unkindness too, and unworthy walkings before me: thus you are bound to love one another.

O that church members and all other Christians would seriously, sincerely, diligently, and constantly mind and practise this grand and indispensable duty to one another, in all their ways and actions, and not lay it aside as a little, useless, or indifferent matter, which they may neglect at their own will and pleasure.

2. As we are indispensably bound to love one another; so we are as absolutely and perfectly bound to walk in a loving and encouraging manner towards one another. Our behavior ought to be such in all things, as to invite all to love us, as holy, humble, and blameless saints, and brethren in Christ. The Lord Jesus expects church members to walk lovingly towards one another, as well as to love one another. They ought, therefore, as much as possible, to provoke and encourage each other, and to remove out of the way of love all such stumbling-blocks as may any way hinder it, as we cannot love a sour, peevish, contentious, and cross-grained professor, with as much complacency as a meek, quiet, humble, affable, and courteous one.

3. Christ hath charged and strictly commanded all church members to live in peace: to be at peace among themselves; to follow peace with all men, and as much as in them lieth to live peaceably with all men. O how often, and with what vehemency doth the Holy Ghost press and enjoin this duty, especially among church members, in the Holy Scriptures! See Psal. xxxiv. 14; 1 Pet. iii. 11; Rom xiv. 19; 2 Cor. xiii. 11; 1 Thess. v. 13; Heb. xii. 14; Eph. v. 3. The apostle Paul earnestly warns church members against all debates, strifes, and contentions one with another, especially in their church meetings, Phil. ii. 3. David tells us, that it is a most pleasant and lovely thing for brethren to dwell together in unity, Psal. cxxxiii. 1, 2. Then how much more pleasant and lovely is it for spiritual brethren to love and worship God in this manner together Christ came into the world and lived here a peace-maker, and pronounces them blessed that are so, Matt. v. 9. He is a lover of peace and concord, especially in his Church; but he is an implacable hater of strife and discord, and will

not endure it therein: much less will he wink at such as are the first sowers of these seeds. The truth is, strivers and disputers in a church are the devil's agents, do a great deal of mischief to it, and are real plagues in it. They greatly hinder edification, and spoil the order, beauty, and harmony there: they are the proud, self-conceited men, who are vainly puffed up with high thoughts of themselves, and their own abilities, because they have got some speculative knowledge into their heads, with a volubility of speech, while they are destitute of spiritual wisdom and humility in their hearts; and therefore they conceive that they are wiser than the church, and more able to manage and order church affairs than their rulers. Their pride and self-conceit make them slight and contemn their teachers, and rise up in a rebellious contention with, and opposition unto them; as the prophet complains, Hos. iv. 4, *This people are they that strive with the priests.* Take heed then of strife and contention, and follow peace one with another, especially in your assembling together about the work of the church. Endeavor to get humble hearts, and then you will not be contentious, but quiet and peaceable.

4. Church members ought to sympathize with, and to help to bear one another's burdens as need requires, Rom. xii. 15, 16; Gal. vi. 2. They ought to make their brethren's crosses, losses, temptations, and afflictions their own. And, when they need the helping hand of fellow-members to support or lift them up, when fallen, they must give it to them freely, readily, and cheerfully, and not turn a deaf ear to, nor hide their eyes from, them and their cries. And, if they are cruel to, or careless of, one another in affliction, our Lord Jesus will require it at their hands, and take it as done to himself. Therefore, seeing it is the will of God, and our indispensable duty to one another, who are members of the church, let us put on bowels of mercies and kindness, Col. iii. 12, and be tender-hearted, pitiful, and courteous to each other, Eph. iv. 32; 1 Pet. iii. 8.

5. Church members ought to exhort and comfort one another, for so is the will of God concerning them. This is not only their teacher's duty and work, but theirs also to each other, Heb. x. 24, 25; Heb. iii. 13; 1 Thess. v. 14. Christians stand in continual need of one another's exhortations and consolations; and if they manage this work well they may be very useful and profitable to one another, and may help to awaken, quicken, and provoke one another, to the love and practice of holiness.

6. It is the will of the Lord Jesus Christ, the Church's head, that her members should be each other's keepers; that they should watch over one another, and admonish and reprove one another, as need requires. It is not meant, that they should pry into one another's secrets, or be busybodies in other men's matters, but that they should watch over one another's life and conversation, that if they do well they may be encouraged; if ill, that they may, by counsel, reproof, instruction, and exhortation, be brought to a real sight and sense of their misconduct, and to unfeigned repentance. By which good work, you will do them, the church, yea, Christ himself, good and acceptable service. Church members should carefully observe, if all do keep close to their duty in the church, or are remiss and negligent;—if they conduct themselves in a holy, righteous, and sober way; or if, on the contrary, they are frothy, vain, proud, extravagant, unjust, idle, careless, or any way scandalous. They should strictly observe if there be any tattlers, backbiters, or sowers of discord; or such as speak contemptibly of their brethren, especially of their elders, (ruling or preaching,) and of their administrations: as also, if there be any such as combine together, and make parties in the church, or endeavor to obstruct any good work which their elders are carrying on, for promoting the glory of Christ and the good of his people, and deal with them accordingly. They ought carefully to observe if any be fallen under sin or temptation in any case, and presently to set their hands to help, to relieve, and to restore them, Rev. vi. 1. They must watch, and endeavor to gain a sinning member, 1. By their private admonition, in case the offence be private; and if that will not do, to take one or two more to see what effect that will have. 2. But if that will not answer the end, then they are bound to bring it to the church representative, that they may deal with the offending brother, and proceed against him as commanded: This is another great and indispensable duty required of church members, that they be not partakers of other men's sins.

7. Church members ought to forbear and forgive one another; for this is another commanded duty, Eph. iv. 2, 32; Col. iii. 13. When a brother offends or does another any

injury, the offended brother should tell him of it, examine the matter and search out the circumstances of it, and see whether he did it unadvisedly, through weakness or ignorance; or whether he did it wilfully and knowingly. If upon an impartial search he is found to have wronged his brother through ignorance or weakness, he must judge charitably of him, and not be harsh and severe towards him, in his carriage or censure. But if it clearly appear, upon impartial inquiry, that he did the injury knowingly and wilfully, then the offended brother must deal with him as a wilful transgressor. He must lay his sin before him, and show him what laws he hath transgressed; what evil he hath done him, what wrong to his own soul, and what offence he hath done to Christ, by breaking his holy laws. He must admonish him again and again of his sin, and reprove him, but not too severely, until he find him obstinate and stubborn. And if God convince him of his sin, and give him repentance unto life, he must readily forgive him. And, if he be once truly convinced of, and humbled for, his sin, he will most fully confess it to his brother, as well as to God, and endeavor to make him amends, and give him all possible satisfaction for the injury he hath done him, most freely and willingly: for it is a certain sign that a person is not powerfully and savingly convinced of, and humbled for, his sin, while he bears off, and must be sought after to make satisfaction to such as he hath wronged; because were his heart really melted into the will of God, he could not be quiet, until he have given all possible satisfaction to his brother whom he has injured, Luke xix. 8. But in case he remain obstinate, and will not hearken to reproof, then the offended brother should take one or two more and deal with him; and if that will not do, he ought to bring it to the church representative, i.e. the elders of the church, that they may see what they can do with him. But if they cannot prevail on him to repent and to make satisfaction, then he ought to be cast out of the communion of the church, Matt, xviii. 17.

8. It is the indispensable duty of church members to hearken to and receive instruction, admonition, and reproof from one another. For if some are indispensably bound at certain times to give them, surely others who need them are as much bound to receive them, Prov. viii. 33, x. 17, and xxix. 1. These are bound to hearken to their brethren's reproofs, counsels, and admonitions, with all humility, patience, and freedom of spirit, with all love, meekness, and thankfulness to God, and to the givers of them: for they are great mercies to such as need them, and they are their real and profitable friends, who seek their good, and endeavor to prevent their destruction. Let it therefore never be said justly of any of you that are church members, that you were reproved and admonished of any known sin by a brother, and that you refused and slighted their counsel or reproof, justified yourselves in your sins, and were displeased with or angry at such as admonished you, and did their indispensable duty to you, under your sin, for your salvation.

9. Church members ought to pray for one another, and that with a real love, fervency, and importunity, as they do for themselves, James v. 16. O with what serious minds and strong affections should all church members pray for one another! They should be much in building up one another, and praying in the Holy Ghost one for another, Jude 20. They should carry one another in their hearts at the throne of grace, especially such as are under affliction, the whole Church in general, and her teachers in particular, Heb. xiii. 18, and wrestle with God for them; for they have the spirit of prayer given them, and audience and interest in heaven, for others, as well as for themselves.

10. Church members should often meet together for prayer and holy conversation, by two or three or more, as they may have opportunity. This was wont to be the commendable practice of our forefathers, when Christ, duty, heaven, and religion lay warmer on their hearts than now they do; and this is still the practice of some, that are now alive. God hath promised his glorious teaching, and his warming, strengthening, sanctifying, and comforting presence to such as do so, Matt, xviii. 20. Church members find time enough to visit one another, and meet together to tell some idle stories, to tattle about other men's matters, which do not concern them, and perhaps to *backbite* some of their brethren, and to prejudice the minds of persons against their teachers and their work, if they do not please them. And will not such meetings have bitterness in the end? Is it not great iniquity for Christians to tempt one another to sin, and to wrong their own souls, by misspending that precious time which they might have employed in the service of God, and one another's spiritual profit.

Men and women were wont to discourse often of the things of God and their experiences one to another, Mal. iii. 16. But, alas! few persons are now to be found, who can find time and inclination for such an exercise. And the reason seems to be, that most are great strangers to God and to themselves, and are so much intoxicated with the things of this world, that they will not attend with any pleasure unto the spiritual duties of religion.

11. Church members ought to encourage one another by their example, to attend regularly on the public ordinances of God's worship in his church. Whenever the church meets for the celebration of the worship of God, all her members are bound to meet together at the appointed time, except in extraordinary cases; otherwise good order cannot be kept, and the public duties performed, for the glory of God, and the edification of the church. By church members wilfully or carelessly absenting themselves at the time of meeting, they give an evil example to others, tempt them to do the like, and cast a stumbling-block in the way of their duty, Heb. x. 25.

12. Church members must be charitable to the poor that are among them, and freely contribute to them according to their ability and *their* necessity. They are indispensably bound to impart their help and assistance to the poor, and to give them a little of their estates. It is a debt which they owe to God, and a duty to them. They will comfort them thereby; but they will much more profit themselves than them. It is a more blessed thing to give than to receive. Wealthy persons are stewards for the poor, and a part of what God hath given those was designed for these, 1 Pet. iv. 10, and therefore, says God, Deut. xv. 7, 8, "Thou shalt not shut thine hand from thy poor brother, but shalt open it wide unto him." The rich must not only give to keep the poor alive in misery, but make comfortable provisions for them, that they may have enough to keep them from the temptations of poverty and pressing wants, and to fit them for, and encourage them in, their work and duty, to God and man.

13. Church members ought carefully, watchfully, diligently, and conscientiously to beware of and avoid whatever may give any just offence or scandal to one another. For we are charged to "give none offence neither to Jew nor Gentile, nor to the Church of God," 1 Cor. x. 32. And our Saviour tells us, that "wo to them by whom the offence cometh," Matt, xviii. 7.

You must take heed of such evils as the following, and avoid them, because they all carry scandal in their nature to your own and others' souls: as, 1. Proud, disdainful, and haughty words conduct, and conversation; for these are grievous and provoking evils, which will justly offend all the observers of them. 2. Sullen, sour, and churlish language and behavior, which is offensive unto all sorts of persons; for this is an evil altogether unbecoming the followers of Jesus Christ. 3. A cross, captious, and contradictive spirit and conduct, delighting in opposition to the judgment of the church and her rulers. This is very scandalous to the brethren, and very reproachful unto themselves. 4. Speaking evil of one another behind their backs; backbiting or publishing their real or supposed evils, before they have been spoken to in secret. 5. Speaking lightly or contemptibly of one another, either to themselves or to others in their absence, as few men can bear patiently to be despised by the slighting carriages of their brethren. 6. Vain, foolish, and frothy discourses, which are very offensive to gracious saints. 7. Earthly-mindedness and greedy pursuits after worldly things; for as these are offensive to God, and hurtful to the soul, so they are offensive to saints. 8. Strife and contention among brethren, and grudging or envying one another's prosperity; as these produce many evil and wicked fruits, and cast blame upon the providence of God, who bestows his mercies as he will. 9. Defrauding and breaking promises. Contracting debts and unduly delaying or refusing to pay them, and disappointing men of their just expectations in virtue of promises made to them. Those also are scandalous, and cause the name of God to be evil spoken of. 10. Entering into a marriage relation with such as are apparently in an unbelieving, carnal, and unconverted state and condition; for this also is very offensive to holy serious men, although many make very light of it. 11. Idleness and slothfulness in your external calling, neglecting to provide for your own house, as that will prove a scandalous sin to others and to yourselves too. 12. Taking up a report rashly against one another of a scandalous nature, giving ear unto tattlers, and busybodies; or being busybodies in other men's matters yourselves, as this will give great offence.

NO. II.122

Quest. Who have a right to preach the gospel and dispense the public ordinances of religion?

Ans. Without some proper furniture, it is absurd to imagine any should be sent of God to the ministerial work. When the ascended Jesus gave to the church apostles, evangelists; pastors and teachers, he gave gifts to men. *Who*, saith he, *goeth at, any time a warfare on his own charges?* What is the furniture, the qualifications prerequisite, according to the Holy Scriptures? A blameless conversation, a good report; experience of the self-debasing work of the Spirit of God; compassion to the souls of men; a fixedness in the Christian doctrines; a disposition faithfully to perform his vows; an aptness to teach the ignorant, and convince gainsayers. Knowledge of languages, knowledge of the history and sciences of this world, are useful handmaids to assist us in the study of divine things. To preach from the oracles of God, without capacity to peruse the original, especially if versant in romances and plays, we abhor and detest. This aptness to teach, however, consists not chiefly in any of these, but in a capacity to conceive spiritual things, and with some distinctness to express their conceptions to the edification of others, in that energy and life, whereby one, as affected himself, declares the truths of God, in a simple, serious, bold, and conscience-touching manner. The difference of this, from human eloquence, loud bawling, and theatrical action, is evident. These may touch the passions, and not affect the conscience: they may procure esteem to the preacher, none to Christ. These are the product of natural art: this the distinguished gift of God, without which, in a certain degree, none can have evidence that he was divinely sent to minister the gospel of Christ.

No appearance of furniture, real or pretended, can warrant a man's exercising of the ministry, unless he have a regular call. That *all may prophesy one by one* is indeed hinted in the sacred records: but there it is evident inspiration treats of what pertains to extraordinary officers in the church; hence there is mentioned *the gift of tongues*, extraordinary *psalms, revelations*: the *all* that might prophesy are, therefore, not *all* the members of the church; not *women*, who are forbid to speak in the church; but *all* the extraordinary officers called prophets, 1 Cor. xiv. 31. The *all* that were scattered abroad from Jerusalem, and *went about preaching the gospel*, Acts viii. 2, could not be *all* the believers; for there remained at Jerusalem a church of believers for Saul to make havoc of. It must therefore have been *all* the preachers, besides the apostles. To strengthen this, let it be observed, that the word here rendered *preaching* is nowhere in Scripture referred to one out of office: that every one of this dispersion, we afterward hear of, are represented as evangelists, pastors, or teachers, Acts ix. 1, 11, 19, and xiii. 1. Parents and masters convey the same instruction that ministers do; but with a different authority: not as ministers of Christ, or officers in his Church. If other gifts or saintship entitled to preach the gospel, wo would be unto every gifted person, every saint, that did not preach it. If our adored Redeemer refused the work of a civil judge because not humanly vested with such power, will he allow his followers to exercise an office far more important, without any regular call? His oracles distinguish between the mission of persons, and their gifts, sometimes called a receiving of the Holy Ghost, John xx. 21, 23.

To render the point incontestably evident, he demands, how men shall preach *except they be sent?* declares, that *no man* rightly *taketh this honor to himself but he that is called of God, as was Aaron.* "I sent them not, therefore they shall not profit this people at all, saith the Lord." The characters divinely affixed to ministers, preachers, or heralds, ambassadors, stewards, watchmen, angels, messengers, brightly mark their call and commission to their work. The inspired rules for the qualifications, the election, the ordination of ministers, are divinely charged to be kept till *the day*, the second coming *of Jesus Christ.* For intermeddling with the sacred business without a regular call, has the Almighty severely punished numbers of men. Witness the destruction of Korah and his company; the rejection of Saul; and the death of Uzza; the leprosy of Uriah; the disaster of the sons of Sceva, &c., Num. xvi.; 1 Sam. xiii.; 1 Chron. xiii.; 2 Chron. xxvi.; Acts xix.

To rush into it, if gifted, or to imagine we are so, at our own hand, introduces the wildest disorder, and the most shocking errors: it did so at Antioch, and the places adjacent, where some falsely pretended a mission from the apostles. This, too, was its effect with the German anabaptists, and with the sectaries of England. Aversion at manual work, pride of abilities, a disturbed imagination, a carnal project to promote self, prompts the man to be preacher. Such ultroneous rushing is inconsistent with the deep impression of the charge, and the care to manifest their mission, everywhere in Scripture obvious in the ministers of Christ. However sound his doctrine, great his abilities, warm his address, where is the promise of God's especial presence, protection, or success, to the ultroneous preacher? Where is his conduct commanded, commended, or unmarked with wrath, exemplified in the sacred words? How then can the preaching, or our hearing, of such, be in faith? How can it be acceptable to God, or profitable to ourselves? For *whatsoever is not of faith is sin*. Falsely this preacher pretends a mission from Christ: wickedly, he usurps an authority over his Church: rebelliously he deserts his own calling, and attempts to make void the office his Saviour has appointed; to frustrate the dispensation of the gospel committed to his faithful ambassadors. For how can they fulfil their ministry, if others take the work out of their hand? How can they *commit it to faithful men*, if, not waiting their commission, men rush into it at pleasure?

In vain pleads the ultroneous preacher, that a particular mission to the office of preaching and dispensing the sacraments was only necessary, when the gospel was preached to the heathen. From age to age, it is *as new*, to children *as new*, to such as never heard it. Nor, when hinting the necessity of a mission, does the inspiring Spirit make any distinction, whether the gospel be newly dispensed or not. *What therefore God hath joined together, let no man put asunder.* In vain he pleads an immediate commission from God: in his infallible statutes, having fixed standing rules of vocation to the ministry, by the mediation of men, God gives us no command, no encouragement, to hope for an immediate call, till the end of time. Absurdly then we allow any to have such a call, till we see *the signs of an apostle wrought in him*. It is not sufficient he be sound in his doctrine, exemplarily holy in his life, active in his labors, disinterested in his aims, seeking not his own, but the honor of Christ, not his own carnal profit, but the spiritual welfare of men: every ordinary preacher is, or ought to be so. But, to this claimant of a mission uncommon, working of miracles, or such extraordinary credentials, must demonstrate he hath not run unsent.

In vain the ultroneous preacher boasts of his feelings; his success; his moving his audience; his reforming their lives; as if these demonstrated his call from God. On earth, was ever delusion carried on without pretence to, or without appearances of these? Let them, who know the history of Popery, of Mahometanism, Quakerism, &c., say if they were. Who knows not, that the Pharisaic sect pretended far more strictness, far more devotion, than the family of Christ? Who knows not, that Satan may, and has oft *transformed* himself *into an angel of light*; his ministers into the form of inspired apostles; and his influences, almost indiscernibly similar to those of the Spirit of Jesus Christ? Who knows not, how oft vainglory, proud and falsely extolling of himself and party, in their number, their spiritual experience and high advances in holiness, mark the distinguished impostor? How oft his sermons are larded with these!

No more tell us, if the sermon be good, you do not regard who preach it. If God has prescribed a method of call, has stated the qualifications of the candidate, has warned against preachers unsent, has oft marked their guilt with visible strokes of his wrath, be ashamed to talk at so arrogant, so careless a rate. Lay it not in the power of the Mesopotamian wizard! Lies it not in the power of a Romish Jesuit, nay, if permitted, of Beelzebub, for a time to preach to you many truths of the gospel, in the warmest strain, the loftiest language? Would you acknowledge the *three* for honored ambassadors of Christ? Tell us not your preacher is wonderfully pious and good: perhaps you have only his own attestation; when better known he may be a drunkard, a swearer, a villain, for you. Suppose he were pious, so was Uzziah; yet it pertained not to him to execute the priest's office. Say not he is wonderfully gifted— speaks like *never man*: perhaps so was Korah, a man famous and of renown: such perhaps were the vagabond sons of Sceva. Say not his earnestness in his work marks his heavenly call: no, such were the Satanic exorcists just mentioned; such was Mahomet, the vilest impostor. To abolish the idolatry, and various other abominations of his country, he exposed himself to cruel reproach, to manifold hardship and hazard of life; about fourteen years almost unsuccessful he persevered in this difficult, but delusive attempt. What hunger, what cold, what torment and death have some Jesuitic and other antichristian missionaries undergone, to propagate the most ruining delusions of hell; all under the pretence of earnestness to gain sinners to Christ and his church. The Scripture, however, nowhere saith, how shall they preach except they be gracious? except they be gifted? except they be in earnest? But, *how shall they preach except they be sent?*

NO. III.123
On the same subject—Who have a right to preach the gospel?

It is expressly enjoined in the word of God that we should earnestly contend for the faith once delivered to the saints. This faith includes all the ordinances, as well as all the doctrines of Christ; and it is no less our duty to contend for the former than for the latter. They have been equally opposed, and there is the same necessity why we should contend for both. Among the ordinances of Christ, the preaching of the gospel holds a principal place, and it hath accordingly, in all ages, met with considerable opposition. Like other ordinances, it hath been often grievously abused, and perverted to the most unworthy purposes. By many who would be esteemed the wise of the world, it is counted unworthy the attention of any but the vulgar: it has been called the foolishness of preaching. The infidels of our time, and some who, by attachment to the Arian and Socinian system, are in a progress to infidelity, cry it down as a human device or piece of craft. This need not, however, occasion any great surprise: the spirit of the world savoreth not the things that be of God, and the enemies of the truth naturally wish to have full scope to propagate their delusions. But it is matter of regret that the preaching of the gospel is, by many who attend upon it, too little regarded as an ordinance of Christ. And some of the professed friends of gospel doctrine so far mistake the nature and institution of preaching, as to engage in it without any other call than their own abundant zeal, and even to plead that all should do so who find themselves qualified. To show that such a sentiment and practice have no warrant from the word of God, the following observations are offered.

I. The preaching of the gospel is an ordinance that Christ hath appointed for the gathering and edification of his Church; and, being a matter of positive institution, all that belongs to the administration of it can be learned only from the rules and approved examples recorded in the New Testament. It is not like those duties that are incumbent upon all, according to the opportunities they have in providence for the performance of them, and which, without any express commandment, could be urged upon Christians by the common principles of moral obligation, such as to teach and admonish one another. And because the obligation to such moral duties depends not upon positive institution, it must equally extend to all, and no person whatever can be free from it. But it is otherwise as to the preaching of the gospel, which is a positive institution of Christ; for it is a duty enjoined upon some only; yea, some are even absolutely prohibited from intermeddling in it, 1 Cor. xiv. 34; 1 Tim. ii. 12: and this could not be the case if it were a matter of common moral obligation. All arguments therefore taken from general principles, to prove the obligation that Christians are under to exert themselves for promoting the cause of religion, are to no purpose here, as they do not prove that the preaching of the gospel is one of those means that all are warranted to use.

II. There is an instituted ministry of the ordinances of Christ unto his Church, by such ministers and office-bearers as he hath appointed. And the preaching of the gospel is frequently referred to as a principal part of that ministry. We read of a ministry of the word, Acts vi. 4; a ministry received of the Lord Jesus to testify the gospel of the grace of God, Acts xx. 24; a ministry of reconciliation, 2 Cor. v. 18; and a ministry into which some are put by the Lord Christ, 1 Tim. i. 12. This ministry is not left open to all the members of the church, in such a manner as that everyone who finds himself disposed, of supposes himself to be qualified, may engage in it as he finds opportunity; but office-bearers are appointed for it by the Lord Christ, Eph. iv. 11,12: "And he gave some apostles, and some prophets, and

136

some evangelists, and some pastors and teachers, for the perfecting of the saints, for the work of the ministry, and for the edifying of the body of Christ." Some of these officers were extraordinary and temporary; they had an extraordinary call, and were endued with miraculous powers, which are now ceased: but the work of the ministry, and particularly the preaching of the gospel, is to continue to the end of the world, as appears from the promise given for the encouragement of those that are employed in it, Matt. xxviii. 20. There are accordingly ordinary officers, pastors, and teachers, appointed for the continued exercise of that ministry.

To these instituted office-bearers is this ministry exclusively committed, Mark xvi., Matt. xxviii. The gospel of Christ, in respect of the public ministry thereof by preaching, is frequently mentioned as a special and peculiar *trust* committed unto them, 2 Cor. v. 18-20; 1 Tim. i. 11, and vi. 20. In all the passages of Scripture where we have any mention of a charge or commission to preach the gospel, it would be easy to show that it is directed only to persons in office; and a variety of names are given to those that are employed in a ministry of the word, all of which are expressive of their peculiar office. They are called ministers, 1 Cor. iii. 6; officers and stewards, 1 Cor. iv. 1; ambassadors for Christ, 2 Cor. v. 20; heralds (so the word preacher signifies) and teachers, 2 Tim. i. 11.

There is no room to plead here, that though a constant ministry of the word, in a pastoral charge, belongs only to persons in office, yet all may occasionally exercise their gifts in preaching the gospel. The word of God acknowledges no such distinction as that between a constant and an occasional ministry of the gospel. It enjoins upon those who are called to the work of the ministry, not an occasional, but a constant exercise of that ministry; so that whether they be paid pastors, or itinerant preachers, they are not to entangle themselves with the affairs of this life, but must be devoted wholly to the work of the gospel, 1 Tim. iv. 13-16; 2 Tim. ii. 4, and iv. 2. And because they must thus devote their time and attention to this work, the word of God also enjoins that a maintenance be given them by those to whom they exercise their ministry, 1 Cor. ix. 7-14; Gal. vi. 6; 1 Tim. v. 17. This is a farther evidence that the ministry of the word is restricted to persons in office, and that they are to devote their time and attention to it, not entangling themselves in the prosecution of a secular business.

III. Those only can be warrantably employed in a ministry of the ordinances of Christ, and particularly in preaching the gospel, who are thereunto called by him, and admitted according to the rule laid down in the word. And none can be warrantably acknowledged and received as office-bearers, to whom that ministry is committed without some proper evidence of their being called and sent by Christ. "How shall they preach except they be sent?" Rom. x. 15. How, without this, can they do it warrantably or profitably? And, without some evidence of this, what ground have we to expect a blessing in waiting upon their ministry? It is not a mere providential sending that is here meant, as if there were no more necessity than abilities, and an opportunity of exercising them; for so the ministers of Satan may be sent, and a lying spirit was thus sent among the prophets of Ahab. But this sending means the call of Christ, intimated in such a way as to warrant the preacher, and with such evidence as may satisfy the conscience of the hearers, in receiving his ministry as the ordinance of Christ. A zeal for God, a strong desire of being useful to souls, and even a persuasion of having the call of Christ, cannot be sufficient warrant to the preacher; far less can the hearers, in receiving him, proceed upon grounds so uncertain.

The apostles, and some other ministers in the beginning of the Christian dispensation, had an extraordinary call and immediate mission by Christ, and this was evidenced to all by the miraculous powers bestowed on them. These powers are now ceased, and it is vain to plead any such immediate call. The ordinary call of Christ to the work of the ministry is intimated by or through the church, judging thereof by the rules laid down in the word; and according to these rules, they that are found qualified and called, are to be admitted to the ministry by them who are already invested with it. The charge is given to the office-bearers of the church, to commit that ministry which they have received "to faithful men, who shall be able to teach others also," 2 Tim. ii. 2; Tit. i. 5. And for their direction in this matter, the qualifications necessary, both as to character and abilities, are laid down in the Word, particularly in 1 Tim. iii.; of these qualifications they are required to make an impartial and deliberate examination, so as to *lay hands suddenly on no man*, 1 Tim. iv. 22, but to admit to the office of the ministry those only, who, by this trial, they have reason to judge are called and sent by Christ.

It is vain to distinguish here between a pastor of a congregation and an itinerant preacher; as if the call of the church was necessary only to the former and not to the latter. If by the call of the church is meant only the choice and call of the people, it is admitted, that this is only necessary to fix a pastoral relation to that part of the flock; but a regular admission to the work of the ministry, by the office-bearers of the church, is equally necessary in the case of all that are employed in it, whether they have a fixed charge or not. Timothy, who had no fixed charge, and though pointed out by prophecy as designed for the ministry, was ordained and admitted to it by the presbytery. And though Paul and Barnabas had an extraordinary call, yet the prophets and teachers of the church at Antioch are directed to separate and send them out, according to the call of the Holy Ghost, to preach the gospel unto the Gentiles, Acts xiii. A principal design of this seems to have been, to set an example of procedure to the church in after times.

It appears, then, that the preaching of the gospel is an ordinance or institution of Christ—that the ministry of that and other ordinances belongs only to those office-bearers whom he hath appointed and commissioned for that end—and that in ordinary cases, none can be acknowledged as sent by him, but such as are admitted to the ministry in the way above mentioned. These observations would have admitted a much larger illustration; but as they are, they may assist an attentive reader to consult his Bible for further satisfaction. It is necessary, however, to take some notice of the arguments urged in support of the opposite sentiment, and of the attempt to prove that every man who is qualified has a right to preach the gospel, without any regular call and admission by the church. And,

1st. It is pretended that this is enjoined upon all that are qualified for it, because Christians are called to teach, exhort, and admonish one another. But even supposing that this were to be understood of preaching, or a public ministry of the word, such directions, though expressed generally, would not apply to all, but to those only who are called to the ministry, according to the limitation and restriction that is laid down in other places of Scripture. There is, however, no necessity of understanding these directions in that sense. The Scripture evidently distinguishes the preaching of the gospel, or that public teaching which belongs to an instituted ministry, from that private teaching which is competent to, and obligatory on, all Christians by the law of love; the latter is enjoined upon some to whom the former is absolutely prohibited: compare 1 Tim. ii. 12, with Tit. ii. 3, 4. Christians in a private station have abundant opportunity, and ordinarily much more than they improve, to exercise their talents in teaching their families, friends, and neighbors, without interfering with that public ministry of the word which is committed to those who are especially called thereto.

2d. Some passages of Scripture are urged, wherein it is supposed all Christians are enjoined to exercise their qualifications in public teaching or preaching: particularly Rom. xii. 6-8; 1 Pet. iv. 10, 11. These Scriptures, on the contrary, restrict the public ministry of the word to those invested with an office, and it is that ministry which belongs to their office that is spoken of. In Rom. xii. persons in office are exhorted to apply themselves faithfully and diligently to that ministry to which they are called, whether it be a ministry of the word, and of spiritual things, or a ministry of temporal things, and that without envying others who have a different office and ministry. And, to enforce this exhortation, the apostle compares the Church to the natural body, ver. 4, in which all members have not the same office, but one member is appointed to one office, and another member to a different office: and so it is in the Church of Christ, ver. 5. The same allusion is applied more largely, 1 Cor. xii. 27, 28, to illustrate this very point. The other passage, 1 Pet. iv. 10, 11, is of the very same import: those in office are called to exercise their ministry faithfully, whether it be in spiritual or temporal things, and are addressed as stewards, ver. 10; "As every man hath received the gift, even so minister the same one to another as good stewards of the manifold grace of God." Some are led to mistake the meaning of these Scriptures, by misunderstanding the word *gift*, as if it meant only talents or qualifications; whereas, in these and many other passages, it means a certain office and ministry to which one is appointed. Eph. iv. 8, 11: He gave gifts unto men; he gave some apostles, some prophets, &c. 1 Tim. iv. 14: "Neglect not the gift that is in thee, which was given thee by prophecy, with the laying on of the hands of the presbytery." Timothy was ordained to the office of the ministry in consequence of special direction of the spirit of prophecy. See 1 Tim. i. 18.

3d. It is also supposed and much insisted on by some, that both precept and example for the preaching of the gospel, by what they call every gifted brother, may be found in 1 Cor. xiv. 31, which is particularly urged in support of their opinion: "For ye may *all* prophesy, one by one, that *all* may learn, and *all* may be comforted." But universal terms, such as are here used, are limited or extended according to the subject; and that even in the same verse, as in chap. xv. 22. In like manner here, the *all* that may prophesy are not the same *all* that may learn and be comforted. The latter may extend to all the members of the church, and even to strangers who might come into their assemblies; the former could apply only to a few. Some members of the church are expressly prohibited from public teaching, ver. 34. Besides, all were not prophets, chap. xii. 29, and therefore all could neither prophesy, nor could warrantably attempt it. The state of matters referred to in that chapter seems to have been this: The church at Corinth was numerous, and had many ministers, of whom the most, if not all, were endowed with some miraculous power, such as that of prophecy, of speaking strange languages, and the like; they were proud of these gifts, and forward to show them, ver. 26, which occasioned disorder in their assemblies for worship; those that had the gift of tongues prevented the prophets, and did not modestly give place to one another. These disorders the apostle reproves, and exhorts them to exercise their gifts in a more regular and decent manner, for the edification of the church. This being the case, it is strange to plead this passage as a warrant for the preaching of the gospel by those who are in no office, and who neither have any miraculous power to prove their immediate call by Christ to the work of the ministry, nor are admitted thereto by the call of the church.

4th. Further, we are referred to Acts viii. 1-4, for an example of the preaching of the gospel by persons not in office. We are told, ver. 1, that "there was a great persecution against the church which was at Jerusalem, and they were all scattered abroad—*except the apostles.*" And it is said, ver. 4, "*they,* that were scattered abroad, went everywhere *preaching the word.*" From this it is argued, that *the Church in general* proclaimed the gospel of the Lord Jesus. But why mention the Church in general, when the method of reasoning used would equally prove that the Church universally did so; and the absurdity of such reasoning must be evident upon a very little consideration of the subject. How absurd to suppose that *all* mentioned in ver. 1, refers to and comprehends all the members of that church, and that all the thousands and ten thousands belonging to it were all scattered abroad, or that they all, men, women, and children, went *everywhere preaching* the word! Are we not told, ver. 3, that some of them, probably many of them, both men and women, were haled and committed to prison? Or, had all the members of the church been driven from Jerusalem, how were the apostles to be employed? Did they only tarry to gather a new church? When it is said, ver. 3, that Saul entered into every house, how absurd would it be to suppose that it is meant every house in Jerusalem, or even every house in which there was a Christian! The expression, also,*everywhere,* ver. 4, must be limited. It would therefore be unreasonable to object against a proper limitation of the word *all,* ver. 1. And about the just limitation of it we need be at no loss. They were all scattered abroad—except the apostles. What reason can there be for mentioning only the apostles as excepted, while there were so many other members of that church still remaining at Jerusalem, but this, that the persons referred to were of the same description in general with the apostles, persons in office, ministers of the church? Others might also be scattered, but these are here spoken of; and Philip, an evangelist, and endowed with miraculous powers, is mentioned as one of them.

5th. As to the case of Apollos, which some urge as affording irresistible evidence to prove that all who are qualified may preach the gospel, a few words may suffice. He spoke boldly in the synagogue, the practice of which is no rule to the Christian Church. He was not yet acquainted with some important doctrines of the New Testament Church, much less could he be acquainted with the ordinances of it. Two intelligent Christians instructed him more perfectly in the way of God. He was recommended by the brethren to the church at Corinth, and there he labored successfully in the work of the ministry. And what is all this to the purpose for which his example is urged? We have no information, indeed, of what time, nor in what manner, he was called and admitted to the work of the ministry, more than we have about many others mentioned in Scripture: but he is expressly called a minister, and is, once and again, classed with the chiefest of the apostles, 1 Cor. i. 12, iii. 5, 22.

Lest these and the like arguments should be found insufficient, recourse is had by some to the plea of pure motives and good designs, with a kind of appeal to the judgment of the great day, and profession of trust, that they are such as will not then be condemned. It is a great satisfaction to have the testimony of conscience to the purity of motives in every part of conduct that is warranted by the word of God, and also to know that the judgment of the saints at the great day will be a judgment of mercy. But every part of the truth of Christ will be determined at that day in exact conformity to what is now declared in the word. And the purest motives and most noble designs are no rule of conduct to any; much less can they give satisfaction to others.

These observations concerning the institution of a gospel ministry, the writer is persuaded, are agreeable to the word of God: if they be not, it would be idle to appeal to his motives in support of them. But he can freely say that they are here offered to the public, not from a desire of controversy, but from a conviction, that at this time it is necessary, on different accounts, to call people's attention to the mind and will of Christ, as revealed in the word concerning this subject. Let not such of the friends of religion, as may be of different sentiments from what are here expressed, be offended at an attempt, in the spirit of meekness, to remove their mistakes: nor let them impute it to envy, pride, or selfish principles. In a perfect consistency with all that he hath advanced, the writer can say, "Would to God that all the Lord's people were prophets."

It is a necessary consequence of what is advanced on this subject, that all should be careful that the ministry of the ordinances they attend upon be such as is warranted in the word. If none can warrantably preach except they be sent, we cannot warrantably attend on the ministry of any but those who we have reason to believe have Christ's call and mission. And if it be an objection against a pastor of a congregation, that he is imposed upon the flock without their choice, it is no less an objection against a preacher, if he be not admitted to the ministry of the word by those whose office it is to examine his qualifications, and judge of his call. It must, however, be acknowledged, that to have gone through the ordinary forms of admission is no sufficient evidence of one's having the call of Christ. The outward forms may be observed, while the spirit and design of them is neglected, and the rule of the word transgressed. Nor can any be acknowledged as sent by Christ, unless their character correspond with that pointed out and required in the word, and unless the doctrine they teach be the gospel of Christ. None can be supposed to have a mission from Christ, who do not bring his message, 2 John ver. 10: "If there come any unto you and bring not this doctrine, receive him not into your house, neither bid him God speed." But when we are favored with the pure gospel, and an administration of it agreeable to the word, let us wait upon it diligently; regarding the preaching of the gospel as an ordinance of Christ, and depending on his promised blessing to make it effectual: for when "the world by wisdom knew not God, it pleased God, by the foolishness of preaching, to save them that believe," 1 Cor. i. 21.

Both parts of this number are recommended to the serious consideration of what are called *lay-preachers*, and of such as favor that scheme. And let all intruders upon the office of the holy ministry, with their deluded votaries, beware lest it should be said to them, *Who hath required this at your hands?*

NO. IV.

Quest. Have not the people a divine right to choose their own pastors and other church officers?

Ans. In those divinely qualified for the ministry, there are diversities of gifts, though but one spirit. As the same food, though abundantly wholesome and nourishing, is not equally suited to the taste, appetite, and constitutions of different persons and nations; so the same gifts in a candidate for the gospel ministry are not equally adapted to every person and place. To secure edification there must therefore be a choice of the gifts most suitable. And who fitter to make it than those who are to enjoy the use thereof, if their senses be exercised to discern good and evil? Can any man pretend to know better what gifts suit the case of my soul than I do myself?

Those ignorant of the fundamental truths of Christianity; those scandalous, profane deniers of the divine original of the Old and New Testaments, or of any truth therein plainly revealed; those neglecters of the public, private, and secret worship of God; those given to cursing, swearing, Sabbath profanation, drunkenness, whoredom, or other scandalous courses, are destitute of capacity and right to choose a gospel minister. The ignorant are utterly incapable to judge of either the preacher's matter or method. The openly wicked have their hatred of Christ, and a faithful minister, marked in their forehead; neither are such qualified to be visible members of the Christian Church. To admit them therefore to choose a Christian pastor would be a method, introducing ruin and we; a method equally absurd as for unfreemen to choose the magistrates of a burgh: rather, equally absurd as if ignorant babes, and our enemies the French, should be sustained electors of our members of parliament and privy council.

Whether visible believers, adults, and having a life and conversation becoming the gospel, have a right from God to choose their pastors and other church officers, must now be examined.

All along from the Reformation it has been the avowed principle of Scotch Presbyterians, that they have a divine warrant to choose their own pastors and other ecclesiastic officers. The first book of discipline, published A.D. 1560, declares the lawful calling of the ministry to consist in the election of the people, the examination of the ministry, and administration by both, and that no pastor should be intruded on any particular kirk without their consent. Their second book of discipline declares that the people's liberty of choosing church officers continued till the Church was corrupted by antichrist: that patronage flowed from the Pope's canon law, and is inconsistent with the order prescribed in God's word. From various documents the assembly of 1736 declared it obvious, that from the Reformation it had been the fixed principle of this church that no minister ought to be intruded into any church contrary to the will of the congregation. They seriously recommended a due regard hereunto in planting the vacancies, as judicatories would study the glory of God, the honor of God, and the edification of men. It is the law of heaven, however, the book of the Lord, that here and everywhere we intend to build our faith upon.

That of Matthias is the first instance of an election of an officer in the Christian Church. No doubt, then, it is marked in the sacred history as a pattern for the ages to come. Being an officer extraordinary, his call was in part immediately divine, by the determination of the lot. Being a church officer, he was chosen by the Church as far as consistent with his extraordinary office. The disciples about Jerusalem (120) were gathered together. Peter represented the necessity of filling up Judas's place in the apostolate with one who could be a meet witness of Jesus' doctrines, miracles, death, and resurrection. The one hundred and twenty disciples chose, appointed, or presented to whom they judged proper for that work. The office being extraordinary, and perhaps the votes equal, the decision which of these two was referred to the divine determination of the lot. After prayer for a perfect *one*, it fell upon Matthias, and he was, by suffrages, or votes, added to the number of the apostles.

Had the next election of a church officer entirely excluded the Christian people, one had been tempted to suspect that Matthias's extraordinary case was never designed for a pattern. Instead hereof, the choice being of an ordinary officer, is entirely deposited in their hands. Never were men better qualified for such an election than the inspired, the spirit-discerning apostles; yet when restrained by laborious attendance to their principal work, the ministry of the word and of prayer, from sufficient leisure to distribute their multiplied alms to their now numerous poor, and directed by the Holy Ghost, they ordered the Christian people *to look out*, choose seven of their number, *men of honest report, full of the Holy Ghost and of wisdom*, who might be ordained to the office of deacons. Judging of the mentioned qualifications, the Christian multitude, entirely of their own accord, chose Stephen, Philip, Prochorus, Nicanor, Timon, Parmenas, and Nicolas. These they presented to the apostles,

141

who immediately ordained them by prayer, and imposition of hands, Acts vi. 1-6. Here, by inspired appointment, the people had the whole power of electing their deacons. If they have the power of electing one ordinary officer, why not of all? If in the case of deacons they can judge of the qualifications of *honest report, full of the Holy Ghost and of wisdom*, what hinders them to judge of these and the like of ministers? If Jesus and his apostles argued from the less to the greater, Matt. vi. 30,1 Cor. ix. 10, who can forbid us to argue so? If it be right and equal for the Christian people to choose deacons who take care of their sacred alms, is it not much more right and equal that they have the choice of their pastors, who take the oversight of their souls?

A third instance of the Christian people electing their ecclesiastical officers, relates to the joint travels of Paul and Barnabas at Lystra and places around, Acts xiv. 23. These two divinely directed messengers of Christ, having ordained (or, as properly translated from the Greek, *through suffrages or votes constituted) them elders* (presbyters) *in every city, and prayed with fasting, commended them to the Lord.* Here it is plainly marked that these elders,*presbyters*, were chosen by *suffrages (votes)* in order to ordination. This the Greek word in our version, by the fraud of the English bishops rendered *had ordained*, plainly imports. The root of this word is borrowed from the custom of giving votes at Athens and elsewhere in Greece, by lifting up of the hand. Wherever it is used in the Greek Testament, and for anything we know in every Greek author, not posterior to Luke, the writer of the Acts, it constantly implies *to give vote or suffrage.* In the text before us it agrees with Paul and Barnabas; because they presided in the choice, and finished the design of it by ordination. Here, moreover, it is evident that the persons chosen for elders *(presbyters)* were set apart to their office, not by a hurried prayer and riotous banquet, but *by prayer and fasting:* and this manner of choice and ordination was used in every church. The very performance of the work of ordination in public conjunction with the church tacitly infers their consent.

Christ's commanding his people *to try the spirits*, to try false prophets, and to flee from them, 1 John iv. 1, 2, necessarily imports a right to choose the worthy, and reject the vile; to choose what suits our edification, and to reject what doth not; for, if we must receive whoever is imposed, there is no occasion for trial, we can have no other. The privilege of trial here allowed to his people by Christ plainly supposes their having some ability for it; and, by a diligent perusal of his word, and consulting his ministers, they may become more capable. Has our adored Redeemer thus intrusted to his adult members the election of their pastors? at what peril or guilt do any ministers or laics concur to bereave them thereof, thrusting men into the evangelic office by another way; thus constituting them spiritual *thieves* and *robbers?* Instead of being *gentle* to church members, as a *nurse cherisheth her children*; instead of *condescending to men of low degree,* and *doing all things to the glory of God* and the *edification of souls*, is not this to set at naught their brethren; exercise lordly dominion over the members of Christ; and rule them with rigor?

In the oracles of God, where is the hint, that the choice of pastors for the Christian people is lodged in any but themselves?—Since men apostolic and inspired put the choice from themselves to the Christian people; who can believe that it belongs to the clergy? Acts i. and vi. When Christ avers *his kingdom is not of this world*, when he threatens judgment without mercy to such as in his worshipping assemblies more readily give a seat to the rich, with his gold ring and gay clothing, than to the poor; can it be imagined that he has intrusted the choice of his ambassadors to men, for their greatness?

There is indeed a haughty objection often stated against the people's choice: Shall a cottager, poor and unlearned, who pays not one farthing of the stipend, and at next term will perhaps remove from the congregation, have an equal choice of a minister with his master, a gentleman, a nobleman, of liberal education, of distinguished abilities, who is head of a large family, has a fixed property and residence in the parish, and furnishes almost the whole benefice? Will you fly in the face of our civil law? Will you plead for the method of choosing church officers, which already has produced so much strife, bloody squabbling, or riot? If Christ's *kingdom*, as himself when dying attested, *is not of this world*, how can outward learning, riches, settled abode, or any worldly thing, constitute one a member thereof? These do not make one a better Christian. No. *Not many wise men after the flesh, not many mighty, not many noble, are called* with a holy calling. How ordinarily do rich men oppress the saints, draw them before judgment-seats, and blaspheme Jesus' worthy name, by which they are called! If worldly privileges and endowments cannot make one a subject of the Mediator's spiritual kingdom, how can they entitle any to, or raise him above his brethren in, the privileges thereof? If by the Son of God the poor cottager has been made free indeed; has been taught to profit; is rich in faith; is a king and priest unto God; and hath received a kingdom that cannot be moved; in the view of the Omniscient and his angels, and every man wise to salvation, how little is he inferior to his rich, perhaps his graceless, master? Your rich man has college education, understands philosophy, history, law, agriculture; but will that infer that he understands his Bible, understands Christian principles, spiritual experiences, and what spiritual gifts best correspond therewith, better than his cottager, who daily searches the Scriptures, and has heard and learned of the Father? How oft are the great things of God hid from the wise and prudent, and revealed unto babes! Christ crucified was to the learned Greeks foolishness; but to the poorest believer the power of God and the wisdom of God. "The natural man," however learned, "receiveth not the things of the Spirit of God, neither can he know them; for they are spiritually discerned," 1 Cor. ii. 14. How easy to find the herdman, or the silly woman, who will endure a trial on Christian principles to far better purpose than many of your rich, your great men!—Your great man is the head of a numerous family, and has great influence in the corner. That, no doubt, is a strong motive for him, if he is a Christian, to be exceeding wary in his choice: if he is so, no doubt his Christian judgment, as far as is consistent with spiritual liberty, is to have its own weight. But while Christ's *kingdom is not of this world*; while in him there is *neither male nor female, bond nor free*; headship over a family can found no claim to a spiritual privilege. Thousands of heads of families are plainly *aliens from the commonwealth of Israel*, without God, and without hope in the world. Many are heads of families who, by neglect of the daily worship of God, of religious instruction, and by other unchristian conduct, ruin the same.

Boast not of the great man's settled abode, boast not of to-morrow, for thou knowest not what a day may bring forth; how suddenly may disaster and death pluck him up by the roots! The rich fathers, where are they? Do the nobles live forever? Shall their dwelling continue to all generations? How often, in a few years, the rich inheritance changes its master, while the race of the poor hovers about the same spot for many generations! What if the cottager attend more to gospel ministrations, in one year, than the rich in forty! what if, removing at next term, he carry his beloved pastor in his heart, and by effectual fervent prayers, availing much, by multiplied groanings that cannot be uttered, he bring manifold blessings on the parish and ministry which he leaves; while your rich man, if wicked, if of the too common stamp, continues in it, for no better purpose than to distress the faithful pastor, corrupt the people, bring down a curse, and cumber the ground! The great man bears the load of the stipend no more than the poorest cottager. He purchased his estate with this burden upon it, and on that account had its price proportionally abated. Suppose it were otherwise, might not a poor widow's *two mites* be more in Jesus' account than all he gives? Will we, with the Samaritan sorcerer, indulge the thought that the *gifts of God*, the spiritual privileges of his Church, *are to be purchased with money*? For money to erect the church or defray the benefice we must not, with the infamous traitor, betray the Son of God in his church—his ordinance, his ministry, into the hands of sinners to be crucified.

It is in vain to mention the civil law: the very worst statute thereof, relative to the point in hand, indirectly supposes the consent of the congregation. It leaves to the presbytery the full power to judge whether the presentee is fit for that charge. If the congregation generally oppose, with what candor do the presbytery, in Jesus' name, determine that he is fit? The last statute relative hereto declared the presentation void, unless accepted. Nor is there in being any, but the *law of sin and death* within them, the law of itch after worldly gain, that obliges candidates to accept. How unmanly, how disingenuous, to blame the civil law with the present course of intrusions!—Since the resurrection of Christ, we think we may almost defy any to produce an instance of bloody squabbling, or like outrageous contention, in the choice of a pastor, where none but the visible members of Christ's mystical body, adult, and blameless in their lives, were admitted to act in the choice. But if at any called popular elections, the power was sinfully betrayed into the hands of such baptized persons, as in ignorance and loose practice equalled, if not transcended, *heathen men and publicans*, into the hand of those who, to please a superior, to obtain a paltry bribe, or a flagon of wine, were readily determined in their vote for a minister; let the prostitutes of Jesus' ordinance answer for the unhappy consequences of their conduct. If they so enormously broke through the hedge of the divine law, no wonder a serpent bit them. But who has forgot what angry contentions, what necessity of a military guard at ordinations, the lodging of the power of elections in patrons or heritors, *as such*, has of late occasioned?

To deprive the Christian people of their privilege in choosing their pastor, and give it to others upon worldly accounts, is the grossest absurdity. It overturns the nature of Christ's spiritual kingdom, founding a claim to her privileges on worldly character and property. It gives those blessed lips the lie, which said, *"My kingdom is not of this world."* It counteracts the nature of the church, as a voluntary society; thrusting men into a momentous relation to her, without, nay contrary to, her consent. It settles the ministerial office upon a very rotten foundation: for how hard is it to believe the man is a minister of a Christian congregation, who never consented to his being such! to believe he has a pastoral mission from Christ, for whom providence would never open a regular door of entrance to the office; but he was obliged to be thrust in by the window, *as a thief and a robber*! If he comes unsent, how can I expect edification by his ministry, when God has declared, *such shall not profit his people at all?* It implies the most unnatural cruelty. If the law of nature allow me the choice of my physician, my servant, my guide, my master, how absurd to deny me the choice of a physician, a servant, a guide, to my soul; and to give it to another, merely because he has some more money, has a certain *piece of ground*, which I have not! How do these qualify him, or entitle him to provide, what the eternal salvation of my soul is so nearly connected with, better than myself, if taught of God?

By patronage how oft the honor of Christ and the souls of men are betrayed into the hands of their declared enemies! If the patron is unholy, profane, how readily the candidate he prefers is too like himself! If a candidate be faithful, be holy, how readily, like Ahab in the case of Micaiah, he hates, he sends not for him! The complaisant chaplain, who almost never disturbed the family with the worship of God; who along with the children or others took off his cheerful glass; sung his wanton song; attended the licentious ball, or play-house; connived at, or swore a profane oath; took a hand at cards; or ridiculed the mysteries, the experiences, the circumspect professor of the Christian faith, is almost certain to have the presentation: perhaps he covenanted for it as part of his wages. For what simony, sacrilege, and deceitful perjury, with respect to ordination vows, patronage opens a door, he that runs may read. Shocked with the view, let us forbear!

N.B. The London ministers in the preceding treatise have a large note respecting the election of ministers, which does not fully invest this right in the people. The editor, therefore, omitted that note altogether, and has inserted this number, extracted from Brown's Letters, in the place of it, as better adapted to the nature of the gospel church, and to that liberty wherewith Christ has made his people free.

NO. V. 124
Of the Ordination and Duty of Ministers.

That the ordination of pastors is an ordinance of Christ, the sacred volumes clearly prove. Through election by suffrages (or votes) Paul and Barnabas ordained *elders* (presbyters) *in every church*, Acts xiv. 23. By Paul's inspired orders Titus was left at Crete to ordain elders (presbyters) in every city, Tit. i. 5. By the laying on of the hands of the presbytery was Timothy himself ordained: he was apostolically authorized and directed to ordain others; and informed that these directions are to be observed, *till the day of Jesus Christ*, 1 Tim. iv. 14, 15.

That not election, but ordination, confers the sacred office is no less evident. Election marks out the person to be ordained; ordination fixes the relation of a candidate to a particular congregation, upon receiving a regular call; while at the same time it constitutes him a minister of the whole catholic Church. Ordination made men *presbyters* and *deacons*, which were not so before. If a person be destitute of the distinguishing ministerial gift, or any other essential qualification, ten thousand elections or ordinations cannot render him a minister of Christ. But solemnly tried and found qualified, he is to be set apart to the ministry, by prayer, fasting, and laying on of the hands of the presbytery.

Nowhere in the heavenly volume do we find either precept or example that Christian people have a whit more right to ordain their pastor, than midwives have to baptize the children they assist to bring forth. Ordination appears to have been performed by apostles, by evangelists, and by a presbytery, Acts vi. 6, and xiv. 23; Tit. i. 5; 1 Tim. v. 22, and iv. 14: but never by private Christians. Could these ordain their pastors or other ecclesiastic officers, to what purpose did Paul leave Titus at Crete to *ordain elders in every city*? or why did he write never a word about ordination to the people, in any of his epistles, but to their rulers?

Thus regularly ordained, the Christian pastor must enter upon his important work. Endowed with spiritual wisdom and understanding; possessed of inward experience of the power of divine truth; inflamed with zeal for the glory of God, love to his work, and compassion to the perishing souls of men, he is to endeavor to acquaint himself with the spiritual state of his flock; and to feed them, not with heathenish and Arminian harangues, but with the gospel of Christ, the sincere milk of the word, diligently preaching and rightly dividing it, according to their diversified state and condition, 1 Pet. v. 3; 2 Cor. v. 11; 1 Cor. ix. 16. Assiduously growing in the knowledge and love of divine things, he is to instruct and confirm his hearers therein. Every divine truth he is to publish and apply, as opportunity calls for: chiefly such as are most important, or, though once openly confessed, are in his time attacked and denied, 1 Tim. vi. 20, iii. 15. Painfully is he to catechize his people, and in Jesus' name to visit and teach them from house to house. To awaken their conscience, to promote the conversion of sinners, to direct and comfort the cast down, perplexed, tempted, and deserted; to ponder the Scripture, and his own and others' experience, to qualify him for this work, must be his earnest care. Faithfully is he to administer the sacraments to such (only) as are duly prepared; and in the simple manner prescribed by Christ. Tenderly is he to take care of the poor; to sympathize with the afflicted; impartially to visit the sick; to deal plainly with their consciences, and to exhort and pray over them in the name of the Lord. With impartiality, zeal, meekness, and prudence, he is to rule and govern the church, to admonish the unruly, to rebuke offenders, to excommunicate the incorrigible, and to absolve the penitent. Habitually is he to give himself to effectual fervent prayer, for his flock, and for the Church of God, travailing as in birth till Jesus be formed in the souls of men. Be a man's parts, diligence, and apparent piety what they will, negligence in this will blast his ministrations, and too clearly mark, that he is therein chiefly influenced by some carnal motive of honor or gain. Finally, he is constantly to walk before his flock a distinguished pattern of sobriety, righteousness, holiness, humility, heavenliness, temperance, charity, brotherly kindness, and every good word and work. Without this his ministrations appear but a solemn farce of deceit, 2 Tim. ii. 4; 1 Tim. iv. 15; 2 Tim. iv. 2.

Can ministers' reading of sermons consist with the dignity of their office? Did Jesus or his apostles ever show them an example of this? No. At Nazareth, when he read his text in the book of Esaias, he *closed his book*, and discoursed to the people. On the mount *he opened his mouth, and taught*: we hear not that he took out his papers and read. Peter, in his sermon at Pentecost, *lifted up his voice, and said*: his papers and reading we hear nothing of. After reading of the law and the prophets, the rulers of the synagogue of Antioch in Pisidia, desired Paul and Barnabas, not to *read*, but to *say on*. Our adored Saviour knew well enough how to direct his ambassadors; yet he ordered them to *go and preach*, not *read*, the gospel to every creature, Luke iv. 20, 21; Matt. v. 2; Acts ii. 14, and xiii. 15. How hard to believe, that he who gives gifts to men, for the edifying of his body, would send the sermonist, whose memory and judgment are so insufficient, that from neither he can produce an half hour's discourse without reading it! How dull and insipid the manner! How absurdly it hinders the Spirit's assistance, as to matter during the discourse! How shameful! Shall the bookless lawyer warmly and sensibly plead almost insignificant trifles, and shall the ambassador of Christ, deprived of his papers, be incapable to plead so short a space in favor of his Master, and of the souls of men?

145

NO. VI.125
Of Ruling Elders.

The rule and government of the Church, or the execution of the authority of Christ therein, is in the hand of the elders. All elders in office have rule, and none have rule in the church but elders: *as such*, rule doth belong unto them. The apostles by virtue of their special office were intrusted with all church power; but therefore they were elders also, 1 Pet. v. 1; 3 John i.: see Acts xxi. 17; 1 Tim. i. 17. They are some of them on other accounts called bishops, pastors, teachers, ministers, guides; but what belongs to any of them in point of rule, or what interest they have therein, it belongs unto them as elders, and not otherwise, Acts xx. 17, 18. The Scriptures affirm, 1st, That there is a work and duty of rule in the Church, distinct from the work and duty of pastoral feeding, by the preaching of the word and administration of the sacraments, Acts xx. 28; Rom. xii. 8; 1 Cor. xii. 28; 1 Tim. v. 17; 2 Tim. iv. 5; Heb. xiii. 7, 17; Rev. ii. 3.

2d. Different and distinct gifts are required unto the discharge of these distinct works and duties. This belongs unto the harmony of the dispensation of the gospel. Gifts are bestowed to answer all duties prescribed. Hence they are the first foundation of all power, work, and duty in the church. Unto every one of us is given grace according to the measure of the gift of Christ, that is, ability for duty, according to the measure wherein Christ is pleased to grant it; Eph. iv. 7: see also 1 Cor. xii. 4, 7, 8-10; Rom. xii. 6-8; 1 Pet. iv. 10: wherefore different gifts are the first foundation of different offices and duties.

3d. That different gifts are required unto the different works of pastoral teaching on the one hand, and practical rule on the other, is evident, 1st, From the light of reason, and the nature of the works themselves being so different. And, 2d, From experience; some men are fitted by gifts for the dispensation of the word and doctrine in a way of pastoral feeding, who have no useful ability in the work of rule; and some are fitted for rule, who have no gifts for the discharge of the pastoral work in preaching, Yea, it is very seldom that both these sort of gifts do concur in any eminent degree in the same persons, or without some notable defect.

4th. The work of rule, as distinct from teaching, is in general to watch over the walk or conversation of the members of the church with authority, exhorting, comforting, admonishing, reproving, encouraging, and directing of them, as occasion shall require. The gifts necessary hereunto are diligence, wisdom, courage, and gravity; as we shall see afterwards. The pastoral work is principally to reveal the whole counsel of God, to divide the word aright, or to labor in the word and doctrine, both as unto the general dispensation and particular application of it, in all seasons and on all occasions. Hereunto spiritual wisdom, knowledge, sound judgment, experience, and utterance are required; all to be improved by continual study of the word and prayer. But this difference of gifts unto these distinct works doth not of itself constitute distinct offices, because the same persons may be suitably furnished with those of both sorts.

5th. Yet distinct works and duties, though some were furnished with gifts for both, were a ground in the wisdom of the Holy Ghost, for distinct offices in the church, where one sort of them were as much as those of one office could, ordinarily attend unto, Acts vi. 2-4. Ministration unto the poor of the church, for the supply of their temporal necessities, is an ordinance of Christ, instituted that the apostles might give a more diligent attendance unto the word and prayer.

6th. The work of the ministry in prayer, and preaching of the word, or labor in the word and doctrine, whereunto the administration of the seals of the covenant is annexed, with all the duties that belong unto the special application of these things before insisted on unto the flock, are ordinarily sufficient to take up the whole man, and the utmost of their endowments who are called unto the pastoral office in the church. The very nature of the work in itself is such, as that the apostle giving a short description of it adds, as an intimation of its greatness and excellency, "Who is sufficient for these things?" 2 Cor. ii. 16. And the manner of its performance adds unto its weight. For not to mention that intenseness of mind in the exercise of faith, love, zeal, and compassion, which is required of them in the discharge of their whole office; the diligent consideration of the state of the flock, so as to provide spiritual food for them; with a constant attendance unto the issues and effects of the word in the consciences and lives of men; is enough for the most part to take up their whole time and strength. It is gross ignorance or negligence that causeth any to be otherwise minded. As the work of the ministry is generally discharged, consisting only in a weekly provision of sermons, and the performance of some stated offices by reading, men have time and liberty enough to attend unto other occasions. But in such persons we are not at present concerned. Our rule is plain, 1 Tim. iv. 12-17.

7th. It doth not hence follow, that those who are called unto the ministry of the word, as pastors and teachers, who are elders also, are divested of their right to rule in the church, or discharged from the exercise of it, because others, not called unto their office, are appointed to be assistant unto them, that is, *helps in the government*. For the right and duty of rule is inseparable from the office of elders, which all bishops and pastors are. The right is still in them, and the exercise of it, consistent with their more excellent work, is required of them. The apostles in the constitution of elders in every church derogated nothing from their own authority, nor discharged themselves of their care. So when they appointed deacons to take care of supplies for the poor, they did not forego their own right, nor the exercise of their duty as their other work would permit them, Gal. ii. 9, 10. And in particular the apostle Paul manifested his concernment herein, in the care he took about *collection for the poor* in all churches.

8th. As we observed at the entrance of this chapter, the whole work of the church, as unto authoritative teaching and rule, is committed unto the elders. For authoritative teaching and ruling, is teaching and ruling by virtue of office: and this office whereunto they do belong is that of elders, as is undeniably attested, Acts xx. 17, &c. All that belongs unto the care, inspection, oversight, rule, fend instruction of the church, is committed unto the *elders* of it expressly. For *elders* is a name derived from the Jews, denoting them that have *authority* in the church.

9th. To the complete constitution of any church, or to the perfection of its organical state, it is required that there be *many elders* in it; at least more than one. I do not determine what their number ought to be; but it is to be proportioned to the work and end designed. Where the churches are small, the number of elders must be so also. So many are necessary in each office as are able to discharge the work which is allotted unto them. But that church, be it small or great, is defective, which hath not more elders than one; so many as are sufficient for their work. The pattern of the first churches constituted by the apostles, which it is our duty to imitate and follow as our rule, plainly declares, that many elders were appointed by them in every church, Acts xi. 30, xiv. 23, xv. 2, 4, 6, 22, xvi. 4, xx. 17; 1 Tim. v. 17; Phil. i. 1; Tit. i. 5; 1 Pet. v. 1.

10th. We shall now make application of these things unto our present purpose. I say then, 1st, Whereas there is a work of rule in the Church, distinct from that of pastoral feeding: 2d, Whereas this work is to be attended unto with diligence, which includes the whole duty of him that attends unto it: 3d, That the ministry of the word and prayer, with all those duties that accompany it, is a full employment for any man, and so consequently his principal and proper work, which it is unlawful for him to be remiss in, by attending on another with diligence: 4th, That, in the wisdom of the Holy Ghost, distinct works did require distinct offices for their discharge: and, 5th, Whereas there ought to be many elders in every church, that both the works of *teaching* and *ruling* may be constantly attended unto; all which we have proved already: our inquiry herein is, whether the same Holy Spirit hath not distinguished this office of elders into those two sorts, namely, those who are called unto teaching and rule also, and those who are called unto rule only, which we affirm.

The testimonies whereby the truth of this assertion is confirmed are generally known and pleaded. I shall insist on some of them only, beginning with that which is of uncontrollable evidence, if it had any thing to conflict with but prejudices and interest, and this is 1 Tim. v. 17, the meaning of which is, the elders or presbyters in office, elders of the church *that rule well* or discharge their presidency for rule in due manner, are worthy, or ought to be reputed worthy, *of double honor*, especially those of them who labor, or are engaged in the great labor and travail of the word and doctrine.

According to this sense the words of the text have a plain and obvious signification, which at first view presents itself unto the common sense and understanding of all men. On the first proposal of this text, that the elders that rule well are worthy of double honor, especially those who labor in the word and doctrine, a rational man, who is unprejudiced, and never heard of the controversy about ruling elders, can hardly avoid an apprehension that there are *two sorts of elders*, some that labor in the word and doctrine, and some who do not. This is the substance of the truth in the text. There are elders in the Church; there are or ought to be so in every church. With these elders the whole rule of the Church is intrusted; all these, and only these, do rule in it. Of these elders there are two sorts; for a description is given of one sort distinct from the other, and comparative with it. The first sort doth rule, and also labor in the word and doctrine. That these works are distinct and different was before declared: yet by the institution of Christ the right of rule is inseparable from the office of pastors or teachers. For all that are rightly called thereunto are elders also, which gives them an interest in rule. But there are elders which are not pastors or teachers. For there are some who rule well, but labor not in the word and doctrine; that is, who are not pastors or teachers.

Elders which rule well, but labor not in the word and doctrine, are ruling elders only; for he who says, The elders who rule well are worthy of double honor, especially they who labor in the word and doctrine, saith that there are, or may be elders who rule well, who do not labor in the word and doctrine; that is, who are not obliged to do so.

The argument from these words may be otherwise framed, but this contains the plain sense of this testimony.

Our next testimony is from the same apostle, Rom. xii. 6, 7, *He that ruleth with diligence*. Our argument from hence is this: there is in the Church one that ruleth with authority by virtue of his office. For the discharge of this office there is a differing peculiar gift bestowed on some, ver. 7, and there is the special manner prescribed for the discharge of this special office, by virtue of that special gift; it is to be done with peculiar *diligence*. And this ruler is distinguished from him that exhorteth, and him that teacheth, with whose special work, as such, he hath nothing to do; even as they are distinguished from those who give and show mercy; that is, there is an elder by office in the Church, whose work and duty it is to *rule*, not to exhort or teach ministerially, which is our ruling elder. He that ruleth is a distinct officer, and is expressly distinguished from all others. Rule is the principal part of him that ruleth; for he is to attend unto it with *diligence*; that is, such as is peculiar unto *rule*, in contradistinction unto what is principally required in other administrations.

There is the same evidence given unto the truth argued for in another testimony of the same apostle, 1 Cor. xii. 28: that there is here an enumeration of offices and officers in the Church, both extraordinary for that season, and ordinary for continuance, is beyond exception. Unto them is added the present exercise of some extraordinary gifts, as miracles, healing, tongues. That by *helps* the deacons of the Church are intended most do agree, because their original institution was as helpers in the affairs of the Church. *Governments* are governors or rulers; that is, such as are distinct from teachers; such hath God placed in the Church, and such there ought to be. It is said that *gifts*, not *offices*, are intended; the gift of government, or the gift for government. If God hath given gifts for government to abide in the Church, distinct from those given unto *teachers*, and unto other persons than the teachers, then there is a distinct office of rule or government in the Church, which is all we plead for.

Of the Duties of Ruling Elders.

1st. To watch diligently over the ways, walk, and conversation of all the members of the church, to see that it be blameless, without offence, useful, exemplary, and in all things answering the holiness of the commands of Christ, the honor of the gospel, and the profession thereof which they make in the world. And upon the observation which they make in the watch wherein they are placed, to instruct, admonish, charge, exhort, encourage, or comfort as they see cause. And this they are to attend unto, with courage and diligence.

2d. To endeavor to prevent every thing that is contrary unto that love which the Lord Christ requireth in a peculiar and eminent manner to be found among his disciples. This he calls his own *new command*, with respect unto his authority requiring it, his example first illustrating it in the world, and the peculiar fruits and effects of it which he revealed and taught. Wherefore, the due observance of this law of love in itself and all its fruits, with the prevention, removal, or condemnation of all that is contrary unto it, is that in which the *rule of the church* doth in a great measure consist. And considering the weakness, the passions, the temptations of men, the mutual provocations and differences that are apt to fall out even among the best, the influence that earthly objects are apt to have upon their minds, the frowardness sometimes of men's natural tempers; the attendance unto this one duty, or part of rule, requires the utmost diligence of them that are called unto it.

3d. To warn all the members of the church of their special church duties, that they be not found negligent or wanting in them. These are special duties required respectively of all church members, according unto the distinct talents which they have received, whether in things spiritual or temporal. Some are rich and some are poor; some old and some young; some in peace and some in trouble; some have received more spiritual gifts than others, and have more opportunity for their exercise: therefore it belongs unto the rule of the church, that all be admonished, instructed, and exhorted to attend unto their respective duties, by those in *rule*, according to the observation which they make of people's diligence or negligence in them.

4th. To watch against the beginning of any church disorders, such as those that infested the church of Corinth, or any of the like sort; and to see that the members of the church attend regularly upon the ordinances of the gospel, as by slothfulness in this, decays in faith, love, and order have insensibly prevailed in many, to the dishonor of Christ, and the danger of their own souls.

5th. It belongs unto them also to visit the sick, and especially such as their inward or outward conditions do expose them unto more than ordinary trials in their sickness; that is, the poor, the afflicted, the tempted in any kind. This in general is a moral duty, a work of mercy; but it is moreover a peculiar church duty by virtue of divine institution, ordaining, that the disciples of Christ may have all that spiritual and temporal relief, which is necessary for them, and useful to them, in their troubles and distresses.

6th. To assist the pastor in watching over and directing the flock, and to advise with the deacons concerning the relief of the poor. According to the advantage which they have by their peculiar inspection of the conversation of all the members of the church, they ought to acquaint the teaching elders with the state of the flock, as to their knowledge, conditions, and temptations, which may be of singular use unto them, for their direction in the exercise of their ministry. The liberal contributions at Antioch for the brethren which dwelt in Judea, were sent by the hands of Barnabas and Saul unto the elders in Judea, Acts xi. 27, 30.

7th. To unite with teaching elders in admitting members into the fellowship of the church, upon a visible evidence of their being qualified as the Scriptures direct. Unto them God hath given the keys of the kingdom of heaven, to open the door of admission unto those whom God hath received, Matt. xvi. 19.

8th. To meet and consult with the teaching elders about such things of importance as are to be proposed to the members of the church for their consent. Hence nothing rash or indigested, nothing unsuited to the duty of the church, will at any time be proposed therein, so as to give occasion for contests, janglings, or disputes, contrary to order or decency, but all things may be preserved in a due regard unto the gravity and authority of the rulers.

9th. To sit in judgment upon offenders, to take the proof, to weigh the evidence and determine accordingly, justifying the innocent, and ordaining censure to be inflicted on the convicted brother, according to the nature of the offence, Matt. xviii. 15, 17, 18.

10th. Whereas there is generally but one teaching elder in a church, upon his death or removal, it is the work and duty of the ruling elders to preserve the church in peace and unity, to take care of the continuation of its public ordinances, to prevent irregularities in any persons or parties among them, and to give all necessary aid and advice in the choice and call of some other meet person to be their pastor, in the room of the deceased or removed.

CONCLUSION.

A Summary of the preceding Treatise on Church Government,
BY QUESTION AND ANSWER.

Quest. What is meant by church government?

Ans. That particular form and order, which Christ has fixed in his Church, for the proper management thereof.

Quest. How does it appear that there is a particular form of government appointed in the New Testament Church?

Ans. As there is as great, if not greater, need of a government, in the New Testament Church, than there was in the Old, all the ordinances of which were most minutely described. Satan is now more experienced in deceiving, and his agents are still alive, and very actively employed, in attempting to waste and destroy this sacred vineyard, if without its proper hedge. Her members are still a mixture of tares and wheat; of sheep and goats: so that there is still a necessity of discerning between the precious and the vile; of trying and censuring false teachers; and of guarding divine ordinances from contempt and pollution. As Jesus gives the New Testament Church the peculiar title of the *kingdom of heaven*, he could not, in a consistency with his wisdom, leave it without any particular laws or form of government, except the changeable inclinations of men. As he was faithful in his New Testament house, he must fix a particular form of government for her, such as tends to her peace, order, and spiritual edification. And, amidst the prophet's vision of the New Testament Church, he is directed to teach his people *the form of the house, the laws of the house,* &c., Ezek. xliii. 11.

Quest. When may a particular form of church government be said to be of divine right?

Ans. When all the parts thereof are agreeable to Scripture precepts; to approved Scripture examples; or are deducible by fair Scripture consequences.

Quest. How does it appear, that Scripture consequences are to be admitted to prove any particular truth or doctrine?

Ans. Because God has formed man a rational intelligent creature, capable of searching out the plain meaning and import, and also the necessary consequences of his express declarations. We find Christ reasoning by a deduction of consequences, when he showed that the doctrine of the resurrection was revealed to Moses at the burning bush; that the sixth commandment forbids angry words; and the seventh lascivious looks, Luke xx. 37, 38; Matt. v. 21, 28. And a great part of the inspired epistles to the Romans, Galatians, and Hebrews consists in such a deduction of consequences. And as all Scripture is said to be profitable "for doctrine, for reproof, for correction, and for instruction in righteousness," 2 Tim. iii. 16, without a rational deduction of consequences, every portion of Scripture cannot answer each of these valuable ends.

Quest. What particular form of church government may lay the only proper claim to a divine right, according to the Holy Scriptures?

Ans. The true presbyterian form, without that lordly dominion and tyrannical power, which has too often been exercised by courts, bearing this name. This government claimeth no power over men's bodies or estates. It does not inflict civil pains or corporal punishments. But it is a government purely spiritual, dealing with the consciences of men, and exercising the keys of the kingdom of heaven, doing all things according to the word of God.

Quest. What are the parts of presbyterial church government?

Ans. It consists of a people, having the qualifications which the Scriptures require; of certain rulers, who are to perform the duties of their respective offices; and of certain courts, in which these rulers sit and act in matters of judgment.

Quest. What are the qualifications of persons who constitute the private members of the visible church?

Ans. They ought to be true believers in Christ, to have a competent knowledge of the doctrines of the gospel, to make a sound profession of their faith, and to maintain a holy conversation.

Quest. What rulers are there in the presbyterian church?

150

Ans. Preaching elders, ruling elders, and deacons.

Quest. Where is the divine warrant for the preaching elder?

Ans. In the Holy Scriptures we find that God hath set some in the Church, TEACHERS: that our ascended Redeemer hath given her PASTORS and TEACHERS: that the Holy Ghost had made some BISHOPS, OVERSEERS, to feed her; and qualifies some for *prophecy, ministry, teaching, exhortation,* 1 Cor. xii. 28; Eph. iv. 11; Acts xx. 28; Rom. xii. 6-8.

Quest. What are the duties of preaching elders?

Ans. To preach the word; to dispense the ordinances of baptism and the Lord's Supper; to administer church discipline; and to rule and govern the church, 2 Tim. iv. 2; Matt. xxviii. 19; 1 Cor. xi. 23-29; 1 Tim. v. 20; Tit. ii. 15, and iii. 10; Heb. xiii. 17; 1 Pet. v. 2, 3. *Quest.* Is the office of the gospel minister instituted by God to continue to the end of time?

Ans. Yes; the ends of it are of a permanent nature, the converting and confirming of the elect, and the silencing of gain-savers, Acts xxvi. 18; Tit. i. 9, 11.

Quest. Where is the divine warrant for the office of the ruling elder?

Ans. From the three following passages of sacred Scripture: 1. From Rom. xii. 5 to 8: "We being many are one body in Christ, and members one of another. Having then gifts, differing according to the grace that is given to us, whether prophecy, let us prophesy according to the proportion of faith; or ministry, let us wait on our ministering; or he that teacheth, on teaching; or he that exhorteth, on exhortation; he that giveth, let him do it with simplicity; he that ruleth, with diligence," &c. Here we have a list of the ordinary officers of Christ, one body, the church. Here is the teacher: *he that teacheth.* Here is the pastor: *he that exhorteth.* Here is the deacon: *he that giveth.* And here is another officer distinct from all them, *he that ruleth.* His description attests, that *ruling* is, if not his only, yet his principal work. He that *ruleth* is here marked by a distinct character, as having a different *gift,* and a distinct work from his fellow-officers. This office therefore must be *distinct.* 2. From 1 Cor. xii. 28, where the *Spirit of God* informs us, that God hath set some in the Church, GOVERNMENTS. These must be understood of *governors,* as *miracles* are afterwards explained of *workers of miracles.* These governments and governors are said to be *set* in the church, not in the state; by God, not by men: they are declared to be distinct officers by themselves. Their title, government, implies, that *ruling* is their principal work. 3. From 1 Tim. v. 17, where the divine warrant for ruling elders shines with more peculiar brightness than anywhere in the book of God: "Let the elders that rule well be counted worthy of double honor; especially they who labor in the word and doctrine." The ruling elders here mentioned necessarily pertain to the church. Two sorts of ruling elders are here plainly distinguished: some that only rule well; others that also labor in word and doctrine. There is not one place in the New Testament, nor perhaps in any Greek author, where the word here translated ESPECIALLY does not distinguish between different persons or things, Gal. vi. 10; Phil. iv. 22; 1 Tim. iv. 10; 2 Tim. iv. 13; and it would be absurd to suppose, that it does not distinguish here also. Therefore this single text shows the divine right of both the teaching and ruling elder.

Quest. What are the duties of ruling elders?

Ans. To exercise ecclesiastical rule in church courts with the same authority as the preaching elder; to watch over the flock; impartially to receive or exclude members; to warn and censure the unruly; and to visit and pray with the sick.

Quest. Where is the divine warrant for deacons?

Ans. From Acts vi., where we are informed of the original and design of their office; and from 1 Tim. iii. 8-12, where the inspired apostle describes their necessary qualifications.

Quest. What are the duties of deacons?

Ans. To look into the state and to serve the tables of the poor, by distributing the funds of the church, according to the respective necessities of the saints, 1 Tim. iii. 12.

Quest. What are the courts in which presbyterian rulers meet?

Ans. Congregational sessions, presbyteries, and synods.

Quest. Where is the divine warrant for congregational sessions?

Ans. From Matt, xviii. 15-18, where, in the Christian form of church discipline prescribed by the Church's Head, the concluding expression, "Let him be unto thee as a heathen man and publican," plainly alludes to the Jewish form of procedure in scandals. They had rulers, and consequently courts in every synagogue, or worshipping congregation, Mark v. 35-39. By virtue of letters from the high-priest to these, Saul had free access to punish the Christians in every synagogue, Acts ix. 1, 2. To these congregational courts it pertained to cast out of the synagogue, and to order transgressors to be held for heathen men and publicans, John ix. 22. Now Jesus, in alluding to these, intimates that similar courts should be in every Christian congregation. In this form of discipline our divine Saviour shows his utmost aversion against private offences being unnecessarily published abroad: and therefore the church, to which the offence is to be told, after private admonition is fruitless, must be understood in the most private sense of the word. The following context evidences that it is a *church*, which may consist only of *two or three* met together in Christ's name; yet, notwithstanding, a church having power to bind and loose from censure; that is, a church having the keys of the kingdom of heaven. It cannot then be the whole congregation or body of the people, as they are in general far too numerous to conceal offences, and to them Christ has given no formal judicial power, Matt. xviii. 18-21.

Quest. Where is the divine warrant for a presbytery?

Ans. Timothy is expressly said to be ordained by the laying on of the hands of the PRESBYTERY, 1 Tim. iv. 14. And the number of different Christian congregations governed by one presbytery, as at Jerusalem, Antioch, Ephesus, and Corinth, proves the divine right of this court. It is shown in the xiii. chapter of the preceding treatise, that in each of these places there were more Christians than could meet in one worshipping congregation, for the enjoying of public ordinances: and yet all these different congregations, at Jerusalem, are expressly said to have been one church, Acts viii. 1: so those at Antioch, Acts xiii. 1: so those at Ephesus, Acts xx. 17: and those also at Corinth, 1 Cor. i. 2. Now the question is, How were the different congregations in each of these places ONE CHURCH? Not merely in union to Christ and mutual affection one to another; for in this respect all the saints are ONE, whether in heaven or in earth. And therefore they are one church in virtue of conjunct government under ONE PRESBYTERY. And in difficult cases, or where a single congregation is so divided into parties that it cannot act impartially; where the difference is between the pastor and the people, a superior court is necessary to obtain material justice.

Quest. Where is the divine warrant for an ecclesiastical synod?

Ans. In Acts xv. and xvi., where we have a cause referred; the proper members of a synod convened; the ordinary and equal power exercised by all those members; the ordinary method of procedure in such courts; and the judicial decrees given by the synod; together with the effect which their judgment, in this matter, had upon the churches.

Quest. What was the cause referred to this synod?

Ans. False doctrine propagated by some Judaizing teachers, who had gone down from Jerusalem to Antioch, and maintained that circumcision and the observance of other branches of the ceremonial law continued necessary for salvation, whereby they subverted some, and troubled other members of the churches there. After much unsuccessful disputing, Paul, Barnabas, and others were delegated to go up to Jerusalem to the apostles and elders about this matter.

Quest. Who were the proper members of the synod convened here?

Ans. The apostles and elders at Jerusalem; Paul, Barnabas, and others, from Antioch; and other commissioners from the troubled churches to whom the decrees were sent.

Quest. Are not the brethren, the church, the whole church, mentioned here as well as the apostles and elders?

Ans. But none of these expressions can mean, that all the members of the church of Jerusalem either were present or judged in that synod; for women, real members of the church, of the whole church, are expressly forbid to speak in the church, 1 Cor. xiv. 34. Church sometimes signifies only a small part of the church, either as delegates or commissioners, and in this sense it is used in verse 3, where the commissioners from Antioch are said to be brought on their way by the *church;* and in chap. xviii. 22, it is said that Paul saluted the *church* at Jerusalem. Now, it is not credible that all the Christian professors at Antioch would attend their commissioners a part of the way to Jerusalem; or that Paul saluted the many ten thousand Christians at Jerusalem, Acts xxi. 20. And the *whole church* does not necessarily mean the whole individual members of the church, more than the *whole world* mentioned, 1 John ii. 2, means every individual in the world. If any, to support a favorite opinion, will still insist that the whole members of the church actually met and judged of this affair equally with the apostles and elders, they may inform us where they obtained a proper place for so many judges to reason and determine with distinctness or order. That the brethren who joined in judgment with the apostles and elders were not private persons, but rather delegates from the troubled churches around, appears from Judas and Silas, two of them being preachers, v. 22.

Quest. How does it appear that the power of all the members was ordinary and equal?

Ans. As every member, inspired or not, acted equally in the whole business laid before them. Paul and Barnabas were delegated by the church of Antioch: and the elders, who convened, had the same power as the apostles. To the elders, teaching or ruling, as well as to the apostles, was the matter referred: both met to consider of it: both were equally concerned in the decision, saying, *It seemed good to the Holy Ghost and to us.* Elders, as well as apostles, imposed the necessary things upon the churches, and authoritatively determined the decrees. In the name of the elders, as well as of the apostles, the letters of the meeting, containing their decision, were written to the churches. And the only reason why the inspired members put themselves on an equality with others was to exhibit a pattern to after ages.

Quest. How does it appear, that this synod followed the ordinary method of procedure in such courts?

Ans. As they examined the cause by much reasoning and dispute. In consequence of mature deliberation they determined the question, and sent letters, containing their decrees, by proper messengers, to the churches concerned. In their disputation they reasoned from the oracles of God: on these they founded their decision; and hence therein they say, *It seemed good to the Holy Ghost, and to us.* And if this had not been to have given a pattern to succeeding ages, all this was unnecessary: how absurd for inspired men to reason and dispute on the subject, when the sentence of one inspired was sufficient for decision!

Quest. How does it appear that there were judicial decrees given by this synod?

Ans. In opposition to the false doctrine taught, they, by a judicial decision, plainly declared, that obedience to the ceremonies of the law of Moses was no longer necessary: and by a decree for promoting decency and good order, they enacted, that to avoid offence, the believing Gentiles should abstain from fornication, from things strangled, and from blood, verse 24-29.

Quest. What effect had the decision of this synod upon the churches?

Ans. They cheerfully submitted to these *decrees*, and were by them conformed in the faith, comforted in heart, and increased in number daily, Acts xv. 31, and xvi. 4, 5.

Quest. But might not this be a meeting merely for consultation, and their decision a mere advice?

Ans. No: for every word here used imports authority. The word translated *lay upon*, commonly signifies an authoritative imposition, Matt. xxiii. 4. The decision is expressly called a *necessary burden*, and *decrees ordained*, which imply power and authority, Acts xv. 16, xvii. 7.

Quest. How does it appear that inferior courts are subordinate to those that are superior; sessions to presbyteries, and presbyteries to synods?

Ans. The true light of nature (which is proved, chap. iii., to be one of those ways, whereby a thing is of divine right) teacheth us, that, if we be injured by an inferior court, we may appeal to a higher court for redress, if there be one. As in the Jewish church there was evidently a subordination of judicatories, so that those injured in the synagogue might appeal to the Sanhedrin, Deut. xvii. 8, 12; 2 Chron. xix. 8, 11; Exod. xviii. 22, 26; Ps. cxxii. 5: therefore as our dangers, difficulties, and necessities are as great as theirs, by reason of false teachers and corrupt doctrines, which were foretold should appear in the last times, 1 Tim. iv. 1; 2 Pet. ii. 1; we cannot, without dishonor to Christ, suppose that he would deprive us of a proper remedy for redressing our grievances, which was afforded unto them:—the gradual advance in managing offences prescribed by Christ himself, Matt. xviii. 19, as his care for the whole church cannot be less than for a single member. If then an inferior judicatory offend or injure us, we ought to carry the matter to another that has more influence and authority. If the offending judicatory neglect to hear this, we ought to tell the offence to the church in the highest sense, that redress may be obtained—the apostle Paul declaring, *that the spirits of the prophets are subject to the prophets.* But the right of reference or appeal from an inferior to a superior court is most clearly evinced from the case of the presbytery of Antioch, respecting circumcision, being referred for decision to the synod of Jerusalem, and their readily submitting to its determination, Acts xv.

Quest. How does it appear that no power of authority is lodged in the body of the people, the private members of the church?

Ans. Although every church member has a right to all the spiritual privileges purchased with the Saviour's blood, and given to the church, as need requires; although he has a right to try the spirits, and to prove all things by the word of God; a power to choose the church officers who are immediately to rule over him; yet the Holy Scriptures allow the exercise of no official power to the private members of the church. Not the Christian people, but their pastors have power to preach the gospel, Rom. x. 15; and to administer the sacraments, those mysteries of God, which are connected with preaching, 1 Cor. iv. 1; Matt. xxviii. 19. Not the people, but their rulers, are divinely warranted. Timothy was ordained, not by the people, but by the presbytery: elders, not by the people, but by Paul and Barnabas: and deacons, not by the people, but by the apostles, 1 Tim. iv. 14; Acts xiv. 23, and vi. 3, 6. Not the people, but their rulers are to censure the scandalous, and to absolve the penitent, Matt. xviii. 18; 1 Cor. v. The Scripture nowhere ascribes to the people any such characters as imply authority lodged in them; but the contrary. Instead of being styled pastors, they are called the *flock*, watched over and fed; instead of overseers, the family overseen; instead of *rulers, guides, governors*, they are called the *body* governed, the persons subject in the Lord, and they are solemnly charged to know, honor, obey, and submit to those that are over them.

Quest. What is the proper method of dealing with persons that fall into scandal?

Ans. If the offence be known only to one or to a few, the offender is to be told his fault secretly, with Christian meekness, plainness, and love. If he profess his sorrow and resolution to amend, the whole matter ought to be carefully concealed; and those offended ought to be well pleased that their offending brother is gained. If, after one or more secret reproofs, he continue impenitent, defending his fault, one or two more Christian brethren, grave, judicious, and meek, are to be taken along, and the offender to be dealt with by them, and in their presence. If now he appear to repent, the several persons concerned in his reproof are, with care and in love, to conceal his offence, lest, by divulging it, they be reproached as wicked calumniators. If the offender contemn one or more such private admonitions or reproofs, or if his scandal be of such a nature that it will necessarily become public, the affair is to be told to the church court, to which he is most immediately subject. And, to bring him to a due sense of his fault, he is to be there dealt with in a prudent, affectionate, plain, and convincing manner. If this prove a means of bringing him to a sense of his offence, the censures of the church are to be executed upon him according to the laws of Christ's house, and the nature of his crime, and he is to be restored to the privileges of the church. But if, after due pains taken by the judicatories, he remain obstinate, he is then to be cast out of the church, and held as a heathen man and publican, Matt. xviii. 15 to 18.

THE END.

FOOTNOTES:

117 | The substance of this Number is extracted from Ford's Gospel Church, printed 1675.]

118 | John xvi. 8, 9; 2 Cor. v. 5; Eph. ii. 1, 5.]

119 [Col. ii. 6; 1 Cor. vi. 19, 20.]

120 [Col. i. 12.]

121 [1 Pet. ii. 5.]

122 [From Brown's Letters.]

123 [Extracted from the Christian Magazine for Sept. 1797—a periodical publication well worth the perusal of the friends of evangelical doctrine.]

124 [From Brown's Letters.]

125 [This number is a summary of Dr. Owen's arguments in favor of the divine right of the ruling elder, with an abstract of the duties which he ought to perform. Although the Doctor was a professed Independent, yet he was entirely different, both in doctrine and church government, from any in Scotland that bear that name, as all who are acquainted with his works will easily observe. The writer of his life asserts that he heard him say, "He could readily join with presbytery as it was exercised in Scotland." And indeed it appears very probable that the difference between the consultative synod which he allows, and the authoritative synod contended for by true Presbyterians, is not so far different as many apprehend, because the decisions of either bind the conscience only as they are agreeable to the Holy Ghost speaking in the Scriptures.]